First Cut

First Cut

Conversations with
Film Editors

Gabriella Oldham

University of California Press
Berkeley / Los Angeles / London

Photo credits: Paul Barnes courtesy of Robert Miller,
Geof Bartz courtesy of Will McIntyre, Donn Cambern
courtesy of Uri Katoni, John J. Dunning courtesy of
MGM, Alam Heim courtesy of Sanford Rackow, Paul
Hirsch courtesy of Irving Sherman, Sheldon Kahn cour-
tesy of Bruce McBroom, Harold F. Kress and Carl
Kress courtesy of Gabriella Oldham, Sidney Levin
courtesy of Lisa Sloan, Carol Littleton courtesy of John
Bailey, Evan Lottman courtesy of Peter Weitzner,
Barry Malkin courtesy of Debra Bard, Emily Paine
courtesy of Jennifer Lewis, Ted Winterburn courtesy
of Katherine Love, Merle Worth courtesy of Wynette
Yao

University of California Press
Berkeley and Los Angeles, California

University of California Press
London, England

Copyright © 1992 by
The Regents of the University of California

First Paperback Printing 1995

Library of Congress Cataloging-in-Publication Data

Oldham, Gabriella.
    First cut: conversations with film editors /
Gabriella Oldham.
        p.   cm.
     ISBN 0–520–07588–9
     1. Motion pictures—Editing.   2. Motion pic-
ture editors.   I. Title.
TR899.043   1992
778.5'35—dc20   91—47713
                                          CIP

Printed in the United States of America

10   09   08   07   06   05   04   03   02
14   13   12   11   10 9   8   7   6   5

The paper used in this publication meets the minimum
requirements of ANSI/NISO Z39.48-1992 (R 1997)
(*Permanence of Paper*). ♾

For Nick, I wish he were here.
He would have loved this one.

Contents

Acknowledgments

Mimi Arsham, Alan Berliner, Lisa Day, Holly Fisher, Lora Hays, Richard Halsey, Michael Kahn, Kay Rose, Larry Silk, and Peter Zinner, film editors whose interviews could not appear in this book for lack of space.

Rocky Schwarz, for his trivia every time I start another project and for not minding my "junk piles." Betty Engel, for when the (micro)chips were down. Miranda Botchway, Alma Gray, LaVonna Wilson, musketeers of the WPC. Carrol Grady and Zoraida Grady, for "multiple" assistance. Tim Couillard, those roses meant so much. For asking and listening: Yvonne Barnes, Kurt Brokaw, Steve Brown, Hope Jensen Leichter, Ted Papoutsakis, Sr. Carol Perry.

Ernest Callenbach, the best editor of the literary kind, and all at the Press who contributed to production.

Fabiana, perhaps you'll be an editor one day. Whatever you do, keep laughing.

My mother, it never seems easy, but it always gets done. Thanks for believing.

Buster Keaton in a scene from Sherlock Jr.
(Courtesy of The Museum of Modern Art/Film Stills Archive)

Introduction

Many people cannot define what film editors are or do. This is understandable, for editors have never been celebrities. When editing awards are distributed, very few outside the inner circle of editors remember who won. Even very distinguished editors are seldom mentioned in a film's publicity campaign; they remain in the shadow of the "big names" involved in its production. Reviewers and the informed public often associate editing with flashy scenes—screeching car chases, fierce battles, demon-possessed furniture flying around the room. Obviously, a lot is happening in these scenes, and *someone* had to put all the little film pieces together. Some people, though, still think such scenes, like everything else in a movie, were "shot that way."

The film industry and audiences in some ways have become incredibly sophisticated in the last three or four decades. Simplistic views of editing, however, have not changed much. Only practitioners of the craft, and those in the industry, audience, and classroom who understand the full filmmaking process, have begun to appreciate the complex nature of editing. Editing involves not merely a theoretical consideration of the effect of one shot upon another, or a linear rendition of a script, or a mechanical measurement of frames. It is *all* that and much more—rhythm, instinct, emotion, psychology, art—and it draws from the total talent of one person, the editor, who collaborates with the director to create a cumulative sensory event.

For starters, editors organize minutiae, intensify subtleties, heighten emotions, and blend countless elements of image and sound to create a film. Unlike film directors, however, editors are not accustomed to explaining their work to an inquisitive outsider. They often respond to requests for interviews with hesitation, a momentary loss for words, surprise that someone is even asking who they are and what they do. But once involved in an interview, like other creative people behind the screen,

1

editors become articulate expounders of their complex art. The twenty-three editors in this book spoke of their profession with ease, animation, and (fittingly) attention to detail. They drew examples from their films and experiences to illustrate major points about what editing is and does. A number of common threads were soon apparent, and the process of editing—often considered mysterious, intuitive, magical, invisible—became defined and comprehensible. For any student of filmmaking, whether as practitioner or analyst, these interviews will throw light on the most critical process of the art.

The image of the editor as a solitary figure in a dark cutting room is a decades-old legacy. Only recently has the importance of the editor begun to be acknowledged by the industry and the public. One major recognition, for example, has been the prominent display of the editor's name in media advertisements, although the name's position or even inclusion in the list is not always consistent. According to recent studies of early film history, the first "editors" were, in fact, projectionists who were asked to splice a couple of single-shot pieces of film together to make up a longer program. Not surprisingly, the physical splicing skill required of editors led to their early reputation as mere mechanics.

The person of the editor may not have been publicly esteemed during the first three or four decades of film, but the process of editing gained professional importance once the concept of narrative structure arose. From the "primitive" one- and two-reelers of Georges Méliès and Edwin S. Porter, to the greatly refined features of D. W. Griffith, Erich von Stroheim, and Buster Keaton, editing became the means to manipulate time and point of view through intercutting, and to intensify emotions through inserts and optical devices. No longer were films presented as stage-like shots simply tacked on to each other. The silent cinema was a showcase for the *image*, and the pictures (plus, of course, a variable number of title cards) flowed as a result of how shots interacted with those preceding and following. Lighting, cinematography, scripting (including titling), acting, and direction were executed with the editing process in mind, for in the cutting room the film would come together. Shots were composed specifically for the sake of editorial continuity.

In the silent 1920s, the critical analyses of V. I. Pudovkin and Sergei Eisenstein elevated editing into a theory and an art form. Juxtaposition was the key principle; "montage" became synonymous with editing throughout Europe, though Hollywood reserved the term for quick-cut, dissolve-laden special sequences. Eisenstein's *Battleship Potemkin* and *October*, Abel Gance's *Napoleon*, and the silent German expressionist films, among many others, not only demonstrated the breathtaking effect of a rapid-fire accumulation of shots (what has evolved into "flash" cutting—a staple of car chases, shoot-outs, television commercials, and MTV). These films also presented simple juxtapositions of emotive images to evoke mood, create subtext and complex abstractions, and pose significant connections where none seemed to exist. Editing, particularly as discussed by Eisenstein, became an intellectual stimulation, the embellishment of a simple narrative with visual richness. Throughout the 1920s, as motion pictures evolved from flickering visions to elaborate narratives, it became clear that the power to enhance every potential of the visual ultimately lay in editing.

Once sound entered film at the end of the 1920s, filmmakers were obligated to combine a greater number of elements in the editing process: dialogue, music, and sound effects. They were more likely to follow the script, a structure that did not always exist or was not rigidly adhered to in silent films. Editing became locked into preserving the flow of dialogue as recorded during production. Only after the novelty of sound had worn off could the use of words, music, and sound effects to enhance the visual become the enterprise of the editor. Overlapping dialogue, manipulating volume, using subliminal sounds and silence, and cutting action-reaction shots to dialogue were among the new considerations faced in the editing process.

The burgeoning studio system swelled with specialists and departments for each facet of moviemaking in Hollywood's Golden Age, and editing was no exception. In the major studio machine, editors were subdivided into A and B editors (for A and B feature films), with assistants, apprentices, and separate departments for sound, music, and montage sequences. With a prolific production rate (for example, MGM made fifty-two pictures a year), projects were assigned to whichever editors and directors were available on a rotation basis. The studios run by the producers (Thalberg, Mayer, Cohn, Warner, Zanuck, Fox et al.) provided their employees (big-name or otherwise) with job security. Editors, for instance, would receive steady paychecks whether or not they worked continuously, as long as they were on payroll. Certain directors and editors were able to work together on successive projects and thus developed a kind of "buddy system" in which the film would be cut by someone who understood the director's vision.

A few editors also exerted great influence on directors and producers. Margaret Booth, who began her career in silent films (and, as of this writing, is still working), conferred closely with Thalberg and Mayer as she moved into a supervisory capacity at MGM. Rudi Fehr (whose interview appears here) was Jack Warner's right-hand man for forty years. In general, however, a stereotype of the editor's personality developed: a quiet, self-effacing, diligent, meticulous cutter, set apart from the madding studio crowd, and editing films in dark rooms to suit the producer and director, who remained the principal creative forces. If anyone critiqued a film from an editorial perspective, the director would usually be cited for its success or failure, although the director's degree of involvement in the editing could vary considerably. As some of the veteran editors in these interviews reveal, certain directors left the selection of dailies to their editors: "Use the good stuff" or "Make it work." Still, the director's was the "name above the title." The editor's name was usually found far, far below it.

The demise of the studio system in the late 1940s and 1950s virtually destroyed job security and created a highly competitive free-lance market. Editors now often speak of the unsettling reality of being unemployed for long stretches, not knowing when the next job will come. They search for comfortable niches with the same family of filmmakers and try to establish reliable contacts. As for the films themselves, studio sets gave way to more location shooting; "tableau" (master) shots—which were seldom cut into and gave a slow pace to many of the films of the 1930s and 1940s—succumbed to shorter shots that quickened the pace and emotional responses. Directors shot from more camera positions and with more takes that might increase options in editing; so film "coverage" increased, obligating editors to organize and reduce the amount of footage sometimes in ratios of thirty or forty to one (ratio of footage exposed to footage used in the final cut). The advent of television also coincided with the crumbling studio system, affecting how films were shot and edited in order to keep audiences coming to the theaters. TV-generation audiences have become conditioned to receiving much information crammed into tight TV time slots. Most editors say they need to remember the level of an audience's visual sophistication and how much viewers notice and absorb in such short durations on the screen.

Still, the greatest challenge in reaching modern audiences and creating outstanding films is understanding one's specialty. Today's filmmaking places enormous responsibilities on each major mind behind a movie: scriptwriter (preproduction), cinematographer (production), and editor (postproduction), who are all answerable to the director and producer. Scriptwriters and cinematographers need to understand all aspects of their respective professions, from mechanics to aesthetics. So too must editors. They need to understand and articulate the inner workings of their specialty—equipment, job pressures, working methods, theories, and instincts. Editors are no longer a pair of hands. In reality, the nature of film, at its best, has never allowed editors to be just that. Rather, the inadequate perceptions of the industry and audience—as well as some of the practitioners themselves—have kept the stereotyped editor in that dark cutting room.

When common responses were distilled from the interviews with these twenty-three editors, a number of characteristics and principles surfaced. Many of the editors here learned by doing. Some found formal book-learning or class-learning to be sorely inadequate to penetrate the emotion and instinct of an editor's creativity. It is very easy, they all contend, to make a beautiful splice. It is not as easy to learn how to edit beautifully.

One universal principle that distinguishes good from bad editing is rhythm and musicality. Many editors were or are musicians (or would have liked to be). Their sense of rhythm, tempo, "the beat" is translated into the intricate alignment of images and sounds. This rhythm is often internal, built into the editor's sensitivity to the image and the word. A sequence in a final film may not even be accompanied by music, yet there will be an inevitable rhythm to the flow of images that transports the audience with it. An editor is especially proud when music written for a scene that was cut *without* music falls naturally into its "visual beat." Editors often cut to music of their own choice, even though it may not be used in the film. This "scratch" or "temp" music evokes a mood or awakens a feeling that helps them enter the emotion of the scene. An editor's innate ability to create a musical flow throughout the film is all the more extraordinary since the film is often scored after the final cuts are made.

Equally important is the subliminal power of editing. Viewers often say that editing is invisible to them unless the film is slowed down and analyzed frame by frame. This invisibility is perhaps a principal reason that editing is seldom considered while watching a movie; it is not as tangible as costumes, photography, music, or acting. Editing is the movement and manipulation of frames, within which more movement takes place, but audiences forget the physical passage of the film itself and become absorbed in the movement of the story. The editor must continually remember both the moving pieces of film and the moving images *on* the film, for both must work together simultaneously. Dozens of joined shots fly past the eye at twenty-four frames per second, and the cumulative impact is of an overall image, emotion, or sensation. Even one shot of two frames (imperceptible to the conscious eye), specially inserted within a longer sequence, can disrupt audience expectations or mold emotional response.

It has often been speculated that editing is a process that draws its momentum from the subconscious of the editor. Editors will agree that successful—memorable—editing makes visual and emotional connections between seemingly unrelated items. One might recall the rich interplay of outdoor sound effects that paralleled the heated argument between Marlon Brando and Eva Marie Saint in *On the Waterfront*. Whether to intensify sounds, insert close shots, return to long shots, cut on, before, or after certain words or gestures—these were all editorial decisions made to portray this couple's relationship through visual and aural elements. Whatever became a part of this sequence had been selected and controlled for its ultimate emotional and narrative impact. Connections between a film's characters, relationships, and environment all derive from a subconscious ability to discover layers.

Editors will continually refer to that "other consciousness" that taps a source of inspiration far beyond ordinary common sense. To enter this dimension, editors have to become absorbed in the film and the cutting so that time, personal problems, the entire room disappear. Editors long skilled in the mechanics of the job (and gifted with assistants who can do the "rough stuff") find the physical work second nature; they can bypass thinking about it to enter a trancelike state. Some attribute this condition to the actual feel of the film and the rhythm they create as they pass film through their upright Moviola or flatbed (editors can also be vehement about which tool they prefer). Electricity flows between them and the film. Their silent attentiveness only masks the busyness of their minds, which juggle hundreds of decision factors for every cut: matching, overlaps, dialogue, camera movement, performance, point of view, sound, music, action-reaction, what precedes, what follows, ad infinitum. This dimension is akin to the process of creation in writing, art, music, acting, inventing—any discipline that reaches into the dark, unknown chaos of raw materials and shapes them into a work that illuminates those who touch the final product. Editors admit, without hesitation, that they are in awe of that process.

The solitary nature of the job stresses organization, discipline, persistence, self-reliance, and tireless devotion to details. Yet all editors recognize the importance of collaboration, particularly with the director, and a generally soft-spoken nature can be an asset to the give-and-take nature of the business. Experienced editors grow confident in speaking up to producers, cinematographers, and composers about what they feel they need to make the film work. However resolute and outspoken they are, though, editors never forget that the director must be the unifying mind behind the project, and they remain servant to that vision. The ideal relationship between editor and director is a close familial one, in some cases spanning decades of trusted collaboration. Editors often describe themselves as assuming various roles for the director: therapist, advisor, hand-holder, mother or father figure, best friend, sounding board, diplomat, even whipping boy. Sometimes the only communication between them is the most sublime kind in which there is no need for words. Yet whatever transpires in conferences and screenings with directors, producers, or other interested parties, there is always the incomparable solitude of the cutting room, where the editor alone joins disparate clips into scenes, sequences, whole reels, and finally the entire film.

The quiet time of actual hands-on editing can be a welcome respite from the enormous pressures on nearly every editor. Of all the roles in the filmmaking process, perhaps only the director's job surpasses it in responsibilities and commitment to the final product. Although they are *post*production, many editors contribute whispers in the director's ear during preproduction and shooting. And editors tend to work beyond the cutting—through previews, premieres, rereleases; sometimes they are even reengaged for television adaptations and reconstructions years later. Unfortunately, film editors (like sound editors, who are even more constrained by last-minute demands) face short budgets, short schedules, and short tempers. One universal editor's lament is that so much money can be spent on preproduction and shooting that the bucks stop before getting to the cutting room.

Despite these limitations, editors are uniformly devoted to their primary responsibility: to make real the director's vision. This duty involves speaking up when they feel the director is too close to the film to see its flaws. Enter the editor as "objective eye." Sifting through mountains of dailies can be a numbing experience, but the editor must preserve a critical distance. Editors develop techniques to keep the material fresh: running different sequences consecutively, sometimes even backward; soliciting their assistants' observations; inviting colleagues for second opinions; audience previews; just stopping work and going off to play. Editors need to control the emotional involvement they develop with a film and learn to let go, as possessive and proud as they may be of a particular sequence. They must objectify the film until every frame— literally—fits into the vision. Many an inspired sequence has had to hit the cutting-room floor because it pulled the film away from its overall focus. Editors must become the translators through which the *film* (not they) speak.

This sticky issue of subjectivity versus objectivity—more broadly, film versus truth—is particularly crucial in documentary film. Documentary editors differ from feature editors in that they usually work from concepts rather than line-by-line scripts, and documentary editors essentially consider themselves filmmakers as much as the directors are. Themes are discovered and abandoned as the story unfolds from the dailies, until the most telling material is selected and arranged. Documentary editors sometimes describe their work with the metaphor of the jigsaw puzzle— finding the pattern of the picture within the thousand fragmented bits recorded by the camera. They are also challenged by the audience's preconception that documentaries are boring; they seek to break away from the traditional didactic lecture-with-pictures format and find ways to give the film a "feature look." They must, however, remain conscious of the reality of their material. They must be ever true to the subject—the real people—without distortion, prejudice, or fabrication. The power of ordering and juxtaposing images is immense, and has been recognized since the (possibly apocryphal) "Kuleshov Experiment" of the 1920s. The Russian director-theorist juxtaposed the same neutral facial expression with three different emotionally volatile images and thereby elicited different audience interpretations of that one facial expression. To avoid bias, broadcast journalism, for example, has prescribed rules for filming and editing. Yet the ongoing challenge for documentary filmmakers and editors is the distinction between film and reality. As the documentary editors consider in these interviews, the choice of where to place the camera and what to shoot already influences the picture of reality-out-there. How much more so can editing tamper with or enhance the "truth"?

In both documentary and feature worlds, however, editors learn to become unaffected by the preconceptions (or the contagious human excitement) of location shooting and unhindered by the responsibilities (or preconceptions) of the director. All editors live by what is in the footage, not what the scriptwriter or director hoped would be there. Editors know they are rewarded for their patience during the grueling chore of watching dailies when special takes leap out at them—a character's glance, a pattern of light, an emotionally charged image. Such footage offers itself as the core of the film, the "heart" around which less compelling material will revolve. Once this heart is located, the film seems to become a living, breathing entity to the editor, despite all its anticipated challenges and problems. Initial feelings of inadequacy and helplessness—"Where can I start?"—which plague nearly every editor, finally drop away. At that point, editing transcends the mundane and ventures into the realm of art.

From the moment footage enters the cutting room to the day the film is "locked," editors are immersed in a complex process of mechanics and creativity. Because their work is essentially intangible, editors are concerned that the profession has too long been misunderstood or even dismissed by audiences, colleagues, and critics. Some editors are troubled by the nagging misconception that they are mere polishers who cut out the "bad stuff" or shorten the film under instruction. Watching an editor work often contributes to this erroneous picture, for an uninformed bystander can easily become bored seeing an editor run the same piece of film back and forth fifty times. It seems senseless, tedious, repetitious, unproductive. But usually, this physical manipulation is part of what triggers the hypnotic state through which editors can enter the deep part of the mind that finds expression, layers, connections. To edit is not merely to *cut*. Editors agree that until one actually faces the screen, feels the film, and embraces the infinite possibilities that lie ahead, one fully understand the intricacies and ecstasy of the editing process.

Editing need not remain arcane and inscrutable to those outside the cutting room. There are a number of comprehensive how-to-edit manuals and famous theoretical studies (see References), which any serious student of filmmaking should become familiar with. But what I have missed in this literature was the person of the editor telling his or her story. My library of film books contained many volumes of interviews with directors, scriptwriters, and cinematographers, and some intriguing collections of interviews with people behind the scenes, among which would be an editor or two. But comprehensive readings that really conveyed how editing looked through editors' eyes were missing.

My own scholarly studies of film have involved close analysis—tearing films apart shot by shot, searching for juxtapositions and layers—so I had a strong desire to understand how editors constructed all these connections. I met with feature and documentary editors on the East and West Coasts who shared generously of their insights. I enjoyed many kindnesses while interviewing: some editors gave me a quick demonstration of the latest video equipment; another invited me to look through memory albums of his years at a big Hollywood studio; at a dubbing session I witnessed an intense discussion concerning the deletion of two frames to make a word sound smoother. I was excited to talk of films that were to be released, as if I were privy to yet-unannounced information from celebrities. Moreover, I was touched that so many editors were willing to entrust me, a stranger, with the emotional (and private) side of their work—their passion for editing, their youthful love of movies, their admiration of (or disappointment with) colleagues and the industry—all described with wit, sophistication, and surprising humility.

My conversations with these editors also disclosed an unexpected camaraderie and mutual respect, considering the general competitiveness and callousness of the film business. The editing field is a tight, supportive network; even when contact is lost between editors, one drop of a name seems to join them again, at least in spirit. Legendary editors like Dede Allen, Jerry Greenberg, Carl Lerner, and Aram Avakian are continually mentioned by those who were greatly influenced or trained by them. Most editors also willingly assume the role of teacher, either to their assistants, who will presumably carry the torch, or to students in film schools. Editors find it incredibly challenging to explain their own or others' works to students, who usually want to be directors or writers. Editing classes should not be a forum for war stories, nor a podium for one editor's favorite methods and formulas. All editing classes, and film history or appreciation classes that include editing (a gap in many curricula), are opportunities to look at old material with new eyes, to tear apart and reconstruct, to make rules and break them, to find and let go. Most important, perhaps, is to be unafraid to reach within and express one's inner voice.

Partly through planning and partly through serendipity (an important force that a few editors mention), the conversations I had with these editors complemented each other in subject matter and personality. Within each broad category of documentary and feature film, where the basic information could have become repetitive, every editor tells different stories and introduces new topics. Thus the interviews as a group present a wide range of information and lore for both the serious student of editing and the interested lay reader. The editors cover such topics as "doctoring" a film, video versus Moviola versus flatbed, the Golden Age, television, second-unit direction, teaching, the assistant editor's experience, stock footage, butt splicers, editor-as-producer/director/writer/ camera operator/audience, *cinéma vérité*, surviving dailies, featurettes, trailers, looping, truth-in-the-news, Oscars and Eddies, point of view, temperaments, voiceovers, commercials, montage, special effects, the "emotional line"—and the list continues. The interviewees' anecdotes about people, places, and things provide unique, practical perspectives on what aspiring or beginning editors are likely to face. There are also conversations with editors in transition to careers as directors and producers. One editor tells of her British background and how she successfully entered the American industry. An interview with father and son editors provides a personal sixty-year history of how editing has changed for the better and worse. Veteran editors balance young editors, and documentaries balance features. Classic films are reconsidered from the perspective of the editors, and what they have to reveal is enlightening.

The interviews have been arranged to present, step by step, the most important structural and conceptual principles of editing. As editors present their unique experiences and examples, ideas will overlap and be reinforced. Side by side, these conversations will stimulate new ways to think about editing. Aspiring editors will find a comprehensive portrait of how an editor begins and grows. Aspiring directors, scriptwriters, and cinematographers will also benefit: by understanding the editing process, they can guide their talents in the early stages to serve postproduction and, as a result, produce tighter, richer films.

Because this is the first book to collect interviews of award-winning documentary and feature film editors in one volume, it is in many ways like the first cut of a film. As is often stated in the interviews, the first cut is the first structure of the whole film which both the director and editor will work with and build upon. No future work can begin without a first cut, however rough and incomplete. And even though the director is the driving hand and the final word, the first cut cannot exist without the persistence and perception of the editor, who sifts through the best *and* the worst to create one special entity. It is the first of many cuts, perhaps, to reach that elusive perfection, but without it, there is no end. Each of the editors who took the plunge into this book have created a first cut once again.

The films are diverse, the personalities are singular. Yet each editor's life and work are bridged by a common understanding of what makes a film successful for an audience. Editors are critical figures in the filmmaking process who balance, manipulate, eliminate, add, shorten, lengthen, mystify, and clarify what is seen and heard and felt on the screen. Almost all editors believe that editing should remain invisible to the eye; only the effect is to be experienced. They are pleased when no one notices the editing, for then the audience is completely captivated by the story. To edit is to respectfully serve the talents of writer, cinematographer, performer, art director, musician, and director; to create a cumulative sensory journey for the audience while the editors themselves remain hidden. This book is a tribute to the hundreds of journeys that these twenty-three editors—and every master editor—have given us at the movies. Here, they become clearly visible at last.

1

Being an Editor

Sheldon Kahn

* See Appendix for complete list of editing awards and nominations.

From his early days of racing through the TV newsroom with "top story" under his arm, to pioneering the KEM flatbed editing system with colleague Donn Cambern, to branching out into producing, Sheldon Kahn never shies from challenges: "As long as I can continually try new and different things, it's fresh every time I come to work." For Kahn, dramatic film is as compelling as comedy, and he comfortably works at both ends of the spectrum, as evidenced by his award-winning work on *One Flew Over the Cuckoo's Nest* and *Out of Africa* and the box-office smash *Ghostbusters*. The first two films also show Kahn's versatility in collaborating with a team of other editors to produce a unified, seamless motion picture.

Kahn's youthful passion for the movies drives him to experiment with film as an editor. Sitting behind a large desk in a comfortable office at the Burbank Studios in California (with a Ghostbusters ray gun on a nearby table), Kahn presents the movie magic of his profession as well as the hard business realities. Although he recognizes the trying personalities, unreasonable schedules, and innumerable decisions that every editor faces, Kahn refers to them in a near whisper as if ultimately they are not the real concerns in editing. He prefers to focus on what he hopes to create with the motion picture for the public and himself.

This interview introduces many basic principles and dimensions of editing, specifically feature film editing. Kahn describes the rich emotional involvement that editors share with film; the intuition needed to unleash unknown connections; the role of the editor as objective audience and storyteller. His experiences reveal how all-consuming editing is in daily and personal life, if editors are to solve problem sequences; his examples illustrate how editors must break rules or make new ones to meet the demands of each film.

Since I was seven, I knew that I wanted to be behind the camera. I wasn't one of these kids who wanted to be a doctor, a fireman, or an actor.

What was the lure to be behind the scenes?

The lure was the knowledge that a lot of talented people were behind the screen helping to put those images there, and I wanted to be part of that process. So from age seven, I focused my education toward going to a college with a great film school so I could learn about all those behind-the-camera jobs. Today I shudder when I think that I applied to one college and one college only, USC, with no doubt that I was going to get into their cinema program. I did, I got into the program, but what a dumb mistake to apply to only one college! Learning about camera, lighting, directing, producing, editing, sound, and writing, I found out very fast that I seemed to shine at the editing process. It seemed to me to be a big puzzle that we're putting together, and sometimes putting it together in a manner that is not necessarily the script's view, but maybe better than the script's view. After graduating, it took me a year to finally break into the film union. I had interviewed at different places and finally got a call from CBS Television City to come in for an interview for the film shipping department. When I left, I said to myself, "Gee, that was good, but I'll probably never get the job," because I knew that a cousin of a TV star and a writer's son from *Gunsmoke* were also applying for it, and I had no family in the business. A week later, I got a call from CBS to come in, the job's mine! Within three or four weeks I got to know everybody, and one day I think I bragged to the boss's secretary that my interview must have been real good because I knew the competition and I had no family in the business. She said, "Oh Shelly, don't tell me that, I know better." I said, "What are you talking about?" She said, "Come on, isn't your father Irving Kahn?" I said, "Yeah, my father is Irving Kahn." She said, "And doesn't he own Acme Lab?" I said, "No!" They had thought that was my father and so that's how I got the job. Sometimes having the right *name* helps you break into the business!

Once you were in, how did you move up?

From carrying cans at CBS Television City, their sister station KNXT needed someone to develop 16mm news film with the possibility that the job would lead to cutting news for TV. I thought I would apply for the job. Of course, I had never seen a processing machine, so the night before the interview, I bought a seventy-five-cent pamphlet that Kodak had on developing stills and the next day I went in and said, "Oh sure, there's developer, there's hypo, there's the button to turn on the machine! No problem!" I got the job and begged the guy who was leaving to show me how to run the machine! He did and I stayed five years at KNXT. Within a few months, KNXT increased its news from thirty minutes to one hour, so they needed to increase their staff. And after three months of being on the monster processor, I went downstairs and started cutting news. After five years, I decided that this was fun but I wanted to get into feature films. I got into assisting and after a few years, I met a wonderful editor named Donn Cambern who wanted to use a new machine called the KEM. It is a flatbed editing machine and very different from the Moviola. I assisted him on two films, *Blume in Love* and *Cinderella Liberty*. The first film on which I was full editor and also coeditor with John Carter was *Mikey and Nicky*, which Elaine May directed. Since I was one of the only people in Hollywood at that time to have ever used a KEM, she wanted my expertise as she was used to this style of editing in New York. After I finished that picture (eighteen months later), I got a call from Michael Douglas, who was producing *One Flew Over the Cuckoo's Nest* in San Francisco. Milos Forman, the director, wanted to work with editors who worked on the KEM. I think I got the job more because of my KEM experience than my editing ability at that time. The rest is history.

Was your approach to editing news very different from features?

Yes and no. The one thing that news taught me was the importance of deadlines. At KNXT I usually got the story that went on at one minute after the show started, but may not have arrived until minutes *before* showtime. So I'd have *seconds* to cut it together and, like in the movie *Broadcast News*, they would hold all the doors open, clear a path, and at ten seconds after six, I would race from my editing room to the telecine department where the projector was, and as they're announcing the story, we're threading it up and just making it on the air. This only relates to feature films as I find it important to get the story on its feet as fast as possible to see if I have everything I need to tell the story. And if I don't, I talk with the director to make sure he is happy or if maybe we should get additional material to make the scene better.

How can anyone survive such pressure?

In all honesty, I'm one of the nuts that find pressure to be fun. Even the pressures of doing a film like *Ghostbusters*—normally you take twelve to fourteen weeks to cut a picture from the time they finish shooting, but we had five or six weeks total. I found it to be a great challenge because we had to make many decisions and be right 99 percent of the time. That added pressure made you do better because many times you could not go back and make changes.

Were special effects a problem for you?

Ghostbusters is in a class by itself in problems because many times the shot consisted of something we could not see when we were editing until it was manufactured by the optical house. Bill Murray may be talking to "Slimer" but you have to use a piece of blank film in place of the character who has to be manufactured later. When you're doing this kind of picture, you're guessing at how long it takes that action to happen, and in *Ghostbusters* you had to guess 99 percent, 99.7 percent correct, because the material given back to you by the optical house would be exactly as long as the leader you put in. Like shooting off the guns, you had to be pretty accurate about how long it took for the ray to hit something, and they would draw it that way. If you made a mistake by making it too short or too long, especially if you needed more of something, you were stuck because there was no more.

Could you overguess and cut down?

"Less is more" is rule-of-thumb with many opticals. When you realize that opticals contain a lot of animation and each frame of animation is very expensive, you try hard to determine how long something is going to be. You don't want to make it twice as long because then the optical costs twice as much money. That becomes a big factor in your editing of the scene. Many times the way you thought scenes were going to look ended up different when they came back because the people manufacturing the optical had a different overview of it. In these cases we might do some last-minute reediting to bring the scenes closer to the way we saw them in our minds. In live-action pictures, if something doesn't work, you can cut it out or change to a different take in order to make the performance between two actors work. When you have an inanimate actor working with a real actor, you don't have that ability to go to a different take of the inanimate actor. You have to make "him" work at all times.

Did you have to act the scene out to determine how long it took?

Yes, mentally you have to act these things out in order to figure out how long it's going to be on the screen. When you're looking at that blank screen, you're seeing images that aren't there!

How about a heavily animated sequence, like that of Marshmallow Man?

In a lot of that, you cut back to the reactions of the live actors. Ivan Reitman and I had discussed how we would make the Marshmallow Man's entrance. As an audience, we learned that Danny Aykroyd is the one who caused this to happen because in his childhood he remembered that marshmallows were important to him. And while he's making that speech, we hear offstage sounds going boom-boom—we don't know what it is yet, but we know that Bill Murray and Danny Aykroyd have seen something unbelievable. I remember Ivan and I discussing how to enhance the enjoyment of the audience by adding as much tension in the development of this character before we see it. Through Aykroyd's eyes, we see something going past two buildings. It's the head of the Man— we're not sure what it is, but we know it's going to be unbelievably great. We could have just had it turn the corner and come straight toward us and you would have seen the whole thing, but we didn't want to do that. We heightened the audience curiosity by showing you a sliver of what is coming, then went to Danny saying something, then another sliver. Finally it turns the corner and you see it in its immensity! The Marshmallow Man.

Is there a standard format for creating tension, whatever the genre?

I'm sure that the "standard" one would say is short tiny cuts would make you more excited than long fluid cuts. Yes, at times you do go to the tricks that you know have worked in the past. The *Jaws* trick of very short shots that get your attention. Absolutely, there are certain techniques you will use in order to heighten the scene that are totally proven. You've got to be very careful, I believe, as the storyteller not to let the audience get ahead of you. And sometimes giving them less information and letting them fill in as the story goes is better than giving them all the information immediately and then they're two steps ahead of you through the film. I hate, for instance, when a writer does a lot of expository dialogue so the scene tells you what the next scene is going to do. As an audience, I prefer not being told what I'm going to see next. I try as much as possible to get rid of that dialogue so that the story tells itself. An example is when someone says, "Well, let's go visit Dr. So-and-so and see if he knows where the Magic Flute is." Then the next scene is they're knocking on Dr. So-and-so's door and they go in looking for the flute! I'd much prefer them saying, "We've got to find out what has happened to the flute, where can we start?" Boom! They're at Dr. So-and-so's door. The way I edit a story, the audience is with me as we go along this adventure. As a film editor, you're looking at the picture totally objectively, not subjectively, and you're trying very hard to pretend you're the audience so that if something is not working, you are the first one to know and can fix it. It's nice to be able to go to the director and say, "Could we cheat something in order to make the scene work better?" I remember when I cut *Same Time, Next Year* with Bob Mulligan. I saw the dailies of Ellen Burstyn the third time she comes back to the cottage and she walks around the room touching all the things that were important in another scene before Alan Alda enters. I felt it might be playing too long and I would be in trouble if I did not have a way to get her into the room faster. So after they shot the scene and I started putting it together, I asked Bob if he'd shoot me one extra shot so that instead of going

A–B–C–D–E, I could go to A–B–E, with just one extra shot to shorten the scene. At the end of the shoot he was able to do it and, if I'm not mistaken, he labelled it "Shelly's Shot."

You talk about being the audience when you edit. Do you actually play a different audience member, like a sixteen-year-old or a fifty-year-old?

No, not really, I can only be myself but I hope my intuition on what is funny or serious in a scene affects other people the way it affects me. This is what I mean by being the audience when I cut a film.

Certainly Ghostbusters *draws a different audience than* Out of Africa.

Yes and no. Audiences, I believe, want to be serious sometimes and want to laugh at other times. I find that to be wonderful because it's so nice to know you can do dramatic pieces like *Out of Africa* or *Absence of Malice* or *Cuckoo's Nest* and still have the sense of humor to do *Ghostbusters* or *Twins*. I find both kinds of films challenging and I know that if I only did one kind of film, I might get bored. I try to find a film that's going to be interesting to me, otherwise I don't want to do it. The director, the producer, and the editor are probably the three people who spend the most time on a film. The editor's there from the first day of shooting till usually it gets into the movie theater. And if it's a project you don't have good feelings about, it's very difficult to get up in the morning and want to come to work. I know when I get up in the morning and go into the shower, the first thing I say to myself is, "What am I editing today?" and I mentally cut the scene in the shower! It's not an eight-hour-a-day job. I find that I make four thousand decisions a day. One of the things that upsets my wife the most is she'll say, "We'll go out to dinner tonight," and I'll say, "Fine, you make the decision where because I've made four thousand today and there's no way I can make another one!"

When you're cutting away feverishly, do you enter another dimension?

Yes, I guess I am in the film.

Are you one of the actors?

No, I'm sort of that omniscient observer watching all the actions of the actors in all the dailies, trying to find the best pieces to make that scene work. Many times I'll find a particular action that an actor has done, and it might have nothing to do with that part of the scene, but I notice that their eyes lit up at a moment as a reaction they might have given to something else, and then I'll use it within a scene to enhance the character. I remember, for instance, in *Cuckoo's Nest*, Louise Fletcher was preparing herself for a scene and Milos Forman said something to her. She sort of sniffed and reacted to what Milos had said because she was registering it in her mind at that point. I noticed that particular attitude as a wonderful reaction to be used somewhere in the picture. When I was cutting the scene in which Jack Nicholson comes back from electroshock treatment where he's walking stiff like Frankenstein, one of the cuts I went to was Louise Fletcher doing her sniff and giving a sideways glance—which was really to Milos Forman, but it looked like it was in the direction of Jack Nicholson. It was a wonderful reaction of her seeing him after his "treatment." It also worked because the costumes never changed, she always wore the nurse's outfit, and she was sitting in many of the scenes. Mostly, it worked for that moment.

That is an amazing film in its use of reactions, as if you never see the person you hear, but you see everyone else.

That was a style of editing that Milos wanted to use on this film, and in my opinion, it was totally brilliant. I don't know of a film prior to *Cuckoo's Nest* that was cut as much on the reactions of other people as opposed to the person who was talking. It's been used since, and it's sort of fun to see a dramatic picture in which they use that style. "Aha! I know where they got that from." Also there were three editors on *Cuckoo's Nest*, myself, Richard Chew, and Lynzee Klingman, and I thought it was miraculous that Milos could form from the three of us this one style of editing where you can't tell the difference between the three people editing. I give him a lot of credit for that.

Is there a distinct editing style between editors?

I find that one of the editors I coedit a lot with is Donn Cambern, and we have seen enough of each other's films to know how we work and the style we work in and it's very easy for both of us to maneuver our styles right into one style of editing. I think that different editors do bring a certain look to a film. I am what I could call a "performance editor," always looking for the best performance from the actors, and I spend a lot of time going through the material, cutting it two or three different ways until I decide, even for the first cut, how the scene should go. I try to bring as much of the performance—it may be in twelve different takes—that I can onto the screen. It's not to say that other editors don't do that too, but I don't consider myself necessarily the best "action editor" in town. I focus on the actor and the performance.

When you follow speakers, it seems fairly easy to know when to cut from each, but when you work with reactions, how do you pace the cutting?

That's like asking an editor how does he know how to cut. It's strictly something that's inside him and it's an emotional thing. When you're in a room with eight or nine people and they're all important to the scene, you've got to keep each one of them alive by seeing each one of them even though they're not talking, and you just instinctively go to them and get what they're doing *as well as* the person who's talking.

Almost as if you're telling two stories.

Or four or five stories at one time, yes, you are. It's the magic of film, that a little bit of information goes a long way. Hold on a reaction from Danny DeVito during a scene, even though the reaction might be a second and a half, then go to four or five more different reactions. You record all of them in your mind and see the whole canvas at once.

Would that cutting be as effective for a film like Out of Africa?

You never use the same style on every film. Every film dictates to you a little different style. It's the old saying of, "If an actor's giving a wonderful performance, don't cut away from it." There's no need to. You don't have to be insecure that the audience is going to be bored. When you're talking about a picture like *Out of Africa*, you just believe in the performances and go with them. It's a different type of story, it's a love story, a romantic story, quite different than the quirkiness and insaneness of *Cuckoo's Nest* where so many people are doing different things and they're all important to the telling of the story. *Out of Africa* is one woman's story and her images are important. The images are much longer played on the screen so you get the beauty of the images that she sees. That's part of the style of telling that story.

Yes, to tell the story at one point you used her voiceover rather than let us watch her performance. Instead, we see the room or the manservant changing the flowers as we hear her reminisce.

I want you to know I get chills when you start talking about that. At the end of the movie when the character is leaving Africa for the last time and telling the manservant who has been so wonderful throughout the picture, "Call me by my first name," it brings tears to my eyes. It's a wonderful relationship between two people. That picture is about relationships. I've seen that film forty or fifty times, and those moments are as stirring and as poignant to me today as they were the first time I saw them.

In the love scene between Meryl Streep and Robert Redford, you used a technique very different from the rest of the film.

We were trying to go for some kind of montage feeling in that scene, and my first mental approach to it was doing 1930s kinds of dissolves, keep it flowing with pretty dissolves and images because this is their first love scene. But Sydney Pollack and I sat down and decided that was so stereotyped for a way of doing a love scene and that there's got to be another way of getting the same message across. To me, the ultimate love scene with dissolves was done with Jane Fonda in the war picture *Coming Home*. It was one of the most erotic love scenes I've ever seen. She's in bed with Jon Voight, and many dissolves lap from one to the next to the next. I knew I could never achieve as good an effect in *Out of Africa* as was done in that picture, so I wanted to do something different. By accident almost, we came up with letting the action go on a particular shot of certain business and *cutting*, moving the action back a little bit, letting it go forward to another point, then cutting to another. When they got in the bed together and Robert Redford starts to move his head down to kiss her, I cut to him getting into the bed again and starting to kiss her again. Those were all different takes of the same particular action that went on in that scene. We felt that we got the best pieces of romanticism out of each piece by doing this style and making it as romantic as we could. That interrupted style was a unique way of telling a love story. The love scene at that point in the film was stylistically different from the rest of the film and we were definitely striving to do that. If it jumped out at you, we succeeded.

Contrast that with Private Benjamin *when Goldie Hawn and Armand Assante walk through the streets. That's a more typical montage.*
    Correct. But it worked for that scene. Another montage in that picture is when she's going through basic training, and we do all these 1930s wipes or "flops" in which we start the basic training with her running through the obstacle course and wipe, then we see her working with the rifle, then wipe out of that to her with the gas mask, then wipe out and see her running. Then when she gets to another obstacle, we wipe to her with a machine gun, and so on, and finally get her through the obstacle course. In a period of maybe a minute and a half, you as audience saw a ten-week period of basic training. For that film, an old-fashioned look worked.

Are you ever so affected by the beauty of the photography, as in Out of Africa, *that you risk slowing the story to include the images?*
    Well, maybe, but I think the advantage of being an editor is that, yes, you may let the beauty of the photography slow the story down, but then you see it on the screen and you know that you need less. And you keep honing it down and bringing it to a playable size. That picture, as I recall, ended up two hours and forty-one minutes long on the screen, and I think the first cut was three and a half hours. We knew we had too much story to tell and we had to bring it down without ever letting the audience know that things were missing from it.

Did you eliminate storylines?
    Or cut down, yes, very much. For instance, the little boy with the broken leg that the Meryl Streep character heals, we took a lot of his story

out, but it still made sense and it worked as part of the movie. Also we had a lot more of the beauty of Africa to work with; unfortunately we had to take it out of the story. This is part of storytelling, slim it down and keep all the enjoyment of it. I remember the first cut of *Private Benjamin* was three hours and one minute long. For a comedy, that was insane. A comedy at two hours is too long. I think Woody Allen has the best approach; his movies are never over eighty-five, eight-six minutes. We finally came out at an hour forty-five, which to me was a little too long. That was challenging to bring it down to that size and keep the comedy moving.

What is the nature of comedy that it must be short and sweet?

I think the audience may get tired of laughing. And you've got to be careful you're not telling the same joke four or five times. It becomes tiring for the audience, they know the joke's going to happen, and you've got to keep it fresh and moving and surprise the audience at all times. It's difficult to do that for more than 85 to 110 minutes.

You can achieve a surprise by either cutting or not cutting. Does that decision depend on what you sense to be the point of the story?

Sometimes by putting little pieces of information into a scene that are not in the script, we can tell a story in the most solid manner and understand why a character feels a certain way. In *Private Benjamin*, there is a scene toward the end where Goldie is going to get married to Armand Assante. When I put it together for the first time, we had a justice of the peace speaking the marriage vows to her in French. We had close-ups in which we could see her thinking, and halfway through the ceremony she says, "Stop! I'm not going through with this." I remember putting that scene together Friday afternoon and being very unhappy with it. At six-thirty, seven o'clock, on my way home, it all of a sudden came to me what I was feeling terrible about and what didn't work. As an audience, you could see she was thinking, but you had no idea *what* she was thinking about. So it came to me in a flash that the way to make that scene work would be to cut to what she was thinking of. As an editor, I'm forcing in the minds of the audience what she's thinking of. I did a very short cut of her first husband Yale doing something bad to her, then cut back to her and a little more of the ceremony. Then she looks over to her father and at that point, I cut to a shot of her father shaking his finger at her, being negative, and then cut back to her at the wedding. Then a little later in the ceremony, she looks over to her husband-to-be and I cut to a shot we've seen earlier where he asked her to sign a prenuptial contract. *Then* she says, "Stop! I'm not going through with this." She realizes that the men she has related to have all done something bad to her and she does not want this to be her life. But that was *not* part of the script. I knew when I cut it together as it was scripted that it was not working for me—Shelly Kahn, the audience—and I felt that if I did not understand why she stopped the wedding, neither would the audience. It had bothered me to the point that I was halfway home when the solution came to me, and I had to turn around, go back to the studio, and make sure it worked. I couldn't wait till Monday morning!

That sequence became even more appropriate because at the end you held the long shot of her walking down the aisle of trees. You used that for credits, of course, but it was like a victory march.

That's *exactly* what it was. Her victory march.

How do you draw the line between subjective and objective when you "force" ideas in the audience? Can that line even be drawn in editing?

I don't know how I draw it. It's just an instinct, in all honesty. I can be wrong as well as right, and therefore that's why in my first cut, I will cut the scene three or four different ways before I decide in my own mind and heart how a scene should play. Part of this objectivity comes from trying to make it work. To feel that the scene is visually and auditorially telling the story.

So objectivity is fitting the pieces together in many ways, and subjectivity is your choice of the best fit.

Yes. The best way that satisfies me in telling that story. And of course, hopefully the director too. I think an editor's best sense is his visual sense, keeping the story moving with all the visuals he has at hand. There is no measurement saying, "The shortest you can have a close-up is two feet, three frames." No. It's what works emotionally. Audiences are very sophisticated today. They catch a short image on the screen, register it in their minds, and understand it. In the old days, in order to cut from one scene to the next, you had to go with long dissolves so that you knew time had passed, it's the next day and another set. Today you can cut from one place to the next. One of the stylistic ways I like to work is finishing one scene in a longer shot, then cutting to a close-up of a person who wasn't necessarily in the scene you just saw. That person will start talking, then I will cut to a longer shot so the audience knows where he is. The audience is surprised by the change and they're taken with it. All of a sudden they say, "Aha! Here we are!"

Then your close-up is the so-called transitional device.

Yes, as opposed to going through a fluid dissolve.

Were there textbook formulas for situations like that at one time?

I believe there may have been. And if there were, I don't want to know about them because, to me, the discovery of how to make a scene work is the most important thing. Not that you should start the scene at this particular point and end it at a certain point, textbookwise. I don't want to know from that, I want to know emotionally what makes it work.

Do you carefully match cuts when you don't use dissolves?

I tend to take liberties all the time in making the scene work. If the actor did not continue with a certain prop, and I have to hide the fact that the cigarette is in the left hand in one shot and the right hand in the next, I try to misdirect the eye to something else that is moving in the next shot so that you don't notice the mismatch. Yes, matching is very, very important, you try to make sure that the action does the same from one shot to the next. But as editor, it's part of the puzzle to make it work with or without that particular action or prop.

Are you aware of mismatches in other films?

Never. Unless I'm bored. If the film is not working, your eye will start wandering the frame of the shot and you might see the mistakes in the shot. But if it's good storytelling, good acting, good editing, good directing, I'm like any other person watching that movie. People will tell me the next day, "Did you see that? Did you notice the microphone in the shot?" Absolutely not. I'm so engrossed in being part of that story.

Do you think editors have had a neglected position in the business?

That's too loaded a question. I think that the most important thing is the script and when you get a good script and those words come out of the actors' mouths, it is absolute magic. There are times when an editor can take a bad script and make it better, but it's very difficult to make a good script bad. A well-written story is very difficult to turn into a bad movie. There are times when through a good editor's vision you can take a not-too-well-written story and make a much better story out of it, usually by what you leave out as opposed to what you put in. The audience never knows what you leave out, they know what they see on the screen and how the story is told. I think the editor as storyteller has a very important function that is part of the scope of motion picture making. But he is not the most important part of that team. He is definitely one of the team that makes it work. Motion pictures, as opposed to other art forms, is a team experience, not a job by one person.

Have you ever had any desire to try another area of film?

Yes, and for Ivan Reitman Productions now, I am producing and enjoying it very much. Do I want to direct? Not at this time, no. It will be a little while longer before I know *every*thing I need to know about producing and I may never want to go on to something else. However, I don't think I ever want to give up editing. It's always a challenge the first time to look at that material and figure out where do I put the close-ups, where do I put the long shots, and so on. All of a sudden your hand moves, your mind starts to click, and magic happens for me. A few hours later, you press a button, sit back and look at that scene, and say, "Yeah, it's working! Wait a second. What if I do *this*? What of the material I *didn't* use? What if I *change* it?" You go back and you shine it a little more and make it a little different. The thing I love most about editing is when I finally get together with the director and we look at the scene, there's a magic that goes on so much of the time. The director will say, "I don't like the scene the way it's put together. What if we try . . . ?" And *I'll* come back and say, "Wait a minute! What if we try . . . ?" And all of a sudden, a third idea comes up that both the director and editor hit on the exact same time. That's when you know you're cooking, you're on the right track, and the scene is going to work. You don't have to say it to each other. You both know and understand.

Do you feel you know everything about editing?

I don't ever want to know everything there is to know about editing. I think then it would be boring. The learning and the trying make editing fun. Those jump cuts in *Out of Africa*, I'd never done that before, but it was something I wanted to try and it seemed to work. As long as I can continually try new and different things, it's like finding the excitement of why it's fresh every time I come to work. I don't know what I'm going to do until I sit with that film, and the film speaks to me and helps me put it together. I'm not trying to be arty. It really is what happens.

Have you fulfilled your childhood fantasies?

I'm not sure but I still am that seven-year-old kid sitting at the Howard Theater in Chicago watching movies. The only difference is today they pay me to watch movies! But I haven't changed. I still have that same love I had when I was seven for being in that dark room and watching someone spin a story for me. The real joy for me, after I've finished a picture, is to go to a theater and watch other audiences stare transfixed. It's working for them and that to me is just wonderful.

2

Becoming an Editor

Emily Paine

1978   *Night Flowers* (Assistant Editor), directed by Luis San Andres

1979   *All That Jazz* (Assistant Editor), directed by Bob Fosse

1980   *The Campaign* (TV) (Associate Editor), directed by Tom Cohen

1981   *The Night the Lights Went Out in Georgia* (Assistant Editor), directed by Ron Maxwell
Community of Praise (TV) (Associate Editor), directed by Richard Leacock and Marisa Silver

1983   *Tender Mercies* (Assistant Editor), directed by Bruce Beresford
Trading Places (Assisant Editor), directed by John Landis

1984   *Graebner High School Handbook of Rules and Regulations* (after-school special) (Associate Editor), directed by Mark Cullingham
The Goodbye People (Associate Editor), directed by Herb Gardner
David Sanborn Concert Film (Editor), directed by Jean Marie Perier

1985   *Static* (Editor), directed by Mark Romanek

1986   *The House on Carroll Street* (Associate Editor), directed by Peter Yates

1987   *Suspect* (Associate Editor), directed by Peter Yates
Homeboy (Associate Editor), directed by Michael Seresin
Sesame Street segment (Editor), directed by Andy Aaron
Crack in the Mirror (Editor), directed by Robby Benson (Coeditors: Craig McKay, Alan Miller, Shelly Silver)

1988   *The Appointments of Dennis Jennings,* directed by Dean Parisot (additional editing)

1989   *The Night's Remorse* (Editor), directed by Max Mayer

1990   *Green Card* (Assistant Editor), directed by Peter Weir

1991   *The Bridge* (Editor), directed by Frank Perry

There is no common pattern for how long it takes to become an editor. Aside from the personality required for the job (and many editors feel they were editors before they ever held a piece of film), everyone must master the tools of the trade. Emily Paine outlines the assistant experience with examples from her work on television and motion picture features and documentaries.

Paine always enjoyed movies, but never realized the importance of editing until she watched friends splice together bits and pieces to make a documentary film. Her father, a commercial producer, introduced her to Bob Brady, who was editing the children's after-school program, *Big Blue Marble*; her reactions to a scene he was cutting piqued her interest in the profession. Paine recalls how essential it was to attend to the tedious nuts and bolts of the cutting room, but to her surprise, she found these organizational demands as interesting as being a liaison between the cutting room and the larger "outside" world of postproduction.

In her many years as assistant and associate, Paine has collaborated with veteran editors William Anderson, Bob Brady, Anne Goursaud, Alan Heim, Michael Kahn, Ray Lovejoy, Craig McKay, Rick Shaine, and Kathy Wenning. Now, as an editor, the feeling of being solo is still fresh and exciting to her.

Complementing Sheldon Kahn's interview, which focuses on his experiences as a seasoned editor, Paine's interview dwells on the beginnings of an editing career. Many of the principles both editors now follow were developed in those early stages of discovery and becoming. An assistant is as devoted to the film as any veteran editor, perhaps even more so because the assistant's job requires persistence through seemingly uncreative chores. Paine stresses a positive, open attitude, not only to master the nuts and bolts, but to develop an awareness of the layers of thought behind every cut.

How would you describe the "assistant" experience?

In a way, as an assistant I felt that I was the total support team for the editor to be able to cut. If the editor has to be distracted by worrying about what I'm doing or about the mechanics of the cutting room, it's a big interference. The editor has to be free. So I felt very important to the project, not because my work was going to show up on the screen, but because the editor couldn't function freely without my providing calm and tranquility in the cutting room. There are a lot of details, it gets very complicated, and it's certainly not a boring kind of job, especially on a feature with a large crew. It's hard at the beginning if you go in wanting to be an editor and you're not interested in the nuts and bolts of the cutting room. Then it can be incredibly tedious wading through all that. I found all of that interesting. I found putting away trims interesting—which is a weird character trait, maybe! You have to like those things because there is a lot of it.

Is that mostly what an assistant does?

It depends on the project and who you're working with. There are some editors who have their assistants editing, which is wonderful. A few people have had good experiences working with one editor for a long time, getting to cut more and more under their supervision, and that's the way they matured as editors. But yes, those are the stages where you learn how to deal with labs and how to handle opticals. You learn how to do everything but cut the film. Running a film cutting room is very labor-intensive. But these are the skills on which you're going to rely. They have to become second nature. You have to know immediately how a cutting room should be organized. The editor has to concentrate on cutting and the assistant has to be able to take care of everything else. There are so many different elements that come into your hands. For example, if the sound editors start to work on a reel and the picture editor changes something, even if he takes out two frames, there has to be a note made of exactly what was changed and the sound editors have to make all other tracks conform to that. Sometimes the assistant has to be the liaison with the sound department or with the composer and the music editor, to make sure they all know what's happening. That's what you are as an assistant. You're the only person who connects that inside room—the room where the director and editor are cutting—with the rest of the team. And at times they don't want to hear what you have to say. Like those six reels that were supposed to be locked are now totally unlocked, and the scenes have been shuffled around and it's back to square one. Nobody wants to hear that. I was not responsible for making sure they did their work, they all did their own work, but I was the coordinator between all these people. I loved the managerial aspect of being an assistant.

Was there a point when you craved cutting film?

After a point, yes. Certainly not initially. I was an apprentice for a long time, about three years, and of course, by the time I was at the end of being an apprentice, I was desperate to be an assistant. My second film as an assistant was *All That Jazz* with Alan Heim. It was a huge job as an assistant. I felt I was pulling my weight, but I was aware that we had a huge crew and a tremendous amount of pressure and it was a complicated job editorially. Plus Bob Fosse was incredibly focused. From nine o'clock in the morning until the end of the day, it was absolutely nonstop. I remember when I first began on the film and it came to be about two o'clock in the afternoon and Bob left the room, I said, "Alan, I'm starving! I can't work anymore. My stomach is growling." He said, "Oh, you're on the Fosse diet." "What am I going to do? I have to smuggle in cottage cheese or something." Anyway, I thoroughly enjoyed being an assistant and then, yes, absolutely, I wanted to be cutting. After *Jazz*, I worked on a documentary with Bob Brady on which I did a lot of editing. My father had introduced me to Bob when he was editing *Big Blue Marble*. I was finishing college and I used to go over to his cutting room and hang out. One day I was watching him edit a sequence with a kid flying up high over a beach. He and I had a very nice casual relationship and I didn't know that it should be anything but that, so I said the sequence was boring. "You don't need all that! Just this little section here, that's the excitement of the shot. That's all you need to use." So he said, "Okay, I'll try that." He was entertaining me. He was willing to let me think I had these great ideas. We had fun and I guess he had the time to be a teacher that way. I went to work for him as sort of a second apprentice part-time; it was that first job you need in order to develop skills and meet people. When he hired me, he said, "This is going to be very different from our visits on *Big Blue Marble*. You're not going to hang out next to me all day, talking about what I'm doing." I went back to work for Bob on the pilot for a six-part documentary, the Middletown Film Project, and I cut a fundraising version of the film with the producer and assembled selected material which Bob needed for the film. It was such a different experience from features. I had never seen raw documentary film before. Here we had documentary footage shot by some of the best documentary cameramen in the country, but it was not like a feature at all. I said, "This is the stuff we throw out!" Between the flash frames; cameras whipping around this way and that. I couldn't imagine how to describe these shots as I used to as an assistant, with copious descriptions of "over-shoulder favor so-and-so." I'm currently editing a feature documentary called *The Bridge* and our cameraman Kevin Keating is brilliant. He creates coverage within a take because, after all, in documentaries you do not get a second take.

Did you follow a script for the Middletown pilot?

No, we had transcripts of interviews which are essential due to the volume of footage and the fact that the structure of the film evolves after the interviews are done. It's easier to go through the transcript and say, "Oh, if I take this sentence and that sentence and the other one, then I can make Emily say whatever." Then you go back and look at the footage where the person says that—and then you find the inflection is off! We used to have a joke about inflections: we have to apply the "inflectionometer" because we're trying to make something sound like it's the end of a sentence that was really the beginning, or it's a question that doesn't work at all even though it looked good on paper.

What would you do when the inflection was wrong but the words right?

Although a lot can be accomplished with clever sound editing, if it sounds wrong you can't use the sentence. You try to find something that sounds more natural or find another way to make the point.

Is the main concern to make the film real to the audience?

Yes, I think to involve the audience with the scene. For example, the audience doesn't have to know that a person got out of the chair or see every little step he takes just to get him to the other side of the room. Some filmmakers use lack of continuity to make a cinematic statement. But in something naturalistic, when you're not making a point of the lack of continuity, you want the audience to focus on the important elements of the story and not be confused. It's mainly taking that confusion out so they don't say, "How'd he get across the room?" If they ask that, they've lost the last twenty seconds of what you're doing. You can come up with these problems in fictional, scripted shooting as well as in documentaries. You can call attention to something with the use of sound if you don't have the picture to do it with. I think in any kind of editing (even on a feature film where everything is supposed to work so beautifully), there are still continuity problems. Sometimes people don't cross the room, yet somehow they get to the other side, so the editor has to figure out how to make the audience *believe* they crossed the room. When I was cutting *Static*, I realized one of the problems in the first scene I put together was that the actors did not complete their actions at the end of a take. In one take, an actor jumped over a fence completely; in another take, he sort of half-jumped and gestured. The two don't cut together. One is real action, the other is fake. In another instance, the character Ernie did not complete his action of getting out of a restaurant booth except in some hugely wide shot that would have been ludicrous to use because we had to cut back in close for dialogue. So instead, I cut to the Amanda Plummer character looking away in the correct direction and used "body rustle" to suggest Ernie getting out of the booth, and it worked fine. I try to suggest to the director and script supervisor to let the actors complete their actions in each take. Sometimes actors are prohibited from completing their actions because of the position of the camera. But if someone is supposed to enter a room, let him enter *before* he starts. If he's supposed to stand up, don't give me a half-rise because that person's energy level in doing that is nothing like when he actually completes the action. As an editor, you become adept at knowing what "cheats" you can and can't get away with. You're always thinking about how to make things work.

What considerations go into selecting from coverage?
    There are a couple of elements. For one thing, if you choose a master, then you choose to use the performances as they were played. If you use coverage, you can change the performances. You can make people wait a long time before they respond, or you can make them jump on another person's line. You create a different reaction to a scene by showing a wide shot with both characters since the audience is objective, or focusing the audience's attention on the perspective of one character over another, if you show one person's reaction to something being said.

So you're always looking for the values within the image.
    That's right, and the image says different things to each audience. You have to trust your gut. I had always heard that close-ups were good in a love scene, but sometimes they can be used to show isolation. Sometimes an over-the-shoulder creates more intimacy because characters are together. Even a two-shot can create intimacy because the characters are together and you can show their body language. In the short film, *The Night's Remorse*, we didn't have enough manipulation of two characters reading their lines, they weren't interacting well, and we couldn't use the two-shot. So we used over-the-shoulders between two characters in order to involve them more with each other. You know, the cut itself is shocking; there can be a tendency to not feel flexible with the material. Sometimes beginning editors or beginning directors can be too shocked by the cut. They might say, "I'm in singles now, I have to stay in singles. As soon as I go back to the master, I've gotta stay in the master."

Why do cuts have drastically different effects? You can have a rush of cuts which people don't notice because they seem transparent. Yet one cut alone can be so abrupt that it knocks you out of your chair.
    I think it has to do with what you're preparing the audience for, what you're asking them to be involved in emotionally in the scene. It has to do with the content of the material. It is also relevant to the sleights-of-hand that can be achieved with editing. The cut should fulfill something in the scene. In *The Night's Remorse*, we cut in flashbacks towards the end of the film. This was actually suggested by an editor friend, Rick

Shaine, who came to a screening. The last scene in the film was really lacking all motivation. A character, who was never major in the film, shows up to kill a Wall Street powerbroker. He has no more reason to hate him than anybody else, he's not a violent man and there's nothing to motivate him doing this. But we put in shots of what that power-broker had done in the past so that it gave the audience memories of his treacheries and created a fuller scene. Nobody at any screening ever said, "What the hell? In the middle of dialogue, I'm suddenly seeing bits and pieces from old scenes." Nobody ever questioned it. Yet in an earlier cut of the film, we tried to build moments between characters with extra cuts, and people screamed, "It's overcut!" There were no continuity problems, there were just cuts that didn't mean anything for an emotional exchange between the characters. We were trying to pump extra life into something that was more satisfying in a simpler form. That created an uproar, while everybody immediately bought the flashbacks which were really inconsistent with the film itself—in fact, the film hadn't even been shot to produce flashbacks. It's just that if the cuts fulfill something the scene needs, the audience will receive and accept that extra pertinent information.

Did you cut to flashbacks or use time-passage dissolves?

We cut to them. They were shots from scenes which had previously been established as flashbacks, and the nature of the character's memory was immediate and urgent, not reflective. Dissolves don't necessarily suggest flashbacks, they can also indicate passage of time in the present or into the future.

Would you say that dissolves have emotional effects on an audience?

Dissolves can create tremendous romance and feeling because they're surreal, I suppose. You're making more of a painting instead of an exposition, not just taking people from one place to another but creating a different mood or reality. Sometimes there are dissolves written into the script and sometimes they don't work. I think that's often because scriptwriters are trying to portray a visual experience on paper and they use a lot of "dissolves to." It's not always necessary to use them in the film. One has to feel free to experiment with a lot of devices. In *The Night's Remorse*, we spent a long time conceiving of flashbacks with dissolves and then the producers came in and said, "You need more punch." The dissolves, in fact, were better, but we needed to feel free to say that the convention we had been using might be completely wrong. I think the ability to fool around with material and go against scripted ideas—which is what you have to do as a documentary editor—can be very helpful in a dramatic film too. You have to know that line between twisting the material inappropriately and using it to create something new. Everybody will cite chapter and verse that the film *has* to end with this scene because that's what we've always discussed. Yet you have to keep an open mind to maybe turning the whole thing upside down. You have to demand that the material give you what you want of it. Eventually it will.

Did you do that with the documentary material for Community of Praise?

Yes. We argued a lot about whether to open the film with a church service with a lot of religious fervor or to introduce our subject family at home and then reveal their religious faith. Eventually we chose the latter. This allowed the audience to experience religion within the context of their daily lives.

Were you restrained in how to present the material because you had to focus on the subject of religion for that program?

Religion really was the focus of these people's lives. They asked so much of God to heal everything, so religion does come in everywhere. You get a different filming experience if you just say, "We're interested in your family," and then see what part religion played. It's like being an anthropologist because you determine the material you get from participants by the way you approach them, how you guide them, what you express interest in. There were two very different schools of thought about filmmaking on the Middletown series. On *Community of Praise*, Richard Leacock shot and Marisa Silver did interviewing and sound. There was nobody with lights, no gaffers. Yet you look at another program in that series, *Family Business* (the program on work, interviewing a fellow with a Shakey's Pizza) and you will see how big a crew was involved. This is bound to affect how the participants present themselves. It affects the editing, too, in terms of how much you tamper with the material. Sometimes on *Community of Praise* we couldn't figure out what we needed for a scene. Do we create extra moments of religious fervor that weren't present? But we kept looking through the dailies and there it all was. "Seek and ye shall find." We got very religious cutting that film!

Could that program ever be taken for a feature? Or is there just a "documentary" or "television" look to it?

I think there is a documentary look which is of necessity because there is no time to relight for different angles and the camera has to be more mobile than for a feature film. But you can certainly make documentaries which people will want to see in a theater, like many of the Maysles brothers' or Barbara Kopple's films. If *Community of Praise* had been cut for feature showing, we would have had time to let things develop more thoroughly. But we had a sixty-minute time constraint and this film had to work as part of a series and deal specifically with religious attitudes. Drama in a documentary comes out because you let things play themselves out. The format you're cutting for determines the material you allow to come through. For example, we couldn't afford just a "dinner scene" in *Community of Praise*, a time for everybody to sit down and chat.

How does an editor pare down all the film a director shoots?

You have to ask of the material what you think should be there, based either upon the script or the experiences of the documentary filming. When I was cutting *The Night's Remorse*, I used to think that, as editor, you've got to be two people cutting a scene. You've got to be the "director of editing," constantly scrutinizing and saying, "That's no good, I want this and this." You've also got to be the mechanical editor getting all this done. It's hard work, you're at a Moviola or Steenbeck all day and it's very concentrated and physically demanding work. If I become unfresh to something, it's because I'm fatigued by trying to find solutions. I have to keep a part of me critical to what I'm doing without losing that critical ability in the face of "I don't know what to do!" Maybe I need to cut another scene, then come back and look at it within the context of other scenes. I like to hear what assistants think; I like to have a body next to me watching. It makes for a different experience.

A silent body?

A silent body! I say, "Sit next to me while we look at this." All of a sudden, it becomes an audience instead of me alone with my material.

Were you a silent body for your editors?

I always worked in the same room with them; I always watched whatever they were doing. Certain editors asked for feedback and others didn't. I remember on my first job as an assistant, I didn't know how to act toward the editor. I had been working in another room all the time. He called me in to look at the scene, but I had *no* idea how to respond. I said, "It works." He shut off the Moviola, looked at me, and said, "I don't want to hear 'It works!' If you're going to make comments like that, I can get a chimpanzee to hand me trims and write down code numbers. You have to *think* about this scene! You have to open your mouth! You have to say what you think!" I said, "Oh, okay." I was intrigued at seeing the pieces come together, but I didn't know how to think about them. I started finding ways. One editor I worked for let me do a lot of cutting. I would screen scenes with him, come up with ideas, then be sent off with, "You got the ideas, you make them work!" As editor, you have to know how to take reactions from assistants because the input is not as experienced as your own, but sometimes they're sharp and fresh to the film. I had an assistant who once pointed out a major plot contradiction that I had absolutely overlooked. She wasn't involved in cutting each scene, so she was more aware of the overall feeling and was able to contribute to that.

How did you finally know you made it as editor?

Editing is a shifting of gears from being a spectator to tackling all the problems, seen or unseen. As an assistant you watch the dailies, you have ideas of how they could be cut, you stand behind the editors and they solve all the problems. Here I watch the dailies, I think how they could be cut, and then *I* cut the film! I solve the problems with an eye to the final effect. Your focus is simultaneously much broader with a view to the whole film, and more specific as each element needs to be just right. When I worked on *Static* and all I had to do was cut the film, it was so much fun. It was a completely different kettle of fish, ball of wax.

Barrel of monkeys.

Absolutely. It wasn't terrifying at all. Well, it starts to be a little terrifying as you approach deadlines. But at the very beginning, when I realized it was up to me to put these pieces together, I couldn't keep thinking of them as tiny images. They have to be *the* characters. You have to look at them with real scrutiny. One thing I learned from and used very much on *The Night's Remorse* is projecting cut film, because scenes play so differently on the big screen. What seems slow on the Moviola is like a snap on the big screen. That's part of the editor's concentration, too, that the little images become more of a bigger reality. When I worked on *Jazz*, I had never seen any of that material projected, and I said to Alan Heim that although you have to know how it plays on the Moviola, you also have to know how it's going to play on the big screen. He said, "That's right." You have to sense what this image size means when it's blown up eight hundred times. Editors develop an internal sense of how things will play on the large screen. That's why it's also important for editors to cut right after they've seen dailies because the ideas are fresh. You become so involved with the characters that it's engulfing. You say to these characters in these little frames, "I want you to walk here. I'd like you to look over here." You get *that* involved with the images on the screen because you have to.

3

Distilling the Documentary

Tom Haneke

As a student in the film department at Boston University, Tom Haneke hated editing. He found it baffling, mysterious, and barely explained except for the mechanics. Securing a job afterward also proved baffling. "When you get a real job, they want to know what you do. You're not a film student anymore. Are you a grip? Are you a production assistant? Are you an editor? What are you?" Haneke worked through low-level film jobs, including picking up the dry cleaning for one boss. After roles as projectionist and assistant cameraman, Haneke wound up in an efficient cutting room and found that he enjoyed being there. The producer liked his beginning work and hired him, and so he jumped from assistant to editor in a year and a half. "I had a role now," Haneke says. "If somebody said, 'What are you?', I could say, 'I'm an editor!'"

Haneke advises students to think long and hard before they choose an area in film because the field is very segmented, and where one starts is likely to be where one ends up. He considers that if his first job had been at a commercial-editing service, he could still be cutting commercials today. Instead, he waded through the making of sponsored films on the history of potato chips and barbecued hamburgers and sales promotion and annual report films, always learning about what made editing work. His earlier experience in a rock band had cultivated an innate musicality that helped him "hear spaces and make moments" in film. As a result of assistant-editor work for producer Allan Miller, Haneke cut his first major film, *From Mao to Mozart*, which won the Academy Award for Best Documentary of 1980. Since then, he has collaborated with Miller on films about Brendan Behan and the world's oldest string quartet. Through editing, Haneke has made music, literature, and dancing more accessible, using the art of film to convey other art forms. He feels that editing is a mystifying process for many because it is slow and invisible. "Students come occasionally and all they see is the Steenbeck and film going back and forth. That's all they talk about. They don't see what you're actually doing."

Once the essential aspects of being an editor are understood, it is easier to recognize differences and similarities between documentary and feature films. For both, music influences rhythm and creates mood. In addition, every film is in search of a story to rivet the audience within its first few minutes. As Haneke says, the documentary's "story" must be found in miles of footage, usually with only a concept of the final film to start with. The editor becomes a scriptwriter, composing with pieces of film instead of words on paper. Haneke believes that the process is one of distilling the truth, the essence of those filmic documents of a life or event. The documentary editor must also grapple with the tension between objectivity and subjectivity while executing the vision of the director or producer. But freed from the restrictions of a script, the documentary editor can make connections never contemplated, or even revolutionize the treatment of the film's subject.

You've cut two Academy Award-winning music documentaries—From Mao to Mozart *and* He Makes Me Feel Like Dancin'. *What's your secret for success?*

I can hear the spaces.

You "hear" visual spaces?

I know how to make moments, where to leave space and where to compress space. I'm not really a trained musician but I'm very musical, I have a good ear. I was in a band in high school, I just take to it. And I've done a lot of musical films. But it's more than that. It's being able to pace and hear the spaces. I can listen to a music track and know the places where you can put the cuts so that they work. I once edited a film which was narrated entirely in Arabic. I was provided with a written translation. It was for some company that wanted to sell an aerospace center or something to Saudi Arabia. So I was faced with editing a film where I didn't really understand what the words were. I knew what they were on paper, but I had to edit to the rhythm of the language. At the final screening, three guys who spoke Arabic came in, sat down, watched the film, and said, "Good!" I hadn't completely missed it. That was using The Force on that one!

Are you on location to suggest material you might need to edit a difficult piece successfully? Request "spaces," so to speak?

No. Editors are hardly ever on location, at least in documentaries. In fact, people will often spend a year filming and then they'll call you up and say, "I'm making this film, I need an editor. Can you start in two weeks?" I think that producers and directors of documentaries would be smart to line up an editor early in the project and talk to him or her about an editor's needs. Describe the events they plan to film and have the editor start thinking out loud about what might be possible in those situations. Then there are technical considerations like room tones, the sound of the room. Most documentary production people don't run room tones. It ends up costing them hundreds of dollars of sound editing and mix time. It's simple, but they don't think about it. As a rule, I don't think it's a good idea for the editor to be on location because you lose the ability to evaluate. I'm really the viewer surrogate the first time I see the film. Sometimes right after the crew comes back from location, we screen the dailies. I don't care how good you are, you can't completely eliminate the feelings you had when you were on location filming the event. You constantly fill in and recall the emotions of that moment when you view the film. *I* don't know what happened, all I know is what's up there on the screen. If I'm not excited, then they missed something, and I have to be able to tell them that something got lost. Then we say, "Well, okay, that's a problem, we can't use it for that." Or I have to figure out a way to cut the footage to convey those feelings. But I *have* to know that it's not there. If I was on location and I got caught up in the whole event, I would have trouble evaluating the dailies.

How do you not feel inundated by the amount of film you receive?

First of all, in dailies there are always one or two scenes that jump off the screen and I would be willing to bet two weeks' salary that those scenes would be in the final film. There's not too many of those scenes, generally. I'm not sure I would get a consensus from other editors or directors on this, but there are millions of different ways to make material work. You can almost make it jump through hoops, put a different spin on it. What are you going to make the material do for you? *Cinéma vérité*, I don't think it ever happens. You can make the material serve what you see as the truth of the situation. It's really in your hands. You have to decide what you think happens in this footage; then you have to take, say, an hour and a half of film of a particular event and make it into a three-minute scene that communicates what you think happened in that hour-and-a-half event. It's the only way you can proceed. You're trying to distill. That's essentially what you're doing in the whole process, distilling the truth, as you perceive it.

But you're manipulating the audience.

Of course you are! That's the point. There's no way *not* to manipulate. Even if you say you're not manipulating, by putting Scene A next to Scene B, you're manipulating, you're leading them on a journey. Seeing a film is an experience in time. You want the audience to be asking, "What happens next? What happens next?" You control the flow of events, the rhythm, the juxtaposition of information. I worry about that because it's so easy to manipulate. You have to be true to the facts, but more importantly, to what you perceive as the truth. Ultimately, it's through your eyes, the filmmaker's eyes. There's no way around that.

Do you have more opportunity to do that in documentaries where you're not as restricted to a script as you are in features?

Yes, when you've got a story, you've got a lot to work with already. Sometimes the material is very clear about what it wants to be. The Beirut sequence in *Mother Teresa*. She went into a war, responded in a particular way, did what she always does, found something that needed to be done and did it. That was easy. We cut that scene in about a week, about twelve minutes of screen time. But it had such a clear line that it almost fell out of the dailies. That was about the only scene in the whole film like that.

Were any of those scenes reenacted, like the coincidence of the cease-fire in answer to Mother Teresa's prayers?

No. Reenactments rarely work, in my opinion. I thought the priest who told that story was good to have in the film because, even though he was a priest, he didn't really believe. At least I didn't believe he did. He was a very savvy, sophisticated man. This is what he's *supposed* to believe but he doesn't really, and I don't think it *seems* that he does, which has a nice double-edge to it. Mother Teresa actually does believe it. That's how she conducts her whole life. That's what I feel is so interesting about her. She is a person who acts without qualification on her beliefs. There aren't many people in the world like that. Because these were religious beliefs, people are a little uncomfortable with that movie. But we didn't feel we could turn her into some sort of white-hat, good-guy social worker because that isn't what she is. It's easy to make her into a feeder of the hungry, those good things everybody thinks ought to be done. But she does them for a particular reason, her religious vocation, and we felt that had to be our focus in the movie. It's a thin line to walk, to let *her* be religious without the *film* proselytizing.

What things did you do editorially to stay on that line?

First of all, we had to tell what she did. You have to assume that the person who comes to see the film doesn't know anything, so you have a big storytelling job. You have to get them interested. The opening ten minutes of a film are really difficult and important. If you don't get them in the first ten minutes, you're not going to get them. In my experience, the beginnings of films are almost the last things to get made. It's easy to make the middle of the film—well, it's never easy, but it's an easy place to start. Sometimes that helps you find out what the beginning is or what it needs to be. In the Brendan Behan film, we needed to tell that he was a writer and he was famous, otherwise why are people watching this film at all? Who was this guy? Most people don't know. He was a poet and playwright of some reputation and he died young, an alcoholic. Plus he was very funny. Those are the major elements of the story. We got all of that into the first two minutes of the film. It was quick, there were a lot of images, you heard his voice, you saw his face, you got a good look, up close, at who the film is about. Then, having done that, we settle down a little and start telling the story.

Do you think you killed the suspense by revealing all that?

No. I think documentaries often bend over backwards to create suspense and I'm often unconvinced. This film is like a wake for Brendan. It isn't really a flashback, but you find out everything "big" at the beginning. Then the details of his life, and all the stories, become more interesting because you know the big picture. We were making a film about a dead guy. That's a very tall order, bringing somebody back to life. At one point, we didn't think we were going to be able to do it. We found an actor who performed a Brendan Behan one-man show. We thought we needed that because we were uncertain we could resurrect Brendan using what we had—photos, a few audiotapes, some newsreels. But the more successful we were, through all the photos and all the reminiscences, the more the impersonator became false, and he fell away and then he fell out of the film completely. With the photos we used every technique I could think of, long slow moves, quick cuts, etcetera. That's all that was left of Brendan Behan. We tried to revive him with what he left behind.

There's a lot of tension in The Second Time Around *because you didn't know whether the couple would marry until the end.*

Right. There's a good example of being lucky and smart at picking a subject. If that couple didn't have those doubts in the middle of the film, I don't know what the film would have been. The researcher for that film was very smart to pick a couple each of whom had been married before. If she had picked an eighteen-year-old couple going into it for the first time, I don't think it would have been as interesting. It was a good choice because they both came with knowledge that made them more reflective and cautious about what they were embarking on again. That's also a good example of how people do ultimately forget about the camera. Usually when you're making a film like that, the subject tries to suck the camera crew into their lives. Strange people are in their living room! It's perfectly natural for you to engage them in some way, and I think the director and crew resisted. They would not be engaged, they were there to observe. After a while—it takes a little while for this to happen—the subjects get tired of trying, and they realize that they have to get on with their lives. And they do. Now I don't think they ever really completely forget, but there are scenes in that film—it's amazing the things that they say to each other.

Like when they're figuring their budget, the man reveals he buys stamps each month for his collection and his fiancée can't believe it.

That's a great scene. We had that scene out of the film at one point, the kind of mistake we make in process. We didn't think the film was moving quickly enough, and actually cut that scene out in order to get to the more solid information which was that they were having economic difficulties. But when we screened it, one of our colleagues in the next room (we invited him in to screen it) said, "What happened to the stamp scene?" And we looked at each other and said, "He's right." It's a great scene because it capsulizes in this one incident what the tensions are between them. But in our haste to "move things along," we lost sight of its value, if only for a while.

From that moment, things began to disintegrate for the couple.

That really is a turning point. There are two points: the "Budget Meeting," we used to call it, and the "Should We Even Get Married?" scene. From that point, yes, things start falling apart for them a little bit. That is, in fact, what happened. But the film is constructed in a way to make you *know* that's what's happening. Things start going downhill, they're tense with each other, they have little fights. Now in real life, it's much less clear. Over two or three weeks, these people are starting to fight with each other, but they're also still nice to each other and sometimes they are just the way they always were. But when you're making the film, you have to make choices based on what you perceive to be the truth. What was the truth of that period in the relationship? You have to cut in a way that conveys that and get rid of all the other stuff, even if it's fact. Yes, they were still nice to each other, they still wanted to get married, but this other was happening. They were having second thoughts. Maybe they didn't even know it at the time! But *we* knew it because we watched it happen in the dailies. You have to develop a principle of exclusion for the material. "I don't want them to be nice with each other now because basically they were having friction there." So you sift through the material, and you get this facial expression from here and that curt remark from there in order to convey that. It was very difficult making a film with no narration and no voiceover. You can waste the viewers' time making them figure out what the hell is going on and they're missing subtleties in the material. Sometimes a line or two of voiceover gets them right into the middle of a scene and helps them see what you want them to see. I believe in using whatever works!

Would you rather whittle a film down to size than add to it?

One of the longest rough cuts I've had was on the Guarneri film, *High Fidelity*, two hours long. The film ended up being eighty-five minutes. I've heard of other editors making nine-hour rough cuts! That's a different approach to making films, cutting and finding the values in the material so that you have nine hours of what seems to be interesting material, and then start to discover a structure. That's not the way I've worked with directors. We look at the material and decide almost right away what we're going to try and do, and then we cut the material to do *that*. If we discover we made a mistake and it's not working, or we missed something, then we go back and recut, but we go for a particular shape almost right away. Which is why we can come out with a two-hour version of what's going to ultimately wind up in the film. I don't just search through the material for all the "good stuff." Again, you need a principle of exclusion. The Beirut sequence in *Mother Teresa* was very clear. In *High Fidelity*, we had hours and hours of rehearsal footage. It's interesting to watch the quartet rehearse, but only for a little while. In their interviews, all four members of the quartet spoke of their relationship as a democracy. How does the material tell you that? Then you have something to look for, an idea to give the material shape.

Did you feel you had to balance the four musicians with each other?

Yeah. What was difficult structurally was that once we would decide to do one thing with one guy, like visit his home, for instance, then we had to do it three other times! So every time you got a peek into their private life, we tried to cut it in a way that reflected back to their life as a quartet. In one scene, the wife of the second violinist says, "Oh, you have the perfect life." Then he responds, "Well, yeah, you know, excuse me, I have to go to Maryland," and he gets up and leaves. So that scene was not only a look at their life at home, the place he lived in, etcetera, but it was also something else about the quartet life. It does seem a good life but they're constantly on the road and it's more difficult than it seems. Another time, somebody makes the comment that the wives don't get involved in quartet decisions because four is difficult enough, eight would be impossible, and that refers you back to the quartet's relationship. So we didn't go to their homes just to go there. We went there to glimpse our subjects away from the others and to find out something else about quartet life. We sort of killed two birds with one stone and hopefully made the trip more interesting.

You used the four "talking heads" interviewed against the red curtain as a pivot for introducing outdoor scenes and rehearsals.

The inevitable talking heads. Those were the interviews shot at the end of the filming. I think you should never sit on a talking head to get information. That's deadly. Get the information in an entertaining and informative way. Don't just plop an expert up there to tell you something. I use interviews and voiceovers a lot. I think only the Brendan Behan film was actually narrated. The rest are always the subjects talking to you, which is different than narration.

How about Promise of the Land?

Oh yes, that was another narrated film. That was a real classic television film, and it had a whole other set of problems. That's the common perception of "documentaries," NBC *White Paper*, a balanced discussion of an issue. Most people who make documentaries aren't making those kinds of films, but that is the public perception of what a documentary is. No wonder that people don't go to see them in the theaters! "They're very informative, but they're not really very entertaining." I think the films I work on are entertaining.

Was Promise of the Land *difficult because it was different for you?*

No, it was kind of relaxing. It's easier. Almost all of your problems are formal. You basically know what the content of the film is, it's already been written down, sequences have been shot in a particular way to serve that. You just have to do the work, keep it going. That program was Depression footage, it was a trip to Thomas Jefferson's house, we went to a tractor show, it was all over the place. The only unifying thing in that film was the idea.

Unlike He Makes Me Feel Like Dancin'. *Cutting there almost creates the personality of Jacques D'Amboise, who teaches children to dance.*

I responded to the subject. When I first looked at the dailies, I felt like I had thirty-five hours of "1–2–3-kick." It wasn't until they did wild track interviews with the kids that the film started coming to life for me. Suddenly you had this interior monologue of what the kids were thinking and what they were going through. There was the one kid who was so happy to be there, he was hanging on for dear life. Suddenly all of those scenes with him in the group took on a meaning that they didn't have before. The voiceover takes you inside the scene. They come to life because you get to go into somebody else's head. The kids were funny, or they could be made to be funny. When these kids answered a question, they answered in three paragraphs minimum!

Actually, you're not showing Jacques D'Amboise so much as he was but as he's seen by the children.

There's a big dose in that film of what he is trying to do and the joy he takes and gives in doing it. He's so hungry to give these kids a chance to experience what he loves so much.

Emile Ardolino also directed Dirty Dancing *and Baryshnikov films.*

Yes, he was a television director for *Dance in America*. It was interesting for him to go through the documentary process wherein he no longer had complete control. A television director has extremely tight control of virtually every image, when to cut from one to another. Emile didn't have that control in the shooting or the editing. It's impossible in a documentary. He found he had to let go in a way that he hadn't had to before. We got along really very well. Editing is always a collaborative process with directors. But they can't make the film play, *you* have to make it. You talk, you look at the film, you say, "What are we going to try and do?" and then they have to go away while you do it. You cut and they respond. They can't sit there and say, "Do this, do that." They might as well do it themselves, then. It's also very satisfying to an editor because you get to make the film. Sometimes you get buried in the material, you fool yourself, and the director is free to come in and say, "Interesting, but not what we talked about." He may give you another idea and you go on from there. You're not just a mechanic when you're editing documentaries.

Were you concerned about fragmenting the dancing, rather than showing it full-body?

You wanted to see the experience the kids were having in these sequences, not that they were good dancers. The kids weren't professional dancers, and that wasn't the point. They were having a good time. Cutting that was a little trouble actually. In fact, I overdid it once. In the final show, there is a professional dancer who is Jacques D'Amboise's adult son. He saw a cut that we did of him and he said, "My something-something turn, you've cut it to pieces!" And I said, "Yeah, I guess we did! Well, we'll go back and fix that if we can." Fred Astaire always wanted to be shot from head to foot, but we were doing something else. The kids' energy and smiles. You wanted to see them smiling, you didn't want to see them extending their toes!

The material really dictates the pace you cut, doesn't it?

It depends on what you want it to do. Montages are extremely difficult for an editor, but they're the most fun, too, because basically when you design a montage you can take material from almost anywhere in the dailies—a smile, a look, a shrug, two lines from somebody. If you can design a tree upon which to hang that material, you can put almost anything in. You can cover a lot of ground, a lot of feeling. If you do it well, the audience feels they're in good hands in that part of the film. You're taking them somewhere in a montage. It's a different kind of pace. Sometimes you need that thickness in the middle of a ninety-minute experience. You need to rush forward sometimes. You get to use a lot of stuff that doesn't survive as a scene because it's not interesting enough. But there's that one little thing in that scene that was the *only* interesting thing in those dailies, which is revealing of the characters or of their attitudes. Montages are very useful, and fun!

An obvious one was the opening of Mother Teresa, *all those shots of the hungry and poor in a combination of slow motion film and photographs.*

That was archival footage. Somebody at one of the rough cut screenings said, "You need to put it on a larger stage." Put her work in a bigger context. We said, "Yeah, how can we do that?" The director got the idea for archival footage, went down to Washington, got a whole bunch of stuff. But it just wasn't working, the images seemed too familiar. I was doodling with it at lunchtime and, you know, a Steenbeck is reostatically controlled, you can go two frames a second, you can go twenty-four frames a second, you can go very fast. I was running it and running it, running it, running it at about eight frames a second—suddenly it took on this dancelike feeling. It became something different, less rooted in—I don't know how to say this. It wasn't just the image anymore. I said, "Let's try printing each frame several times." I had never done that before. So we tried it and it took on almost a dancelike quality. It made you look at things in a way you weren't used to looking. We took every frame and printed it as many as eight or ten times and it became very elongated, very effective, I think.

In the opening montage, there's one slow-motion image with Mother Teresa's back to us and she's gently pulling a blanket over a man. You also use that later in the film as a photograph. Why the repetition?

To recall you to the opening. Some images obviously have such raw power in themselves. The dailies tell you that right away. One of your tasks is to place them for maximum effect. You can waste good images if you come to them too quickly or in the wrong place. You can fritter them away. You have to recognize the strength of the material and set it almost like a jeweler. In a lot of documentaries you have to give a little history, that's almost pro forma. But the audience is not ready to hear a lot of history at the beginning of the film. They don't care! They don't even know what the subject of the film is yet. If you're going to be strictly chronological, you say, "This person was born here and they grew up da-da-da-da"; that's classic chronology. We're not interested in that. The viewer has to become invested in your subject enough to want to know those things. If you look at the Behan film, the Guarneri film, the Mother Teresa film—the three that have histories in them—they all come twenty or thirty minutes into the film. Earlier than that, you don't care. It goes in one ear and out the other.

You introduced chronology in High Fidelity *with each musician's childhood photographs.*

That's like a hook, though. That serves a couple of purposes. It's charming and you find out what the film's about, you hear their voices, you see their faces. But the part about going to school together and what their personal lives are comes much later. You always have to be aware that this is an experience in time, it's got to be finished at one hundred minutes or eighty minutes or ninety minutes. You can't ever forget that. A film is a journey. It's just not one thing after another. One interesting thing, another interesting thing, another—you get tired of that after a while.

Do you yourself research the subjects before you start work?

I do some reading, but only after I've seen the footage. I don't want to fall prey to the problem of knowing too much already. I want to come to it cold. I have to be able to recognize when the material is confusing or incomplete. If I already know about it, I won't recognize those problems. It's very difficult to maintain that distance. After you've seen the film four hundred thousand times, it's not fresh.

How do you keep it so?

An audience helps a lot. When you invite two or three strangers into the cutting room, even if you're not looking at their faces—while they're watching, you can *feel* their reactions. You know when you want something to go faster, when it's not working. You can fool yourself when you're watching it by yourself, but suddenly it's up there on the screen, people are watching. Something tells you, "This Is Not Working."

And it's not that the people leave the room?

No, it's not like they're coughing or yawning or anything! You just know. You suddenly feel, "This is not good." You feel your hand reaching for the fast-forward! "Let's get through this section!"

Have you ever had to rip something apart and start from scratch?

I do it all the time. "Oh well, this didn't work!" After a while, the whole film is on index cards, and you take something at thirty minutes into the film and move it up to the front. "It wasn't until I got to that point that I was sufficiently charmed or engaged, so let's put it up there." Of course, that's a house of cards. Everything falls apart because one thing is leading to the other. Suddenly you move it and you've got to change everything else around. But that's the process.

Both Mao to Mozart *and* High Fidelity *contained concert pieces that surround the action. Did editing those pose particular problems for you?*

Yeah, there's a problem. These are world-class musicians, but if you stay too long on those performance pieces, you stop the film dead. These are not concert films. The only time you see a whole movement in the Guarneri film is at the very end where we just let them sit down and play. We felt at that point you were ready—okay, enough words, here they are. You've seen them go through fights, soul-searching, how they do what they do. Now let them do it. But if we'd done that in the middle, it would have stopped the film and then where do you go? So in the performance sections, we usually arrive in the middle of the piece and let it end, then go off somewhere else, or we let it begin and leave in the middle. You always have to be on your way somewhere. Some music lovers find that a little frustrating, but I think it ultimately serves the film.

In Mao to Mozart, *Isaac Stern plays his piece and then you cut at a precise moment to a student playing the same piece.*

That's very deep into the film. That's like a handoff. "Okay, I've said all I can say. Now you do it." It's like he's handing off to her, that's why he went to China.

That scene comes right after the phenomenal monologue where the Chinese professor is describing his torture during the Revolution. You decided to keep that one lengthy shot intact?

Actually, it's not, there are about four pieces. That was a two-hour interview. It was a question of letting him tell the story. That's an instance where the talking head is everything, not just information. He went through the Revolution. It's written all over his face. So he deserves to be up there on the screen. A lot of him in the film isn't like that. He leads you on a tour where you don't want to watch him tell you about the conservatory he runs, you want to see the students instead. He's your guide through that, but it's mostly voiceover.

Watching the professor's face was like day and night compared to the cutaways of interviewer reactions to the speaker in Promise of the Land.

Cutaways—deadly device! A classic television device. I think it's lazy. Cutting to close-ups of somebody's hand fiddling with the paper! It's always more interesting to see what they're talking about than to see them talking about it, unless it's a situation like in the China film. The professor's experience is so etched in his face, his whole demeanor, how he holds his body, the kind of dignity with which he tells that story. Then it's not just a talking head, it's more. If I had my druthers, you would never see a talking head just giving information. But often viewers say, "Who the hell is telling this? What am I hearing?" In *He Makes Me Feel Like Dancin'*, there is no sync picture for the interviews with the children because it didn't exist, they were wild track interviews. But you know intuitively who's talking by the way the words are placed over the pictures. It isn't always the actual kid, but you're seeing the kid who's feeling what the other kid is talking about, so we marry the two. You come away feeling like you know that it's *this* kid who's talking. You're not adrift.

In High Fidelity, *you identified speakers with their names on the screen, unlike other films.*

Lower thirds are a difficult device. We did it in the Guarneri film, but I don't think people read those things or remember them for more than fifteen seconds. I never remember them and I'm an editor! "Is this the expert from MIT? Who is this guy?" But that's what happens when it's information. We just felt there's four guys and the manager, you get them all mixed up. So we identified them a few times for you.

It didn't matter after a while.

That's exactly the point. That's what you hope, that it doesn't matter. In Brendan Behan, there were a million people. We're obligated to identify them and we hope that what they're telling you tells you, in some sense, who they are. You get to know Brendan Behan's wife pretty quickly and it's important that you know she was his wife. About the second or third time up, you know and then you don't have to worry.

Back to the treatment of a concert piece. In High Fidelity, *during the Beethoven finale, you weren't just using the master shot of the quartet on stage, but were cutting to instruments or hands and faces. Did you find it difficult to match music with this visual fragmentation?*

That performance was shot several times. There were two concert versions, two cameras each, and lots of inserts. I can find my way through a score. I can hear who's leading because I have "depth of field" when I listen to music, so I know who I'm interested in watching. I meticulously go through all the material and log what pictures are available for every measure. What are my choices? I have an extreme long shot from the left side of the balcony, I have a close-up of the cellist, I have this, I have that. There's a lot of cuts in that scene. Now you want to see the quartet because you've spent so much time with them and they have spoken in such detail about how they do what they do. You want to be in the middle with them while they're playing. You don't want that long-shot concert look. But you do want the four of them together too, and in various combinations, because that, of course, is what the film's about. The needs of the individual versus the needs of the group, and how somehow they mesh those very strong individual personalities. The music is great in and of itself. But it's even more fun, more accessible, when we can glimpse the process involved in making it. The door's opened up a little bit, we can peek in.

Are you on some other level when you cut something like that?

I'm not thinking so much anymore. I say, "When do I want to leave . . . *now!*" and I cut there. Before I had cut any music at all, I was around an editor who had done music films. I said, "How do you know where to cut? Do you always cut on the downbeat?" He said, "No, sometimes you cut before, sometimes you cut a little after, sometimes you cut in the middle." I know what he means now. You have to feel it. I had a great device on the Steenbeck that saved me a lot of time. It was an electronic footage counter with a button where I could zero the counter. I could listen to the music track and, at the right place, press the button at the cut point. Then I could play it back, go over the music again—there was a plus and minus sign going off and on with the counter—and if that little light went off at the right place, I knew I was in the right place to cut. I was usually a frame or two late because of reaction time, so I could back it up two frames and rezero the counter. Then I could be certain that, musically, that cut was in the right place before I even made it. I would have to look at the picture to see if it was appropriate or even if it would work visually. But I knew it was in the right place. It saved me a lot of time.

Could one frame make a big difference?

In music, inevitably one frame makes a difference. We're talking about one twenty-fourth of a second. I can see it and you can feel it. I know you can't see it, but you can *feel* it. It does make a difference and you have to be willing to spend that time to get it exactly right. You have to be efficient and have a long attention span to be a good editor. A very long attention span.

Do you cut lengthy talking scenes as you would a piece of music?

Somewhat. I get impatient, I want to condense. I virtually always want to compress when I'm editing and multilayer things. People interrupt each other when they're talking. If they're arguing, you want it to feel and sound like an argument. There's a scene in the Guarneri film when they're arguing about playing a particular piece of music. In the cut, they're talking on top of each other, interrupting each other, because that's in essence what they were doing. But not actually. It was all single-camera coverage. One camera. But we cut it to convey the energy of their discussions and it looks like a multiple-camera shoot. The guys were looking at each other back and forth, exchanging glances, etcetera—those were all editorial decisions to distill the feeling of the scene. I think that's true to the feeling, but there's a lot of compression in that scene. Who's fighting, what are the other guys thinking about the fight, how are they positioning themselves physically to the fight? Are they leaning to this side, are they leaning to that side? That's all editorial. Done with reaction shots. It doesn't happen by laying the dailies up there because it didn't happen that way. It happened over hours, the whole circling process. You can't do that in a film, you don't have that much time; you have to make it happen editorially. Faster, faster. I always want it to get faster—until we get to that place in the film where we want the long space, the big empty moment, where things are ringing and you're alone with your thoughts. There's a moment in the Isaac Stern film when the professor has just told you what he went through during the Cultural Revolution. I think he said, "They wanted to kill us all because we taught them Western music." It's a big statement. Then you cut to what ultimately is Isaac Stern playing the concert. But before you get to Stern, you see three big reactions, three faces. That's a "made" moment, a manufactured moment in the film where nothing happens except silence and those faces, and that statement rings. That's the design. You really want that to set in. When we first put it together, we cut directly to Stern. It didn't work at all. It had a completely different effect, actually. It was almost like Stern was chastising the audience for not allowing Western music. But putting the audience in there *makes that moment*; it's *their* experience. They think about what happened to them and what they're hungry for now. Just three shots. Three faces. Those shots came out of the big audience reaction roll. Pictures of audience. What do you do with them? You could do a million things. Where do you put them? As I said, that's a manufactured moment in the film in order to tell the story we're telling. In the reviews of the film, more than once people said, "The camera always seems to be in the right place at the right time."

Bet you love that!

Well, you do in a sense because they're not aware of the editing. You're not supposed to be aware of the editing. But it's amazingly naive about the process of how you make a film like this. It's only in a fast cutting montage that people ever notice the editing. People don't know what editing is—even my friends who *know* what I do. I turn off the sound and I show them pictures. "See? Cut, cut, cut." I turn on the sound, you know, effects, music, etcetera. "See, that didn't happen that way. We added all that in later." So what? The whole film should go somewhere.

So it doesn't matter to you that people don't know about editing?

Every once in a while it matters! It matters because people often think of me as a technician, which is not what I am at all. I'm a filmmaker. A documentary editor is a filmmaker, as much as the director, every bit as much as a cinematographer. You're crafting the entire experience. You're not just cutting out the bad stuff, the fog frames at the front of the film or where the camera shakes. "The camera always seems to be in the right place at the right time!" Lucky me!

How do you decide how much sound to include on your tracks? Some of your soundtracks are very dense.

I think it enriches the film.

Are all those sounds distracting to the viewer?

I don't know. Do you think it's distracting?

In some cases. Sometimes I wasn't even aware of them.

It's not working if it's distracting. It's not arbitrary at all. The sounds are very carefully placed. If it's distracting, then it's just not working. I do have very dense tracks on my films. That is definitely something I would say is a style that I like.

Would you consider that your style of editing, then?

I would be very reluctant to talk about style. I approach the problem at hand and I try not to repeat myself too obviously. But yeah, I do have very dense tracks. There's a lot happening, there's not much dead air. Things are weaving in and out all the time. Somebody says something in voiceover, then something jumps up off the sync track immediately that I think is connected. Whether it is or isn't, that's up to the viewer to decide. In the Mother Teresa film, we always ran the ambience tracks of the location under the sync interviews, so that when we cut away to the "talking head," you didn't leave the film and then come back to it. It's always there in your ears. Be it a New York street sound or a Beirut war effect or the sound of the hospital, wherever you are, it's there under the voice track. You're always *in* the film, you don't leave it for the interview and then come back again. The sound does that.

You must have approximated the chaos of war with such dense tracks.

In the Beirut sequence, when Mother goes to evacuate the kids from a bombed-out hospital in the West, we knew that it had been chaotic. We mixed that right up against the red line, I wanted that as loud as it could be, the chaos of it, noisy and echoey. We reinforced that in the mix. So finally when she brings the kids back from the war zone to her shelter, it's quieter. It gets peaceful. You don't know that's how we did it, but you feel it happening. It's another way you reinforce the disparity of the two situations. Similar images, sisters and children, you need to know what you think about them in order to figure out a way to make them work for you; otherwise, they're just raw material. Image, image,

image, image. What do you want it to do? In this case, the soundtrack makes you *feel* the effect Mother had on those children.

You also chose to keep one lengthy quiet shot of a sister massaging an agitated child in bed.

That's an example of when not to cut. There's a camera reposition in the middle of that scene, the kind you would cut out automatically. It would have been possible to cut out that camera move—go to a close-up of the sister, then back to the hand. But the director and I thought that to cut in the middle would be to falsify in a way. Just to leave it intact seemed the right thing to do, to watch it. To make you watch it. That's probably the most powerful scene in the film. No cuts at all.

How do you feel when you make a connection like that? To cut or not to cut. Suddenly there's a spark.

Excited. Enthused. Encouraged. The more material you have, the harder it is, but the first time you screen the film, it all seems to go in and stick. I take extensive notes, of course, but I just remember that I saw an image of someone looking in a particular direction doing a particular thing, and when I'm finding my way through a sequence, I start to make connections. People don't hire me because I'm a good splicer! The mechanical side of editing is like driving a car; it seems mysterious and complicated until you learn how to do it and then you just use it to get where you want to go. To be an editor, you need the ability to see connections between things and a desire to order them. Life needs an editor sometimes. If we could only montage this party, cut to the core of this graduation speech. If we could only get *this* next to *that*, everything would be clear. You can't do that, but it's appealing to think about.

4

Film as
All the Arts

Carol Littleton

Carol Littleton often refers to literature, language, and music as powerful influences on her editing because, in fact, these were her areas of study before she took up film. Her plunge into the French language by watching French movies during her music studies in Paris introduced her to the hothouse world of French film culture. Her early exposure to New Wave films molded her perspective of cinema: it is the best medium to portray art because it is an "extraordinary cocktail" of *all* the arts.

Because of her broad arts background, Littleton feels the need to diversify her film work, to keep her "diet" from becoming too rich on feature films. She has cut negative, sound, music, documentaries, commercials, American Film Institute Fellows' projects, and television movies. Even though she loves narrative films, Littleton welcomes other projects whenever she can squeeze them into her schedule.

Added to her editing responsibilities is Littleton's position as president of the Editors Guild Local 776 (West Coast), for which she ran (not expecting to win) after she witnessed her assistants being exploited and grew aware of the conflicts between union and nonunion editors on West and East Coasts. Her experiences in this office provide an insider's view of the gradually diminishing schism between locals.

Littleton also proudly acknowledges how much she has learned about editing from her husband, cinematographer John Bailey. "We get to work on the same film once in a while, when the director's brave enough." By osmosis, seeing how he responds to images, she believes that her eye has become even more trained to find those visual elements with which she can create the magic of a movie.

As Tom Haneke did for the documentary, Littleton explores the nature of the feature film as a distillation of music, drama, literature, painting, sculpture, and choreography. Side by side, their interviews suggest curious parallels between the mindsets of documentary and feature editors.

Again, rhythm and music are vital to both, and both need to lift story-telling into compelling forms. Like the documentary editor, the feature editor must find "truth" in the fictional work in order to make an emotionally rich film—although, as most editors admit, they can only work with the material (good or bad) that the director and cinematographer give them.

What do you consider most important in feature film editing?

Making movies is telling a story in its simplest form. I was reading a book not too long ago about David Lean. With the revival of *Lawrence of Arabia*, someone in the book was asking how he has been able to have such a long career and his films are not dated, while many of his colleagues have not had the kind of career he's had nor have their films survived. David Lean thanked him for having that idea and didn't know if he agreed, but one thing that he could say was that, to him, film is simply telling a story. Simplicity is the key. And I think that probably is the best advice for any editor. Just simplify one story to create pure life and emotion. In fact, editing is a lot like writing. You are rewriting a film. You have a script but you're rewriting a script with the film. It's not like editing in publishing. It is not a matter of omitting and corrections. It's very different, I think. You become a writer, but you're writing with images, you're writing with music, you're writing with performances, you're writing with all the things—intangible things as well—that make an emotional event.

So you are editing for the essence that will progress the story.

Right. Let me give you an example. In *The Accidental Tourist*, the first cut was very long, and this is the problem that you have any time you adapt a novel to film. You need to capture the essence, you're never going to be able to include all the detail. My assistants, of course, had read the novel and read the script and now we're working on the first cut. So we start to talk among ourselves. What do we think really needs to be dropped? We're talking about the structure. Everybody liked something different: "Oh, I am really moved by this." "Yes, but what about that?" "And what about this?" "And what about *that*?" Everybody had their pet scenes and their pet moments, things that were their favorites. But being able to talk about them, you began to realize, well, is that telling a story or is that just a predilection that you have? Having those conversations among ourselves, we began to realize, "This scene is very much like another scene, maybe we don't need two scenes that are alike." For instance, there were a lot of dog training scenes. In the novel there were many because that was a device for Macon and Muriel to get together. In the film, there were five or six, and there ended up to only be three. That's because they in fact were repetitive. *Everybody* loved that dog—that pooch was incredible. It took us a long time to be able to say, "All right, let's be rigorous and think about what is structurally important." We just simply had to think about what elements move the story along, at the same time giving you emotional peaks, emotional moments, throughout the film. From the standpoint of structure, you can't afford to have anything that is repetitive.

One almost has to be well versed in various art and literary forms to understand the differences between each of their structures.

My education was primarily studying literature and music, so the skills that I acquired studying nonfiction, novels, and poetry from an analytical viewpoint are directly applicable to film. When I was in college, I studied my third year in Paris, which happened to be at the height of the New Wave in film. I had really never gone to movies other than to Saturday matinees when I was a kid. To be exposed to directors like Truffaut, Godard, Rivette, and Malle was extraordinary to me. I discovered that film could be something other than escapist fare, and that a great deal of art and vision was involved. I was there studying music, trying to fight my way through the French language, and it helped my French to see a movie several times. Well, after you've seen a movie two or three times, you pick up on things other than the story. You begin to see the various elements which constitute filmmaking style. How did they get that effect? Photographically, isn't that interesting? The use of music, isn't that amazing? So I had an awakening to the notion of movies as art. I also went with a friend to the Cinémathèque and saw the most moving film that ultimately made me decide that I wanted to work in film. I didn't know about the editing yet, but I recognized the emotional impact of film which is as great or greater than any novel, as great or greater than any symphony or literature. I saw Pontecorvo's *The Battle of Algiers.* A pivotal event for me in my professional life certainly, because I think in the back of my mind, that's when I decided I wanted to pursue a career in film. I just didn't know how to go about doing it. So I stumbled around for two or three years and finally found myself in the cutting room and said, "Oh, this is what I'll do."

Why does film have a greater impact than literature or music?

I think because it is both. It's sort of a double whammo. Film is, after all, very musical, extremely musical. Throughout my college career, I flitted with the notion of being a musician. I've played in an orchestra, enjoyed it but never was convinced that I had what it took to be a professional musician. I think the skills of performing music are closely related to the skills of editing. You have to work on something until it's right, you can't give up. Not only is it what you do with your instrument, but what you do in playing with an ensemble. You have to perform expressively. I remember the years that I was playing in an orchestra, it wasn't enough just to toot out the notes. You had to do it in such a way that it was moving, and also you had to play with the others. As in editing. It's a question of balance, a question of what's going to happen, what's the music, what's the director's statement, what are the actors doing? All of those have to be orchestrated into a whole. That's what the editor does— to a degree, I mean. Clearly we're under the supervision of the director, interpreting his work. Yet there are many ways in which we influence the film. So why did it affect me more than literature and music? I guess because in a way film is terribly musical and it is also narrative. It has characters, dramatic progression, structure. All of those are also in music and literature. Film is just an extraordinary art, a twentieth-century art form.

And, of course, the visuals?

Oh yes. Let's not forget that! It is a moving picture after all. An illusion as well. Having the combination of story, music, *and* image is an extraordinary cocktail. I work in Hollywood and there's no denying that it's a business; a film is very, very expensive. We have to answer to the demands of a business, but also the demands of an art.

To go back to your musical performance metaphor, some people can be technical wizards when they perform, yet lack something—

Have no emotional interpretation whatsoever.

Yes, and others may not be perfect but play with great emotion. Is editing similar?

I think so, yes. Many people have the technique. I don't think there are quite as many who can make a film purely emotional at the same time. It's as though you have to rub your tummy and pat your head simultaneously! Recently, I was involved in arbitrating a film credit. Two editors worked on the same material, with the same director, same shots, same script. It was interpreted by two different editors, and the two versions were radically different. Clearly I couldn't be an editor without thinking that whoever edits the movie makes a difference, but actually seeing the difference was so amazing to me. The editor's influence on the material was extraordinary. That to me is mind-boggling. I don't think about that everyday. If I did, I would tremble in my boots because of the responsibility involved—I couldn't think about it! A group of editors were looking at the material because of the credit dispute to determine who had the largest artistic contribution to the material, and it wasn't a difficult decision. But it was a tremendous responsibility. We would rather let the editors involved come to some happy compromise with the producers and the director rather than have it come to such a point where people are so disappointed and hurt, and feel so denied that *we* have to settle the dispute. These cases of credit arbitration can be very difficult to judge. You're getting into that area of what makes someone a technician and what makes someone—I hate to use the word because it sounds so affected—an "artist." I cringe when I say that. A lot of editors know technique better than I, believe me, and those same editors can take material and just can't move you. You can have a violinist who can really play, a pianist who can do anything on the keyboard, and you're not moved. Or you have someone like Horowitz, who takes tremendous liberties with the material, and you are in tears when you listen to him. Something about the language of music goes beyond obvious technique. Something that touches a chord in all of us that is communal, that makes us emotionally involved.

Is that drawing out of personal experience?

I suppose so. *Places in the Heart* was a very unusual film. That film was the most directly related to my experience in life, having grown up in Oklahoma, near that part of the country. Certainly not in 1936, but I felt I knew those people, that culture, that way of being because it's very close to my grandparents' experience in life. That life has disappeared because of mass communication, and those regional differences in how people look at reality are fading quickly. And to see that small community (seen through Robert Benton who is clearly an original director) was wonderful to me because it was so personal. That whole Protestant way of looking at the world, that rigorous life, the emotional crosscurrents of a small town, all of those were part of my experience in growing up, so being able to express them in film was a special treat.

And your first feature took place in France, where you studied.

Yeah! *French Postcards.* The irony is that it was a story about the very thing I did, which was third year abroad, and it was shot where I lived. Purely coincidence. I was there in 1969, I went back in 1979 to recreate what I had lived ten years before in a movie!

Have any other films drawn so deeply from your experience?

I don't know. Let's hope not *Body Heat!* Maybe fantasy! Film is somewhat magical, don't you think? And when you start to try to define magic, there's not much left. You take a film and wonder, "What about this movie brings me to tears every time I see it? Or brings me to laugh every time I see it?" There's something eternally magical about its elusive qualities.

E. T. is a prime example of a magical movie.

Oh sure. Some films you make as adult films and the kids love them. We made a children's movie and adults loved it. I think Steven Spielberg and Melissa Mathiesen, who is the writer, knew that they were making a parable, that this film was going to have an extraordinary appeal for adults and youngsters. They didn't want to make just a kids' movie, they had a story they wanted to tell and it was very important to both of them. But we didn't know it was going to be a hit. We loved it. We were delighted by it. Everybody just loved that "little guy." But we didn't know if an audience would hoot when they saw it or if they would take it as something real. We had no idea. I remember when we were in Houston to preview the film, Steven leaned over to me at one point and said, "Do you think people will be able to accept E. T.?" I said, "I really don't know. I'm scared about it." And he said, "If they will accept E. T., I think they'll go with the film and believe it." So we really didn't know until it was shown to that preview audience, and they ab–so–lute–ly loved that picture! Unlike any preview I've ever been to, before or since. And it was not just a kids' audience, it was very mixed. Probably six hundred people.

That's a great example of how film is a collaboration of all the arts: lush music, special effects, beautiful images, captivating story.

It's a perfect example of how one person, the director, does have his vision and the sense to know what people are good for what things. Steven knew that John Williams's music was right, he knew the casting was right. That's a perfect example of a director supervising all aspects of film and allowing his collaborators to exert their influence as well.

As an editor, how are you responsible for some of that magic?

I'm thinking about the film I'm working on now, *White Palace*, another film based upon a novel. There is a quite explicit sex scene in it, a lovemaking scene. There were also several scenes like that in *Body Heat*, and to some extent there was a suggestion of it in *Accidental Tourist*. I had to stop and think what makes something prurient, pornographic, versus emotional. It's not just that suggestive material is more erotic than explicit material. It has to be more than that. There has to be something that touches a chord that somehow is felt by all of us. There has to be *something* that does that. Now I'm not aware of it when I'm working. You're dealing with the material directly and it's telling you what to do. I don't impose myself on the material, at least I hope not. I'm searching for something that is—for lack of a better word—more magical, more spiritual, more elusive than just explicit material. Many times I will be totally unmoved by a film, I think because there was no attempt to reach inside the material and tell the story, yes, tell the feelings. Like in a rehearsal in an orchestra, the conductor stops and says, "Well, that's good for technique, now let's do it with feeling."

Could you take unmoving material and make it moving?
Well, you can try. You can certainly try.

Would that be conscious?
I don't think it's conscious at all. I think you start finding ways to make the characters connect. Actors are really the custodians of their characters. Editors can peel away the skin and get down to the essence of that character by very judicious choices, but the actor has to do that work. That's our big job, respecting what the actor has done. We have to be the actor's best friend. We have to get inside the work. That's very exciting, by the way. I've never tried to act so I don't know if I understand acting, but I try to understand behavior, what rings true and what doesn't. I try to interpret acting vis-à-vis human behavior and make it as truthful as possible. I'm attracted to performance movies, ensemble movies, certainly *The Big Chill, Places in the Heart, French Postcards, Accidental Tourist.*

I remember that incredibly moving scene in Accidental Tourist where you remain on William Hurt as he reveals his pain to Geena Davis. By staying on him, you almost see his pain seeping out of him into her.
He delivers the letter explaining why he can't come to dinner. She sees him and pulls him through the doorway into her house. She knew what he needed at that moment. She's able to embrace him. It's like a balm, it's like a wash of love. I think all of us go through life hoping there will be that moment when someone is there to take care of us when we're needy. I think we've all had that, either the fantasy or the real experience, just that lovely beautiful thing that love is all about. When I saw that in dailies, I was in tears. I was moved by it even before we put it together. As he told the story about his son and why he couldn't have dinner, she understood instinctually what he needed, and during that time she pulled him in and allowed him to speak, to say everything. When she realized that there was nothing else he could say, she simply took his hand and led him to bed. Because we've worked together so much, Larry Kasdan and I, we have a kind of unspoken language. And working together on *Accidental Tourist* was the height of that level of communication. While he didn't tell me what to do in cutting the scene together, we talked about the scene before I started working, about what he felt the essence was and what was important to have happen in the scene. We talked about Geena's performance and about Bill's performance, and after that he trusted me to put it together. To my knowledge, it didn't change much at all over the course of editing the picture. It was extremely well acted,

beautifully directed, beautifully photographed. You'd look at the dailies and you'd just know it's perfect. All you'd have to do is follow your nose. The scene was covered well because Larry wanted to have as many options as he could in the editing, rightfully so, but in our talking it through and looking at dailies, it was very clear what worked and what didn't. You have to have the faith that you're going to recognize what is really good and put it in the film. You don't have to manipulate the footage or do any tricks. Many times the less you do, the better it is.

Are there added complications in working on a film adaptation? Extra steps in translating to film that you don't have with an original script?

When you work on a film like *Accidental Tourist*, you want it to seem as though it's unfolding in front of you as in real life. Larry wanted to be true to Anne Tyler's vision and he wrote the adaptation of *Accidental Tourist* trying to be faithful to her vision. There is something very stately about Anne Tyler's work, something very intricate as well. The ideas and the metaphors, if you will, the symbols are almost axiomatic, and Larry wanted the film to be that way. It has a European feel about it, very leisurely, yet it sweeps you on and catches you emotionally. It's intense and dense emotionally. At the same time, it's elegant and stately and extremely reserved.

That was the nature of William Hurt's character, too. His line at the end—that it's not how much you love a person but who you are when you're with them—was his growing realization of emotional expression.

You put your finger right on the scene that didn't work initially. We had to reshoot it. When we screened the picture, we had a difficult time with the last few scenes in Paris. How do you treat Sarah, the Kathleen Turner character, so that she is not discarded like an old piece of clothing? How do you treat a marriage with respect and dignity at the same time it's falling apart? The scene that we had really didn't convey that, and so Larry went back to the "writing board" and reshot it. Also, the very first scene in the kitchen (which in the novel takes place in the car) was shot first of all in the car going from the airport to the house. It was too searing a scene, too tough—it was tough in the novel. The wife tells him *every*-thing on her mind and she is angry at his closed-down emotions. People couldn't take a scene that angry and that spiteful and that emotional so soon in the film. A movie has to earn its right to be emotional. Starting out with something like that overwhelmed people and there was never another scene in the movie that intense or with that high a fever pitch. The scene between Sarah and Macon in the first reel is a composite of two scenes which were dropped from the movie. In the novel, when Sarah says, "I don't want to see you anymore . . . I'm getting a divorce," that was searing and audiences didn't recover from it. The material had to be removed.

Those were problems with the script, though.

Well, problems in adapting the novel to the script. A novel works in certain ways, and a script has to work in others. Sometimes you discover those things when the film is edited and so you preview it. You realize that the audience's breath is taken away or they are misled into thinking it's going to be a certain kind of movie and it's not. If we could all make a movie correctly from Day One, it would be done! But things happen.

How do you handle humor when you have a large number of characters?

I'm really drawn to what you'd call "inner comedies," where the comedy is derived from behavior and character. I am not drawn to gag comedies, slapstick. I'm really interested in comedy being born out of the frailty, the foibles of man. These comedies of manners are sometimes difficult to appreciate in script form because the humor is created by the acting and direction. When we were doing *The Big Chill*, I remember distinctly that Columbia was very concerned about the picture. When we showed the film the first time to the people who were in charge of the studio then, nobody laughed. Larry and I were perplexed. Barbara Benedek and Larry had written a comedy—admittedly it was a *different* kind of comedy, not the usual fare for Hollywood movies. Nevertheless, it was a comedy about a group of friends who come together to mourn the death of a friend who had committed suicide. We were dumbfounded no one saw the humor of the film. Shortly after that, we showed it to a preview audience—this is before studios had a series of marketing screenings, which I think are absolutely ruinous for a film. We took it to preview in Seattle one night and then to San Jose. Two different groups of people, a professional sort of yuppie audience versus a more middle-class, larger spectrum of people. Both groups laughed uproariously. Then the studio realized they had a comedy! They didn't realize what kind of film they had until the audience responded.

Had you changed it in the editing?

We hadn't changed it at all. We had a very large flashback sequence at the end of the movie which we had pulled from the time the executives saw it because we were experimenting. Otherwise we hadn't changed it at all. I think that happens a lot, executives really don't know what kind of film we have until we show it to an audience.

Why did you say marketing screenings were ruinous?

Well, screenings for audiences are very valuable when we're making a movie. But I think quantifying an audience with marketing research is harmful and deleterious to making unusual personal films. They start to become more and more homogenized, more and more alike. What makes film so fabulous is that it reflects the ideas and the way the director feels about that material. But to emasculate his vision by going through a series of marketing screenings—I just don't get it. In the old days, the studios were run by gentlemen who really knew film, all aspects of film. Now a lot of people running studios come from business schools, MBAs, and rely heavily on marketing. They look at a film as a product. Yes, it is a business but it's highly personalized. An unpredictable, unscientific thing we're doing that doesn't have rules and regulations. No sooner do you make up a set of rules than the person who breaks them is the one with the hit movie! Screenings with an audience, yes, I take very seriously, and the responses while I'm watching the movie. The directors I work with also take that very seriously. What's valuable about screenings is having the immediate reaction of an audience. But quantifying that experience, putting it into numerical formulas is useless.

Do you think that is one reason why some editors feel anonymous? If a director can feel "quantified," how much more so an editor?

I don't mind being anonymous. I prefer it. For myself, I do not have the personality it takes to direct a film. I know that I am most comfortable in an editing room dealing with the intimate problems of the material that you're not even aware of when you're looking at a movie. I don't mind being anonymous or having my work in a sense being taken for granted. Editing is just another part of making a film. I feel I exert a certain influence on it. I don't control it, I just influence it. I hope that I could work in a climate of trust where the director feels he would be able to use my ideas, my feelings about the material, the criticisms, the praise, all for the good of the movie. Our job is to interpret and respect the material at hand. Certainly respect the style, performances, composition, writing, lighting, every aspect. We are a very respectful lot!

Are you involved in other areas of production and postproduction?

Oh yeah. I probably am a nuisance in that way. A lot of editors say, "Well, I've cut the picture, now I'll hand it over." But I am very involved—I don't know that I really even need to be, but I enjoy it. I want to have my hand in everything. On *White Palace*, we had a run-through to talk about music and the fur was flying in the cutting room! Everybody was saying, "No, this is right. No, that's right." That kind of creative argument and exchange of ideas was exciting. But no, I don't do the music editor's work, the sound supervisor's work, the ADR work. They have their work to do. I just want to express my opinions and hear the opinions of others. I want to make sure everybody understands the movie, that we're all working on the same film. Arguments start the creative juices flowing and allow people to have more opinions, to change yours or elaborate. I'm a facilitator with a brain and a heart. I'm not a computer. But I do manipulate the film with my hands and my brain and my heart.

And a Moviola.

I work on a KEM actually. If I worked on videotape, I'd do the same thing. It doesn't really matter what you edit on. They are just tools.

You have two additional interesting perspectives that must influence your editing film. One is being married to a cinematographer.

I've learned an awful lot from John. My eye has become trained by being with him and seeing how he responds to things visually. We go to a lot of movies, art shows, photo shows, art museums, and his eye is constantly at work. And to talk about what he sees, by osmosis my eye has become trained. He sees film in somewhat the same way I do, that the cinematography should be unobtrusive. It should serve the story. It should be another dramatic tool. The visualization of the film is another dramatic tool and it should not overpower the material. The style should be dictated by the material. A lot of the ways he looks at film are precisely the ways I do, we're just doing different things. We get to work on the same film once in a while, when the director's brave enough!

Secondly, your confidence as an editor must have evolved much from your experience as president of L.A. Local 776 of the Guild. How did you get so involved with the union?

I am essentially an apolitical person, but there are events in one's professional life which can galvanize one into action. I was working on a film for a major studio and my assistants were being exploited. So I called the union representative and he came over to talk to us about it. My assistants and I put an end to that violation of our contract by going through the proper channels in our local. The episode made me think about editors as workers in the Hollywood system. I also started thinking about the ways that nonunion editors were being used in Hollywood without the job protection the union provides, and about the extraordinary number of editors in L.A. at the time, nonunion editors who were being excluded from the union because of our protectionist notions. The more I talked about these inequities, the more outraged I got. One of my assistants, in fact, said, "If you feel so strongly about it, why don't you do something?" So an election was coming up and I thought, "Well . . . " Even before I got the idea of running for president—even before I was totally surprised by having been elected, there were changes taking place within the union structure. But the biggest change that clearly needed to take place, which should have taken place years ago, was to open the doors to all qualified people—which we have as a result of our contract in 1989. If people can do the work, they should be given the opportunity, and the last place they should be blocked is by other editors. Furthermore, we were creating a large, highly qualified, cheap, nonunion work force, and it was starting to be very destructive for us as a group. Now that we have opened the doors, more and more postproduction work is unionized because those editors in L.A. who are qualified can be members of the local if they want to be. It has created a very large pool of organized labor. You can't get a movie made without an editor who is in the Guild. I think that's quite a turnaround. Now we are approaching producers with the notion of having a national editors Guild, so the different locals that are spread across the country can be consolidated.

Is there a schism between East and West Coasts?

I think that is healing. I've done some pictures in New York and I've done a number in L.A. There are a lot of editors who work on both coasts, and I know people who have bad feelings about it because they have been blocked from joining either the L.A. local or, in my case, the New York local. But as we begin to realize that we can take charge, we can find a way to make it more workable for everyone, those feelings are becoming diffused. We've now had two years of talks with New York. Those feelings of "us" and "them" are slowly changing to ideas of "we" together.

Are there differences in editing styles between New York and L.A.?

The biggest difference I've found in New York, quite frankly, is the level of serious commitment to film. I think because the competition is fierce in New York, there are very few jobs, and in order to survive you have to be very, very committed. In L.A., there are a number of editors who see working with film as a great job and are not that committed to film other than the paycheck. But I'm making sweeping generalizations. Of course, instances on either end of the continuum can exist anywhere in any profession at any time. You also have to realize there are all kinds of work in L.A.: commercials, documentaries, television films, long-format television films, short-format, series, mini-series, features, on and on and on. The work is more restricted in New York. The other difference I've found is that because New York is a small community, it's somewhat inbred and the system of networking is not as familial as in L.A. There's a lot of networking and cooperation in L.A. because, while there is competition, it's not quite as severe. I'm talking in the broadest terms. Also because New York is not a film town, people have interests in many other things. You can be in film and feel you are part of a larger community of artists. In New York there is everything—theater, film, music, dance, literature. A general awareness of the culture at large is perhaps greater in New York. In L.A., because we are a movie town, Hollywood, it's ingrown, we feed upon ourselves a lot. Another big difference is how a cutting room is organized. In New York, there is a lot more paperwork and busywork for the assistants than in L.A. I don't know why, but I'm amazed. There's a terrific amount of record making in New York that I find double work. What *I* expect from an assistant is a person who's eventually going to be an editor.

Who wants to be an editor.

Who wants to be, absolutely. Clearly they need to do assistants' work. They need to run the editing room. I want someone to deal with the outside world smoothly so that I can work, so whatever they do to organize the work is fine with me. I just want it done neatly so that I can find a piece of film at any moment. More than that, I want my assistants to be film critics. They're my first audience. When I have problems with a scene and I'm pulling my hair out, I invite my assistants in to take a look and I want them to give me their honest opinion. I don't want them to praise me. I want them to think what they would have done had they had a chance to work on that scene. Think about what works and what doesn't work and why. I don't want someone who says, "I don't feel it works." That's not enough. It needs to be articulated. That stirs me up too. I can be looking at one set of problems and completely ignore what needs to be dealt with because I had a problem in matching or with a performance. They can open up an area of thinking that I perhaps have not even thought of. They get to participate and, for selfish reasons, I get to use their brains! I want them to see themselves as future editors. Given a certain set of problems, how would they solve them? I have a bit of mother hen in me. I hover around, I want everybody to be happy. People should be able to do what they want to do.

Might an editor ever teach a director something?

Editors are put in a position many times of—I don't want to say "teaching school" because that sounds so condescending—but we are in a position of sharing our knowledge with directors who may have less, and guiding them through the treacherous labyrinth of making a movie. Editing is different today. We are more involved in the dissemination of knowledge than we had been. When we were working within the studio system, editors were assigned to projects and worked primarily with the producer. There are a few directors who have a large body of work, Steven Spielberg, John Huston, but most don't. Editors, cinematographers, production designers, and so on essentially have more experience than directors do. Making a movie can be a terrorizing experience for a first-time director, or for a second or a third or a fourth, you know. Cutting your teeth as a film director is difficult because directors now have to generate their own material, generate interest, get the actors, raise the funds and so forth. So directors now have to do a whole lot more than directors in the past. It's easy for editors to have a body of work because we're on a film probably every nine months, and before you know it, you've worked on quite a few. But directors simply don't have the opportunity to work on that many films if it takes them two or three years to put a project together, direct it, and get it released.

Would you say the editor follows the director in having the final say on the film?

Those lines are blurred by the time you have gone through the editorial process. It's not like the film goes through "the editor's stage" or "the director's stage" or "the producer's stage." Film is such a collaborative work that I can't say at any point that editing has all that much to say about it ultimately. Obviously when people solicit my opinions, I'm not shy about giving them. But I wouldn't be so sure of thinking that what I say is necessarily what everybody's going to do. It often occurred to me, though, that if the director really knew how many decisions we make as editors, how many decisions seem unimportant but in the conglomerate influence the film extraordinarily, I think they would want to edit themselves. Either they don't have the patience or the inclination, or they would rather have the input from another person in the hopes that the material could be treated in any number of ways and become better through collaboration. I would like to think that the film, having gone through the director's filters and the editor's filters, and then once again through both, would be better than what either might do on their own. I think that occurs most of the time.

But for all of that, not every film is a success.

Oh no. If we could make blockbuster movies, every movie would be one. There are so many variables. To its contemporary audience, *Citizen Kane* was a mess. It's become a film classic, a breakthrough film for American cinema. Think of all the Nicholas Ray films, those B movies. They were not considered great films at the time. Now they are certainly cult films and they represent filmmaking that is a genre in and of itself in film noir. Making a movie is like going to Las Vegas, it's a huge gamble. I recently saw a film about the cold war. They started making the film probably a year ago and it's being released now. Look what has happened to the world in a year. The cold war is over, really. This movie is suddenly dated and probably doesn't have an audience at all. Taste is fickle. You can make a jungle movie one year, and the next year people aren't wanting jungles, they're wanting Antarctica! This year's hit is next year's memory. Very few films become classics and they were usually too unique to be "popular" at the time they were released.

Then again, one movie can spawn thirteen clones.

Yes, and you have carbon copies until you can't bear it!

I'm sure you wouldn't want to work on clones one after another. In fact, you have a diversity of feature and documentary credits.

I like to alternate. A few years ago, I did *Swimming to Cambodia* with Spalding Gray. One man behind a desk. It had challenges: multiple cameras, three performances shot live, stock footage from *The Killing Fields*. I love narrative filmmaking, and it is very satisfying, but sometimes the diet can become too rich. I cut commercials from 1972 to 1977, I had my own company. I cut my teeth doing American Film Institute Fellows' projects. I haven't cut news stuff, but I've cut negative. Telling a story, no matter what form, is what's fascinating to me. I enjoy life in the cutting room. The irony is that when I thought I was going to be a professional musician and I was in school in Paris, I said, "This is an incredible city! What am I doing in a practice room? I love music but I don't want to practice hours in a dark room. I would like to have some social life!" What am I doing now? I'm spending eight, ten, twelve hours in a dark room! I might as well be in a practice room.

But it's different, isn't it?

Yeah, it is. When I'm working, the life that goes on in the screen is where I am. I'm not in a dark room, really, I'm inside that screen. I hate to say it, but I'm a voyeur. I'm seeing something that wasn't there. When I start a film, the racks and bins are empty, the benches silent, there's no film going through the machines. The dailies come in a little at a time. I say, "In eight or nine months, what is nothing—because they haven't even shot the film yet—is going to be on the screen." Now that's incredible. I have a real thrill as the film comes in because I realize very shortly I'm going to have an encounter with it. When I'm in the dark, alone, and I'm looking at the film for the first time, it's very exciting. Then when the director comes in, you're dealing with the mind and heart of the person who has *the* most intimate knowledge of the film. You go through problems together, talk, hash it over, find solutions. It's you two at the end. It really is magic. We're sort of alchemists. We put a lot of elements together, and we're hoping to make it gold.

5

Flashback, Flashforward

Harold F. Kress
and Carl Kress

HAROLD F. KRESS

1939   *The Adventures of Huckle-berry Finn* (Supervising Editor), directed by Richard Thorpe
Broadway Serenade, directed by Robert Z. Leonard
It's a Wonderful World, directed by W. S. Van Dyke
Remember? directed by Norman Z. McLeod
These Glamour Girls, directed by S. Sylvan Simon

1940   *Andy Hardy Meets Debutante*, directed by George B. Seitz
Bitter Sweet, directed by W. S. Van Dyke
Comrade X, directed by King Vidor
New Moon, directed by Robert Z. Leonard

1941   *Dr. Jekyll and Mr. Hyde*, directed by Victor Fleming
H. M. Pulham, Esq., directed by King Vidor
Rage in Heaven, directed by W. S. Van Dyke
Unholy Partners, directed by Mervyn LeRoy

1942   *Mrs. Miniver*, directed by William Wyler
Random Harvest, directed by Mervyn LeRoy

1943   *Cabin in the Sky*, directed by Vincente Minnelli
Madame Curie, directed by Mervyn LeRoy

1944   *Dragon Seed*, directed by Jack Conway and Harold S. Bucquet

1946   *The Yearling*, directed by Clarence Brown

1948   *A Date With Judy*, directed by Richard Thorpe

1949   *Command Decision*, directed by Sam Wood
East Side, West Side, directed by Mervyn LeRoy
The Great Sinner, directed by Robert Siodmak

1950   *The Miniver Story* (United States release version), directed by H. C. Potter

1953   *Ride Vaquero*, directed by John Farrow

1954   *Green Fire*, directed by Andrew Marton
Rose Marie, directed by Mervyn LeRoy
Saadia, directed by Albert Lewin
Valley of the Kings, directed by Robert Pirosh

1955   *The Cobweb*, directed by Vincente Minnelli

I'll Cry Tomorrow, directed by
Daniel Mann
The Prodigal, directed by
Richard Thorpe

1956   *The Rack*, directed by
Arnold Laven
*The Teahouse of the
August Moon*, directed by
Daniel Mann

1957   *Silk Stockings*, directed by
Rouben Mamoulian
Until They Sail, directed by
Robert Wise

1958   *Imitation General*, directed by
George Marshall
Merry Andrew, directed by
Michael Kidd

1959   *Count Your Blessings*,
directed by Jean Negulesco
*The World, the Flesh, and
the Devil*, directed by
Ranald MacDougall

1960   *Home From the Hill*, directed
by Vincente Minnelli

1961   *King of Kings* (United States
release version), directed by
Nicholas Ray

1963   *How the West Was Won*, di-
rected by John Ford, George
Marshall, Henry Hathaway
*It Happened at the World's
Fair* (Supervising Editor),
directed by Norman Taurog

1965   *The Greatest Story Ever Told*
(Supervising Editor), directed
by George Stevens

1966   *Alvarez Kelly*, directed by
Edward Dmytryk
Walk Don't Run (Supervising
Editor), directed by
Charles Walters

1967   *The Ambushers*, directed by
Henry Levin
Luv, directed by Clive Donner

1970   *I Walk the Line* (Supervising
Editor), directed by
John Frankenheimer

1971   *The Horsemen*, directed by
John Frankenheimer

1972   *The Poseidon Adventure*,
directed by Ronald Neame
Stand Up and Be Counted,
directed by Jackie Cooper

1973   *The Iceman Cometh*,
directed by
John Frankenheimer

1974   *99 and 44/100% Dead*,
directed by
John Frankenheimer
The Towering Inferno, di-
rected by John Guillermin
(Coeditor: Carl Kress)

1976   *Gator*, directed by
Burt Reynolds

1977   *The Other Side of Midnight*,
directed by Charles Jarrott
(Coeditor: Donn Cambern)

1977   *Viva Knievel*, directed by
Gordon Douglas

* See Appendix for complete list of awards
and nominations.

CARL KRESS

1966   *Alvarez Kelly*, directed by
Edward Dmytryk

1967   *Luv*, directed by Clive Donner

1970   *The Liberation of L. B. Jones*,
directed by William Wyler
Watermelon Man, directed by
Melvin Van Peebles

1971   *Doctors' Wives*, directed by
George Schaffer

1974   *Rape Squad*, directed by
Robert Kelljian
Sugar Hill, directed by
Paul Maslansky
The Towering Inferno, di-
rected by John Guillermin
(Coeditor: Harold F. Kress)

1976   *The Blue Bird*, directed by
George Cukor
Drum, directed by
Steve Carver

1977	*Audrey Rose*, directed by Robert Wise	
1979	*Man, Woman, and a Bank*, directed by Noel Black	
1979	*Meteor*, directed by Ronald Neame	
1980	*Hopscotch*, directed by Ronald Neame	
1981	*Looker*, directed by Michael Crichton	
1983	*Stroker Ace*, directed by Hal Needham	
1984	*Cannonball Run II*, directed by Hal Needham	
1986	*Rad*, directed by Hal Needham	
1987	*Body Slam*, directed by Hal Needham *Bloodsport*, directed by Newt Arnold	
1988	*Hollow Heads*, directed by Tom Burman	

Television

* *Singing Whales: The Undersea World of Jacques Cousteau* (David Wolper)
Sofia (David Wolper)
Rafferty (Warner Brothers)
Deerslayer (Sunn Classic)
Lost in London (GE)
Airwolf (Universal)
Honolulu Run (Universal)
Legmen (Universal)
Paper Dolls (MGM)
Braker (MGM)
Generation (Embassy)
Matlock (Viacom)
B. L. Stryker (Universal)

* See Appendix for complete list of editing awards and nominations.

Together, father and son Harold and Carl Kress span more than sixty years in the business and have cut many of Tinsel Town's memorable films. While the tinsel glitters in Harold's memories, however, it is tarnished for Carl who faces a different industry than the one his father knew.

Harold quickly became friendly with some of the biggest names at MGM, including Irving Thalberg, L. B. Mayer, William Wyler, Barbara Stanwyck, Greer Garson, Spencer Tracy, and Katharine Hepburn. He boasts that he once made Garbo laugh: he had forgotten to shut off the sound as dailies were reversed, and Garbo's backward chatter amused her so much that she insisted on viewing outtakes in reverse for days afterward. Harold was a pioneer in Cinerama editing techniques for *How the West Was Won*; and he was capable of scolding top directors like George Stevens, who tilted the cumbersome Cinerama camera on *The Greatest Story Ever Told*. "He tilted it a little and the disciples started walking down the hill on a slant! I said, 'You can't do it, George.'" From his auspicious introduction to Thalberg to postproduction supervision forty years later, Harold remembers primarily the friendly security of the studio system.

Carl Kress's career has followed a difficult route. He describes himself as the whipping boy for George Cukor during the first United States–Russia collaboration, *The Blue Bird*, because he was closest to the director and vulnerable to his frustrations on this troubled film. Carl is outraged at the megabuck business Hollywood has become, and laments the overwhelming number of hopefuls who venture into the movie industry, only to be disillusioned. "I don't know what working a year is all about," Carl says. "I was honestly scared to put my salary on the line to buy a house because I knew six months down the way I was going to be off for two or three months." Perhaps his longest job, on *The Towering Inferno*, was

83

also his greatest disappointment. He still feels, as does Harold, that their joint Oscar failed to guarantee getting better work. Carl's determined hopefulness for the work he loves ekes through his words, however, and he continues to cherish those moments of kindness from directors who value his speed and ability to "make the film sing."

Harold, why don't you start by describing how you began at MGM?

My father was very well known in Hollywood, he ran a restaurant on Hollywood Boulevard. He started the Chamber of Commerce, and he and Cecil B. DeMille started the Hollywood Athletic Club. Because of the 1929 crash, my father lost three million dollars and we all went to work. I was going to UCLA to be a lawyer and worked at night as a host in my father's restaurant. One night an old friend of my father's, who was the right hand of Irving Thalberg, came in and asked what I was doing. I said I was studying law at UCLA and working at night, and it was getting awfully tough. He said, "Why don't you come out to MGM? Thalberg could use some smart young men like you." The next morning I was in Thalberg's office for one hour and forty-five minutes! Here's the head of the studio, he was like a god then, but he spent an hour and forty-five minutes talking with me about the picture industry. I was overwhelmed. He said, "Would you like to come to work?" I said yes and met the head of the film editing department who put me in what they called the Test Room. MGM had all the stars, but when directors wanted to cast a picture besides the leads, they would decide who would be tested and screen tests from the big stock company. MGM also had a school with a gymnasium where the actors learned fencing, dancing, everything. Those tests would go into the cutting room, I would label them, send them to the projection room, pick them up and bring them back. It was dull after a while, so I asked permission to start cutting some of the tests and work with the directors. I would ask them, "Do you want to change it?" and they'd say, "No, that's fine, very good work." Then I got a call to come to Thalberg's office again, he had found out what I was doing. They were getting ready to do the crowd scenes in China for *The Good Earth*. Thalberg said, "I'd like you to receive and catalogue the film. You'll have your own small cutting room up in the balcony." I was to receive over one hundred thousand feet of film minimum with the treks and the drought. To make a long story short, I was on *The Good Earth* for three years. Oh, I asked Irving Thalberg if I could take a week off to get married. He said okay. A year later, Carl came along and I was still on *Good Earth*. He was two years old and I was *still* on *Good Earth*! The amazing thing is that the picture cost three million dollars. I couldn't imagine what it would cost today. We were still working on it the night of the premiere, sticking in time lapse inserts. Remember the planting of the seed, the tree growing in winter and summer? We put those in the night we premiered. Anyway, that's how I started.

How did you finally become an official editor?

I remember as an assistant on one film, I had to finish the cut because the editor was working on another picture. Every day I ran dailies for the director, Robert Z. Leonard—"Pop." On the last day of dailies, he asked, "Who's cutting my picture?" I said, "Pop, I'm staying at night on my own time to put together a first cut for you." He said, "Have you ever cut a picture before?" I said, "No, sir, but I'm getting the hang of it! Could you give me a week?" So he came back in a week and we projected it, and Pop never stopped once. I'd been in projection rooms with editors running sequences and the directors would press the stop button and say, "This is wrong." That's what I was expecting. Pop never stopped once. The picture was over, he turned to me and said, "You know, I can't tell you what the hell to do. This is one of the best first cuts I've seen. Are you doing anything for lunch? Let's go to the Brown Derby." I'd never been there, we went to lunch and talked. He said, "Your last name is Kress? I know your father and mother, Sam and Sophie Kress." Then he said, "You're going to be a great editor. I want you to come to my office Monday morning. I'm going to take you up to the executives. I want you to meet Mr. Mannix." He was the hatchet man for Louis B. Mayer, he used to be a bouncer. So Monday morning I went to Mannix's office. He said, "Is this true what Pop says about you?" I said, "Yes, sir." He said, "Pop wants to give you a lot of money and he wants you to get credit on the screen as editor and he wants to give you back pay from the day he started shooting. And if I don't give it to you, he's going to quit the studio!" Well, he was just having a good time with me. It was the biggest check I ever received.

[Carl] How much did an editor make?

[Harold] In those days, I think it was a hundred dollars a week. Sixty dollars for an assistant. Then they buzzed Mayer's office. That's how I became an editor.

What impressed Pop so much about your work?

Just that he could find nothing wrong. It was perfect storytelling, and I worked hard. I did a lot of things myself because I didn't have assistants under me and I couldn't ask anybody. Pop shot for editing, just like Willard Van Dyke and Vic Fleming. They knew their scripts well. They didn't get too artistic, they just told the story. Van Dyke had been in the Marines before he went into the motion picture business and he directed just like the Marines. He was in every morning at five o'clock. He laid

out the work he wanted to do that day. If he finished at three, wrap. If
he finished at five, wrap. But he got that work done. He camera-cut, only
shot up to a certain line in the script and cut. He knew he would go to
a close-up, pick up the end of the scene, another two-shot, wrap and that's
it. So you could only cut it one way. And he never ran the film himself.
We had to be on the set at eight in the morning to tell him whether the
dailies were good or bad. Most of the times you'd tell him they're good.
Once I had to tell him he made a mistake, I thought he'd stick a knife in
me. They had rehinged the door of the set but nobody told Van Dyke,
so the actor went through the door as it was one way and when he came
in, it was different; you couldn't cut the shots together. They had to
reshoot.

Did you ever work with the famous "montage team" at MGM?
    Vorkapich and Balbusch, wasn't it?
    [Carl] Way before my time.
    [Harold] Yeah, they'd come down to the cutting room and take film.
Our assistants had the most trouble with them—"You can't take that
film." They thought they were running the whole show. They did background for main titles, time montages. I don't know. The editor should
be able to do a montage. An A roll and a B roll and send it to the optical
department, that's all. When I was young I built a film library in the cutting room with outtakes of music and I'd mark the cans "love theme,"
"chase," "rapid music," "slow music." Even though I was not a musician,
I had a great feeling for music. And I developed a theory ever since I
started editing: never run film silent, even if you have to put wind on
top of it. On *The Yearling*, I was getting this beautiful film daily from
Florida, cutting about seventy thousand feet of film of the boy romping
through the woods. But I couldn't find the music for it, I had nothing in
my cutting room. But one night as we were playing a newly acquired recording of Mendelssohn's "Midsummer Night's Dream" and I heard the
scherzo, I knew I had my music. I took the record to the studio the next
morning to transfer it to a soundtrack. I swear, I put the first note of music
on the first frame of the picture, with no fooling around, put a start mark
on it, projected it, and it was just fine. It's in the picture today!

It fit perfectly?
    Perfectly. I called Sidney Franklin and I said I had something very
important to show him. I tipped the projectionist off, "When we run this,
don't do what we usually do with the dailies. Darken the room, wait, *then*
start it." He did. When it was over, Sidney Franklin was crying. Margaret
Booth was there and she was crying. I was crying, it was contagious. Sidney came over and hugged and kissed me, sobbing in my face. He said,
"That's the most beautiful thing I've ever seen." And Margaret, with tears

in her eyes, said, "That was something. How did you do that?" I said, "I just found the music off a phonograph record." They calmed down and called Louis B. Mayer's office. Here comes the whole board, the so-called board on the third floor. L. B. Mayer was on one side of me, I forget who was on the other. L. B. could cry at the drop of a hat, but here he was bawling! He said, "Who made this?" And Sidney said, "Harold did it." That was one of the best moments of my life.

What story were you telling through those images and music?

I was telling a story beginning with a boy and his fawn romping through the woods and all the other animals start joining in. One animal would go off in one direction and another, the sun is setting, and in the last shot the boy runs after the fawn and disappears. It wasn't Disney, but it was like *Fantasia*.

So you were in control of your own montages, basically. Did you have input into the transformation montages in Dr. Jekyll and Mr. Hyde?

I directed them. I got assigned to *Jekyll and Hyde* and asked, "What about his changes?" They had hired thirty animators and had close-ups of Spencer Tracy on cells because someone had sold the producer Victor Saville on this idea. They spent seventy-five thousand dollars just doing that—you know, like thumbing through those little books of animated movies when you were a kid. When I got the film, I couldn't even run it. I said there's got to be another way to do this. I woke up in the middle of the night and got an idea. I ran other versions of *Jekyll and Hyde* with John Barrymore and Fredric March. They always start on him, cut off to the side, cut back to him to start his struggle, cut back to his hand, and so on. I wanted something else. The first guy I talked to was Jack Dawn, the head of the makeup department, and asked, "How many times would you have to stop the camera on Tracy?" He said, "About thirty-six." Then I got the idea of sitting a camera on a barber's chair on wheels to dolly the camera back and forth. The camera was normally bolted to the floor with a chain, and you never racked it over. Next to the camera, I got an old camera from the still department, set it up, and hired an artist. Then I went to Tracy—he and I were great friends. I explained the idea to him and he asked, "Do you think it could work?" I said, "I can't tell you but it's a lot better than that crap I saw on that other piece of film." I still had to tell Saville. I explained it to him and said, "I talked to Jack Dawn about this and he said it's fantastic, and I talked to Spencer Tracy and he thought it would work, and Victor Fleming, the director, liked it." Saville fired me! I went home. About an hour and a half later, Victor's assistant called me. "We've stopped shooting." "What do you mean?" Spencer Tracy, Ingrid Bergman, Lana Turner all stopped because I was fired! Mannix the Butcher called me, "What happened?" I said, "I just gave the producer a great idea which was okayed by Tracy and Fleming and your producer fired me." He said, "Get your ass over here." I was scared, everyone was scared of Mannix. I went over and there's Fleming and Tracy. "If they stop shooting, it's going to cost us fifty thousand dollars every day they stop." I said, "That's not my worry. I just thought I had a brilliant idea." To make a long story short, they told L. B. Mayer why the picture was stopped, Saville was sent back to London, Fleming was made producer *and* director, and I shot the four transitions. Just a series of staggering dissolves. Each one was shot differently, we used different light effects on the second and third, and the last one was strictly his death mask. I dreamed it all up.

[Carl] I'm hearing stories I haven't heard before!

How was it for you growing up in the home of a famous editor, Carl?

Well, my story in no way relates to what you've just heard. I can't really recall what it was like living with a famous editor. I just knew that he was never home, he was working all the time. As far as a cohesive family life, it was mom and me. I remember I used to go flying in Clarence Brown's airplane, swim in his pool and play in his private lagoon. Greer Garson was pretty friendly with me. When I came to the studio, as much as I can recall, I was on the set more than in the cutting room. The Kress name was pretty well known because of grandfather too. But my beginning in editing was nothing like Harold's. I spent ten years as an apprentice and an assistant before I was allowed to cut film. There was an eight-year rule when I got into the business that you couldn't cut during that time, and when you had your eight years, you went out and tried to ask somebody to let you cut their movie. They'd say, "What have you done?" and you'd say, "Nothing." It was like being between a rock and a hard place. Very frustrating. When I started, I was in the splicing unit at MGM—they were still hot-splicing film. I would stand at a hot splicer eight hours a day, scraping film and running it back and forth. I stayed there as an assistant four years, then went to Columbia with Harold, spent another four years, went on to David Wolper, spent a couple of years. I got frustrated and left film.

What was happening to you?

I did not tolerate the resistance I was getting because I *knew* I could cut. Whatever genes were in Harold transferred to me. Cutting was easy for me.

[Harold] He still cuts faster than anybody.

[Carl] I didn't know how to deal with the frustration and the suppression I met. I left town for a while, took a break, came back and was going to be assigned as an assistant on *The Liberation of L. B. Jones*, William Wyler's last movie. The editor, Bob Swink, usually did the second unit directing for Wyler. I hadn't been in the room for five minutes, hardly knew the man, and I said, "Hey, can I put the movie together for you?" He said, "Yeah, sure." "Excuse me?" "Yeah, sure." "Do we have to go through the office and tell Mr. Wyler?" "No." It was that easy! After ten years pounding doors and begging, just like that I get a break!

You were at the right time and right place.

Yeah. To this very day I'm not so sure my last name has helped me. I don't know if it's been a deterrent or a help. Sometimes I've thought it was not good to be in Harold's shadow or footsteps. I liked working with cameras and when I got out of the army, I tried but just couldn't crack that closed door. The cameraman's union was really a closed shop. When Harold said there was an opening in splicing, I said sure. I guess I thought that was the only way I was going to get into the business.

Did you find photography helpful in editing?

I think my eye for the visual setup has helped me cut better. I let the image on the film take me. I don't force film to do what I want it to do. I let the film tell me and I'll say, "Oh, that's good" and manipulate it. Yeah, I think it probably helped.

Once you got into editing, did you find a difference between how your father had cut and what you were being asked to do?

Oh, a world of difference. What was sad for me was that I was getting to do my first picture with a gentleman Harold had worked with. Willie Wyler was a great guy, we would go to his house and run dailies. What happens? The man dies! That was my first out at bat. My second one was with Melvin Van Peebles who directed an avant-garde black movie, *Watermelon Man.* What happens? He leaves town and practically disappears. These were not my choices. My start was a good run, but it was nothing like Harold's tales. In 1969, 1970, the producers were a different kind of men than Harold's kind. Not friendly, no warmth. That was twenty years ago and if anything, in my opinion, it's gotten worse. There are a few editors in town who do hook up with the same directors and producers, guys who have made a "family," but only a few. Harold worked thirty years under one roof, he didn't have to sell himself. I have to sell myself at least twice a year. I've sold myself over forty times in the last twenty-one years. And I'm not really a good salesman. I don't have that ability. I'm known for speed and I'm good. Put me in a room, give me the film.

[Harold] It's a different world. It's hard for me to understand his days looking back on the opportunities I've had. I've been all over the world. Producers have sent me and my wife to England. Airplane tickets, hotel reservations in Paris, a week in Munich.

[Carl] I love my father dearly, but I envy what he went through. Because I have had personal problems with abuse and things like that, I've told my mother and my father on more than one occasion that I don't have the tough skin and the mental makeup to handle the roughness that is out there. I look at Harold and say, "He didn't have to do it. Why can't I have it like he did?"

[Harold] I don't think I'd be able to do what he does. I couldn't handle it. I've never asked for anything. I was asked to do things so many times, I didn't have to ask.

[Carl] When I confronted Harold some years ago about cutting for TV, he said he wouldn't. I *have* to cut TV in order to make a living. There was a time when he said he wouldn't do it. I don't have a choice.

[Harold] If you restrict people like that, I don't know how they can do a good job. I wasn't brought up that way. I was brought up if you needed an extra day or two, all right. Or they'd say to a director on the set, "You're a day behind," and the director would say, "What do you want me to do? Stop shooting?" Of course they didn't want him to. If you want a good picture, it takes more time, even another day or two.

[Carl] I think the movies back in the Golden Era are the best films ever made. They'll be classics until the world dissolves.

[Harold] I can still run *Random Harvest* and get a tear at the end, when Ronald Colman opens the door of that cottage. Not only women, but men get their handkerchiefs out. Pictures with feeling. Maybe once a year, today, you have a picture like that.

[Carl] I think the art form has resolved itself from being whatever it was when it started, but the basic goal of "taking out the good stuff," looking for the actors, making something lead the pace—that's basically the same since I saw Harold's first movies. They were glorious, great films. The movies he had the opportunity to work on are far beyond any movies made since the mid-sixties, even if they cost two hundred million dollars.

Is that because of better stories or acting in the old movies?

I think it was because of the men who ran the business. It was because of the Warners and the Cohns and the Mayers and the Zanucks. They were filmmakers. Nowadays we have guys out of Harvard Business School running the studios. It's not anywhere near the same. Yes, in those days it was a business and they did make movies for a million or two, and they didn't expect the film to be a flop, but they were still being made by moviemakers. Today, they're out to make a big buck.

How about current heart-wringers like Terms of Endearment? *Is that the success of the story?*

I'm definitely on the screenwriter's side. I don't believe there can really be a good movie unless it's written. It's got to start somewhere. If you get directors who are good, they can interpret. But you can't interpret something unless it's written down.

[Harold] When I teach college, students will ask, "What do you feel is most important?" I say, "Well, the word comes first." I developed a course for the International Student Center in Westwood called "The Movie Is Made." I start with the script and on ten Monday nights, I bring in a screenplay writer, director, producer, agent, musician, art director, actor, and so on. At the center I started with twenty-eight students and when we finished we had standing room only. You know, certain great things happen to you. When we finished, a student stood up and said, "Harold, we're so glad you came." He brought out a little Oscar and he had typewritten and pasted on the plaque, "With appreciation for all you have done." To me, that has more importance than the big Oscar.

[Carl] Speaking of Oscars and big moments, I wasn't even here to go upstage for the biggest moment in my life and receive my Oscar for *The Towering Inferno*. I was in Russia being the whipping boy for George Cukor because he couldn't make *Blue Bird* work and he berated me because he didn't have anybody else to berate. *Inferno* was another disappointment in my life, again because I think I was hooked up to Harold, namewise. Harold had an automobile accident well before *Inferno* was even close to being done. Movie magic hadn't been shot. The dramatic scenes had been shot, but let's just say the meat of the movie had not been done, right?

[Harold] Yes.

[Carl] Irwin Allen called me up when Harold was in the hospital and said, "We have to press on." I said, "Well, of course. Do you want any help?" *Inferno* was the fifth or sixth movie I'd been on. I said to him, "I'd prefer that you allow me to make an attempt to finish the movie myself." So they kept on shooting, the film poured in, I think I had two assistants, and I just kept cutting.

[Harold] I didn't get back until they were dubbing.

[Carl] As I said before, I let the film lead me on. I'm extremely fast and I don't let film become difficult. I picked up Harold's secrets of not running film back and forth too many times and making a decision. Whatever feels right, just mark it and get on with it. Put the film up on a rack and don't look at it until it's all done. So I kept on cutting, kept on cutting. First thing I knew, the movie was done, we were screening, soon it was on the dubbing stage. Harold came back, he took it on previews. It was really 75 percent my editorial, 25 percent his. The movie got an Academy Award for its technical merit because it was a réally slick movie. Editorial-wise, there was a lot of movie magic that they probably weren't even aware of: one shot of a miniature, cutting to a taller one, cutting to a real building, and making all that work. It wasn't difficult for me. But because nobody realized that Harold wasn't even around for that time, word got out that Carl got an Oscar for hanging onto Daddy's coattails. I've discussed this with Harold. I burned on that for quite a few years. What are we supposed to do? I can't ask him to take out full-page ads in the trades and say, "You know, my son cut the movie because I was in the hospital." That's Hollywood. I couldn't even get big-time after that because I was told that was the rumor.

[Harold] And I wasn't there. That's the truth.

[Carl] I wasn't looking for a guarantee, but the Oscar didn't do for me what it's done for a lot of people.

Can you simplify editing on films with such large amounts of footage? With these "disaster films," you're always building tension because every turn puts the characters into another catastrophe.

[Harold] A lot of that has to do with the script.

[Carl] Yes, I was going to say that there were some heavyweight writers on *Inferno* and *The Poseidon Adventure*, and because of the way the scenes were connected and kept going through the film, you were following the words.

[Harold] *Poseidon* was easier to cut. It was one of the very few pictures that had to be shot in continuity. You had to shoot everything before the boat went over, then everything from the inside had to progress through until the passengers got to the top. We all took cameras when the ship turned over in the big set, even I had a camera. We had the actors go up a stepladder and jump off, and I would set my camera in one place and have my eight people jump off and fall through; then I set the camera in another spot and the same people would go up the ladder and jump through. How those cuts came in handy. They asked, "Why are you shooting all that phony-baloney?" I said, "Wait till you see the picture." You know how you can use cuts like that.

It's easier to cut "flash" because you can insert a lot of elements.

Oh, a dinner table sequence is the hardest sequence in the world to cut. Like on *Jekyll and Hyde*, ten days of shooting fifteen people at the dinner table. You can imagine how many hundred thousand feet of film. Or in *Mrs. Miniver*, where Greer Garson finds the German soldier and invites him into the house—ten days shooting for two people in the kitchen.

[Carl] I did a movie with Robert Wise called *Audrey Rose*, it was heavy talking. You have to keep a momentum going so the audience doesn't get too itchy. In twenty-one years on the bench, my big moment was with that movie. I haven't had the opportunity to get stroked like Harold talked about getting stroked—I don't think the stroking men are out there anymore. But after we ran the film, Robert Wise, gentleman that he was, said to me, "Carl, you've cut things in that movie that I didn't even know I shot." I'll carry that one around forever.

[Harold] That was true with John Frankenheimer on *The Horsemen*. He had been to Afghanistan and shot the buzkashi game and the treks through the mountains and came back with thousands of feet of film. I had never heard of Frankenheimer, but one day the head of production at Columbia called me. "Harold, we're having trouble. Frankenheimer is not happy with the man who's editing the buzkashi game." I said, "What the hell is a buzkashi game? Does the editor know what a buzkashi game is?" He said, "Well, he's supposed to . . . " "How much time did you spend with him?" "I spent ten or fifteen minutes telling him what a buzkashi game is." I said, "Well, if you want me to do it, you'll have to spend an hour because I never heard of the goddamned thing! All right, I'll do it, but on the condition that I talk to the editor." I did. The editor said, "Harold, you're not hurting my feelings. I don't know how you're going to get along with this guy." I told the assistants to strip all the film, put it back in dailies form, and we ran half of it that afternoon. Then I went to see Frankenheimer. "All right, tell me what a buzkashi game is and how you see it play." It's a yearly celebration. Tribes fight with a dead goat's body filled with sand, helter-skelter, and the more times they drop it in a circle than in the field, it counts. So I started putting the film together and made it as exciting and rough as I could. I got six loops of horses' hooves and screaming, reversed the sounds so they were going faster, took it into the dubbing room. I called Frankenheimer over and played the hell out of it until the screen was shaking with sound too. He said, "Jesus Christ! That's what I want. I'm bringing some men from *Sports Illustrated*—they want to know what a buzkashi game is—and this is the best way to show it." See, if you search the film, you find things. In another Frankenheimer picture, *I Walk the Line*, I needed a close-up of a girl, and the only shot we had was an over-the-shoulder of Gregory Peck. In the last third of the picture, in a similar scene, Frankenheimer did shoot close-ups and in one, the girl had a tear in her eye. I wanted something like that in the front part of the picture, but she was wearing a different dress, so I took the close-up to the head of the optical department and said, "Could you blow this up just to get rid of the dress?" The close-up came back and I put it in the first sequence. Never told anyone about it. Ran the first cut and Frankenheimer said, "The picture looks great." We ran it a second time and when we got to that point, he pushed the reverse button, ran it back and said, "Did I shoot close-ups *here*?" I said, "No. That's from the last sequence. I only used her eyes welling up and the tear running down her cheek." He said, "That's fabulous."

How do you handle close-ups in dialogue scenes?

[Carl] I've noticed that a lot of editors with four hundred or five hundred foot takes of people talking will play the principal speaker and then think of where to go off to the other person. I've found an easier way—I don't know if Harold taught me this or not. I just play the person who's talking and let him do his whole speech until the other person talks. For however long my A character on camera is talking, I mark the beginning and end. I leave it in the machine and then start playing the other person—the same amount of time, but listening to the other person. Then I start working with that reaction shot of the one who's *not* talking, pull that picture out, and put it where the second person is talking. I like to do that because it lets me flow more freely within my style of editing. I think an actor's best moments are when they're not talking. I look for those moments in any dialogue scene. Many times I will go to the person listening probably more than to the person talking, unless the person is saying something very specific for the story point. I'd rather go to a good reaction. It does more for the dialogue.

[Harold] Kate Hepburn, I used to play miles of film on her. She was the greatest listener. And Tracy, he had good reactions without moving his head. Just with his eyes. As Carl said, sometimes those are better than moments when the action is happening.

[Carl] As I said before, I let the film dictate to me. I let my visual eye and my editorial brain work on automatic. I think that's what has made film editing easy within this family affair.

Can you intellectualize about that a little more?

I think intellectualizing gets you pretty screwed up sometimes. I see a lot of film editors run the Moviolas back and forth before they even make a mark. They're always worrying about, "How do I look going from this cut to this cut to this cut?" If you start to intellectualize, you're going to bind up and go real slow. The KEM can sometimes do that to you because if you get three of those picture heads loaded up with film and see all that's going on, you start saying, "Wow, this wouldn't be bad here, but look what *he's* doing," and you get slowed down something fierce. I'm not saying two frames don't make a difference, but I don't let it stun me the first time through. I don't think about it when I'm going to line up my picture. When I start passing through it the second time, then I'll say, "Gee, I let somebody make a turn and I didn't let it finish and I don't like it, so I'll either not let the turn start or I'll add frames and let the turn finish." Then I'll fix those things. But if I miss them the first time out, it's okay. So I'm not a great intellectualizer. I am personally and adamantly against film editors who have to intellectualize and get so wrapped up about a cut. If you've got a good director who knows what he's doing, he's going to give you stuff that's good. There's just no getting around it. I'm like Harold. I give my director his picture within at least five days after he's finished shooting. Not too many people can match me for speed and there was nobody who ever could match Harold, because we just sit in the room and we cut.

[Harold] We've never played the outside film business.

[Carl] Just stick to my guns. Sit there, do my work, and go home.

So you're reacting out of your emotions to the material. It touches you, it upsets you, whatever it does, and then you refine it.

That's how I do it. That's how you do it too, isn't it?

[Harold] If I didn't like it, I'd go down and tell the director. But most of the times, it's the same. I didn't spend a lot of time dwelling over this or that. It's shot. I have to make the best use of it I can. Why should I aggravate myself? I just cut it as smoothly and as nicely as I can and I put it away. When we used to have hot splicing, my assistant would bring the film in, the girls would splice it, and he'd say, "Should I get a projection room, Harold? You want to run it?" Well, they didn't know me very well. "Put it away. We'll look at it in a week." How can you be a judge after you've just spent two hours cutting a sequence? I've seen some guys who can't wait to get it spliced. They yell at their assistants, "Splice it! I want to see it right away!" How can you be the judge of what you've done? You've just cut it.

[Carl] One of the greatest inventions ever made for the cutting room was the butt splicer which allows you not to lose frames and you can experiment. You can always fix any mistake. I've gone into some cutting rooms and—I'm not going to exaggerate—there is a stack two inches high of cuts only an inch or so long. Frames, frames, all over the place, because these editors do what I was taught *not* to do. They cut their sequence and fine-tune it the first time out. They come into my room after I go through a first cut, and they might find two-framers that I take out for the negative cutter if I'm cutting back into a scene real quick, but that's *all* you'll ever see in my room. I try to make it easy on myself the first time. I try in the most polite way to tell them, "Why do you make it so hard on yourself? Why don't you try this?" Some of them are changing slowly, but I guess they see things differently. Some of them have ego problems; when the director tries to change an internal cut, they get hurt. They get bent out of shape. I say, "It's only a piece of film. Come on, it's the director's prerogative."

If you're doing a montage or a documentary, where so much is what the editor conceives, could a director's change be taken more personally?

I did a Jacques Cousteau program where they shoot reams of 16mm footage. They come back and you sit with the director and writer with

four-by-five index cards on the wall about what they think "could be."
"Here's the story of the singing whales." You have to go through ten,
twelve hours of film. *You* have to make a story for them. They lock you
up in the room and say, "Call us when you're ready." Yeah, it got a little
personal because I got more into it. You get storylines you didn't even
think you had. It's really phenomenal.

Do you consider the audience when you cut?

[Harold] Once in a while. If you start dwelling on them, you're lost.
Do it for yourself. If I like it, then I think the director will like it. Go by
your instincts. If you don't, then you're not a sure person. Why should
you doubt yourself? Sometimes it's lousy, but 90 percent of the time
you're going to be right.

[Carl] I'd say 75 or 80 percent.

[Harold] I have had people who go to movies twice a week say to me,
"What did you do in moving pictures?" I tell them, "I was a film editor."
They ask, "What do film editors do?" I tell them.

What do you tell them?

Editing I think is a part of the film you don't see. Even some people
in the business don't know what editing is. You ask them to talk about
editing and they can't because they don't see it. I think it's only the film
editor and the director who know. Do you think anybody actually watches
for editing?

[Carl] I think it's the impression of editing they see.

[Harold] Who would think of watching a picture just to see editing?

*You spend so much time at it, wouldn't you want the audience to know
what you do?*

Well, we don't want the audience to know it's a film.

[Carl] I think film editing is like the editing of *Vogue* or *Cosmopolitan*
or a novel, or what an editor does on a newspaper. Everybody knows
about books, magazines, and newspapers. There's an editor on every one
of those. It's their responsibility, if I'm not mistaken, to throw out what's
not so good to read or what's not a good picture. As a simplification, that's
basically an editor's job with film. He reads the whole story and once he's
got his story cut and he sees it, he decides what's not really working and
what could be better. For someone who doesn't know what a film editor
does, you can equate it in that way. That's basically what we do.

[Harold] That's a good explanation.

[Carl] If you have a movie finishing at ten thousand feet, and they
printed one hundred thousand, you're putting away ninety thousand feet
of film. That's the editor's job. In a novel, when you read it as 325 pages,
maybe it was 513 first. Well, some editor at Doubleday went through it
and helped the writer say, "Don't you know we can get rid of this? This

doesn't help the story move along." So if we switch that over to film, the ninety thousand feet of film that we put away is the same. It doesn't do anything for us.

[Harold] One of the toughest editing jobs I've ever had was for *The Iceman Cometh*. It was shot with three cameras and it was an all-dialogue picture. You couldn't change the words—that's a classic, you know. Ten years after I cut it, I got a call. "We're trying to recut some of these pictures for rerelease and we're having problems with *Iceman*." I said, "That's going to be a hell of a picture to cut. How can you cut Eugene O'Neill? How much has to come out?" "Fifteen minutes." They made me a picture-track print and, I tell you, I worked all day long. I just started cutting whole sentences out. The first time I went through the picture, I got eight and a half minutes out, then another six. I went through it three or four times and finally got eighteen minutes out. I said "Oh God!" all through the picture, I ruined O'Neill's beautiful dialogue in some instances. But you have to do it for a purpose sometimes.

You certainly followed that picture to the end, even over years. Is it usual for editors to stay with a film to the end?

In the so-called golden days, the editor always followed the picture through the ADR work, through looping. Spencer Tracy hated doing looping, but if I were on the stage with him and asked him to do it, he would. Editors worked with musicians. I worked with Al Newman on *How the West Was Won* and I had the guts to go to him when he was scoring the picture and say, "Al, I think you're making a big mistake. That music introducing Jimmy Stewart paddling his canoe sounds like a mystery picture. He sounds like a mad character." Al said, "You really think that?" So he wrote new music, completely wide open music, beautiful. He said, "Harold, you're right. I thought about it, got up in the middle of the night, and wrote a new piece of music!"

[Carl] But this is how I see the system work now. An editor is paid to an answer print, and in any union job, that's a rule. But in the job I'm doing now, a movie of the week, they're taking us off once the picture is locked—meaning the director and producers have put their notes in and the editor is finished. We're losing two or three weeks of paychecks because they're not taking us through the dub or anything we would normally do. Now either you keep quiet because if you open your mouth you kill the work you've done, or you're putting a big black mark by your name as a rabble-rouser. So you keep your mouth shut and take it.

Harold, do you think you had more security because editors were thought of more specially at the studios?

The picture was special. I always felt responsible for my pictures. A good editor should have that feeling. I wanted to be in on the music, on the sound effects, on the dubbing, and I think an editor should be. When I was president of the union for two years, I fought for recognition for the editor. I started the fight to get editors' names raised up on the credits. Now we get screen credit, and some producers and directors give advertising credit too, but that took a long time. On those MGM lists, we usually were down at the bottom. Finally, we crawled up to the middle, then we got underneath the camera, then we got on top of the camera. We're the directors' best friends and the directors helped move us up. We asked the Screen Directors Guild to help and they said, "Sure, we'll fight for you." The big directors wanted the best editors.

[Carl] That's what's frustrating for me now. I'm fifty-two years old and I've been in the business for thirty-one years and I can't crack this so-called inner circle that's around.

[Harold] You don't have the big studio feeling anymore. It was like being in a country club going to work.

[Carl] The business is so far gone to greed and so out of hand. When I read the business section of the paper where they print the salaries of these Harvard business guys, it turns my stomach. Nobody is worth thirty-five or forty million dollars of salary. I don't care what he's turned for the company. I don't think it's good for the business or good for Hollywood for a technician or a grip or somebody to see that one man has earned that much money in one year. All these guys have to do is sit around a table and say, "We're going to put a stop to this," and you'd see the whole thing start to come around. They could change this place in a year if they force the issue. But no, there's too much money to be made.

[Harold] I could always talk to L. B. Mayer on the phone. And producers, directors, actors used to give you gifts at the end of each picture. I've got gold cuff links coming out my—like Jean Harlow, she didn't want to sit in her dressing room alone so she would come down to the cutting room. She'd ask, "Do you have anything to drink?" No. The next day, down comes a twelve-bottle case. There's none of that now.

[Carl] I think there is *some*. You would think you can deal with people in your same business, right? But I remember I put a note in the office mail to a very big director, saying something about myself like, "I'm Kress Junior, if you need any help, let me know." The note came back to me, unopened, stamped "We do not accept unsolicited material." It was a letter, not a script! I mean, this man who puts on his clothes just like I do wouldn't even open my interoffice note because it didn't come through the proper channels.

[Harold] It's a different world.

[Carl] I'm not knocking anybody, but the business isn't as warm and as sweet as it was. I feel sorry for kids who have stars in their eyes expecting to make it. You have to have patience and be willing to suffer and do a lot of nonunion stuff. Colleges tell their students, "Okay, now go into Hollywood and make a living." Oh my God, it's hard.

[Harold] Some of them get in.

[Carl] Some of them do. But it's tough. I'm not the only frustrated human being in this town, believe me! Just open that window and yell, and you'll probably have a hundred right downstairs.

[Harold] There was nothing like the Golden Age.

What would they call this age?

[Carl] Nickel?

[Harold] It wasn't golden, really, moneywise.

[Carl] No, the money wasn't, but I'd almost go for the friendship and the security. I wish it could be again as it was of yore. I wish it could change.

6

The Essential Film

Geof Bartz

1969 *Hiroshima/Nagasaki: August 1945*, produced by Erik Barnouw (Coeditor: Paul Ronder)

1971 *Part of the Family*, produced by Paul Ronder
Beauty Knows No Pain (*60 Minutes*), produced by Elliot Erwitt

1972 *The Great Radio Comedians*, produced by Perry Miller Adato (Coeditor: Aviva Slesin)

1973 *The Men Who Made the Movies* (Three Episodes: Howard Hawkes, Raoul Walsh, William Wellman), produced by Richard Schickel

1974 *Last Stand Farmer*, produced by Richard Brick
The America's Cup Finals, CBS Sports

1976 *Pumping Iron* (Coeditor: Larry Silk)

1977 *Lifeline: Dr. Randolph* (*TV Pilot*)

1978–80 **Lifeline* (Producer/Supervising Editor), NBC
*Lifeline: Dr. Duke (Editor)

1979 *The Body Human: The Sexes II*, CBS (Coeditor: Bob Eisenhardt)

1980–81 **The Body Human: The Body Beautiful* (Producer/Supervising Editor)
*The Facts for Girls, CBS Afterschool Special

1981–82 **The Loving Process: Woman*, CBS

1982 *Andrea Doria: The Final Chapter*, produced by Peter Gimbel and Elga Anderson

1983–85 *Stripper* (Producer/Supervising Editor) (Coeditors: Bob Eisenhardt, Larry Silk)

1983 *Going for Laughs*, HBO

1985 *The Great Pleasure Hunt: Japan*, HBO

1986 *Saturday Night Live* (two short films)

1986–87 **The Wyeths: A Father and His Family*, produced by David Grubin

1987 *Four Lives: A Portrait of Manic Depression*, produced by Jonathan David
Bodywatching, CBS

1988 *Inside the Sexes*, CBS
The Living Smithsonian, produced by David Grubin
The Making of the Sports Illustrated *Swimsuit Issue*, HBO, produced by Maysles Films and Susan Froemke

1989	*The Best Hotel on Skidrow* (also Codirector) *The Great Air Race of 1924*, produced by David Grubin	1991	*LBJ*, produced by David Grubin (Coeditor: Tom Haneke)

* See Appendix for complete list of editing awards and nominations.

Geof Bartz's articulate responses come from more than twenty years of documentary film experience and ten years as a teacher at Columbia University's film school. Originally, Bartz studied marine biology at the University of Notre Dame, where he was introduced to the intriguing possibilities of assembling pieces of film to tell a story. Once he had edited his own little film in the trunk room of his dormitory, he abandoned the science major and carved a niche for himself in the New York documentary world. Science still played a part in several of his projects, particularly the pioneering prime-time NBC television series *Lifeline* (thirteen episodes), for which he received Emmy Awards as producer and editor.

Every editor needs to be adept at editing any subject, and Bartz's credits show his diversity. He is personally most proud of *The Wyeths: A Father and His Family*, which shows the power of a documentary editor to turn an informational "talking head" program into a vibrant, emotional portrait. Perhaps the two most popular films he has worked on have been *Pumping Iron*, which made Schwarzenegger a household name, and *The Making of the Sports Illustrated Swimsuit Issue*, one of the largest-selling videotapes of all time. Bartz remembers the latter as one of the most difficult projects he ever worked on, with a footage ratio of 100 to 1 and only forty days to cut. He recalls *Pumping Iron* as a tremendous editing feat that combined the rigor of the *cinéma vérité* approach and the mass appeal of a fiction film—a daring attempt for the time.

In this interview, Bartz gives a practical analysis of the mechanics and structures of editing, from "paper cut" to final cut. He also speaks of finding the core or heart in the dailies, around which he begins to construct the entire film. In searching for this essence, the editor must also adopt the perspective of the viewers. As their surrogate, the editor can respond to their needs as well as to those of the film.

Would you describe your start in film editing?

I went to the University of Notre Dame from 1962 to 1966 and intended to become a marine biologist. But at that time, there was a growing interest on American campuses in European filmmaking, Bergman, Antonioni, and Fellini, primarily. I got involved with the people who ran the film society and eventually took the only film course offered. I remember the teacher describing how films were put together, that you can take shots from different angles and make a choice of how to join those shots together. I never realized that. I always felt that what you saw on the screen was the way it came out of the camera. I wanted to try something like that, to take a shot of somebody coming into a house from the outside, and join it to another shot of that person entering from the inside, and give the illusion that the person came in the door. We figured a way to raise money to make a movie would be to show a risqué art film like *La Dolce Vita*. We made four hundred dollars in one night! With that money, we went to New York. I was obsessed by the song "Downtown," so we filmed all these images of what it was like to be downtown in New York City. Back in Indiana, a priest let me set up a little editing room in the trunk room of the dorm. I had a splicer, glue, a moviescope, and a projector. The first time I ran the film through the projector, it fell apart! But I stuck with it and, after about a month, showed it on campus. I had more fun doing that than anything I'd ever done before. That finished my biology career.

Did you go to film school then?

Yes, Columbia University, where I got an MFA degree. I expected to become a teacher myself, but a teacher there, Paul Ronder, said, "You've got a real talent for editing. Why don't you pursue this?" He hired me to edit some films that he was directing. Through his encouragement I decided that's what I wanted to do.

What was your first professional position?

In 1969, I was an assistant on the CBS show, *The Simon and Garfunkel Special*. About two or three weeks before it was to air, they let me sit in on a big conference about the film. At one point I piped up and suggested that they take a scene that was second from the last and use it as the opening scene because it looked more like the beginning of the film than what they had. The two editors, Ellen Gifford and Luke Bennett, supported me on that, and the next day they tried it. It really worked well. As so often happens in filmmaking, what you think is going to work and what actually works don't necessarily go together. You have to be alive to what's there, to the feelings on the screen, and not what's in your head about what's supposed to be there. After it was over, the director, Charles Grodin, shook my hand and said, "Thank you for that idea, I really appreciated that." When you're starting out, praise like that feels great. Then 1969 to 1975 was a period of transition from an assistant to an editor. Elliot Erwitt, the photographer, asked me if I would cut a film he was producing and directing called *Beauty Knows No Pain*, about cheerleaders in Texas. I began to get a reputation as a good editor for independent documentaries. Eventually, I met Bob Fiore who was to shoot a film about bodybuilders based on a book called *Pumping Iron*. He said, "I want to recommend you as the editor." That was my first break to work on a feature documentary.

Was documentary film something you automatically gravitated toward or did things just move in that direction and you followed?
   A little of both. When I was in film school, documentary filmmaking was the most exciting thing going on. *Cinéma vérité* was beginning to take off and people eagerly awaited films like *Salesman* and *Gimme Shelter*. As a documentary editor, you really work as a writer for the film since there is no script. You're writing a film with images, and you're solving structural problems as you go along. Documentary film was also a way to become an editor quickly. I was loath to go through five years as an apprentice to a feature editor. In features, the challenge is to get the actors to appear natural, to get performances to work. You've got the opposite problem in documentaries: you have people who are real, but you've got to find the story, the structure, and the dramatic and entertaining way to make it work.

How much of Pumping Iron *was based on the book?*
   George Butler and Charles Gaines published photographs and text about a year in the life of some bodybuilders, among them Arnold Schwarzenegger, Lou Ferrigno, Mike Katz, and Franco Columbo. The book, which was done either one or two years before the film, was like research notes for the film. The film wasn't just a remake of the book.

Pumping Iron *feels like a mix of documentary and fiction. Was the outcome of the body building competition expected, or did the ending develop as the film was shot?*
   There were certain scenes that were recreated in the film, after the fact, just small ones. The main thing about that film, from an editorial point of view, was that Larry Silk, the coeditor, and I saw it as a way to break away from *cinéma vérité*, which was how most documentaries were made at that time. The *cinéma vérité* aesthetic frowned upon using music, voiceovers from the characters, and narrators. The idea was to take the pure footage as you shot it, the synced dailies, and shape the film using that and nothing else. That was believed to be more truthful. Whether it's more truthful or not, it didn't capture a large audience. Most people

found those films too hard to understand. We decided to make this film entertaining, so we were going to go against that aesthetic and bring back music, voiceover, narration, whatever we needed to make the film fun for people to watch. We spent a lot of time listening to records to get temporary music that we cut to before the film was scored; that wasn't done much in those days.

Why did you retain the shots where focus blurred and sharpened?

That was the way people shot back then, so it seems very dated. This was the end of the whole *vérité* style, with a lot of the searching for focus that the cameraman would do when he was shooting with zoom lenses. Nowadays, editors don't leave that in; back then, it was considered cool.

What was the dramatic focus you were aiming for in the film?

The struggle in these kinds of films is a struggle between telling a story and giving information, between making an entertaining film that has characters and story, and giving information about a subject that people don't know anything about, like bodybuilding. People wanted to know: Are these guys all gay? Are these guys narcissists? What happens to you if you don't work out, do you just turn into a big blob? There's a whole list of questions that everybody says you've got to answer in the film. The problem is, once you get a story going, you can't stop it and just do a report on bodybuilding. You can't suddenly switch gears into what's called an informational mode of filmmaking. If you do, you break the rhythm of the story. Whatever information we got in, we tried to integrate into the telling of the story. As when Arnold talks about the "pain barrier" as integral to his training, which is part of his rivalry with Lou. But we never could get into narcissism and homosexuality; it always stopped the flow of the story. The questions had been asked and there was interview material, but either we weren't smart enough to get it in, or we were smart enough to leave it out! At any rate, we couldn't use it in a way that was part of the story. It took us a month to look at all the dailies. I think the ratio was 100 to 1, and there were subplots that were filmed that we just didn't use. The big struggle editorially was to get the story of Mike Katz, the Jewish bodybuilder from Connecticut, and his rivalry with Ken Waller into the film because there were some very moving things there. But that was really peripheral to the main story, which was the competition between Arnold and Lou. We had originally structured the film to show Arnold and Lou training, then Mike and Ken training, then everybody goes to South Africa; then there's the Mr. Universe contest between Mike and Ken, and the Mr. Olympia contest between Arnold and Lou. The problem was that you lost the focus of both stories that way. By the time you got to South Africa, you didn't want to see two bodybuilding contests back to back—one of them was hard enough to take! Eventually through screenings and suggestions, after maybe twenty-five different rough cuts of this structure, it evolved that the smaller story of Mike Katz would be thrown into the beginning of the film, in a way you don't ever realize quite where you are.

Did you find a way through the editing to convey the different personalities of the contestants?

What we tried to do is tell a story, and part of telling it was to contrast Lou and his father from working-class Brooklyn, with Arnold and his buddies in bright sunny California. It was funny to see the two of them in parallel. Larry Silk cut Lou's training sequences and I cut Arnold's. Then over a long period of time, we intercut the two of them. They just played off each other. It wasn't that we were creating the personalities, but we were creating the tension between the personalities. For example, in the film *Stripper*, the five principal characters in the film were not chosen at random. We took a long time to come up with those five women, and they were selected in the casting process, just as George Butler had selected Arnold and Lou in the casting of *Pumping Iron* because they each represented qualities that would play off well against each other. In *Stripper*, there is the character of the older woman at the end of her career versus all the younger women just starting out; ballsy, feisty women versus introverted, shyer types. You don't want to have everybody the same, you want a variety. It's like making soup, you want to have different tastes in it.

In Stripper, *the story of another competition, three of the five major characters were the finalists. Was that a coincidence?*

There were actually seven finalists, not five, and only two of our characters got into the finale. We had to create—through the magic of editing—the third one. We played loose with that whole contest, partly because we were one of the sponsors of the contest, and partly because unlike the Mr. Olympia contest, it wasn't a real contest. It was a vehicle to allow women from different parts of the country to get together. A lot of people criticized the film because of the convention, but had there not been this convention, it would have been the story of five women in five different parts of the country whose lives never would have come together. We didn't manipulate the judges' verdicts; we just found other ways to come up with our version of what happened at the end.

How do you organize the material for the films you edit?

Since each film has a different structural problem to it, you try to solve some of the logistical problems when you organize the material before you edit. Most editors follow a rigorous procedure. If you do your work right, it helps you get to the final film. First, you screen the dailies with the producer, talk about them, and take notes. I take very loose notes, some take quite detailed notes. However you choose to do it, at the end of that process, you have seen all the dailies and have notes on what you've seen. Then as editor, I make "selects" of that material. That is, I mark the parts of the film that interest me and have my assistant remove those parts from the rest. That usually boils the dailies down to one-third of what they were originally. That's the material I work with. So now I've seen the film twice, once as dailies and once while marking selects. Now I look at it a third time with the producer or director, just as selects. Usually things are a lot more lively than they were as dailies, but you still haven't come up with a structure. That's the next step, the "paper cut," which is a structured intellectual approach to the material. "I think we should start with this scene and then we'll go to this scene and maybe this stuff should be at the end." The rest of the process is working out the final film through a series of rough cuts, screenings, recutting and recutting. Just like a writer, after taking notes and doing research, will sit down, write a screenplay, and rewrite it and rewrite it. It's a very similar process.

With Lifeline, *you also covered many locations and many characters in thirteen episodes. Can you give some background on that series?*

As far as I know, *Lifeline* was the first prime-time documentary series in the history of television. There were projects like it planned in the mid- and late-sixties at ABC, but they never got on the air. It was a landmark program that way. Because doctor shows had always been popular on television, NBC agreed to finance the pilot for this series, and the producers, Al Kelman and Bob Fuisz, chose a pediatric surgeon. We attempted to make a real-life soap opera out of the material rather than a straight documentary. In other words, we treated the material in a dramatic way rather than in an informational way. We wove together all the stories that came into the hospital so that we would leave one hanging while we picked up another. It was a dramatic treatment of real material, of documentary material, which hadn't been done that often before. We used music, we used a little narration to orient people as to who the doctor was and what the particular medical problem was. But we didn't try to get into the medicine in any scientific way. It was there the way it would be in a fictional doctor's TV show. NBC loved this. I was made coproducer of the series, and supervising editor over eight editors.

Did you find certain editors matched the material on certain doctors better than others?

Yes. In fact, there was one case in which two editors came to me and said, "Can we trade material?" One was working on the film about a brain surgeon, the other was working on the film about a pediatric surgeon, and they really wanted to trade. Even though they each had already put a couple of weeks into it, I thought it would be in the best interests of the series if they traded since the material would then better match their personalities. It was an exciting project because nobody had ever done anything like it before. We never knew from day to day whether we could pull it off or how it would be accepted. There were no guidelines or rules to go by other than the pilot which became a model, an approach to this material. There were scenes at home and in the hospital that the location producers would film the way you film fiction. They'd set it all up, do several takes, which goes back to the old way documentaries were done, where things were treated in a more scripted fashion. There was also the material with real patients that came into the hospital. We didn't recreate the operations. But because some dramatic license was taken, we were asked to put a disclaimer at the end of the film.

How did you approach the Dr. Duke episode that you personally edited?

He was a trauma surgeon, so everything he dealt with was an emergency. I would try to find the case that had the longest piece of continuity with the most twists and turns in it. With Dr. Duke, there was the black woman who had been in a car accident; she went through two operations and it was not clear what her outcome would be—she finally died. That case had enough continuity that you could start the show with it, come back to it in the middle, and end with it. Other material was slotted into it either to relieve heavy moments, as the scene of the kid with the broken arm; or to bring back more tense moments, as in the case of the Jehovah's Witnesses who were stabbed. It was fundamental dramaturgy that nobody really had tried in documentaries before, as far as I know—juxtaposing material based on its moods and its dramatic power. On a structural level, that's what editing or writing is about, balancing things so that there are contrasts and relief. It goes all the way back to Elizabethan dramaturgy, right? A funny scene following a tragic scene.

Once you had selected the cases, would you then decide whether you needed fillers, like scenes of the doctor at home?

The film producers would be filming that stuff all along. The Dr. Duke show was different than most of them in the series in that I made the decision that I would never let the audience see the doctor outside of the hospital until the end. In a typical episode, after a big operation, you would next see the doctor playing with his kids, so that you got a break in mood. But in the Duke episode, I tried to find ways to vary the moods *within* the hospital and save the home footage for the very end.

How did you editorially relieve the static nature of the operating room setting? I'm reminded of the shot of the blood tubes inserted during the operation on the Jehovah's Witnesses.

That's an interesting story. In that operation, neither of the two women would sign a paper authorizing that they could be given blood. So the doctors gave them blood, explained to a notary public why they had to do that, the notary gave the paper to a judge and the judge okayed it. But that sequence of events wasn't very dramatic. So I reversed the order and had the notary take the deposition first. The audience thought that she took it to the judge, the judge came back with this order, and *then* the blood was administered. That to me was a more exciting sequence of events. Also, those tubes with blood going through were not blood being administered but blood being sucked out! They were suction tubes from the operation. But they worked at the end of that scene because the whole theme was the necessity for blood. When I saw those shots, I thought this was going to be great in this scene even though that's not literally blood being given because it paid off the scene, and it paid off in a visual way rather than a verbal way. That's one example of what I, as an editor, find important to stress. Look at material not just for its literal content but for what it can symbolize, or for its expressive value, apart from what it actually is. This is something that people in documentaries don't often do because they're very interested in the truth. I'm not saying that you should deliberately falsify something, but shots have a literal meaning and they also have an emotive meaning. You've got to be very aware of the emotive content of the shot. Another example is at the end of the Dr. Duke episode. There is a shot of him staring at the sunset, he takes his hat off and looks kind of sad. Well, that shot was from a camping trip, a sequence that didn't end up in the film. He was camping and at one point they panned over as he looks out at the sunset. But using that shot after he had operated on all these people and finally gets out of the hospital, to me that shot said a lot about his inner struggles. It had a reverberation that it simply did not have as part of the camping trip. In fact, it looked ridiculous in the camping trip!

But isn't that sort of taking license with reality, especially in cinéma vérité?

Cinéma vérité doesn't emphasize the poetic quality of material so much as the accumulation of real moments. That's not to say there's not a lot of poetry in great *cinéma vérité* films like *Titicut Follies* or *Welfare* or *Salesman*. There's a lot of subtext there. But the editors don't create that feeling so much as cull it out of the material. What we were trying to do in *Lifeline* was give the editors a little more freedom, to have fun with the material and not be so tied down by the literal reality. We were really trying to create a new form of entertainment and weren't that interested in the literal truth of what was going on.

How did you merge entertainment and truth in the Wyeth film?

The Wyeth project evolved out of a bigger concept that Smithsonian World wanted, which was a film on "family." At first, David Grubin, the producer, felt that the Wyeths would be just a part of that bigger film. But then he discovered that there was this rich, rich story of the life and death of N. C. Wyeth, and that all five of his children were still alive. The Wyeth film looks like other films that are a combination of interviews, photographs, film of paintings, home movies; cutting back and forth between the various members of the family who were in their early to late seventies, reminiscing about what it was like growing up with this astounding father who was a creative genius. He was a devoted father, but at the end of his life, he felt he had failed as an artist, even though everyone now says that he's one of the two or three greatest illustrators in the history of American painting. Frankly, when I was hired and told that it was going to be five people in their seventies talking about their father, it did not sound like the most exciting thing in the world. But when we began looking at the footage, here were five very different people who were extremely alive and full of both intelligence and emotion, which is pretty rare. Grubin's direction was somehow to tell the story of the life and tragic death of N. C. Wyeth through the voices of these children. The most famous is Andrew Wyeth; but then there's his brother, Nat, the inventor; the oldest daughter, Henriette, a painter; Caroline, who was a bit of a recluse and also a painter; and Ann, a composer. I made selects of the best of the interview material from each of the "kids." Then my assistant and I made about twenty-five categories of topics and organized the selects into those topics. For example, one category was how N. C. looked. And there was a big category about what happened when he died.

How did you finally make N. C. Wyeth come alive?

In looking at the topics, an idea for an order and a structure began to emerge. But I wanted to dive into the heart of it, which was the story of his death. I felt that really was the most powerful material. Somehow by working with that first, the rest would fall into place. It was the part of the film with the greatest story element. To me, that made the film interesting in a way it wouldn't had it just been "What a great guy he is" and "What an unhappy man he died." It was also clear from the dailies that the hero of the film wasn't Andrew or the daughters, but Nat Wyeth. Nat's four-year-old son was in the car when the train hit N. C. The death of Nat's father was double-edged: not only did he lose his father but he lost his only son at that time. There was also a suggestion that the accident might have been suicide; no one's really sure. I gravitated towards that and started working on that material right away. Then we went back to the beginning of the film, worked towards that point, and eventually created a montage ending. Fortunately, people kept talking about N. C.'s death without ever spelling out how he died, which was pure serendipity, because it gave us a kind of tease effect. What did happen, and how did he die? I worked intuitively, through the emotions of the material. I kept moving the pieces of the story around until they felt right to me. I didn't try to think about it too much. I did the thinking when I made up and organized the topic categories, but beyond that point I stopped thinking about it and started reacting emotionally.

Can you keep the material fresh since you work with it so much?

It's hard, and the only way is to get away from it a bit. Every editor is going to have the experience where on Monday night they think they've cut the greatest thing in the history of film, then on Tuesday morning it looks awful. Another way is to screen it with other people to sense how they are reacting, and it makes you look at it in a different way. I also have the habit of backing up two or three other sequences and playing into the scene I'm working on, so that the tone of the current sequence seems to grow out of the tones of the other sequences. For instance, in my recent film, *The Great Air Race of 1924*, I finished a sequence where one plane sinks in the ocean and the pilot is very sad that he's out of the race. You wouldn't want to have another sad sequence follow that. Scenes should either echo a little of the feeling of the previous scene, then begin to take you away from it, or radically contrast with it. Even though documentaries are supposed to be about information, to me what's interesting is moods, the relationship between moods, and the way you can contrast them. Almost the way a screenplay writer approaches it.

Would an example of such a contrast be when you used total silence to underscore the sequence of Andrew Wyeth's paintings?

Yes. That's one of the things I was most proud of. After we describe how N. C. died and the effect it had on Nat, we talk about the effect of his death on Andrew and how it affected his painting. He was very close with his father; in fact, his father never sent him to school and taught Andrew how to paint. Andrew went from being a pretty watercolorist to somebody who painted quite bleak visions. When it came to that sequence, nobody said, "Let's not use music." It's just that when Andrew said, "This is the effect of my father's death on my paintings," and then you cut to the paintings, it seemed like the emptiness of nothing, rather than using music, was what it was about. That's what happened to him, that he experienced this terrible void in his life. It's very effective on television because you hardly ever hear nothing!

Did you feel obligated to use only the sister's compositions?

We thought Ann's music would play a role in the film. I didn't expect to score the entire film with her music, and in fact, she sent over recordings of her music that were at least twenty years old. You could barely hear them. I wasn't all that taken with it. But then I started to play them against the footage and in some peculiar way, I guess because she knew her father so well, the spirit of that music was very much the spirit of our film. That film would not be half as powerful without the music. Ann's footage is an example of how a scene is transformed while editing. At the end of the film, she is seen playing the theme song on the piano that you heard throughout the film. It has a very nice feeling, and it's used to carry credits. That scene was originally intended to introduce Ann, it was a standard way of meeting somebody. But it stopped the flow of the story so I pulled it out. But at the end, we said, "Let's use it for credits," and it felt absolutely perfect at that point.

How did you decide to include the poignant footage of Nat's baby at a birthday party during the discussion of his death?
At first, all we had of the little boy was one photograph of him when he was two. Then near the end of our work, Nat's other son came by with film footage he found in his father's basement, footage that had been sitting in the can for forty years! Incredible home movies of the same little boy. It allowed us to recut earlier scenes so that you had a greater feeling for the boy before the accident. It made the tragedy of his death much more powerful. Oh, he was a beautiful little boy. The photograph of him at two didn't do any justice to how utterly charming he was. We showed Nat playing outdoors and cavorting on the water with the little boy, and the boy at the piano. When it was revealed that the boy died in the auto accident along with N. C., we took footage of him at his second or third birthday and "step printed" it, that is, converted it to slow motion, when he was blowing out the candles. Nat talked over it about the effect of the death. But not in a maudlin way. Nat never cried, but it was clear that it had probably been the most painful thing in his life. Being able to cut away from his interview allowed us to condense a little of what he said and change the emphasis slightly. In structuring the film, in looking at the dailies, the pivotal point was also the point that was the most difficult for David McCullough, the interviewer, to get to. McCullough knew he eventually would have to ask Nat about the death of the little boy. The way he asked it was brilliant: "What would you say to your father now if you had a chance to see him again?" Nat went on with what a great guy he was and what a great painter. Then his face became like stone; he stopped for a minute and said, "Of course, I would ask him about the death." That moment was really what the film was all about. It was the hub around which the rest of the film got structured.

It actually became the hub once you started to work with the film.
In making the selection of dailies, I try to be alive to what's the most interesting footage, without thinking too much about how I'm going to

put it together or what the story is. When you look at the selects, you go through yet another process, which is to figure out where in that mish-mash is the story, and how much of it really is sustainable. In *The Great Air Race*, a couple of people reminisce about how two of the four pilots hated each other. As interesting as that footage is, we're unable to get it into the film. It's so provocative that you want to go to another level of significance, but there's nothing beyond the statements that they hated each other. It provokes without being dramatic. Since there's no material to resolve that, it's out.

Did working on either Pumping Iron *or* Stripper *influence your cutting of the Wyeth film, as in the use of photographs?*

In the Wyeth film, we would cut to photographs in order to advance the story, and to allow us really to cut down and cut through interviews. In *Stripper*, we used historical photographs of Western saloons and strip-pers at the beginning of the film to give a broader context to what this film was supposed to show, that stripping didn't start yesterday but it is a part of a tradition. I honestly don't remember how we concluded that we would use childhood pictures of the girls at the end of *Stripper*; that idea was there from a very early stage. We tried to avoid cutting to photo-graphs during interviews, which is a traditional documentary style. The Wyeth film is a traditional documentary filmmaking style, talking heads, voiceover, narration, stills, movies. Other than that, I was influenced only in that the most interesting films I work on are films that can tell a story. That there's some epiphany or payoff with a dramatic conclusion. For example, in *Stripper*, we centered the action around the women prepar-ing for this convention; the convention helped unify it. *Pumping Iron* was another story of competition. The Wyeth film really is a different bird. *The Wyeths* is a film where you work a great deal from transcripts; it's a film about thoughts, ideas, and feelings, with very little action. The action is implied action. In films like *Lifeline*, *Stripper*, or *Pumping Iron*, the action is much more dominant, and you have movie scenes. The feeling of cutting those films is different.

How do you determine the various demands of each film?

As a documentary editor, you find that all the different kinds of films basically fall into two categories. One film is interview-driven, like *The Wyeths*; portrait films with a great deal of voiceover, people reminiscing. The interviews are the spine of the film. Then there's action films, like *Lifeline*, where the interviews play almost no role. You're not learning as much about the inner workings of these doctors as you're experiencing them in their daily rounds, feeling what it's like to be a doctor. Then films like *Pumping Iron* and *Stripper* are a combination of the two. There's ac-tion, but you also stop and have interviews, see photographs, then move on. That's an amalgam or hybrid of the two. When *cinéma vérité* was around, those films were almost purely action-driven. There were no interviews, no narration, no music. When I'm asked to cut a film, I can tell what my experience as an editor will be by a description of the type of film it is. You approach the action film more visually, constantly trying to find the shot. You're given an enormous amount of material and you have to find something that is decently composed and has significance. You know it when you see it. With interview films, you're not looking for shots as much as for moments of revelation or information that you can weave together, hopefully, in an artistic way, to tell a story. But in both cases, you have to be aware of rhythm.

Rhythm keeps the audience involved in the film, doesn't it?

Rhythm is at the heart of all of this. What makes a film interesting and palatable to an audience, even though they may not know it, is the rhythm of the film, the way you structure the highs and lows. What you *don't* let people say is as important as what you do let them say; what you have to cut out to make their sentences clean and have resonance so they're not spewing on forever. It's the part you don't see when you watch the film. That's the creation of the rhythm. And that's the part of the craft that's really interesting, that fine-tuning, that honing, so that when you're done, you look at the film and say, "This is the essence of those dailies. This is the essential film." All you ever have is your own intuition and your own instincts about it. That's the scary part and also the fun part. Since no two people are alike, each person will approach this task differently. Among professionals, though, there is a common film language, a shorthand that you can talk to each other.

Only among editors?

Or among producers who have been at it a long time and have been in cutting rooms. What most young producers lack is experience in postproduction, which is in many ways the hardest part. Not that it's not hard to get on the phone and make a film happen. But when it comes to making a movie out of raw dailies, it helps to have a lot of experience, to have made mistakes and screwed up, but have suffered through.

When you say shorthand, do you mean a tacit understanding about what each of the principals wants for the project?

There's that. And a kind of shorthand about how you will construct a scene, like, "We'll do voiceover here and then come out and do a little of this." For example, Dave Grubin said to me just as I was leaving, "Well, now you're in the sequence that goes bam-de-bam-de-bam."

In those words exactly?

I knew what he was talking about, yeah!

Is this shorthand why many people don't understand what editors do?

Editing is done behind closed doors in little rooms. I've had this experience many times of walking by cutting rooms where other editors were working, and looking in and saying, "That's idiotic! What are those people doing sitting in front of those little machines?" But when you're doing it yourself and get excited about it, and there are those times, at midnight or whenever, when suddenly something comes together, it's very exciting and exhilarating. I think that within the industry, editors are appreciated, but I'm not sure that many people understand what's involved in editing. I remember at my father's funeral, this woman came up to me and said, "I want you to meet my son someday, he runs a camera shop." As if somehow the fact that he ran a camera shop and I was a film editor put us in the same field. That's an extreme example. But you do tend to feel a little neglected. I'm sure it's a lot of the way writers feel in fiction. Directors, producers, actors, camerapeople get the credit, and actually the structure they're working from is a screenplay. Most people think of *Citizen Kane* as Orson Welles's film, not Herman Mankiewicz's.

Do you think certain personalities tend to become film editors?

Absolutely. Usually introverted, thoughtful types. The wonderful thing about film is that it attracts all different kinds of personalities, it needs all kinds of personalities. Shooting a film and editing are really different. Shooting is very practical, down-to-earth, nitty-gritty stuff. Editing is much more concentrated, much more interior and quieter. I think somebody who's spent time in the cutting room is going to be a better director, and I think they will know much more about what an editor needs to make a scene work.

Do you find that editing is affected by the audience for the film?

Very, very much so. That's the other thing besides what kind of film you're making, whether it's a talking head, interview-driven film or an action film. Is it meant for a theatrical audience, a network audience, a Home Box Office audience, or a public television audience? Those are very different ways of approaching the material. In this day and age, you would never approach a film for the networks the same way you would a film for public television. Public television is the most satisfying to work for because there is no demand for slickness. Most networks require their nonfiction programs to be slick, to look like TV, "keep things moving." Home Box Office stresses entertainment values. It doesn't necessarily have to be all that slick, but it always has to be entertaining and, if possible, titillating. The feature audience is the real tough one because you have to convince them to plunk down seven bucks these days to come into the theater. You really have to work at making the movie something people want to see. That it's not just good, but it's very good.

Do you become the audience when you're cutting?

The editor is the surrogate audience, the person who doesn't have feelings about the characters based on whether or not they like the actors, whether they're nice people or not, but simply how they are in the film. You have to pretend that you're that audience. Sometimes I try to imagine what my mother would like to see! Often late at night when I'm alone, after I cut a sequence, I will literally sit back from the machine and imagine that I have a can of beer or Coke in my hand, turn on the machine as if I were turning on the TV, and see if I would want to stay tuned to what I've just done. You have to separate your critical self from your creative self. In a sense, you become the director at that point, or the audience, saying, "Do I want to watch this or not?" When you're working on a feature film and screen it for a preview audience to test its structure, you can feel the vibrations from that audience. Sometimes *literally* vibrations, if they start moving around or coughing. I think Shaw, or maybe Oscar Wilde, said, "The worst sin of all in drama is to bore somebody." Meaning, is the film moving in a direction that is emotionally and intellectually satisfying?

In summary, what would you like people to know most about editing?

That it exists! People don't realize that somebody sits there and makes thousands and thousands of decisions before what they see ever gets on the screen. That they've gone down hundreds of wrong paths before they've ended up with the final film. I think the reason most people don't understand editing is that there's nothing really comparable in their own lives. People have taken movies, they've written letters, they've seen directors in other movies. They don't understand these things really, but they think they do. Editing is the last analysis. Unless you have unlimited resources and can continue shooting forever, the buck stops in the cutting room. Either it works there or it doesn't. I think sometimes the reason directors and editors clash, if they do, is that editors can be the voice of doom, or the messenger carrying the bad news: "Hey, you know, Harry, that doesn't work very well!" And you know what the Greeks did with their messengers of bad news. The thing that's most annoying is when people say, "So you're the one that cuts stuff out." As if there was a big long thing and you cut it down to size. Often there is just a big mishmash of material. It's as if somebody gave you all the pieces of a jigsaw puzzle and no picture of what that puzzle is supposed to look like. Maybe there's three or four jigsaw puzzles all mixed up. You've got to put those pieces together and make a picture. If you can get that across to people about editing, that would be great.

7

Telling Stories

Tom Rolf

1989	*Black Rain,* directed by Ridley Scott	1990	*Jacob's Ladder,* directed by Adrian Lyne

* See Appendix for complete list of editing awards and nominations.

Tom Rolf comes from a show-biz family. His Swedish father and Norwegian mother were both actors. When he was one year old, his widowed mother remarried an American dance director who had been Shirley Temple's dance director and later a contract director at MGM during the 1940s. The family left Sweden and settled in California, where Rolf wondered what to do with his life. When he asked his stepfather how to become a film director, Rolf recalls that "he said if he had to do it all over again, he would try to be a film editor. The editor is able to judge and make the decision what to use and what to throw away. He thought that experience was invaluable. I took that to heart." Rolf served eight years as apprentice and assistant editor before cutting *The Glory Guys*, written by Sam Peckinpah, a film he calls "no worse than any of the rest of those Westerns with the cavalry and Indians." He laughs at the title of his first solo effort, an Elvis Presley film called *Clambake*. "It was possibly the worst vehicle for Elvis but I was just desperate to get in." Rolf has since edited classic television series such as *The Big Valley* and movie classics such as *Taxi Driver*, and has settled comfortably into life as a successful feature film editor.

Rolf's thirty-some years in the business have given him what he calls a hard-nosed approach to the people and the work he handles on each project. He elaborates on a concept shared by many colleagues: editing is manipulating the film to manipulate the audience. He also enumerates *Story!* a number of his "minor rules" of editing—then adds that there really are no rules of editing. However, he has developed his set of preferences, primarily to hunt out the story in every film.

balance and emphasis

Editors are like the old storytellers who used to sit around the campfire. They knew when to accentuate one part of the story and balance the other part so you would draw the kids into these marvelous images.

What does good storytelling depend on?

If you play too much on one side of the screen and not come around and play on the other, it starts tilting and it's uneven storytelling. It's a matter of cadence and rhythm. As a guiding force, I tend to cut on punctuation. Any kind of hesitation gives me a place to get in and come around the other side. But to cut arbitrarily in the middle of the word drives me crazy. Some people do it, and I think that's just carelessness and/or they don't have the ear for it, or they disagree with me! So be it. We're in the same field as the storytellers but we're providing the images. We're not just using your imagination like radio (when I was a kid, I loved listening to the radio), but we're showing you what's there. So you have to be careful of the rhythm. At the end of *WarGames*, when there were so many different elements coming together—there was a bomb, a nutty colonel, codes—they all had to mesh. I think I went back and reworked three and four times until I felt the rhythm was right.

How about imagination for graphic scenes?

You're lucky you didn't see how the killing of Andy Garcia was originally planned in *Black Rain*. We literally decapitated him. You saw the head leaving the body, rolling down the trunk, and bouncing on the pavement! We previewed it and people jumped out of their seats. And when we had Sato slicing off his finger, people couldn't handle it. He was so good at what he was doing that people believed he was cutting his finger off. I'm not a fan of that kind of stuff, even though I know it has to be sometimes. I did a picture called *The Hunting Party* years ago where Gene Hackman shoots with a telescopic rifle at a man hunched over a campfire some hundreds of yards away. They had a charge set in the back of his head and it blew the back of his head open. When it was in the theaters, and even when I cut the movie, I never once looked at that scene.

When you were cutting, you wouldn't look?

I would not look in the Moviola. I couldn't, it was too horrific. I cut by listening to the soundtrack and then marking it.

In Black Rain, *you ended up stylizing the decapitation scene.*

Yes, I used slow motion only because you really can't believe what you're seeing unless it's slowed down. But I must admit that personally I do not like slow motion at all at any point, unless it's needed to graphically explain something that your eye probably would not catch at normal speed. We had some problems with that on *Jacob's Ladder*—bizarre angles and lighting with dark scenes—and if you didn't slow the action down a little, you probably would see only part of what was happening.

You used an unusual time maneuver in Taxi Driver *when you dissolve on Robert DeNiro several times while he's walking up the same street. As if time passes but he hasn't gone very far.*

That was Marty Scorsese. He had a great vision about doing things that take you to another plateau. You don't quite understand it, but you're not supposed to. It's just visually stunning to look at. *Taxi Driver* was quite an experience for me. Because there was an enormous time problem, they had to get somebody right away to start cutting. When I came in, it had all been shot, just sitting in the room. I looked at it and said, "Who the hell is going to look at this? This is depressing!" This was long before we had the voiceover narration of DeNiro's character, Travis, so things were very loose. It was a hard thread to get. There was a lot of DeNiro and Albert Brooks and Peter Boyle improvising. They'd say something one way during one shooting and then turn the words around shooting it another way. To try to get it to make sense was a nightmare.

Was there a script?

It was more of an outline as opposed to a final shooting script because those guys did a lot of improv. You know that scene with DeNiro: "You're talking to me?"

It's a classic.

It is now, but when I was cutting the scene, I said, "What is this? What can I cut? There's no coverage." It was a full shot and a close shot, all on DeNiro. There were no reverses—oh yeah, I had an insert of him pulling the gun. I just wanted a little more coverage on it, a few more options. I didn't have any. The whole montage of DeNiro making his gun slide back and forth and cutting the bullets was really hanging on one setup on each of those actions. The options were nil. Yet because DeNiro was so maniacally good, it worked, and it's the scene everybody quotes.

Have you found that sometimes even with a lot of material, you still have difficulty finding options?

Well, with *Black Rain*, we got over six hundred thousand feet of print which is a lot of film to go through. But the story was constantly being changed by the writers because the Japanese would not agree to certain locations and/or times, and as we were shooting we were writing, which never bodes for a peaceful transition. Storywise, the female lead was never fully developed—she didn't make any sense at all. Her story was cut down. Remember after Michael Douglas escapes from the airplane and runs back to her for help? Originally they walk into that very bizarre set with the neon which is what they call a "love hotel" in Japan—these are hotels where couples can go to spend time together because their own homes are so small and cramped. There was a whole sequence of her putting Douglas up for a time, bringing him food and so on, and because it was cut down, the scene kind of sticks out like a sore thumb because you don't know where you are. We tried to suggest that we were back at the nightclub where she was a hostess by playing the music that was similar to the music we played earlier in the scene. But it is a confusing element in the movie. We ended up with a three-hour and seventeen-minute first cut—totally unmanageable. So to get it down to where we are, which is around two hours, we had to sacrifice. A lot was capsulized and some was "accordioned" together to make it move faster.

Crunching can create "mistakes" that trivia buffs enjoy finding.

Take the whole sequence at the end of *Black Rain* around the Japanese farmhouse—which is actually Napa Valley, California, where we shot it because of the problems we had in Japan. Michael Douglas crawls up the hill to the house and our Japanese hero providentially arrives in time to save him from a fate worse than death. I always wanted to go back and make it a little more believable, but I never had the chance. There was a big dialogue scene there that we cut out and that was another reason why it doesn't quite make the sense that it should. In one cut, Michael is up behind a wall, looking to see because he hears voices coming through. Rain is literally bouncing off the wood. Next cut comes and it's all bright and cheerful! Nobody ever said anything. When putting it together, I said there was no way anybody would believe this because it was so obvious. In *New York, New York*, when DeNiro and Liza Minnelli are on their way to his interview where he's going to play his sax, sometimes their taxi is stopped, sometimes it's going forward, sometimes it's stopped to the side. I remember Scorsese would say, "Cut it anyway," and I'd say, "Marty, you're crazy," and he'd say, "They'll never notice." Nobody did, nobody ever cared. You assume it's doing what you expect it to be doing and Marty was dead right. Because the *cuts* make sense and/or because the tension is heightened and/or because the music is driving, all of a sudden that element is no longer important. It's amazing that it works as well as it does.

You labor over frames and see the problems, but the audience is moved along by the cumulative effect.

Exactly. It's amazing what you can get by with. I know the things that I do in the cutting room: flop shots, make people look the other way, make the action go backwards, make jump cuts in the middle of the film and have things scoot out of the way. Things I never would have thought of doing years and years ago because I thought that the film, and therefore the negative, was inviolate. You couldn't do things like that. Now I do it without even thinking about it.

When you talk of long films, that brings The Right Stuff *to mind.*

Yeah, I still firmly believe that it's too long. We had an enormous push to finish because of a release date that was an absolute commitment; hence the number of editors who were on the film. I was absolutely stunned when it was nominated for an editing award. There were sections of it that were rather well cut, but it had no real continuity. It didn't have any real consistent rhythm and style. Maybe other people wouldn't notice it, but I feel the lack of consistency. There again, an awful lot of film. Of course, the champion was *Heaven's Gate* where the film never seemed to stop. Self-indulgence beyond belief. Michael Cimino had a magnificent eye for framing and mood, exquisite. But if nothing else, he defeated himself by the scope he insisted on making the movie in. Cimino had thousands of extras in costume and he'd insist on checking everything himself, like looking at every bead to make sure it was up to period! He had hatters who knew how to make hats out of beaver pelts. Everything had to be absolutely authentic. We know the history of that film, don't we?

Could that film have been saved in the editing?

No. There wasn't enough story. If there's not enough fiber, you can't make anything out of it. It falls apart no matter what you do. I can truthfully say it's the only bad experience I've ever had working since I started in films. Eventually, I just could not communicate with Cimino. He would talk to my assistant and my assistant would talk to me—it was childish! When I left about three or four months before the opening, I had that terrible feeling we all get when we have a little self-doubt. "Maybe I'm wrong. Maybe I'm the one who screwed up." I refused to take another job just to wait and see what would happen when the picture opened in New York. I called a friend at United Artists the next morning and said, "Well, what happened last night?" "We yanked the movie." It was a bittersweet experience. Nothing helped the picture or the seventeen months of my life that I spent on it. People who have seen the shorter version say it's even more muddled than the long version.

With the inconsistent style of The Right Stuff, *possibly because of five editors, can you conclude that there are individual editing styles?*

I think so. I mean, there are no absolutes in cutting films. I do have a couple of self-imposed rules that are about as close to absolutes as they can be. I try never to do certain things, like I hate to cut straight in. I try never to leave an empty frame of anything for any reason; there always has to be something, even if it's a mood that you want to try with a sound effect like crickets or birds. I never put music in when I run a cut with a director because I think music gives you a false sense of confidence that the scene is working. The one false element in any movie is the music. It's totally emotional and out of left field, and I've always had a little problem with it because I think it tends to support the picture. To run a cut, put in a few sound effects, like gunshots or birds or wind, whatever the story is, just so it isn't totally dry. I'd much rather hear if the story is working. Then you know that when you augment it with music, you can make it that much more compelling. Putting music in too early allows the fat to remain on the film because it becomes more acceptable.

Do you have any other rules?

I like to overlap a lot, a personal preference. Another of my minor laws, I never let an actor start his dialogue offstage. He should start onstage and then segue into whoever else is reacting to it. I hate when people start talking offstage and *then* you cut to them. It annoys me.

Does it disorient you?

Yeah. It feels like you're trying to correct a mistake. It doesn't look normal or real. That was something Cimino liked—"pulling the cut around," as he called it. Hearing something and *then* going to it. To me, that is always confusing. You'd hear a sound, you wouldn't know where it was coming from until it was revealed, and it jerked you out of the story for that finite second. I try not to do that.

How about a lot of speakers?

If there's some way to include everybody in the scene most of the time, it becomes a smoother, homogeneous kind of scene to me, rather than having the two principals looking at each other and talking. This is important in any kind of courtroom drama where you have to keep everybody alive. Dining room scenes can also be tough. Passing the food, serving, pouring, etcetera. Trying to match all the action can drive you nuts!

You prefer action scenes?

Action I find very easy to cut. Action dictates itself. A guy shoots a gun, it's going to go somewhere, and you have to show where that is. It's a matter of style how you do it. Action is really boring. Every time you get in a car, it's a chase.

Is it boring to cut?

Yeah, and boring to see. If I get another tire squeal in my life . . . !

The chase has been important in many of your films.

There have been a lot of chases. That's why I'm bored!

You must have loved Black Rain, *then.*

I know, I know. But they were a little more stylistic. By the way, those motorcycles in the chase at the beginning of the movie never ran longer than a hundred yards at any given moment total. It was the same hundred yards repeated over and over again and cut in a different way. It's amazing how you can create a rather lengthy chase.

Do you feel there are required ingredients to a chase scene, like inserting close-ups of the cycles?

Maybe stylistic things the director wants to do. If you show the throttle handle of the motorcycle so it has some ancillary part into the story—that the two riders are going very fast, or if you show the brake pedal to augment the action, fine. But to have an arbitrary cut of, say, the engine would make no sense to me.

Perhaps the energy of the chase demands a high number of quick shots?

Well, that can happen, if you think using the shots is being smart and stylistic. Once you get something going, you hate to slow it down unless it's resolved. I did *Ghost Story* with Fred Astaire and Melvyn Douglas, what we thought was the magic cast of all time. I joke about that film and say that to get Fred Astaire to move across the room, you had to have a reel changeover before he got there! (He was an older man then.) So you lose energy when you have something like that, obviously. You've got to cheat, you need cutaways to jump people around.

Did you elongate the flights in The Right Stuff?

Yes. A lot of that was throwing models through the air. We had guys up in San Francisco standing on A-frame ladders and throwing models. And you'd try to catch them on film. We had a lot of special effects in wind tunnels. But everything was all pieces put together. All the shots of John Glenn in his space suit or when he's orbiting were shot absolutely rigid with the camera totally fixed. So we revolved them in the optical printer to give the illusion that it was in space, because otherwise it was just this guy sitting! There were a lot of special effects to make it look a little more authentic.

Do you consider yourself a filmmaker?

No. I am part of the filmmaking process, and hopefully a good part of it, but I am not a filmmaker.

Would you say that as part of the process, an editor might get lost in the shuffle? Be anonymous?

I think it's a role that is thrust upon editors because of the egos involved, and we're above-the-line or below-the-line people. Since you're dealing with diplomacy, it's a difficult position to be in sometimes, and if you have a very big ego yourself, then you've got a problem. If you're bright enough to discuss a problem or try to change somebody's mind because it makes sense, great. You could be strong in that way. When someone says, "What do you think?" and you say, "I think it's shit and you ought to reshoot it," that's strong enough! But you can't be a lackey, you have to be your own person. Some people just refuse to take any kind of criticism, they feel it's all personally directed at them. Editors have to be malleable, have a good sense of humor, and be patient. I'm basically a lazy editor, so the first time I cut something, I try to make it as good as it can possibly be, knowing in the back of my head that I'm going to go back and change it anyway because it might be good for that sequence but it might not be good for the overall picture. But I don't think *consciously* that I have to go back and compress the picture. So I make my overlaps, stretch my dialogue, fill my tracks. I do all the things that many editors in their first cuts don't bother with. They call it an assembly. I never make an assembly. I make a first cut. I do not like what I am doing to be referred to as a rough cut.

Is the audience in the back of your mind too?

I try to put myself in their place. Audiences have become savvy over the last few years because of television, and they are constantly assaulted by visual images. Editors should know and learn what audiences expect and give it to them. Don't use a piece of film that has no relevant merit to the sequence. It disappoints an audience and they're puzzled by it. They don't understand why they shouldn't be seeing what they are used to seeing in their mind. All of that works into making a smoother, seamless kind of cutting. There is a saying, and I believe, that the best cut is the one you never see. I believe that by and large, except when you want the cut to be seen because you want to shock somebody and rattle their cage a little. But the unseen cut is the way it should be. You don't want to remind people they're looking at a movie. You want them to go through the experience, be the voyeur of the story.

the best cut is the one you never see

What would you say is a seen cut?

Say in an intimate scene between two people. The film almost dictates where you want to be with the flicker of the eye, the intensity of the look. Is it better to say "I love you," bang, then cut to the reaction? Or is it better to say "I love you," hang on it a beat to show the emotion of the person delivering the line, then go for the reaction? It's a matter of choice. Either way, there's a different result for the audience looking at it. Are their sympathies with the guy who said the line, or the girl who said the line? Or is the audience saying, "Don't believe him, he's going to screw you over!" It's how you play it. If you find the frame to cut on at *that* right moment, the audience will be totally satisfied because they are ahead of you and they know that guy is telling a lie, or whatever the situation is. Say in *Taxi Driver*, the whole montage of "You're talking to me?" All those cuts draw attention to the film. But when DeNiro is sitting watching *American Danceland* on the television and he starts to kick the set over, you know what's going to happen. You know it's going to go over, and it does. That's a different style of filmmaking: telling a story. Speaking in generalities, seamless editing is more satisfying. When you look at some old movies on television, the footage was pretty sparse back then so there weren't many choices. They shot a lot of stuff in masters; in comedies, for instance, the comics who had been honed on the stage played their numbers in a master scene. They didn't break it up into little close-ups and everything. It's a very simple look. Now audiences are much more sophisticated. They want to see a different pace and images and colors, you name it. I bought a tape of a film I had seen many, many years ago when I was working as a kid on ships. I ended up in Buenos Aires and went to see *Sahara* that had been dubbed in Spanish. I didn't understand a goddamned word, but I understood everything that was said in the picture, it was so beautifully pictorially enacted. I didn't have to understand the words, the story was there. When I worked on the TV series *The Big Valley*, it was the old classic style. The big masters. The show lent itself to that. We had a lot of extras and stock shots of farming areas.

Do you think because the old-time big master style is gone, it's more intimidating to cut from all the coverage you are given?

Oh sure. When I was in Sweden, I once had thirty thousand feet of film with no slates, nothing. I had the feeling, what do I do? But the film spoke of itself. Film does. It's positive film, you can put it back together again. Some assistants think they've broken the mold if they cut the film. When I made a mistake, it was so obvious that I'd correct it.

You like to fix mistakes at the beginning anyway, right?

You bet. A lot of times you want to get lazy. "Aw, I'll fix it later." Once you do that, you're sunk. You think, "When I go through it again, I'll catch it." You never do, or if you try it's too late. Too many things are happening all the time. You've got to run through music, or sound effects comes and grabs the reel and they've already laid down the Foley, then you have to change that too. Then the looping guy has the loop footage count so you can't change that. What you should have taken care of in a minute and a half or five minutes is now all of a sudden in the pipeline. Gone! Then when you see the answer print, you say, "Look what I did wrong!" Having seduced myself a few times by saying, "Aw, I'll take care of it," and then being caught, I don't do that anymore. Nobody came to me and said to do it. It's a self-inflicted pain.

It doesn't seem that editing is a job for procrastination.

No. Schedules nowadays are inhuman. On *Black Rain*, we worked almost four months seven days a week. Seven days after a while becomes a mélange, you don't even know what you're looking at. On *Jacob's Ladder*, our producer knows exactly where the money is going, so he doesn't want me in seven days a week. And I say hallelujah because I don't want to be there seven days a week, no matter what they pay. You need those extra days to get the batteries going again, or you'll never catch up.

Returning to your storyteller analogy, do you think you are in the best position to manipulate your "listeners"?

Good storytelling can only go so far. I think you can augment. You can help the story that's being told by the script and by the actors by making your audience feel what you want them to feel. Fear, obviously, you can do it in a cheap way. Blood splatting on the screen. But that's not what I consider terrifying. Terrifying is walking down a dark hallway and not knowing what's on the other side of that door—and suggesting that something is. That's one way of manipulating. How long do you prolong it? How many creepy steps does he go down into the basement? And once you get there, you better deliver. You better do it to satisfy your audience. If they see a joke building and you hold back a little, they'll get pissed off. With *Jacob's Ladder*, if the story is told correctly, it'll be one where at the last minute you go, "Oh my God!" It'll just turn you inside out.

That's a combination of what's been shot, acted, written. And, of course, edited.

It's all part and parcel. As I said, I'm not the filmmaker, but I am part of the process.

8

Sparking Life, Shaping People

Paul Barnes

1973–77   Staff Editor and Soundman for George C. Stoney Associates
Documentaries include:
The Shepherd of the Night Flock: A Portrait of Pastor John Garcia Gensel (1976–77)
Fair Housing Project (1976)
Vera and the Law: Toward a More Effective System of Justice (1974–75)
They Call It Wildcat (1974)
Planning for Floods (1973–74)
Hudson Shad and *Hudson River Series* (1973)
St. Peter's: A People on the Move (1973)

1977–78   *How the Myth Was Made: The Making of Robert Flaherty's "Man of Aran,"* directed by George C. Stoney (Consulting Editor and Soundman)

1978   *No Maps on My Taps*, directed by George T. Nierenberg

1979   *Free Radicals* and *Particles in Space*, and experimental animations by Len Lye (Post-production Supervisor and Editor)

1981   **Wasn't That a Time!*, directed by Jim Brown
Between Rock and a Hard Place, directed by Kenneth L. Fink (also Associate Producer)

1982   **Say Amen Somebody*, directed by George T. Nierenberg

1984   *Pumping Iron II: The Women*, directed by George Butler (Coeditor: Susan Crutcher)
Woody Guthrie, Hard Travelin', directed by Jim Brown
Musical Passage, directed by Jim Brown

1985   **Statue of Liberty*, directed by Ken Burns

1986   *On the Move*, directed by Merrill Brockway

1987   *Heaven*, directed by Diane Keaton

1988   **The Thin Blue Line*, directed by Errol Morris

1990   *The Civil War*, directed by Ken Burns

1991   *Coney Island*, directed by Ric Burns

* See Appendix for complete list of editing awards and nominations.

Because he is also a teacher, Paul Barnes discusses editing with a precision that comes from having to explain an intuitive, ephemeral process in concrete, practical terms. His mentors at New York University Film School were George Stoney, Carl Lerner, and Larry Silk, whose courses he enrolled in multiple times because he enjoyed them so much. Barnes started out as an editor at George Stoney Associates on various sponsored documentaries, skipping long years as apprentice and assistant. But his real love was feature films (after seeing *North by Northwest*, he concluded, "I've gotta do this somehow!"), and documentaries became an acquired taste through his work with Stoney. Barnes finds that his work in documentaries is still strongly tempered by his love for narrative film. As a result, he aims to make documentary films more entertaining than audiences generally consider them to be.

After an ideal work situation at Stoney, Barnes free-lanced through a rough time and paid his dues by cutting what he considered "truly junk." At the 1976 Flaherty Film Festival, he met George Nierenberg who offered him his breakthrough film, *No Maps on My Taps*. The film was widely shown on PBS and toured America and Europe along with a live performance of the three dancers in the film. From then on, Barnes has learned to merge his school learning (shot-by-shot analysis) with an innate sense of rhythm and his love of people in order to realize the vision of the director. Because editors are in the shadow of directors, they naturally risk anonymity and invisibility. But Barnes vehemently criticizes film critics for not learning more about editing to understand and acknowledge the editor's vital function in a film. He points out that each major craftsperson in a film—scriptwriter, cinematographer, editor—trades off with the next at preproduction, production, and postproduction, respectively. Although each becomes the director's collaborator at a different stage of a film, the editor remains the ultimate counterbalance.

Do you really believe editing is an intuitive process?

I think it is. I think if you just get a key to solving an editing problem, suddenly that problem can be unlocked. When I took Carl Lerner's class the first time, I was cutting a dialogue scene and I had never done sync dialogue before. Luckily, he was going through a dialogue scene in *Klute* and showed how you can overlap dialogue from one shot to another. Someone would say something and if you overlap it on a reaction shot of Jane Fonda, she would start to talk and then overlap the end of her sentence on Donald Sutherland; then an abrupt cut to Sutherland where you would begin and end his line; then cut to Fonda with a pause and she would start, then overlap on Sutherland. There was a dramatic, rhythmic flow to the delivery of the dialogue against the action and reaction shots of the actors. Suddenly it was, "Of course! That's how you do it." And I had just been cutting: Actor A says something, cut, Actor B says something, cut, Actor A says something, cut, Actor B says something, cut.

Before Carl showed you the tricks, did you think your work was great?

Oh God, no, it was so blocky and horrible. I was just baffled. What do I do? Carl showed me how you could smooth out the rhythms and make the visual cuts disappear by putting sound *over* the cut and create a lovely flow, as well as showing me that the actor reacting to a line is often more dramatic *to see* than the actor delivering the line. I immediately went back, recut the scene, and it began to work a hundred percent better. Those kinds of keys allowed me to take off.

How did those keys help you in your musical films?

Overlapping is a basic principle that helps you, certainly with making bridges with music. Carl taught me that as well, taking a score and beginning a theme on Scene 13 and running it across the beginning of Scene 14 to help make the transition. One thing I'm not sure I learned from him: I have a kind of innate musical sense. I've never been trained as a musician, I don't know how to read music, I've never played music. But there's a kind of musical rhythmic feel that I seem to have, and in my approach to cutting, I think the rhythms I produce are very musical in terms of when there's a pause, and placing something new on a pause as if a new instrument is coming in. Carl gave me some clues: If you make a music edit and side by side it doesn't seem to make sense, sometimes if you bang a hard chord or a word of dialogue or a sound effect on top of this rough cut, it might carry. Beyond that, I think it is a feel that I have as far as how to cut things against music, or how to best show the performer in terms of the angles.

Although you've mastered these tricks, do you still find a scene might not work?

Oh sure. You have an idea, an approach, and I try to put the film together very quickly so I can see a result fast. Parts of it might w< other parts are just horrible. By looking at where the problems a can start to finesse it. If the concept is totally wrong, I'll just start over. Film is mysterious in that you can control it only so far and it still wants to be what it wants to be. I've got the tools and tricks at hand, so I just keep molding it. It's rare when the first cut will stay. Sometimes it happens, but most of the time you go through two, three, four, five different versions until you arrive at something that is working well. Then it is a question of finessing even from there.

Do you work closely with the director in finessing these versions?

I feel as though in editing a documentary, I'm writing the film with the director. I prod him, I goad him to tell me what he likes about the material or what he doesn't like or what's important to him about a certain scene or a line of dialogue or just a shot. I try to get inside the director's head. What is his vision of the film? What is he trying to do? Also, to get the film footage in my head, to memorize it, to feel it as much as possible. Once I've got those two things inside me, then I can start to shape his intentions or concept or vision. The two of us are shaping it together. That's where the best experiences come, when I have a real active collaborator in the director, that I've absorbed his material to the point where I'll start a sentence and he'll finish it. It's not really my film. I feel that is the function of the editor, to realize the director's vision and make what he's had in his head or his heart up there on the screen accessible to everybody.

What are your visions then? How do they fit in with the director's?

I bring my own personality and feelings and thought to each project. I develop certain attitudes to the material as I'm watching it, and I convey that. I love people and I gravitate towards the characters in the films, even when the story is not strong or the theme is hit-or-miss. In looking at the dailies, it's the quirkinesses of the characters or deciphering the essence of the character and how I can build that character through the film. That is helpful to directors, especially when they come from production and have had problems with these people on the set. Sometimes they can't be objective to their material, or they can't see through all the problems and hassles in preproduction or production, and they can carry that baggage into the cutting room. Another function of the editor is to become the objective eye for the director, a fresh eye, so you can help him strip away some of those things he's carrying in. On *The Thin Blue Line*, Errol Morris had a dislike for the attorney who handled the appeal, to the point of almost not wanting to put him in the film at all. The appeal was a crucial part of the story that we had very little material for, and a lot of that information was conveyed by the attorney. I felt there was a detachment and coldness about the way he was approaching the case which I found interesting, and to me it was a part of the cynical philosophy that Errol has anyway. The way this attorney was handling Randall Adams's case was an essence of the way the case had been mishandled from the start. I kept pushing that to Errol. He never liked the guy, but it was essential to the narrative line, and the character was a part of this whole miasma that Randall found himself caught in. I pushed him to keep it, and it's in the final film.

Other than including the material, what other things can you do in editing to enhance the character?

Cleaning up people? All the time you make people look better than they are! Again, that's a kind of function of the editor, you want to make everybody look their best, or if it's their worst, look their worst. If that's the essence of who they are and the way they function in the narrative, it's important to bring that out. We're always cleaning up people, whether it's a fiction film, an actor's performance, or a real person in a documentary. To give the best presentation possible of who they are, good or bad, without going over the top. One reason I like documentaries so much is the complexity of the characters that gives you a richness, all kinds of colors, things you like, don't like, and allowing those to filter through. Errol falls in love with his interviews, and he lets them run. In *Thin Blue Line*, the interviews hold on the screen longer than most do. Errol would often want them to go even longer. Randall's lawyer Edith was at times a problem. Errol found Edith so funny, her excesses so endearing, that he would want me to allow her interviews to continue for another two, three, four lines. To me, there was a point where Edith was suddenly becoming annoying and aggravating or exasperating, almost destroying what she had said in the first part. We were trying to make a point come across, whether it was a narrative point or a character point. He would want her to do two or three more lines and it would upset the whole balance. I said, "You can't do that because now Edith looks bad and we're not going to believe what she said before. I think we're going too far." I was often trying to pull him back from becoming too excessive and steering the characters off course. In *No Maps on My Taps*, one of the dancers, Chuck Green, had a mental health problem. George Nierenberg and I both loved him, but the material with him was hard to use because he was so inarticulate that if we used too much of it, it was annoying, scary, or exasperating to the audience because you couldn't understand him. I kept saying to George, "The less of Chuck, the better." If we left him as a mysterious presence, the other two dancers were so articulate that they could talk about Chuck and we would understand his brilliance as a dancer and his history without Chuck saying it himself. Doing that allowed the audience to take Chuck in. You admired his dancing, feeling great sympathy for his problem without going overboard rubbing it in the audience's face. That subtle approach with Chuck, in terms of the editing of the character, was very effective. One of the best reviews of that film in *The New Yorker* called Chuck "The King Lear of Tap." It was exactly what George and I were trying to do.

Balancing characters was also important in Pumping Iron II: The Women. *Did the first* Pumping Iron *influence your cutting of the sequel?*

There was a difference between the two films because *Pumping Iron* was much more *cinéma vérité*. What George Butler and his cinematographer Dyanna Taylor were trying to do with *Pumping Iron II* was give it more a feature film look, a slick look, so I didn't have shaky cameras and jump cutting. I shifted gears and decided to approach it more like a feature than like a *cinéma vérité* documentary.

What is the feature approach in cutting a documentary?

Again, it's my whole interest in narrative films, since that's where my love of film grew. I approach a documentary as if it is a feature, to bring out the story values. I make it look as much like a feature film as possible. In situations where there's only one camera shooting, I cut the scenes as if there were multiple takes, or as if there were three cameras shooting. Try to cut them so I've got a master shot, cut to a two-shot, cut to a close-up. If I can cut from those three shots, it almost seems like a narrative film in the way it's structured, without resorting to documentary tricks of a newspaper cutaway, something like that. When I was starting to do documentaries, *cinéma vérité* was beginning to die out. A lot of the documentary directors I began to work with had aspirations to become feature directors, and they would always say to me, "I want it to look as slick as possible, I want it to look like a feature film." It was a whole change in the style of documentary, and in my role as editor, I'm responsible to give them that style—without sacrificing the material. If there's a shaky camera movement and the content is great, I'll argue like crazy to keep it if it plays into the story and the emotion.

Did you attempt to give Statue of Liberty *a slick look even though, of all your films, it appears to be the most traditional of documentaries?*

I wanted to work with Ken Burns because I had seen his Brooklyn Bridge film, and I was bowled over because I had never seen anybody use archive material so effectively as narrative. You felt so wrapped up in the story of Washington Roebling and his wife and building the bridge, you were being told a story. At times it felt live. It's a challenge in a way— using still photographs and abstract live shots and portraits of people, and trying to make that story come to life. That was our approach in the first part of *Statue*. Strip away all the didacticism except where the information plays into the story, and build to a climax.

That's where pacing is vital.

Very much so. That's another thing I think about in my own style. Not to toot my own horn too much, but I prefer a slower, more elegant, stately style of cutting. I'll let a shot play. If it plays when it holds, I'll just hold it. I don't go nutty cutting rapid-fire. When we were beginning discussions, Ken said, "We want to make the audience feel as though they're living in the photograph." And by holding the shots longer or doing gentle moves in and out of the spaces and revealing different details of the photo, often it does seem to come to life in that regard. So the mood is built on the pace and you can feel yourself in the photo without cutting like a madman. Also when you're dealing with static images, there is a mobility in the audiotrack that you can utilize almost in a contrapuntal way to the images. If the images are moving at a slower pace, the audio can actually be going faster. You can put a faster piece of music against a more slowly cut photo, and the combination of the two balances each other out. Or if the voice is so compelling that the information or the evocative sound effects we've laid underneath provide a mobile or active feel against the static images, it's almost as if they're moving faster.

In addition, you used sound effects, like crowd noise and bells ringing, under certain photographs.

That was an attempt to evoke reality and bring it to life. That's something we're doing in the Civil War project. The entire nine episodes is like the first half-hour of *Statue*.

You keep referring to the "first part" of Statue. *There really is a different feel to each half of the program. Was that intentional?*

It was. Ken didn't want it simply to be a narrative history, he wanted to deepen the theme of the film. It's not just how was the statue built and brought to America, but what does the statue mean to us as a nation. Some of that thematic material is built into the narrative story. It's the reason the statue was built, why Bartholdi created it, why it was brought to the States. But Ken wanted to go one step further, really question. Has America held up to the ideal that the statue represented? How have we achieved those ideals, or failed? The second part was harder to cut because it was more free-form. We didn't have a story structure to fall back on, and I always find it harder to make free-form structure work. It took us longer to cut the second half-hour than the first to get it to a point where it was working well.

You used startling techniques in the second half with the fast motion of the boat crossing the river and the advertisement montage.

Those were conceptions Ken had before we started to cut. In that second section he wanted the fast-motion trip to the statue because he knew people would be expecting to see it, but he wanted it over with fast. That generated his idea to do the pixilation. He also knew that he wanted to deal with the commercialization of the statue, also in montage fashion, so when I began, he had gathered all that material already.

How did that film help or hinder you when you moved on to Diane Keaton's film, Heaven, *with its rapid cutting and montages?*

Heaven, I think, was sort of my experimental phase. My style had evolved to this stately, elegant way of cutting, holding takes longer and making it look like a feature film. I thought, "You're getting a little too staid. Maybe it's time to open yourself to other possibilities." The great montages like Eisenstein's "Odessa Steps" or the end of *Bonnie and Clyde*, those fantastic fast-cut montages fascinated me. One thing that was attractive to me about *Heaven* was that Diane did want to cut it fast. She had gathered all of these phenomenal heaven images from feature films and industrials and wacko documentaries from the 1920s through the 1950s, intending to cut them with interviews which were, by and large, extremely quirky. One reason she chose me was because I liked the people so much, whereas other editors were saying they were too weird, too bizarre. I loved jump cutting the interviews for two reasons: one, visually, I loved the jagged rhythms you could create by jump cutting interviews; secondly, I loved that I didn't have to resort to stupid cutaways to mask that you've eliminated a piece. Further, it allowed us to compress people's statements. You could cut out all the boring stuff and only use the good stuff. When you cut it together, it had a very lively flow to it. Where I used stock in documentaries, it was always very traditional. *Heaven* allowed me to smash it up, use it more experimentally. I love the opening of the film where Joan of Arc from Dreyer's *Passion* is menaced by a 1950s industrial clock, tormented by time.

Was that kind of thing pre-scripted or did you invent?

Heaven was the most free-form of all the films I've done. That's why it took over a year to cut, because you could go in any direction. That particular montage, Joan and the clock, was my idea. After absorbing all this material, we were groping for how to open the film. Diane knew she wanted to do the universe, the stars and planet and explosion at the very beginning, and then go from there. I said, "Diane, look, your whole theme is 'Are you afraid to die?' and 'Are you going to heaven after you die?' People are afraid to die and consequently afraid of time, the clock.

Why don't we take Joan, who had the most terrified expression—" (and Diane loved Falconetti) "—and menace her with the clock!" She saw what I was driving at and agreed to give it a try and we shaped it together. The track also kept evolving. We started with a strange piece of music by Sakamoto, combination rock and New Age, and some simple clock effects. Then Diane found this educational film, *How to Tell Time*, I built a track that repeated, "What time is it? What time is it now?" and we had that running against Joan for a while. Then Diane found a sermon from a crazy preacher doing a takeoff on the Peggy Lee song, "Is That All There Is?" so we combined that with the "What time is it now?" and built this multilayered track. Montages of sound as well as images, and kept layering them. Fast cutting can become a jumble, a mess, and I think the real art of it is making it clear. The "Odessa Steps" sequence from Eisenstein's *Battleship Potemkin* is a prime example, or the killing at the end of *Bonnie and Clyde*. You can learn so much from the rhythms, placement, and repetitions of shots, the way every aspect of the montage is carefully set up and prepared for so that when you break and go rapid-fire, the audience is always grounded. They know where they are and what those little pieces of film represent. Whether I achieved it in *Heaven*, I'm not sure; to some people, a lot of it looks like a jumble. But I'm still terribly fond of the film personally. One of the reasons why the film bugs people so much, I think, is because we confront them so heavily with death, in perhaps too jokey a fashion. About three months into cutting, Diane's grandmother died. It made her very angry, questioning why. I also had a very good friend die a few months before I started the film. We brought a lot of that anger into the project, perhaps too much; we were pummeling people to the point where it wasn't funny anymore, or too black, too assaultive. I think we were trying to exorcise ourselves.

Can previewing help you change the tone of a film like that?

I love to screen. As an editor and a director, you get a kind of writer's block. The visceral or emotional effect of the material starts to recede after a certain point. I try to keep in mind that feeling when we finally made it work, when it brought tears to my eyes even after working at it for three months and yet we still have three months more to go. You've incorporated all of your concepts and ideas and crazy experiments into the piece to the point where you're not quite sure what more to do. Screening with an audience is almost a shock, but boy, does it break you out of that block. For directors, it's often terrifying. Diane had only made one short film before *Heaven* and never showed that to anybody. I thought she was going to have a nervous breakdown the first time we screened the film! In *Pumping Iron II*, George Butler loved giving the audience xeroxed handouts for their responses and we could extrapolate material from that.

I try to go by consensus in making changes. If twenty people out of forty we invited say something's wrong with a scene, we should pay attention to it. But directors often will listen to the last person they talked to and immediately want change. I try to be very diplomatic or mellow with them. Directors who get stale want to tinker with stuff that works like gangbusters and that's when I get fierce!

You mean they don't remember their first reactions to the material?

They do, but directors are so anxious and doubtful. The weight of the film is on their shoulders. They'll watch a scene and feel it, then two months later, "What happened to the scene?" "Nothing, it's the same way it was two months ago." "But I don't feel it anymore." "Don't you remember when you *did* feel it?" That's when you need to get them in with an audience—they'll feel it with the audience or at least see the audience responding. Still sometimes they worry. Some idiot from the audience will say, "That scene didn't work for me," and they'll come back the next morning, "We've got to do something! So-and-so said this." And you go, "Yeah, but who else said that? It's only your crazy aunt!" Sometimes you want to put locks on the doors and say, "Stay away!" The ending of *The Thin Blue Line* was so powerful and so moving—it was cut early and not tinkered with a great deal. Right when we were about to lock the film, Errol started with, "It doesn't work, it's not fast enough, it's not slow enough, should we put something in?" Finally three-thirty in the morning, he said to me, "I think we should speed up the photographs with David Harris, take out some pauses in his speech." My heart dropped because I felt the rhythms of David's lines, the pauses, where the cuts were falling on the photos, the structure of the photos, everything seemed right on the mark to me. I was worn down and said, "All right, fine, I'll try it for you." I cut it, he said he liked it, I kicked him out at four or four-thirty. I started to get the reels technically ready to send to the sound cutters in San Francisco to meet the deadline for sound editing. Errol came back in the morning and said, "I couldn't sleep all night! I think we ruined David's scene. Put it back the way it was." I just went, "THANK YOU! BLESS YOU!" We restored it, and it's the way you see it now. As an editor you're a hand-holder, a therapist. You've got to keep them from going too far, wrecking something that works well, and always openly be responding to their ideas for making it better.

How did your new-found style on Heaven *work for* Thin Blue Line?

I had to do a lot of adapting for Errol. Errol likes to hold shots forever. On *Heaven*, I was doing a lot of motion cutting, cutting on the movements within the shots, especially on the stock footage. When I started on *Thin Blue Line*, I began the montages, like of Dallas or the crime scene, cutting those very, very fast and always on the motions. Errol said, "No! That's not what I want. Longer, longer, longer." The crime reenactments are somewhat fast-paced, but there's again a counterbalance to it. Often the shots start still or with little movement at the head, then there's more movement in the middle of the shot, then a kind of dead patch, no movement, at the end of the shot. Cutting to the next shot, it's still again, then movement comes in, and then it goes still. Even though the pieces are short, they almost always had dead space at the head and tail, so that you're not cutting from movement to movement within the shots, which I was doing initially and which is a common technique. I finally realized what Errol wanted and adapted my cutting accordingly. The frames are almost like still frames with movement in the middle.

Each reenactment feels mathematically designed, with inserts of images like the milkshake container thrown from the police car. Did you literally measure the placement of these inserts to increase tension?

Many of the shots were similar. Obviously, we had differences but with a basic pattern, starting at the high shot and then going closer, the same thing sort of broken down. Errol had shot a bunch of 16mm material and when I started cutting, I had that on hand. He didn't like the lighting so he was intending to reshoot it, but I said, "Let me cut some sequences and at least give you an idea of how it could possibly work." It actually helped confirm for him his direction to dramatize the killing. From there, he hired a production designer to do storyboards; some were based on shots he had done and then a lot was completely new ideas that he hadn't been able to realize in that aborted 16mm shoot. We thought too from the start about staying close, doing extreme close-ups, not showing wide shots except where helpful, and trying to abstract and pull it apart. That generated ideas for him—the cop spinning, the flashlight falling, the milkshake, the body hitting the ground, the feet under the car. Staying away from faces, keeping them in shadow, seeing body parts instead of full figures. I was forceful about that. One place where dramatizations tend not to work in documentaries is when you've got the full figure and it's an actor, obviously. We did want to create a tension with the reenactments and we knew they were going to be repeated. The repetition was going to be a part of the style of the film. At the same time, we didn't want them to get boring and lose that tension. The idea was that every time we did a scene of the killing, we would cut it differently and make people tense up as the cop was approaching the car. Philip Glass's music provided a lot of the tension for the film and played into the repetition of the scene itself. Errol wanted to show the shooting ad infinitum. We learned in early screenings that we were turning people off because the cop was getting shot too much. Finally I said, "Let's shoot the cop the first or second time, and then bring the cop to the car, but don't shoot him. Let the audience feel him coming up to the car, but cut away before he's shot. That will create a different tension." We decided to do that and in the middle of the film yanked out a lot of shootings. Almost all the reenactments were little montages. Again we discovered it was too monotonous, so two-thirds of the way in, a couple of reenactments were single shots; or instead of an elaborate ten-shot sequence, it became three shots; in a couple of cases, I think just one shot. We changed the pattern of expectation, too. Even though you returned to the same place, there was a slightly different feel each time. The killing that comes right after it's announced that Randall is guilty is the most horrendous one: the police officer's body twists, you see those squib shots in the back, close-ups concentrating on his body. It was the most gruesome and very fast cut—it didn't have the dead heads and tails. The one you had seen prior to that was a single shot of him walking. So you know you were getting into a climax at that point. Even though it's the same thing, we changed them each time and made them slightly different. Stripping away a lot of the shots and bringing it back at the crucial moment. When it's revealed in full intensity, it's at the most emotional moment: Randall's monologue about being convicted, about the D.A. not caring, intercut with the electric chair.

Was cutting between interviews or reenactments easy because you could make transitions with images of swinging watches or taillights?
All that actually evolved in the course of the cutting, especially the graphics, the headlines in the newspapers. Coming out of *Heaven* where Diane said, "Jump cut the interviews," I felt so liberated. Then I came to Errol and I said, hopefully, "You don't mind using jump cuts, do you?" And he said, "No jump cuts!" So we would get ideas about how to bridge an interview by using a paragraph or a word from a newspaper, and that became a prime binding device to eliminate jump cuts, as well as a stylistic thing. When I started cutting, Errol said three elements interested him as far as the structure of the film. First, the interviews themselves which are the main structure. The second structure was dramatizing the killing. And third, the objects and graphics that expressed the case; those were going to be the main visual elements, apart from the killing—the watch, the milkshake, newspaper headlines, the photo of the gun, the license plates. They all became fetishistic objects to Errol, emblematic of the general weirdness of the case. The only problem he posed for me—besides the "No jump cuts!"—was he wouldn't want to cut Randall and David together. It was okay to cut together Randall's two lawyers or the three cops or David's three friends. But I could *never* cut Randall against David. It was forbidden. I always had to put something between them.

Like in the opening, I use the close-up of the flashing police light between the first two pieces of Randall and David as a bridge.

Was he afraid Randall and David together would create bias?

It was that. He didn't want the standard documentary good guy/bad guy opposition. You could *hear* them adjacent, but something always had to be in between them visually. He hated when I intercut people telling the same story, or people contradicting or responding to what someone has just said. That was a common investigative journalistic documentary technique that he hated. He preferred if Edith tells her story, then we cut to someone telling another part of that aspect of the case but not a *direct* response, not a direct amplification. It's their point of view, it's not answering Edith. Now you're going into the cop's head for what he thinks, never making direct, blunt juxtapositions between statements. More like we enter Edith's world, float around in there, then cut to the cop's world and float around in there. Sometimes juxtaposing interviews was a visual thing with Errol. He liked the way the shots of the three cops looked together. He had designed those backgrounds and liked the way they were cut. There was also a problem cutting Randall and David together because Randall's shot was so dark and David's was lighter and predominantly orange. There was almost a black-and-white quality to Randall's shot, an orange-greenish in David's. In a standard documentary, many people don't care about the visual look of the film, and hanging weird-looking things together gives many documentaries that ragged look. But Errol was very concerned about the look of his film and it made sense visually not to put Randall and David together—besides what it meant philosophically. Errol knew the potential of the material to become a kind of *Sixty Minutes* investigative journalistic piece, and he was torn between that (which may have been an easy way to make the film) and maintaining his own aesthetic style which he had established in *Gates of Heaven*. Even though he knew he had a moral responsibility to help Randall as much as he could, he didn't want to give up his own style to achieve that. So there was always a tension about how we could do both. There was also an epistemological aspect to the film that intrigued him very much. I always kept fighting against that because it seemed too detached.

The concept of "the thin blue line" between law and anarchy?

Yeah. My first impulse was, we're going to tell the story of Randall Adams and help get him out of jail, I don't care what your philosophy is. Even though he's done something very good in helping get Randall out of prison, I don't think that has changed Errol's cynicism at all. He feels that injustice could happen to anybody, and he wanted to maintain that view in the film. Finally I had to come to respect that, even though it's not my own philosophy. It was difficult cutting the film in that I had to mold it according to his view and not regard my own feelings. But once I recognized that, I felt responsible to his vision and kept trying to achieve that. There was always a hard balance between telling the story, making the audience understand that Randall was innocent, and maintaining this cynical overview. We had some earlier cuts of the film where it wasn't even clear that Randall was innocent. If things could be a little obscure or confusing, Errol loved it; it was like the confusions and obscurities in the case itself. He didn't want to use narration or title cards or graphics to simply explain something. We could have used a paragraph in the newspaper, isolate a sentence that might have made something clear. But often he would fight against that kind of clarity. We always walked a high wire, I thought. It's a very, very risky film.

Do the participants see the film as you cut and offer their opinions?

Sometimes. In *Say Amen Somebody*, the Barrett Sisters came to the cutting room a few times. They'd spot a few bad music cuts and help us fix them up. If I cut a piece of music out and made an awkward bridge, they could tell me it was musically off. Since I don't know music technically, I go by feel and so I worked to fix it up for them. Dolores kept asking me to make her arms look thinner! I said, "There's a limit to the editing, Dolores!" On *Wasn't That a Time!*, Ronnie Gilbert came to our screenings, helping us steer things that were going off.

Pumping Iron II, Wasn't That a Time!, and Say Amen Somebody prepared for concerts or competitions. Was that deliberately structured as in "We're going to make a film about getting together and having a . . . "?

In those films, we knew the performances would be the climactic moments. It's always helpful to have that structural linchpin, especially with documentaries. But each evolved somewhat differently. Initially, *Wasn't That a Time!* was going to be a film about Lee Hays of the Weavers, but their get-together worked so well and the four of them enjoyed it so much that the Weavers said, "Maybe we should do a reunion concert. Let's go to Carnegie Hall." The get-together happened in May, and in November they did Carnegie. So Jim Brown shot the May reunion, then shot Carnegie (about one-third of the film's material), then we began to cut. As we cut, what was important about their story became clearer, and the structure for the film evolved out of cutting only what we had. Then Jim could go out and shoot more material very economically. Ronnie Gilbert's interview was shot on a four hundred foot roll, about twelve minutes; Pete Seeger's was also a four hundred foot roll. We knew exactly what we wanted them to talk about, a certain period of their career or their character; we could see exactly where we needed to fill in the holes in their story. We also restructured the Weavers' rehearsal scene in Lee's house, which we *say* is the rehearsal for Carnegie Hall. It was actually the rehearsal for the May reunion outside. A gigantic lie there! But we had to do it because between the reunion in May and Carnegie in November, Jim had no money to shoot any of the actual preparations for the concert. The only thing we had was a little of Carnegie backstage, but none of it actual rehearsal. We originally had the rehearsal placed before they sang in May. It was always deadly there, pacingwise. Once they said they were getting together, you wanted to *immediately* see them sing, and the rehearsal interrupted that flow. We yanked it out of there and I said, "Let's make it the Carnegie rehearsal."

It worked perfectly.

It did, even though they're in the same clothes! But there's so much material between when you saw them sing in May and finally see them at the rehearsal, supposedly the rehearsal at Carnegie. The film clips are there, they talk about their first records, you forget what they wore, so it wasn't a problem. But I have to admit it's a lie.

Don't you feel uneasy about that when it's a documentary?

You do have to consider the ethics of lying when you're working with this material. But my rule of thumb is, is it faithful to the character, to the story, to the feeling of what's going on? If it rings true, then I feel it's okay. In that scene, I'm sure that's what a rehearsal before the Carnegie concert was like. It's faithful to what could have happened. If it's something more serious, a political or social issue, or something revolving around a case like *The Thin Blue Line*, I want to be sure things are not distorted, except where people are distorting it themselves.

To be careful your juxtaposed images wouldn't bias subliminally?

Well, I think they do! Intercutting the judge with the *Dillinger* footage in *The Thin Blue Line* is pretty biased, I must say! But given the style of his form, Errol felt he could take license. He told me when I started, "I want to use the film clips *Boston Blackie* for Emily, the surprise witness, and *Dillinger* for the judge." I was all for giving it a shot. It adds humor and I don't mind demeaning those two characters. Errol kept saying to me it's not that far out of reality. "It's their dreams. It's Emily's dream and it's the judge's dream." What Emily says corresponds to what the woman does in the *Boston Blackie* footage.

Yes, Emily said she always wanted to be a detective.

Right. And so with the judge, that romanticism of police work and how that plays into his hard-nosed attitudes towards getting the cop killer at any cost. In both senses, it adds to their character. Even though it's a projection by the filmmaker, it's within the realm of possibility of what's in their heads. It is a fictional device. In a sense, Errol was trying to, almost like a novel, enter their heads and see what was inside by using stock footage instead of words.

How much do mechanics of editing intrude on your creative process?

I find that when I cut, I almost get into a Zen-like state, an intuition that almost occurs naturally. Once I'm in the process of cutting, putting one shot next to another shot, overlaying music, I'll see how it works on this shot; then I get an idea on how it's going to go on the next shot, and I put a third in and it's totally off the wall and I try something else. My mind starts working rapidly and I'm not always aware of the process. Oftentimes the room disappears, all there is is the screen. I've been cutting so long that the mechanical operations are automatic, so I don't think about the splicer or the film or labeling. People can come in and out of the room and I won't be aware of them. I'll get a tap on the shoulder and practically jump through the ceiling.

How long does it take you to get into that state?

It's fairly automatic. I've got myself trained to dive into it, almost at will. I'll sit down first thing in the morning and go until lunch or a screening.

Does the feel of film help create that state for you?

I like the manual manipulation of it, and for me the time involved in manipulating it to cut allows me the time to think. It's automatic, it doesn't intrude, so I can be thinking about what I want to do. The mind works creatively, not on mechanics, but the mechanics allow it. I'm a little afraid of video editing. I asked a friend of mine how he felt about video editing on a new system called Laserdisc, and he told me, "It goes so fast I can't think anymore." Which doesn't sound good, but I do want to try it and see what might happen.

Do you suppose the very first cut you made that worked was an intuitive one? Or did you plan it?

Now it's a funny combination. I can look at two pieces of film and say, "I can cut it there because I know it's going to work." A lot of editors I talk to say to me, "I don't know how I do that." It may be because in preparation for teaching, I've sat down with some of my films and tried to analyze what I was doing. I've also analyzed *Bonnie and Clyde*, which I use in my class. I started to realize some of the common tricks I was using. Some came from Carl Lerner, but he never explained it all really technically. I've been able to analyze by cutting on a movement from one frame into a movement on another frame how that makes it appear more seamless. I may be a bit more aware of how those tricks work than other editors who do it intuitively. I'm not always sure if I'm getting it right or not, but sometimes I can say what will work—this movement matches that movement, these compositions are similar, they will clearly cut.

Like the visual contrasts in the opening of Pumping Iron II: *the glitz of Las Vegas versus the sensuality of the women athletes.*

The opening really spells out a lot of the complementary and contradictory aspects of the themes of the film to me. One was the kind of commercial, almost freak-show aspect of bodybuilding which perfectly suited Las Vegas, so that to me was represented by the neon. The strength and beauty of the women's bodies were almost in direct opposition and that was the design of the opening—the neon, the glitz, in opposition to the strength and beauty of the women athletes' bodies. We liked the suntan machine shots—the way they look was a photographic accident because if you look at a tanning machine, a yellow light comes out, but the way the film reacts to the light, it made a bluish tone. That gave a kind of sci-fi quality to the images which built into the "woman of the future" idea. That too played into the design. I also played around with how images were juxtaposed, like the pan that goes along one woman's arm which has the strong vertical of her veins running through it, and cut to a shot which has the vertical neon tubes. It seemed a direct analogy to the vertical of her arm.

Was there a turning point when you changed from a mechanical editor to an editor of "connections"?

I think there was. On *No Maps on My Taps*, which was the first big film I did, I was terrified and didn't think I was doing very well the first three months. Then I had a breakthrough. We brought five people into a screening room when we were having trouble, and an editor friend of George Nierenberg's said, "This is going to be a really good film, but I'm not into it until about twenty minutes in. I don't feel the film until the scene with Bunny Briggs and his uncles, reminiscing about how Bunny started as a child dancer and supported his family. And Bunny begins to cry remembering his mom who died. It was very emotional, a lovely scene and very personal, and it clicked for me." I said, "That's it! That's where you *feel* it." So we took the second fifteen minutes of the film and made it the first fifteen minutes, a full juggle. You've got to let the audience feel first, then you can explain anything in the world afterwards. For me, film is the most powerful as an emotional medium. I think intellectually it often leaves a lot to be desired. If emotion and intellect can go hand in hand, they become strong. That was a real turning point for me, because I had been trying to do things by rote. I had done fifteen minutes carefully explaining who each dancer was, how they related to the history of dancing, step by step, ponderous and didactic; then we got personal.

It was the wrong way to go. From that time on, I approached cutting any film differently. I look at the dailies differently, isolate character moments that you *feel*, think about those first. Then think about how to wrap the other material around that.

Around the heart of the film.
    Exactly.

9

Touching the Heart

Anne V. Coates

1989   *Farewell to the King,* directed
by John Milius (Coeditor:
C. Timothy O'Meara)
Listen to Me, directed by
Douglas Day Stewart

1990   *I Love You to Death,* directed
by Lawrence Kasdan

1991   *What About Bob?* directed by
Frank Oz

* See Appendix for complete list of editing
awards and nominations.

During the cutting of *The Elephant Man*, Anne Coates broke her wrist skiing over Christmas vacation. She had promised to have the film ready in January. In the best theatrical tradition the show went on, and just as John Hurt had to suffer his special makeup to play his role, Coates performed her task, even with her arm in a cast.

Such dedication to her profession began when Coates was a teenager at school in England. She was dazzled by the ability of film to turn "fairly long-winded, boring books" like *Jane Eyre* and *Wuthering Heights* into magical movies that everyone could enjoy. She was determined to direct. There was little that women could do in film at that time except continuity ("script girl") and editing. Coates selected the latter field, hoping to emulate other directorial greats like David Lean* and Robert Hamer, who had also begun as editors. "You couldn't work in films unless you were in the union, and you couldn't be in the union unless you worked in films, so the back door was religious films or, nowadays, commercials." Coates worked in religious films, to the relief of her family who had hoped, to no avail, that the inspirational content would deter her from pursuing such a frivolous career. Upon joining the union, Coates applied for work as second assistant editor at Pinewood Studio, where she was asked if she could perform all the necessary tasks of the role. Her earlier experience had barely introduced her to splicing, but she said certainly she could do it, sought a little help from editing friends, and bluffed her way through.

At the time of this interview, Coates was hoping to renew her collaboration with David Lean on his long anticipated saga *Nostromo*. But she also looked back proudly on her career to date, which includes having edited—and reedited—the British cinema classic, *Lawrence of Arabia*. Notwithstanding such epic achievements, Coates is especially proud of

---

*David Lean died in 1991.

being an editor who loves to cut "little films," those gems of stories with full-dimensional characters. Coates also comments on some of the similarities and differences between British and American editing, and the growing cooperation between the two continents.

I remember one of the best compliments I ever had paid to me was by the British director, Carol Reed, who said, "I've had some great editors work for me, but I've never had one with so much heart as you." I've always treasured that remark.

How does an editor find heart when, essentially, all editors are working with the same equipment and concepts?
How do you explain a Laurence Olivier as opposed to other great actors in the theater? He had that little special edge. It's your choice, isn't it? The way you choose the pieces, the order in which you put the pieces together. I cut very much by what the actors give you in their eyes. I was taught early on to look for that in a performance. I suppose it's something you see that works, a rhythm you have in yourself.

Was there an influential editor in your career?
I was lucky because I was assistant to the editor, John Seabourne. He was very old and very experienced, and I worked closely with him. He was also slightly deaf, so often he didn't hear the notes the director gave him and I would tell him what to do. He frequently went home about four o'clock to tend his gardens and he'd say, "Finish that sequence," which was great experience. He taught me the most of anybody, I think. He taught me to be ruthless, not to fiddle around with matching and such things, but to go for the heart of the scene, for the drama, and always keep your mind on telling the story through the pictures.

But how do you get to that heart?
I don't know. I think editors don't get a lot written about them because it's not easy to explain what we do. It's what we feel. An instinct. You have that flair and instinct—I guess you're born with it. It's a fact that assistants can't learn, really, until they're actually editing because then they're suddenly faced with, "Why does one cut on a particular frame?" You have a whole heap of frames in every cut! Some instinct tells you. It must be something in you as a person.

Is it a question of entering the film somehow?
I don't go into one of those moods or trances, however you describe it. I'm very laid-back as an editor. I mean, I'm very strict, I like a well-run cutting room and well-trained assistants. But once it's running smoothly,

I like a pleasant atmosphere. I don't think you should be the kind of editor who chews fingernails and goes wild. You aren't necessarily going to be a better editor for doing that. Of course you worry, we all worry, but you should enjoy the work. There was an editor who should be absolutely nameless who was cutting a film once that took place in Antarctica. I went into his cutting room on a warm day, and he was sitting there in an overcoat with a scarf around his neck. And I said, "What are you doing?" He said, "Well, I'm trying to get into the mood of the picture!" I think that's carrying it too far.

Method editing!
Indeed.

How long does it take you to find the heart?
It varies. I always feel when I start on a film that I'm never going to get it, that I'm not anywhere near what I should be doing. I used to say to my husband and kids, "My God, I've lost my touch!" Then suddenly I'd cut a sequence and get excited. After that, things fell into place. It's a magic that suddenly comes to you. The moment doesn't necessarily come with a particular sequence. You just find you've hit your stride, you might say, and you find that little core you're looking for in that film. I don't know why that happens. You know, when you lecture to film students, they're always asking you about rules. I don't cut by rules. Every film has its problems and I tackle every sequence freshly. On the other hand, my daughter who is at university in England took a film course in which they studied my "style"—very much to her amusement and mine too. Maybe if you asked the students there, they would know what my style was, but I'm not aware of a style. I would like to think that I can cut all types of films. I particularly love black comedy, like *I Love You to Death*. Recently we ran one scene from that film for the unit, and one of the associate producers came up to me and asked, "What was your psychology behind cutting that scene?" I said, "Well, I don't really have any psychology. I just mark the film, cut it, and hope for the best." That wasn't the answer she wanted, and my crew nearly died with laughter because they heard me and they knew. I'm more a doer than a talker.

You need versatility with films like The Horse's Mouth *and* Becket.
They're so different, aren't they? But the one thing they did have in common was a great deal of dialogue. *Becket* had beautiful speeches and was shot in a fairly theatrical way. Peter Glenville was mostly a theater director. I came off *Lawrence* onto that and it was a bit shattering because *Lawrence* had so much material and *Becket* had long, quiet dialogue scenes shot without much cover, and the very neat death in the cathedral. There was a very complicated scene to cut in *Becket*: the men on the

horses at the beach. I always believe that you can cut any two shots together, it's just that you can cut some better together than others. And there's always the *one* place where you can make them the best you possibly can. This scene was tricky because the horses never were in the same place. You couldn't control them from take to take, they were all over, facing this way and that. And it was important to cut on a certain line if you wanted to get the faces as it was a very dramatic scene.

The horses must have appeared to jump cut.

It didn't appear like that, if you look closely. It catches at the right moment when a horse turns one way or other. One of my favorite cuts was from a very long shot of the beach to a big close-up of Becket's face.

Didn't you feel obligated to insert a medium shot?

Not at all. That's what I mean by the fact that I never work with formulas or rules. In another situation when they'd been estranged, the king says, "I'll go and see Becket," and I made a direct cut to Becket coming in the door. A lovely cut, nothing very complicated. Hal Wallis said to me, "You can't do a direct cut. You've got to do a dissolve in there. He's fifty miles away." I said, "So what? It's a great cut and very dramatic, and goes right to the heart of the scene." He never mentioned it again and it stayed like it was.

Since editing is so subjective, could you and the director both have correct but different views of a scene?

I think so. But that's where the director must decide because it's his movie. Very often there are instances where an editor has cut scenes that he or she has thought were better, but you have to change them to the way the director wanted them—eventually! I never objected to directors coming into the cutting room. I always thought it was their movie and I like working closely with them and exchanging ideas. I also spend quite a lot of time on the set watching the director working. I started this when I was a young assistant. The "floor," where they actually make the film, was and still is so fascinating to me. When I started, I was meant to take film from one place to another, but I would sneak onto the floor and watch the film being made. Not coming from a film family, someone would ring me up and the person who answered would say, "Oh, I think Anne's on the floor with the director." That used to cause a lot of amusement! I still go down to the floor, I think it's very important. You assimilate a lot by watching the director, hearing him with the actors, seeing what he changes from one take to the next. Also he'll often run over and talk to you, just discuss something with you in passing. A lot of editors in England objected strongly to the director coming into the cutting room. There were articles written in the magazines that the director's place is on the floor and not the cutting room.

Editors said that?

Those were the editors who are probably not working now! Yes, yes, oh, some of them really resented it. They felt the picture was theirs. I know editors even nowadays who have great problems in doing what the director wants them to do. I think you should work very closely with your director and find out exactly what it is that he wants to say or create, and then work towards that. If you come up with something that's a great idea, you should always show it to him or talk to him about it. But your first loyalty, really, is to create what the director first saw as his picture. You've always got to try everything even if you know it's not going to work. Basically, I think one should show them what they want to look at, and then hope they'll see how bad it is! I have a video setup attached to my KEM, so if I think the director is spoiling a scene, I'll video it so I've got it to show him. I can always put it back the way it was. Sometimes they say, "Oh, well, you were right in the first place, go back to the original." So we've got a record of it. If the director wants to compare, if he wants to see what he's done and how it was before, you can watch it up on the screen. Not many editors are using the system I use. We video our dailies so that we always have the equivalent of KEM rolls of them on video. But I cut on a Moviola. I find it absolutely essential to get to know the material on my Moviola. We used this video system first on *Greystoke* in England. It's not worth it if you're not going to have a great deal of material. On *I Love You to Death*, Larry Kasdan resisted the system a bit to begin with, but loved it in the end. The sound department loved it when they had to come in later and change lines; they could put the videos on and immediately find the other takes.

That's rather considerate of you.

Well, I like to have a happy relationship. As a mother and being used to handling children, it helps a great deal in handling directors.

Is that the way you felt about David Lean?

I was terrified of David. I've told him this. I was only a young editor when I did *Lawrence of Arabia*. I'd cut a couple of decent films, but I was very much on the way up at that time.

How did you come to cut Lawrence?

My husband and I were shopping at Harrods on a Saturday morning and bumped into an assistant director named Jerry O'Hara. I asked him what he'd been up to and he said he was about to do a test of Albert Finney for *Lawrence of Arabia* (it was actually called *Seven Pillars of Wisdom* in those days). I half jokingly said, "Have you got anybody cutting it?" And he said, "I don't think we have." So I said, "Give me the number of who to ring." Luck is very often a good factor. But it's not only luck, you have to be a little pushy and follow up on things. So I rang up the production supervisor who said they hadn't got anybody to cut the test, and he would check with David, but for fifty pounds a week, I could do it, with no assistants or anything. I thought, to work with David Lean, it was well worth it! Monday morning I turned up. David was doing a fantastic test with Albert Finney—two scenes, one in the map room and one in the desert—and I cut the film. After we had finished the first of the sequences, David asked me, "Did you cut that material?" "Yes." "Well, go and fetch it and we'll show it." I was terrified. The whole unit was sitting there. I said, "You can't show this to everybody." He said, "Don't be silly, just go and get it." Shaking with terror, I brought it back and showed it to him. I was so frightened I didn't see one cut. At the end David got up and said to the whole unit, "That's the first piece of film I've ever seen cut exactly the way I would have done it!" I felt great, it was very flattering. But I still thought that another editor was going to do the film. A couple of afternoons later, Sam Spiegel said, "Would you like to come up to London with David and me in the Rolls Royce?" I rang my husband and said, "Sam has just asked me to go with them in the Rolls." He said, "It obviously means they're going to offer you the picture, doesn't it?" I said, "I doubt it, I doubt it." But sure enough they did. It's luck plus perseverance. You've got to make your own luck, really. To be cutting for David who was known to be one of the greatest editors ever was nerve-threatening. But he loves being in the editing room. He finds the floor tough going, particularly with the pictures he does—big crowd scenes and that sort of thing—and everybody always looks up to the director and expects him to make instant decisions. *Lawrence* was very complicated to make because they were shooting in the middle of the desert, miles from anywhere, with five thousand mouths to feed and two complete kitchens and water and fridges for the Europeans and the Arabs. It was complicated logistically.

Was it complicated to cut?
It was complicated partly due to the great deal of material and a great many choices, but of course, David had some scenes well worked out. At first, I mostly saw David when he was directing and I would take the film to where he was on location. I would run the dailies with him sometimes in a church, sometimes in a hall. I was going to go to Jordan but there was no means of running dailies there, so David didn't see me for the first eight months. I didn't cut a lot then, as I had to wait for David's notes, then I cut. After the eight months in Jordan, they stopped shooting for three months to write the second half of the script, so I was able to run all the material that David hadn't seen during the eight months he was in the desert. I used to go once a month to Spain to run film with David and then come back and cut it. Even then, he was very much the

director. But once he came back to the cutting room in England, he became his old editing self. He's happy and relaxed in the cutting room; he's another person. I learned a lot from him, obviously, and we worked closely together because we had a very short time. We took thirteen months to shoot the film and four months to cut it! We just cut phenomenally, when you think about it. Seven days a week, until about eleven o'clock at night. Sam Spiegel had already arranged the premiere for the Queen, and you can't really alter the Queen! I now look back and wish we had had a little more time to finesse some of the scenes. In fact, we never saw the whole film until the first screening for the press.

Has Lawrence *been restored to its original intention?*

We put back all those finesses that we could have done but were too late to do once the negative was cut. It is a much better film now. So much meaning was taken out of it. I was extremely lucky to be available to do the restoration. The studios had cut it down for television, too. I had done the two original cuts, but under studio control.

I imagine that being under another's control, the studio or even the audience in preview, can affect the initial vision of the director.

I can't tell you how much I am against previews right at this moment. I've just been through previews on *I Love You To Death*, and I know that before we previewed it, we had a better picture. I still do think it is a very entertaining and amusing film, even though it's not done that well businesswise. We took it to preview and it didn't get such good write-ups. I think a lot of people don't like black comedies and there's nothing you can do about it. What you have to do is make the film the best you can within that genre. We were never going to please all the audiences, so we would have done much better going with what we believed in and not being swayed by what they thought. There were several really good dramatic scenes which shocked a few people. In one scene, Kevin Kline hits Tracey Ullman, and her mother comes in and says she should do something. The next morning, he tries to make it up with her, she slaps him back, and they fall onto the bed. Now every married couple has had this happen, they start by struggling about and end up making love. These two characters had a great attraction for each other, but people called that marriage rape and walked out. It was a marvelous, very dramatic, and very real scene, but we had to tame the picture down. We were so busy trying to get the preview numbers up, including shooting a new ending that cost two million dollars or so. Not to sound snooty, but some people who fill in preview cards can't even spell. The picture had every chance to be good, and I think we bastardized it by making it a much flatter, more simple picture. Not shocking. The picture should have been more shocking. It was a shocking story of a woman hiring killers to murder her unfaithful husband. I think the accountants and agents who run the studios these days are too influenced by statistics. By Friday midnight, they know how much a film is going to make every weekend, how much it will make in its first week, that sort of thing. I only remember this happening in the last few years.

Is there a way to change this trend?
The Directors Guild is trying to stop things like colorization, bastardization, and so on. With *Lawrence*, it's become fashionable to put films together again, finding "out scenes" and putting more back in than they took out. *A Star Is Born* was restored before us, but that was done with a lot of stills. Because of the restoration, I received a lot of acknowledgement as editor—which I think is great for *all* editors. I was taken to premieres, I was interviewed, I went to Cannes. The press conference there was the most terrifying experience I ever had. We were all up on a dais before all these cameras. I was sitting next to Tony Quinn so I was sure they would ask him the first questions. But the first questions came right at me! Why had we done the restoration, what we took out, what we put back. You know how it is when you're scared, your mind goes blank. I couldn't remember what we'd taken in or out, or the complex reasons why we cut it down. But I managed to get by in spite of the fact that on a big picture like *Lawrence*, Sam Spiegel and David Lean didn't really talk to me about why these things were done, so I basically never knew all the reasons it was cut down.

Now that you've answered their questions, what did you put back?
A lot of the early exposition in the map room explaining Lawrence's personality and where he came from. The scene on the balcony where Allenby was conning Lawrence into returning—we didn't put all that back, unfortunately, because Jack Hawkins was dead and the sound was completely missing in half that scene, it was impossible to dub it with another actor. A scene between Lawrence and Ali before he goes off to battle the first time. Some were pictorials. One scene looks like a pictorial but isn't because when Lawrence rides down into Auda's camp, enjoying himself, he could possibly be riding into an ambush but didn't know it. We put back some of the walking across the desert. We had thirty-one miles in film! Somebody, not me, worked that out one day. That's a lot of work.

Did you feel the pictorials ever becoming repetitious?
I used to worry about the length of it sometimes, but David said, "Hang on to it, Annie dear, hang on to it!" When we put the music and atmosphere on, the shots seemed just right. I don't know that without him saying to keep those scenes as long as they are that I would have

done it on my own. You have to keep an open mind when you edit. Some-times you do a great cut on a scene, you think it's terrific—and it is, in itself. But either it doesn't have a place in the film or you only need part of it because when you see the whole film together, you find you have it earlier and it has to go. David once said to me, "Part of what makes a great editor is what you take out, not just what you leave in." Sometimes I would say, "David, you can't lose that, it's fantastic." And he would say, "Out with it, out with it." One brilliant director I worked with many years ago, Robert Hamer of *Kind Hearts and Coronets*, used to shoot me stuff that seemed as if it wouldn't cut together on purpose to see what I'd do with it.

Was he playing a game with you?

Yes, he liked to take actors out left and bring them in right. I had to find something I could cut away to, put between the two. Or even just jolt. It was great training. I wouldn't be beaten, I'd always find some-thing. It's your job as editor to make it work. Though I think all the shots in *Lawrence* hold in the cinema, I don't know whether they hold on video—it wasn't made for video. There was no such thing as video then—it wasn't even made for television. The extraordinary thing was that cinemas were actually selling out of cold drink. Crossing the desert af-fected the audiences so much, they were very strongly carried into the desert. My mother and brother were at the first screening of *Lawrence* and I had to get them endless cold drinks at intermission!

Did the atmosphere also affect you in cutting those scenes?

I think so, because at one point we got to feeling and thinking that it was very hot and slow. People were apparently mesmerized by the noise that we put on the camel's feet and the bits of mirage. We tried to get that feeling into it. Which is why they went to sleep and fell off.

The audience?

Oh, no, no, Lawrence and his companions. No, hopefully, we got the audience into feeling mesmerized.

Your editing paralleled that slowness versus, say, a battle scene.

Lawrence was a very carefully paced film. David loved the desert and wanted to convey Lawrence's love for the desert as well, which was very important. Most people would die if they saw all that desert, but for him it was challenge, excitement, it was where he wanted to be. Like editing, I think it's hard to explain this huge fascination with the desert, but we tried very much to get the emotion he felt. Riding the camel across the desert, going to Arabia—Lawrence was so happy to be part of it. We used shots of him when he looks around and sees the singing and riding. He's in his element. He never was particularly happy—I think this is fairly clear in the film—when he was back with the British in the officers' mess. He didn't feel at home with them.

Your job then was to identify moments when the audience needed to enter Lawrence's head.

That's very important. We used shots of the sun blazing down, or a very, very long, slow shot. Also Lawrence's attraction and fascination with Ali—those two had a very close relationship. One scene had to do with going into Lawrence's head. Lawrence expected to be shot down when he came to the officers' quarters in his Arab clothes and defies Allenby. Allenby is pretty rude to him to begin with, then realizes he can be useful to him so he starts to praise him and sweep him off his feet. I think it was one of the most moving scenes in the film—the military band is playing, Lawrence and Allenby march down, everybody salutes, and Lawrence is listening to every word said to him. David did this swirling move with the camera across the balcony as part of the idea of being inside his head. David didn't expect people to understand it as such, it was just a subliminal way to think. David always says, "I'm not an intellectual." He just has an instinct of what's right and what's wrong.

Is he economical when shooting?

Not particularly, no. Occasionally, if he really knows exactly what he wants. But mostly on his films, he shoots a lot of cover because he knows that in the cutting room it's good to have cover, even if you know what you want to do with it. The only director I've worked with who was really economical with what he shot was Sidney Lumet on *Murder on the Orient Express*. I practically had no two ways to cut on the film. Even if he had close-ups, he often didn't want to use them. I had to fight to get them in because he got it so in his head the way he wanted it to be. He was very nice to me, but he's for speed, time, and motion. I'm very quick, but I'm not used to working so regimented. He did an interesting thing on *Orient Express* in the interrogation scene when Albert Finney was questioning the different passengers in the carriage. He was walking up and down the train talking, or he'd be sitting, get up, and walk back and forth to talk to them. Sidney shot everything facing one direction toward Albert coming in, talking to people, coming out again, then wheel in the next couple and do that part of the scene from that direction also. About four weeks later, Sidney turned around and did all the pieces that went into each sequence. That's not easy to do. Usually if you don't do the reverses on a scene as you go, it's very difficult, it's not going to match, and the actors' moods will change. That was quite amazing. I don't know anybody else who's done that. Cutting all in his head and keeping the performances exactly the same.

You also worked on The Elephant Man *which was based on a stage play. Do you think that, through the editing, more could have been left to the imagination about his deformity?*

As they did on stage? I think it was right to show the Elephant Man for cinema audiences. I think it was probably right *not* to show him for stage audiences. The two have different expectations. The kind of horror that he looked was a plus for the film, in a way. I don't think it would have been right to have him more gruesome, but showing the amount we did was, I think, a right decision. There never was any decision *not* to show him. Originally, the director David Lynch wanted to show the Elephant Man when the doctor Treaves sees him for the first time at the freak show and cries. Mel Brooks, who was the producer of the picture (though he kept very much in the background), said that he wanted the scene shot two ways: so that you could see the Elephant Man at the freak show, and then so that you only saw him later when the nurse sees him for the first time in the hospital. David decided to only shoot it so you saw the Elephant Man when Treaves sees him. When Mel Brooks saw it, he said, "I don't think it's right to see him there. I want you to cut it so that you don't see him until the nurse sees him." So we went back into the film and I had to cut the first part so that you don't see the Elephant Man. We had to completely lose sequences and blow up frames. Being black-and-white and grainy, it didn't matter very much, so we blew the Elephant Man off the side of the screen and cut away from him just before you see him. It was quite a challenge from an editing point of view. I think maybe the film could have been better if the scene had been shot without seeing the Elephant Man in the first place. It was a challenge not to lose the important elements of that scene and do just what you were asking about earlier: *not* see him. I kept stressing the emotion that was in those early sequences. We actually could have seen him much earlier, but it was very right not to see him.

It was more poignant to watch Treaves crying at the Elephant Man off-screen and imagine what he was seeing.

Oh yes, of course. You get preconceived ideas and that sort of thing. John Hurt was made up to really look like the Elephant Man. They did research at the London Hospital where his mask is; I went to see his remains there. When John was in his mask, you really felt he was the Elephant Man; I found myself helping him along up steps. You felt that you had to look after him, this was someone delicate. We shot every other day because John couldn't have that makeup on every day, and we'd shoot as late at night as we could. The makeup dragged on his face; the first makeup they made took his skin off. He used to go in at four o'clock in the morning and it would take four hours, I think, to put it on. We didn't shoot with the Elephant Man for about the first three or four weeks of shooting, only the scenes with Treaves and Bites. The first day we shot with John, we did the lovely scene when the Elephant Man is talking to Treaves's wife about his mother: "What a disappointment I must have been to her." When we ran the dailies in a very small theater, all the secretaries and people who generally didn't come to dailies came; the theater was full. David was curious, "What are all these people doing here?" I said, "They're crew. There's nothing you can do about it now." Toward the end, everybody started sobbing and rushed out of the theater because they were crying so much. David was then delighted that they had all come. I had a great lump in my throat, I could hardly speak. It was really most affecting.

Is such a scene easier to cut because it's easier to find the heart?
It was interesting to know exactly how much one should use of the character and get in the right bits without capitalizing on him. Just have enough and then cut away. *The Elephant Man* was a huge success on video. A lot of younger people didn't go to the cinema to see it. Some of my son's friends told me they'd seen it on video. I said, "Well, why didn't you go to the cinema?" They said, "We didn't want to get upset in front of the girls." Men in particular were frightened to cry in front of their girlfriends. That was one of the reasons it had this enormous success on video because people could be alone in their own sitting rooms.

How did you develop those haunting elephant montages?
They were very much David's mind. It was difficult for him to get over to me what he wanted to do there. We did a lot of experimentation because we had to go through him, through me, then through my assistant who would order from the laboratories. We tried a hundred different speeds with the woman's head turning and the elephant roars. There was no way the image would work without putting the sound on it. It wasn't always easy to explain what we were doing, but sometimes I'd put a piece in that I liked and David would think it was great. Nowadays it would be easier because we would put all those takes on video and David would be able to mix how he wanted it and experiment. The montage where the Elephant Man goes to the theater and sees the pantomimes onstage was shot as a straight sequence, not as a montage. It didn't come off well straight, it was extremely flat. Between David and me, we had this idea of making a montage. We had the music before we had the montage, so we worked from the music and made up this quite entrancing little montage where we superimposed the floor with twinkling silver over the dancing. You got completely what you wanted from the Elephant Man's reactions. It took on a dreamlike quality which it wouldn't have had the other way. I think a perfect example of a montage was at the beginning

of *Orient Express* where the little girl was stolen, which was made up partly of what I cut and partly what Richard Williams did optically with special effects and animation. Those were like the old montages where newspapers spin, calendar pages fly, and little bits of action come through. They were quite an art; generally speaking, I don't think we do that anymore. That's a marvelous way of telling time.

With montage, one associates Eisenstein, who had formularized it almost mathematically.

He could explain it. You'll find some editors can. I remember after I'd been cutting a few years, I picked up Karel Reisz's book on editing and started reading it. God! I realized I'd been doing all these things wrong all these years! I decided that it was better not to read the book. It was full of rules and regulations of what I should or shouldn't do, how many frames I should leave before somebody speaks—that's just not the way I work at all. I'm much more off-the-cuff, and I think I always was. My first film was *Pickwick Papers* and it was the director's first film—the blind leading the blind. The first few days I was having a lot of difficulty cutting the film, and I was showing it to the director every night, which is quite a rare thing to do. We saw dailies at lunchtime and I'd show that cut sequence every night. Very quick for a new editor! I knew that they weren't that pleased with what I was doing, and the more they're not pleased, the more nervous you get. Then the director shot the courtroom sequence and, I don't know, I just did a great job on that. It's a lovely cut, with interruptions and looks from the characters. They all loved it. I suppose that great moment changed my life. I think that if you have the chance for a break, take it; if you've got what it takes to be an editor, you'll come through even if you make a few mistakes. There's only so much you can learn as an assistant, and great assistants don't necessarily make great editors. It's a different kind of mind altogether. You can have theories coming out of your ears, but if you don't have that feeling, you're not going to survive. Anybody can cut two pieces of film together once they know the theory of editing, which is not very difficult. Once at a film school in England, I remember showing *Greystoke* footage of the baby Tarzan. You could have made ten stories out of the thousands of feet of film there was of this little baby. You could make him look up at the apes and be happy to see the apes swinging about, or you could make him look at the apes and be really sad because he couldn't swing. You could make him stand up and look as if he was going towards the apes, or look as if he's running away and falling over. Playing with the leaves, eating the leaves, a little piece of the apes—this is simplified editing. You could make so many different emotional stories out of the footage just from three or four shots of film.

That's the essence of juxtaposition.

That's right. I also used to show a film I cut about World War I pilots, a story about how these kids would go out completely untrained to fly these airplanes. I made aerial battle sequences out of three different films, *Blue Max, The Red Baron,* and *Darling Lili,* library stock which we bought. We had real planes and also radio-controlled miniatures with twenty-foot wingspans and tiny electronically controlled planes, then real miniatures and footage with the live actors flying, firing guns, smiling, all sorts of things. I made complete battles out of this where the airplane is shot down and the plane blows up—but it wasn't the same plane because I used whatever I could get. We had such paucity of material that I had to use footage from different films of planes hitting each other and breaking up. But no one ever noticed. When Malcolm McDowell came in to see the film, he couldn't believe it. He said, "I saw this flyer doing amazing things, shooting down planes, and suddenly I realized it was me!" But these were not scripted sequences. They were just ideas that I made up out of having material. Instinctive. You make it up in your head. In the bath.

Yes, some editors like to "cut" in the shower.

I'm not a showerer because I'm English and it's too cold to shower! I was brought up with no central heating, so I like to lie in a nice hot tub. I don't really try to think there, I'm just relaxed, I guess.

Do you start cutting when you see dailies?

I like to sit back and watch them like an audience, enjoy them, laugh at them, or cry at them. A lot of editors start cutting dailies when they first see them.

Ever feel overwhelmed?

Occasionally. When I've got seven cameras and thousands and thousands and thousands—

Of people and camels.

Exactly. Sam Spiegel and I used to run the camels at double-speed because they get up so slowly! But normally I just sit back, get the impact, and enjoy it. When I see dailies a second time, then I start thinking. It isn't until I get the film on the Moviola that I really start cutting. Different films bring out different things in you.

I imagine that, of all your editing credits, it would be easiest to remember Lawrence of Arabia *because of its epic proportions, the reconstruction and, of course, David Lean.*

Yes. But often it's the little films that I've been very proud of. *The Bofors Gun,* which I'm sure nobody ever heard of, was a little gem, I thought, with a very good director, Jack Gold, who has never been fully recognized. I cut several films with him, including one that I produced, *The Medusa Touch*.

What makes these films so special?

The story they're telling, about real people you get to know and understand. You get inside their lives and souls and care about them. I like to think that I didn't just do big epics. I may do a little film before I begin *Nostromo*. In action films, the characters are not often human beings. These small films were about people and their problems, particularly in the English background. Usually they cost only three or four million, not like here in America where they cost 30 or 40 million.

Besides weather and budgets, what other differences exist between British and American editing?

For one, sound editors work much more closely with picture editors in England and they start on a film before the end of shooting. Here they don't start until more or less you've got a final cut. In England, usually you have one, two sound editors at the most on a crew unless you're on a huge picture. They have very good but larger crews here; even on a simple picture like *I Love You to Death*, we had four, five sound editors. It's just a different concept. In America, they start late and work in a shorter time. Ours start right up front. For *Greystoke*, our sound editor came on early to get ape sounds. There's also a difference in the cutting bench. I have a British cutting bench which has sacks to hold the film; I had one made here. I'm surprised all editors don't have one. If you don't want a sack, you could just have doors that fit in and come out. It's much better for the film to be in sacks. In America, the film is all over the floor. Another of the main differences is that in England we make smaller pictures and we have to work much faster. We've got a reputation for being slow but that's not really true because, generally speaking, we don't have the money. In America, there is much more retake and shooting of extra scenes. In England, we don't do that because we don't have the money to do it, generally. I think American cinema had quite an influence on British editing, as did the French New Wave. A lot of direct cutting. Opticals, dissolves, and fades became very unfashionable. You know, such a simple thing like somebody crossing a road? You don't need to see the person go through that and cross the road and match it. The British were still matching their cuts when the Americans would be jumping people all over to get along with the cutting. So when British films came over, they were considered very slow. Through the 1950s and particularly the 1960s, the younger editors getting their breaks changed that. In the old days, I watched editors who would painstakingly match arms going up.

I think editors cut more for drama now. In England, we make small indigenous pictures like *My Beautiful Laundrette* and *My Left Foot*, which have a style of their own and become hits. I thought *My Left Foot* was extremely well cut, and I'm sure it was the way the director conceived it. They hit right to the center of scenes, which I love.

How have editors been regarded in England?

Well, at the time of *Lawrence* and *Becket*, there wasn't even a British editors award. You see how little the editors were thought of? They didn't even have an award, like the Oscar or ACE [American Cinema Editors] awards. The British award didn't come about until several years later. When I was first in the business, editors were not considered at all, that's for sure. David Lean always says that *he's* much more thought of in America than he is in England as a director. I met Kenneth Branagh the other day and he is already aware of this situation in his career.

Is there an explanation for that attitude?

I don't think the English like success very much. It's something in them. They like people when they're on their way up. As soon as they get up there, they start knocking them. I didn't realize till I came here that I am more highly regarded in America than in England. I don't think they like success very much. I haven't worked on a British-British picture for a long time; my films are really all American pictures that I've worked on in England, most of them brought over here and shown to the heads of the studios and previewed here. So they are American films really. That was why I'd been over here so many trips that I knew I'd fit in. When I got the chance to do *Raw Deal* about four years ago, I came over with two suitcases and never went back. One by one, my children followed me here, and they've all gotten great jobs in the business that there was no way they would have gotten in England.

Have you become "Americanized"?

I don't think so. I don't feel I've been Americanized. I think shortly I will be able to do what I've always wanted to do, which is work freely on both sides of the Atlantic. It's going to be very exciting in 1992 when Europe opens. England is going to have to compete on a very high level— they don't want to be left out of a united Europe. In fact, there seems to be a resurgence of filmmaking in England now. David loves Pinewood Studios, it's his favorite, and wanted to shoot *Nostromo* there, but he's discovered it's full. Shepperton Studios is full. All over the last five years. The government is taking a little more interest in the film industry and they've put up about eight-and-a-half million dollars of seed money—by our standards in America, that's not very much, but it was a million-and-a-half before, so it's a great change.

Do you think the growing competition will make a difference between American and British styles of editing? Or is there a difference?

I don't think there is. Each editor is different. Given the same sequence, I think you'd find all editors would get to the same point, but they'd all get there in slightly different ways. I judged some student films last year. They were each given a sequence of *Dynasty* to cut. Thirty students from all over America—all of them were trying to get to the same place, but some were way off the wall, some did extraordinary things. Some tried to make their editing look flashy; they were doing things for effect, not because it was telling a story. That's really the first important thing for an editor, to help tell the story. That's what you should always keep in mind. All editors everywhere have different styles, it does not depend on country. But what's interesting to me is that almost every year for the last ten years at least, there's been a British editor nominated for an Oscar. At least three, John Bloom, Thom Noble, and Jim Clark, have won in the last ten years. The year I was nominated for *Elephant Man*, another British editor, Gerry Hambling, was also nominated. A lot of British editors are working over here now. They're obviously popular. And I think there'll be more and more coming to America. I think that speaks pretty well for British editing. When you think of how few films we make and how few English editors there are compared with Americans, that's really rather remarkable.

10

Maximizing the Moment

Bill Pankow

It would be easy to characterize Bill Pankow as a horror-genre editor, based on his filmography at this time. But he quickly asserts, "I want to be known for good editing." He echoes nearly every editor when he says that the material dictates the cutting and guides the editor if he or she is open to the material at all stages of the process. Whether hired for horror film, romance, or comedy, Pankow would feel ready to meet the challenges of each because he is open to the film's potentials.

Pankow is equally quick to acknowledge his roots. During his early studies at New York University Film School, he discovered how well editing suited his soft-spoken, meticulous personality. After school, he remembers his "baptism of fire into everything" when he juggled jobs day and night to get hands-on experience in the professional world. But being associate editor to Jerry Greenberg on a number of Brian DePalma's films was perhaps Pankow's ideal education. Many of the principles that have become ingrained in his techniques he attributes to Greenberg, who was willing to hire him as an assistant based on Dede Allen's recommendation, even though he had never served in that capacity. That confidence in his potential helped Pankow grow into the successful editor of such diverse films as *Parents, Casualties of War,* and *The Bonfire of the Vanities*. He emphasizes his give-and-take working relationships with assistants who will one day carry on the tradition as editors. He wants to set an example for them, hoping that they will say, as he does, "I love to come into the cutting room and work."

Pankow's interview analyzes the complex nature of building tension and suspense in any film by careful pacing and point of view, playing with time, and maximizing the material to heighten the visceral response of the audience.

What did you like about editing when you studied film in school?

Editing was a job that no one on a crew that you get assigned to in film school really wanted to do, so I was interested in doing anything I could jump into quickly. In school, as well as in the film business, it's very difficult to make a movie if you don't have any money. Even though they allow a certain amount of film and equipment, unless you have money to finish the film yourself, it's difficult to get it all done. When I finished school, a friend of mine working on a low-budget film shooting in Vermont asked me if I wanted to be their liaison here in New York, to pick up the film at the airport, bring it to the lab, have it developed, work with a bona fide union assistant editor in New York synchronizing their dailies, then put the film on the plane in the evenings and send it back to Vermont so they could view it. Of course, this was not for any money, just for the glory of joining in a project. I ended up learning a lot of technical things like handling negative and track negatives, things you don't necessarily do hands-on in a feature film. I liked the fact that we were among the first to see the product of what was done on the set. A lot of editors, particularly assistant editors (which I was for many years), have a compulsive nature to get things neat and orderly and organized. The bigger the film, the more footage it has and the more challenging it is. And the idea that as an editor you could organize these images—in any way you felt like or chose to—was intriguing. I thought if I could somehow be a part of that, it would satisfy some creative drive I had. Ultimately it did.

Many of the films on which you were assistant or editor seem to be of the horror or mystery genres. Is that your specialty?

That's just coincidence. I have done a lot of mystery, thriller, horror, whatever, but I don't have any particular proclivity or bent toward them. I would like to do lots of different films. *Casualties of War* was a challenge to me, and I would like to do comedies and action films. There's a lot to be said about doing a so-called dialogue picture; it's a challenge to make that as interesting as you can with what the director wants to do, as much as an action film where you obviously have a lot of fast cutting and movement to work with.

Are there techniques you use in the horror genre that you may never use in, say, a romance or action film?

Sure. There are suspenseful moments, certainly at the first blush of editing, and sometimes they stay into the ultimate cut of the film. I milk suspenseful moments for whatever they're worth; if I've overdone them, I back off. I consciously maximize moments of suspense, maximize their potential, whereas in a romantic film or a "dialogue" film, that may not be what's called for because of the nature of the piece.

How do you know how to milk something for tension or suspense?

The director, especially someone like Brian DePalma, speaks to you in the dailies. They shoot the film in a certain way and it has to be cut the way it's presented because sometimes you don't have a lot of other options. I put in all the film shot for a particular sequence, use at least a representative sample of every single angle in an appropriate place, as well as elongate each moment as much as possible with the film I have. When I view that, I may find I've made it too long or put in too many angles that I don't need, but that's how I start. I just jam in every single thing I'm given for as long as it will go, then pare it down.

Is it hard to keep the material exciting?

For me, this work is not the kind I leave at the workplace. When I'm in the middle of editing a sequence or a scene, my mind always works and thinks. Even when I'm walking home to the train, it comes into my head. I try not to get locked into what I've done. In other words, the first time I'll cut it full and look at it. I keep an open mind, adding representative samples of each angle to the piece. This reminds me of all the angles that were shot, and I may decide on a series of shots or even one pair of shots that I think is the best right now. I will go ahead and still try other angles, because sometimes I'm surprised that what I didn't think of right away opens up new avenues. The first approach for me is to cut as scripted. I would never remove or do anything differently than is in the script without consulting with the director and coming to an agreement. You have to start somewhere, that's really a foundation.

Have you sometimes found what works on paper doesn't work visually?

No, not really. Dialogue may take up several pages, obviously, or the exchange between two characters may be in two shots and fill up a whole page. Then at the end of that, there may be a *single* line that says, "Four cars crash through the building, the roof caves in, and all the fire engines arrive"—only one line on the page but fifty thousand feet of film with some directors! So I've never felt that what I got on film didn't work for what was on paper, unless there was something missing or the angles didn't go together. Then we would discuss it and remedy it.

You served a long association with editor Jerry Greenberg. Can you describe that experience and your responsibilities as an associate editor?

Being the assistant editor, the first assistant editor, if you will, means running the cutting room. In addition to that, instead of working closely with Jerry while he was editing, I had an opportunity to edit parts of the film on my own. Often another assistant or the apprentice would work with Jerry in my stead next to him. It just meant I cut certain scenes or sequences or reels, rather than half or all of the film. In *Dressed to Kill,*

I did the end scene at the restaurant where Nancy Allen tells the boy about the penectomy and the prosthesis, a man turning into a woman, and the madhouse scene, the dream where they go into the madhouse. I edited the scene in *Still of the Night* where Roy Scheider comes to Meryl Streep's house when she's getting a massage. What's wonderful about working with someone like Jerry is that, even though he is the editor and will pretty much do whatever he feels is correct, we have an interplay as there is between editor and director; there is a relationship between editor (Jerry the editor) and assistant (in this case, me) which allows me to feel I have input. It's a learning experience to be in on his thought process.

On The Untouchables, *you were coeditor with Jerry.*
    Brian hired Jerry to do the job. Jerry was not available when the shooting began, so he asked me—I'm sure he discussed this with Brian first—if I would start cutting until he became available, then once he did, the two of us would finish up the film. I'd like to lay claim to the so-called Odessa Steps sequence. That sequence, the Bridge sequence, and the big stalking shootout at the end were all scenes Jerry had edited.

Did you cut the apartment scene where Sean Connery was "killed"?
    Yes. I was very happy to see that Brian was pleased with that.

You switch point of view within that one sequence. Initially, you look through the killer's eyes as he watches Connery from the window ledge in a tracking shot; indoors, you switch to Connery's perspective.
    That was how the scene was shot. Connery turns the tables on the killer and begins chasing him. The tables are turned once again when we see the machine gun close up. Then we see the point of view of the machine gun and the killer. The audience is always kept involved and hopefully this maintains tension and excitement.

DePalma uses lengthy shots where the camera tracks or "roams," as in the museum scene in Dressed to Kill. *Does that restrict your creativity?*
    Obviously it does restrict the editing because you would be locked into that shot, although there have been occasions when a shot of that type has been cut into without the audience knowing. In *Body Double*, in particular, Jerry very cleverly edited into a scene and you wouldn't know it. But no, whatever the film calls for. There will be sequences that need to be edited, and there are sequences where a long tracking shot works very well. It's a point of view shot which works extremely well to create tension and suspense. I certainly would never second-guess a director and imagine that he or she shouldn't use that sort of long sequence. It's to the film's benefit that that shot can sustain the drama they're working on.

Some of your films have been compared to Hitchcock. Did you study the "masters of horror" while you were editing?

I didn't feel a need to do that. What I had hoped was that, maybe through osmosis, everything I had learned in an editing room, and all I had seen cumulatively from other films, would allow me to make my own judgments about how films go together to work most suspensefully. On occasion, after I had completed a sequence, I would view one of those films and see how someone else had done it. If there was anything terrific, I would steal it immediately!

How did you know you wanted to steal it?

It strikes you dramatically. I would analyze it and see why it did strike me. Is it because a sudden image came, or a sudden image I was expecting *didn't* come into view? Was it staccato editing all of a sudden? I would see what worked for that film and compare that with how it worked for what I was doing. If anything, combine some of the idea.

Is there a concrete way to measure the pacing of a sequence?

I like to think it's intuitive. If one would tap out a meter for each cut or group of cuts, chances are they would fall in some rhythm. It's gratifying to me when I put music to a sequence that I've edited, say a tension sequence that is silent, and everything falls into a rhythm. It lets me know that I have created a rhythm that seems to work. It's hard to say how one arrives at that from shot to shot. It's just a timing you feel while you're working. The manner in which I work, which is on an upright Moviola, helps me feel that sense of timing. It has something to do with the sound of the machine and the length of time it's running through and how you feel about it. I'm not sure how that timing is created, but when it's wrong you know it right away. That's how you back into it. I prefer to cut some things silent. I become familiar with the dialogue to the point where I know exactly what the characters are mouthing. I often prefer to edit a group of shots without listening to any dialogue. Only after I'm satisfied visually with it do I then add the soundtrack, view it, and decide if adjustments have to be made on that basis. The only things I've ever edited to music were the two music videos I worked on. Bruce Springsteen was a performance video, Frankie Goes to Hollywood incorporated some bits from *Body Double*. In neither case was there a narrative structure, so we were free to do whatever we wanted. With the Springsteen piece, "Dancing in the Dark," we used his performance and I underlined what he was singing with different angles or camera movement to help enhance the song or the performance.

All to the rhythm of the music?

In that case, it definitely was. Most of the time it was probably on the beat. That seemed to work for that. It depends.

Some of your sequences start in silence and music is added later.

Yes, that's a conscious decision made by the composer and the director. Sometimes the editor comes in on that decision to include or exclude music at various points. Very often, there will be a score written for the entire scene and then in the mixing process, it might be decided to only use it in a certain section.

Can you create humor with editing? I think of the gag in Parents *starting with the shot of the attack on the school psychologist, followed immediately by a shot of the parents barbecuing meat.*

Sure, you can occasionally add a visual tag or end the shot abruptly or catch someone in midsentence to make a point, and sometimes that point is humorous. Sometimes it may be an allusion to another film, or what the actor is known for, or a part of the film that you've seen earlier. Most of that has to be scripted, but occasionally you can do something visually or with the sound to make the most of it. You can create that.

Would using details be part of a definition for creating tension? For example, you don't need to see every step a person takes crossing a room, yet in some tense sequences, you include shots of walking feet.

Yes. One thing you need to create tension is time. If it takes a certain amount of time to create tension, there will be a certain surprise or shock or payoff at the endpoint. It's not necessarily true that the longer you take to get there, the more powerful that moment will be, but you do need time to build up the audience's expectation, and either deliver or not deliver something intentionally. You need to use that time to the best advantage. To use the audience's mind. You want the audience to be in the character, to feel what the character is feeling in that time, so that at the endpoint they will experience what the character experiences. That helps an audience's enjoyment of a film. I don't know how to create those moments quickly, it takes me time to build them. I could take a week doing it, then work on other parts of the film. If I wasn't satisfied, I would perhaps go back to that sequence for another few days. Sometimes it's good to edit a sequence and get away from it a little bit. When you view it after a month, your perception of it will change and you'll find a way to blend it in better with the rest of the film.

What makes you select one image over another? As when you suddenly cut to Kevin Costner's eyes during the roof chase in The Untouchables.

That's one of Jerry's scenes, but I subscribe to his theories wholeheartedly. Eyes are very expressive. With visual images, we fractionalize the action. Many things are unique to the film medium as an art form which we as editors can use creatively. Cutting to someone's eyes or *an* eye or a hand twitching—these images that a director provides can enhance or underline a character's feeling. Film is wonderful because the slightest motion can convey some inner feeling or emotion. A raised eyebrow or a slightly upturned lip on a stage would be difficult to perceive, but in film could have tremendous meaning. Yes, on my part, it's always a conscious decision to use those images, either when the director intended them (which is most of the time), or when I think they would be effective.

Do you think techniques like split screens distract audiences? Dressed to Kill *used it to show two characters speaking on the phone.*

It's been said to me that audiences don't like those devices. I don't agree. Everything in filmmaking is an artifice. Depending on how well it's blended into the drama or the emotion of what we're seeing, it can be effective. *Dressed to Kill* is an excellent use of split screen, which Brian has used in many of his films. In that film, it underlined the split personality. We have an image in one scene where Michael Caine sits in a chair and a mirror on an armoire reflects a television. The shot was set up that way, that's not an artificial laboratory-produced split screen. I think Brian always has a clear mind of what effect he wants to achieve.

Do your choices to retain those devices then come from the material?

The material speaks to you either in how it goes together or how the performance or action is underscored or underlined by the editing. We have to look first at the film, present it in the way that makes the most of it, and go in any direction it takes us. Bob Balaban had great ideas for optical effects in *Parents*, the dissolves with the boy running in his dream. In that case, he wanted those devices and we maximized them.

How did you maximize the many dialogue scenes in Casualties of War?

Again, we presented the material in the best way. If it's dialogue, present it in the way that makes it clear to the audience what they're supposed to feel about what's being said, or what the character is feeling about what is said, and what effect it's having on the person being spoken to. Maximize the material by either pausing or not pausing to make the dialogue more powerful and dramatic. Most actors put nuance into their performance. I wonder if sometimes they're afraid that the editor won't recognize the little things they add to their character. Nuances might be easily edited out if we were not conscious of them.

As in Meryl Streep's monologue about her father's death at the end of Still of the Night. *No cutting at all.*

Absolutely. Most editors recognize when to cut away and when to stick with the money. That was definitely a case where we wanted to stick with it. Both Jerry and Bob Benton felt strongly about that. It's important to be conscious of everything the director and the actors do to present this visual drama, to be mindful of all one sees. Certainly the performance is the biggest part, and you have to respect what an actor does in the film. Some actors will be very similar from one take to another, some will give a slightly different bent from one take to another. How those nuances are used often depends on the edge—if you can call it that—that the character takes on in the course of the film. It's nice to have those subtle differences available to you in the performance.

How can editing imply or stylize material that is not subtle? Take the buzz saw sequence in Scarface, *where the gore was implied offscreen, not graphically shown.*

As an editor, you have several tools to work with. One is your mind, one is the film you're given, and another is the audience's imagination. Perhaps that's the most powerful tool you can use in film, the audience's imagination and emotion. When you imply something, you often lead them to a point beyond which the images they conjure in their minds are more powerful than what you show them. By taking them to that point and choosing *not* to show more, you can make that suspense or horror more powerful. Use the imagination that you know the audience brings to the film. In that way, for instance, you can stylize violence by choosing *not* to show the ultimate act or choosing to show pieces of it.

You must have faced such decisions in Casualties of War *with how much to show in the rape and murder scenes.*

Brian consciously decided not to be graphic with the rape scene. We played out—and as the editor, I used—as many of Michael J. Fox's close-ups as I had. Sometimes that results in overlapping the character a little, in terms of where they are physically, because you want to maximize the shots. The emotion grows by what we read on his face. By *not* showing what's happening to the woman, we feel what Michael J. Fox feels, we understand the horror from his point of view. The character's point of view plays a tremendous part in *Casualties*. Most of the film is from Michael J. Fox's point of view, and the audience can get behind that and identify with him. Once you've established that point of view, you don't necessarily have to show a lot because the audience understands that character and knows what he's feeling from his performance.

Did you have more graphic material to choose from if you needed it?

Not in the rape scene in particular. A good instance of maximizing emotion is the scene where the men decide to get rid of the girl on the railway bridge. When they go around the group to decide who's going to kill her, that leads up to where I visually used what Brian had given me to create the suspense he wanted, over whether or not it would ultimately be Diaz who would kill her. At the moment where Diaz would stab her, Michael J. Fox fires his rifle to attract the attention of the Vietcong on the opposite bank. That changes the whole story and that suspense is ended. I maximized the moment by taking time, leading up to the endpoint of that sequence. Once at that point, all hell breaks loose with the shooting. Then when she's stabbed, the whole idea follows about her rising from the dead, if you will, and staggering down the tracks. Again, a case where we maximized all that Brian had shot and all the ideas he wanted to visualize there, showing as many pieces of the woman as I had and going back to her as many times as I thought the audience could stand it, *and* as many times as worked dramatically, intercutting her with all the other action going on. There was very little shot that was not used. I think the sequence is powerful because you also see it through *her* eyes. By juxtaposing her point of view, what she feels, with what Michael J. Fox sees and feels, you create a strong emotional reaction in the audience. Another powerful sequence was when Michael J. Fox was in the hooch with the woman after she had been raped by the others, and he tries to gain her friendship by giving her the cookie. For the first few days, we couldn't help crying just looking at the dailies. What I had hoped, based on that gut reaction, was to have this moment hit home with the audience. I made it as much a tearjerker as possible. Later, of course, Brian came in and we pared it down and made it just the right size. Again, that was a case where the performance leads you to make something happen for the audience.

As another example of the emotive content of an image, there were brief shots, especially in the hooch scene, where Fox and the girl were photographed at a skewed angle.

Yes. Brian uses that angle several times in *Casualties of War* and for me it represented things that either apparently sound normal—like the captain saying this was not really so bad—or look normal but are really askew. The camera itself tells us that and I use it to that effect. You see it when Sean Penn pulls Michael J. Fox out of the hole and during the shooting at the end. Again, in the hooch, here was a man trying to be tender with this abused woman. It's easy to say, "Isn't he a good human being?" but something is not quite right about the situation. She shouldn't be there, he should be doing something else. The angle, just as the juxtaposition of the images, says this to the audience.

That's certainly subliminal.

But the audience knows they're feeling something. I'm presenting that shot in such a way when they're so involved in what's happening that it has an emotional, internal effect on them. They don't stop and think, "Gee, here's a Dutch angle, here's a skewed camera, what does that mean?" But rather it has a subliminal effect as part of the whole of what you want them to feel in the scene.

Are these distinctions and decisions learned-by-doing?

It's learned by what the material leads you to do, by how the film comes together, how the characters behave, what the film becomes as you edit. It's hard to preconceive any of that. You can't say, "In the next two years, I'm going to work on three pictures that have violence, and in one we won't show everything but this one we will show more." In editing, there is no set way. There are probably a lot of wrong ways to do things, but there's no one right way. There are many ways where things can work very well. A particular film and a particular director's vision lead you to edit in a particular way. With good material, of its own volition—and in spite of a bad editor (if there is such a thing), it's going to come together. By the same token, if the material is good and the editor is also good, it's going to be beneficial for everybody. I don't think there's any such thing as a bad film, and then an editor comes in and makes it good. By the time we get the film, it's already acted and shot— there's a limit, obviously. Editors can only work with what they have.

Having had such a wonderful teacher as Jerry Greenberg, how do you carry on the tradition with your assistants?

People who enjoy their work probably do it as well or better than people who don't enjoy it and who don't have anything else that they feel like doing. The emotion and creativity of the job help you make the leap from being around pieces of film in a room to involving your mind in what those images can ultimately do on a screen. I let those who work with me know that, even if they're just cataloguing the film or putting away trims, it's all part of my process. It's all important to what I do, otherwise I can't proceed. I include them by asking their opinion on how I've pre-sented a certain scene or sequence. By involving them, they will become interested in what I do. And that works on two levels: if they're interested in what I do, they will do their job more thoroughly for me; it also helps them be interested in the process enough to want to do it themselves. If they want to do it themselves and they're on my wavelength, it helps me do my job better. I assume that if they're working with me, editing is what they want to end up doing! There's an innate drive that makes people do what they want, like people become bankers because they really like business and people go into or stay in fields because they enjoy them. Enjoyment is the key. I really like what I do, I find it very satisfy-ing, very challenging. I love to come into the cutting room and work. I learn from every experience and every person I come in contact with. I take away something that teaches me more about what can be done the next time.

Does editing style change with each experience on a film?

I guess there are people who have one certain style. It could be almost coincidental in that if an editor does an action film well, then someone doing another action movie may want to hire that editor. So you could say that editor has a fast-paced, bang-bang-socko style. But that same editor, given another film with different material, will probably do a wonderful and totally different job. Overall, there are certain subtleties of style, like the way you handle dialogue. Some editors have no qualms about overlapping dialogue and use that to further the drama. Some editors don't like to overlap dialogue and find the punctuation of the end of the line or silence is what they use to change shots. I don't preconceive how my style is going to work from one film to another, even from one scene to another. It depends on what is given and how it ultimately comes out the other side.

For the audience.

Right. If they're involved, they won't see anything except what you want them to be involved in. If the film affects you in a great way—whether it's a scary way or a touching emotional way, I like to think that the editing helped that feeling. The actor, actress have a lot to do with that, the cinematographer—where he or she puts the camera—obviously the director's vision are all part of creating that feeling. We as editors add to that. When the film works on the level it's intended to work, the editor has contributed to that effectiveness, emotionally or spiritually. Getting the audience's involvement. We choose to present those images at those times. To keep the audience hooked into that emotion or action is what we want to do.

11

"Percussive" Editing

Paul Hirsch

1970 *Hi, Mom!* directed by Brian DePalma

1972 *Sisters,* directed by Brian DePalma

1974 *Phantom of the Paradise,* directed by Brian DePalma

1975 *Obsession,* directed by Brian DePalma

1976 *Carrie,* directed by Brian DePalma

1977 **Star Wars,* directed by George Lucas (Coeditors: Marcia Lucas, Richard Chew)

1979 *The Fury,* directed by Brian DePalma
King of the Gypsies, directed by Frank Pierson

1980 *Home Movies,* directed by Brian DePalma (Editing Consultant)
The Empire Strikes Back, directed by Irvin Kershner

1981 *Blowout,* directed by Brian DePalma

1982 *Creepshow* (*The Crate*), directed by George Romero

1983 *The Black Stallion Returns,* directed by Robert Dalva
Footloose, directed by Herbert Ross

1984 *Protocol,* directed by Herbert Ross

1986 *Ferris Bueller's Day Off,* directed by John Hughes

1987 *The Secret of My Success,* directed by Herbert Ross
Planes, Trains, and Automobiles, directed by John Hughes

1988 *Steel Magnolias,* directed by Herbert Ross

1990 *Coupe de Ville,* directed by Joe Roth
Nuns on the Run (Consultant), directed by Jonathan Lynn

1991 *Hutch,* directed by Peter Faiman (Coeditor: Adam Bernardi)

* See Appendix for complete list of editing awards and nominations.

Paul Hirsch's early nonfilm endeavors in New York were a precursor of things to come. He majored in art history at Columbia College, where he spent hours in dark rooms looking at projections on the wall. At Columbia Architecture School, he studied structure and design. And there was music: Hirsch's high school experience as a percussionist guided his rhythm and timing. His studies in the different arts have helped him develop "editing equations" (Editing is like . . . architecture, sculpture, choreography) to help describe what he does in film.

Hirsch was smitten with making films in architecture school when he was assigned a photographic essay to shoot people and their surroundings. After wielding a 16mm Bolex and discovering the thrill of stopping and reversing frames on a viewer, Hirsch abandoned architecture for film. "I had all this footage and I didn't know what to do with it. So I thought I'd better learn about editing." He delivered packages for a film company, worked for a negative cutter, and assisted on trailers. He remembers the first project he was ever assigned to cut was "the 8mm film shot by the boss of the company on his vacation in South America." Hirsch also worked on featurettes, documentaries about the making of a feature film used for publicity. Before long, he met Brian DePalma and cut *Hi, Mom!*, his first feature credit as editor and the first of eight collaborations. Hirsch proceeded to cut films in nearly every genre and to win an Academy Award for *Star Wars*. "I felt I had achieved more than I wanted to in editing, and there really wasn't any room for me to grow anymore." He discovered himself at a fork in his professional life.

This interview presents an editor in transition. Hirsch looks at directing as a way of growing again. "Directing a movie is painful," he acknowledges, as are various aspects of editing, like screening dailies. "But if I'm going to experience pain, it should be a new kind!" Hirsch does not discount a return to editing in the future, but for now he is headed toward directing. The bond between editing and directing is inextricable, and Hirsch can once more draw from his experiences as he moves into the next phase of his career.

Hirsch's discussion of tension builds upon Pankow's treatment of the subject. His analysis clearly shows how music and filmic rhythm combine to create intellectual, emotional, visual, and auditory climaxes. As both men separately have worked on a number of Brian DePalma's films, an interesting scholarly study could be done of the construction of tension, suspense, rhythm, and illusion by two different editors. Such an analysis would undoubtedly illustrate how editing style is an extremely difficult term to define. Although editors develop their own preferences, which they may repeat from film to film and which seem to constitute unique styles, how much really is "individual" and how much is due to the director's own style and what the film itself requires?

Godard said, "Photography is truth, and film is truth twenty-four times a second."

Do you believe that?

Film is truth, but it's all an illusion. It's fake. Film is deceptive truth! When you cut back and forth between two characters having a conversation, one of them may have been shot in the morning, the other in the afternoon. And every line spoken by each of the characters might have come from a different take. Film is not true twenty-four times a second because by joining two pieces of film shot at different times, you're implying that they happened consecutively, in the instant it takes to see them, when in fact they may have been shot months apart. One of the old definitions of art is deception. The Artful Dodger—it's all about deceit. All a fakery. When you see close-ups of Meryl Streep and Robert DeNiro in a scene, it looks as if they're talking to each other at that moment, and the emotion going on is happening between them at that moment, but it is all an illusion. So the shooting of the movie is the truth part and the editing of the movie is the lying part, the deceit part.

The manipulative part.

Well, manipulative has a—

Negative ring to it?

So do lying and deceit! In the theater there's more willing suspension of disbelief, whereas when you're shooting a movie, people are constantly judging it against their perception of reality. They say, "Oh, that looks phony, that set looks phony. People don't talk that way." There's a constant comparison to reality. Editing is very interesting and absorbing work because of the illusions you can create. You can span thirty years within an hour and a half. You can stretch a moment in slow motion. You can play with time in extraordinary ways. There was an invisible wipe in *Obsession* in a 360-degree pan. The idea was to have a continuous pan that would cover, say, twenty years from the time Cliff Robertson is bulldozing the land to when it's all green and landscaped and he's in the same place looking at the monument to his dead wife. That wipe joining two shots made it possible to bridge that time span.

You've worked with split screens in some of the DePalma movies. How does that affect the depiction of time in film?

Basically it takes the audience out of the movie. It takes them out of any kind of reality that you've created. The technique works on an intellectual basis. At its best, it can give you two different perspectives on the same event, or give you more information than you can get from a single frame at a time. It can show the simultaneity of things going on at the same time. But you don't *feel* anything. Engaging your intellect takes away from feeling what's happening.

Do you consider feeling more important than thinking in a film?

Personally, yes. If you want to engage the audience's interest, that's one thing, but if you want to involve them emotionally, it's a device I would stay away from. In *Carrie*, Brian shot a whole sequence in split screen and locked himself into it by including camera stands and lights and sandbags in the shot so that half the frame was unusable. When he looked at it all put together, everybody said, "You can't make this whole thing a split screen. This is horrible." So he finally gave up and said to me, "Just recut it any way you want." I put back as many full-frame shots as possible, but there were some shots where I wasn't able to use the full frame and I was forced to go back and forth between split screen and full frame a bit. Then of course, we ran into a problem of screen direction: there was a big close-up of Carrie on one side of the screen and she's supposed to be looking at things happening on the other side. At one point, she was looking from right to left, and then in the same shot she turned and looked left to right, so it looked like she was looking off the screen. We did a trick where we moved the panel across the frame, so that the direction of her look made sense. It got very complicated, more than we bargained for. Historically, split screen has worked best in phone conversations, such as in *Pillow Talk* or *When Harry Met Sally*. And Coppola did it without an optical in *Tucker*, he had people talking long-distance on the same set. People have played around with it.

How did editing help create tension in these early DePalma films?

Suspense is created in an audience by presenting them with the threat of something awful happening within a given time. You can't have suspense unless you are working within a limited time framework. The famous example of that is *High Noon* where they had a picture without any tension that was made to be very tense by the introduction of periodic cuts to a clock showing the clock getting closer and closer to noon. So in a sense, in all suspense sequences, you have to have "a clock" going. You set the clock in motion and then you can play with that time by either elongating events or compressing them. You play on the audience's sense of time elapsing against this deadline. The anticipation of the dreaded events can be heightened by accelerating the rate of the cutting so that it gets faster and faster and faster until the clock strikes twelve!

You as editor also have an internal clock built into you.

Right. You can increase the tension by shortening the cuts. Sometimes I would do it mechanically in the sense of counting the number of frames in each cut, and I'd say, Well, this cut is sixteen frames, I'm going to make the next cut fourteen frames, then twelve, then ten, then eight, and six. You can't do it totally mechanically, but you can approach it that way, then make adjustments, depending on the images and how quickly they read on the screen. The audience's nervous system starts to respond to the impact of the cuts, and their heart rate and heartbeat and everything starts speeding up along with the pace of the cutting and creates a feeling of excitement.

That's certainly true with Star Wars.

In *Star Wars*, the end of the battle scene is exactly the same editing problem as dumping the bucket of blood on Carrie. It's the same scene in a way: the Death Star is going to blow up the planet or they're going to dump this bucket of blood. That's what you're afraid of. The difference between Brian DePalma and George Lucas is that Brian makes the dreaded thing happen whereas George saves the day! Anyway, if somebody is tied to a log and struggling to get free, that's kind of boring. Physical difficulty is boring. However, if the log is tied to a buzzsaw, then it becomes interesting because you realize the clock is going and they're running out of time. Or somebody's tied to a train track, it's boring unless there's a train coming! That's what I mean by starting the clock. If somebody's tied to a track and you cut to a train approaching, you've created an element of tension because you're saying, "Time is running out." You can't create suspense without telling that to the audience.

How do you approach cutting montages? You had a number in The Secret of My Success.

I'll try to find a piece of music which I think will be right for the scene as I imagine it to be when it's edited, and I use that music as a guide for me to cut the picture to. If I pick the right piece, we can use it as a guide to the composer in writing the final music, or sometimes we license the actual music and use it in the final score. Editing can then be the conjoining of movement and music. Editing is like a lot of things, I'm always comparing it to other things. It's like architecture in terms of the way you get involved in structure. It's like sculpture in the sense that you can take away or add on and make adjustments the way you do when you're modeling clay. And in another sense, it's like choreography, which is the organization of movement through space over a given period of time, usually against a piece of music. Editing can be the organization of two-dimensional movements on the screen within a given period of time, perhaps set against music. When you're cutting a sequence to music, you're choreographing all the movements within the frame. It can be a physical movement by an object or a person, or it can be a camera movement. It's "motion" pictures. You try to organize the motion that's in the frame in a way that captures the music as a dance will capture the music. In *Footloose*, for instance, the trick of the opening sequence was to try to find the movement of the feet that most closely reflected what was happening musically in the measure that it was set against.

And later on too, when Kevin Bacon dances in the barn.

Now the dancing in the barn was a difficult sequence because they changed the music, so he danced it to one song and then we replaced the song with another and had to reedit because the dance he did to the original song didn't work when the new song was put in its place. It was the same tempo, but the phrasing, the lyric, whatever, didn't work. If you change the music, you change the scene. You have to change the picture to reflect the music. I'm told by music editors that I'm one of the few picture editors who will change a picture to work with the music; some picture editors won't change the picture. I feel it all has to go together and sometimes it's easier to move the mountain. I always wait to cut negative until I see the picture against the music so that I can still keep making adjustments in the picture to match the music.

What was the story behind the art museum montage in Ferris Bueller's Day Off?

That's an interesting one because the piece of music I originally chose was a classical guitar solo played on an acoustic guitar. It was very arrhythmic and sort of conversational in its style, and very personal and nonmetrical with a lot of *rubbato*. I cut the sequence to that music and it also became nonmetrical and irregular. I thought it was great and so did John Hughes. He loved it so much that he showed it to the studio but they just went "Ehhh." Then after many screenings where the audiences said, "The museum scene is the scene we like least," he decided to replace the music. We had all loved it, but the audiences hated it. I said, "I think I know why they hate the museum scene. It's in the wrong place." Originally, the parade sequence came before the museum sequence, but I realized that the parade was the highlight of the day, there was no way we could top it, so it had to be the *last* thing before the three kids go home. So that was agreed on, we reshuffled the events of the day, and moved the museum sequence before the parade. At the same time, John decided the problem with the museum sequence was the music and he came up with a song for it. We put the song over the scene as it was, and the cutting didn't work at all. Everything was off because the cutting was tied to the idiosyncratic performance of the classical guitar piece, so I had to change the picture to reflect the music. Because the music was regular, the cutting then became regular, and I didn't like it as much. Then we screened it and everybody said they loved the museum scene! My feeling was that they loved it because it came in at the right point in the sequence of events. John felt they loved it because of the music. Basically, the bottom line is, it worked.

That was a poignant sequence because it seemed the emphasis shifted to Ferris's friend Cameron. The film assumed his point of view as he was growing up to confront his father.

That was deliberate. Essentially, the picture was always about Cameron and what effect this "day off" had on him. He changes, Ferris doesn't change. The protagonist is usually the one who changes. But that was built into the material, frankly. There was a sequence at the museum where Cameron was staring at the Seurat painting and he gets closer and closer to the dots and is absorbed in the little girl and begins crying.

Ferris's line at the end, urging us to stop and notice things because life goes so fast, seems emblematic of the editing process. Could you comment on how editing helps us notice, or not notice, little things?

Well, all the stuff that's done outside the editing room is really designed to be edited. The amount of work that goes into the script, the set, the costumes, the lighting, the shooting, the acting, all that is devoted to accumulating the raw materials that go into the editing room as dailies. Dailies are unwatchable, except if you're being paid to do it, and they come out to be the movie that you are willing to pay to see! So that transformation of boring, unedited film into something that is an emotional experience is what happens in the editing room. It's the magical point in the process of making films because you're creating an illusion about time. By manipulating time, you can create the impression that things that are impossible in real life can actually take place. It involves making choices about which details, in all this mass of footage that you get, to include and in what order. That's sort of reduced to its barest minimum: editing is choosing what's to be in the film and in what order.

What about in Steel Magnolias *where you had to balance six lives while they interacted?*

That's part of the writing also, but for instance, in cutting a group sequence with a lot of women, you'll find at times that you've been away from one of them for a while and you cut to her just to keep her alive in the scene, or else you lose track of her. So that's a part of the choices you make. *Steel Magnolias* was a problem because I thought the performances were so good I never wanted to cut away from anybody. But if I didn't cut away from anyone, I would never show the other performances that were going on in reaction to the action taking place.

Why didn't you underscore the hospital and death scenes with music?

I think to put music on that sequence would have really made it into a TV movie, and that was the only scene in the movie that I was absolutely convinced could not have music. Georges Delerue agreed. In fact, I toyed with what would happen if we put music on this scene. I got the saddest piece of music I could find, "Adagio for Organ and Strings" by Albinoni. I put that music on that scene and it made the material *less* sad. It made the sequence more bearable, and the idea of that sequence is that it should be a difficult sequence to bear. Make it easy and then it's a TV movie! Dramatically, it's supposed to be unbearable.

Tension was created there by the spare use of hospital sounds.

"Quiet" is an effect. And not having music is a way of scoring as well. Where the music *isn't* matters as much as where the music is.

You played with that concept earlier when the daughter is having her diabetic attack in the beauty salon.

There was sound. There was a very strange chord that swelled up. It wasn't music, it was more of a musical effect. A strange dissonant chord and the strings swelled, and we put the voices into echo at the same time as the camera pushed in on her face. The idea was to convey the impression that we were inside her head. That was what we were doing, and the music helped us make that leap out of reality into a new sort of internal reality. We're now hearing the voices as she heard them as the attack came on her. The music in a way was the attack. As she takes the orange juice and starts to recover, the music goes away. One of the things I feel very strongly about and enjoy doing more than anything is putting music against film. In my new job with 20th Century–Fox, I worked as a consultant for a British comedy called *Nuns on the Run*. One of the things I did was to throw out the music and put in a new score, which was tremendous fun.

You're certainly drawing on your musical and art backgrounds.

I majored in music in high school. I was a percussionist, which has a great bearing on the way I approach my work. And at Columbia College in New York, I majored in art history, so I spent a lot of hours sitting in dark rooms looking at projections on the wall—a precursor of things to come, I guess! The way percussion is related to editing is that it's all about time, dealing with different portions of time, dividing time into very small bits or different bits that relate to each other in different ways. I like to say that I learned more about editing from Beethoven than from anyone else! For example, study the sonata allegro form and the rhythmic structure of Beethoven's symphonies in terms of statement of theme, development, recapitulation, and so forth. You can create punctuation by the timing of the cut. If you establish a certain pace, and then change the tempo at a certain point, you break the rhythm and that can act as a period on a sentence. If you want to start a whole new paragraph, sometimes it's important to use a dissolve which the audience interprets as a paragraph or a chapter.

In Obsession, *at one point, you had seven dissolves in a row, as Cliff Robertson meets the woman who looks like his dead wife. But in* Steel Magnolias, *you cut from season to season. What were the feelings behind choosing two different passages of time?*

Well, I had edited DePalma's *Hi Mom!*, *Sisters*, and *Phantom of the Paradise*, which were all very kinetic, hard-edged, straight-cut, quick-cut films. *Obsession* was a romantic mystery and wide screen, and I wanted to adopt a more lyrical style because I felt the material required it. It's a very stylized picture in terms of the look of the film, the location, the subject matter, very lush and romantic, and I felt that dissolves were appropriate. In *Steel Magnolias*, we did use dissolves in a couple of places. We dissolve to the baby when he's having his first birthday. But a lot of times the cut was dictated by the fact that the "button" on the season we were leaving was a joke. One of the outs is when Shirley MacLaine says to Olympia Dukakis, "The older you get, the sillier you get," and she answers, "The older you get, the uglier you get." It's a big laugh, so it didn't make sense having a dissolve coming on top of that line. The cut is the punctuation for the button on the line.

Is that a rule for cutting comedy?

I don't know if you can expound any kind of rules or principles, but I do know that you can sharpen a laugh with timing. It's intuition. The only thing I've ever worked by throughout my career is how it feels to me. I've never tried to second-guess how a director is going to like this. Or the audience. My only approach has always been, how do I make it good enough for me? Intuition is the only thing you can go on.

Did you have difficulties editing special effects on Star Wars?

I have a motto. "If there's a problem, there's a solution. If there's no solution, there's no problem." You can't get upset about things you can't control. But it was a hard job. George Lucas designed the picture as a heavily encrusted jewel box with thousands of little diamond solitaires. Every single one of these effects was like a little ornamentation and every one had to be put in place, so it took a lot of time for Industrial Light and Magic to put each of the elements into a single shot. There was a lot of detail in it, more than the average film.

You certainly have a variety of films to your credit.

Yeah, I've done comedies, musicals, suspense films, action films, sci-fi. Then when I did *Steel Magnolias,* I finally did a drama, which I had never done.

Have you ever done documentaries?

Early in my career I did featurettes, which are documentaries about the making of a feature film used for publicity purposes. The first thing I ever cut was one on *The Thomas Crown Affair,* a ten-minute featurette they asked me to cut down to three-and-a-half minutes. The client liked it and gave me an assignment to do a featurette from scratch for *Chitty Chitty Bang Bang.* I did a montage to the song and learned how to say "Chitty Chitty Bang Bang" backwards—"nyab nyab itich itich."

I'm sure that's come in handy for you. How about directing?

I'd like to direct a feature film. That's what I'd like to do.

Is that where you're headed?

That's what I hope.

Directing and editing go hand in hand.

Yes, the director is shooting material designed for the editor, so it seems to me that editing is good preparation for directing because you can see what works and have an idea of what you need to go out and get.

Are you able to watch for editing when you go to the movies?

I'm usually not aware of the editing on first viewing, unless it's great or horrible. Horrible is everything botched, it doesn't make any sense at all and you can't figure it out. Horrible is horrible. Like rotten eggs. Great editing takes your breath away. Every moment is nailed to perfection and you're dazzled by the film.

Wouldn't that take you out of the film?

Only to the degree that a great performance will take you out of the film. When you watch Meryl Streep, you can say, "What a brilliant actress," and still be involved in the film.

Can you watch your own films?

It's very painful just because I've seen them so many times. See, when they come out to the public, fresh and new, to me they're dead. A film is sort of like a living, breathing organism as long as you can make changes in it. Once the negative is cut, the film is mixed, the optical track is married to the picture negative and you have a composite print, which is the way the public sees it, then to me it's a mummified corpse! It's no longer alive, it's an artifact that has no life. It's just a thing and I can't watch it. It's unbearable. And this is the cruel trick that the film gods play on the worshipers at the shrine!

Have you become frustrated with editing?

In my case, it's not that I was unhappy doing it. I was happy, and then at a point when I became dissatisfied with my potential for growth—you know, a man's reach should exceed his grasp—I felt I had achieved as much as I wanted to in editing, and there wasn't any room for me to grow anymore. So I just felt I had to take a shot at trying to achieve more than that. A year from now, I may be back in the editing room. I'm not ruling it out. Being away from it, I may find that there are things about it I didn't appreciate. I was just getting burned out doing it over and over again. Looking at dailies is painful.

Editors say it is an exhausting process.

It's painful! Looking at answer prints over and over again is painful. I mean, directing is painful too, from all I understand. But if I'm going to experience pain, it should be a new kind instead of an old familiar kind.

Do you think other editors feel frustrated because they are underacknowledged for their work?

I think that the good editors have been undermined by the poor ones. There are some editors still working who do it sort of "by the numbers," who don't have any feeling of showmanship or don't have an instinct for what's right. They put the film together as best they can in their relatively inept way, then go to screenings with the director and take notes about what he wants changed. They're functioning as a pair of hands, they're not contributing, and therefore they're not really worthy of respect by creative people who bring the movie together. There are editors out there, working professionally, who don't have a clue as to what editing is about. Then there are editors who take a very active role. They try to elevate everyone else's work, and they're in a position to do that as an editor. It's their job to make everybody look as good as possible—the actors, the cameraman, the director, the screenwriter. The editor is the final filter before the film reaches the audience. If your standards are high enough and you can apply them to every aspect of the film, you can make a difference.

How will you treat your editor when you're a director?
    With the respect he or she deserves.

Keeping the Beat

Donn Cambern

1989   *Ghostbusters II,* directed by
Ivan Reitman (Coeditor:
Sheldon Kahn)

* See Appendix for complete list of editing
awards and nominations.

1991   *The Tender,* directed by
Robert Harmon (Coeditor:
Zach Staenberg; also
Coproducer)
The Butcher's Wife, directed
by Terry Hughes

After more than thirty years in the business and still going strong, Donn Cambern describes himself as having been "on the cusp" between the demise of the old studio system and the start of the free-lance hustle. He has seen major changes in both the mechanics and the look of editing. He was, in fact, instrumental in shifting both. With Sheldon Kahn, Cambern developed the organizational system for the KEM flatbed. Whether it is used for cutting, viewing, or both (and the debate between Moviola and KEM partisans continues to this day), the KEM expanded the editor's capacities. Cambern also speaks of his famous counterculture film, *Easy Rider*, as pioneering the look and impact of editing in the late 1960s.

Cambern's film experience has been imbued with a lifelong love of music. Much of his discussion returns to the many musical considerations that challenge editors: the subliminal effects of rhythm, "eyeball riffs," the art of the "cheat" to enhance rhythm, and the natural running-time of a perfectly edited film. His argument on the latter point invokes Toscanini and challenges the television networks that chop out minutes from classic films to fit in commercials. Cambern has intriguing views on ego in editing, and how little room there is for it if the film is to be successful. He believes, as many others do, that each film dictates its treatment and presentation. His discussion of style adds a new aspect to those discussed in the preceding interviews. Attempting a definition, Cambern says that style may lie not so much in an editor's preferences for certain techniques, but rather in the style of caring that each editor contributes to films.

Your background was a mix of film and music, wasn't it?

My father was a music publisher affiliated with Carl Fisher, an old New York publishing firm. My mother was a professional harpist, joined the L.A. Philharmonic in 1919 when she was eighteen. She was probably the first woman in any major orchestra in the United States. After about fourteen years, she started to get into radio work and played at almost every studio. In the RKO days, the Astaire and Rogers days, she was in those orchestras, and every time I hear the harp in a film like *Top Hat*, I get a particular delight out of it. I probably heard the harp before I was born. So music played a very important part. I knew I had a very strong desire to find some facet of the motion picture business because I loved movies tremendously. I used to set the marquee every Wednesday and Saturday night in a movie theater in town so I could have free admittance. It was always in my blood to get into the business. Consequently, when I started university, I majored in music with the purpose of writing music for films. I did some scoring of films back in the late 1940s, early 1950s at UCLA, but once I graduated I started to realize I had certain limitations musically and found myself thinking more about using my music skills in editing. I was able to get a job at Disney's in 1953 as a messenger and talked my way into the editorial department, became a music editor there. I was at Disney's until 1959, went to Fox as a music editor under Lionel Newman, and then to UPA. I worked on one of the most delightful shows, *Mr. Magoo's Christmas Carol*. Over at Desilu I did some *Untouchables*, and started with Earl Hagan who was a well-known television composer doing shows like *The Dick Van Dyke Show*, *The Joey Bishop Show*, *Andy Griffith*, *Gomer Pyle*, and *I Spy*. Spent several seasons with those people, then formed a music editing and sound effects company with shows like *Tarzan* and *The Monkees*. I got bored with music editing and thought more about picture editing. One day a man walked in—the proverbial man walked in the door with a movie, looking for help editing. That movie was *2000 Years Later*. Believe me, I had never really edited a movie at all. I just had watched. In a sense, editing is like the old guild process that's trial and error and you learn from other people. There are very few textbooks and the more you get your hands on the film, the more you understand how to manipulate it. The film was independently made. We worked very hard during the week and usually on Friday nights we would screen at the Beverly Hills Hotel for potential investors and try to get another eight or ten thousand dollars to shoot more. I asked Jerry Sheppard, the supervising editor of *The Monkees*, to look at the material I cut because I wanted someone's opinion who knew more about editing than I did. He was doing the Monkees picture *Head* and didn't want to do *Easy Rider* next, so he recommended me. I met Dennis Hopper, we got along fabulously, and that's literally how *Easy Rider* came into my hands. That just opened up a whole new avenue for me.

You were also instrumental in developing the KEM system. Can you describe that experience?

I had become aware of the KEM while doing *Blume in Love*, with Shelly Kahn as my assistant. This was in 1971. I had heard about the KEM and thought it was a tool with wonderful possibilities. The director, Paul Mazursky, liked the idea very much because of the size of the screen, the flexibility in using the machine, the ability to immediately compare one performance against another in the movie. The KEMs used up to this point had been in *Woodstock* and in documentaries, so in essence we were starting completely fresh. We had to train ourselves on the KEM and go through a period of dealing with the mechanics—just like learning to drive a car, a pure mechanical sense. Film basically travels left to right, so when I'd make a mistake, usually being terribly out of sync with dialogue to picture, I would back up right to left, find that point, analyze what I did wrong, and tuck that into my experience. Shelly, in the meantime, was dealing with building rolls of film to make them usable for me, and devising a coding system to *find* the film easily. The KEM system has evolved into a far simpler system than the Moviola system, and we all played a great part in doing that. After some time, the KEM became user friendly, as they say. Usually, once the film is put into a first cut, which is the editor's real first attempt to get the film on its feet, the director would look at it and say, "But I remember there was a certain close-up where she did so-and-so and . . . " So you'd go back to the room and look for the shot. Sometimes it was never shot or it was on B negative and never printed! Sometimes you'd find it at the bottom of your trim bin. The KEM system removed all that searching because whatever was not in the film was on rolls in sync that you could play on another picture head on the same machine. And you could say to the director, "These are the takes that were printed, here is everything. Did you mean this one or what other?" Then you could take that piece and put it in place of the other piece. It became a marvelous tool for the director to do comparisons. We were literally the first to devise that system. It used to be that to find film, you would look at a piece, see the code number, and tell your assistant, "Give me code number so-and-so." They'd look through boxes to find that one roll of film. Or they'd go to the code book and then to the rack to pull it out. As it is now, I'll look at a code, say "Bring me the B3000 box," and that's it. It's a direct line of communication and the whole system is predicated upon laying your hands on the film that much quicker. Interestingly, at Warner Brothers where we were doing *Blume in Love*, I'd invite other editors in the "compound area" to come in any time to try the machine, watch me work. Nobody came in! It's one thing when a man who has been on the Moviola for forty years is not interested, but I didn't understand when someone my age or younger wouldn't even give it the time of day. Shelly and I were unconsciously looking to find a way into a very difficult business and gain new experiences. So Warner Brothers was the first major studio that had a major film edited on a KEM. When I went over to Fox, they bought their first machine, then I went to Universal and they bought their first. There was a lot of squawking because it was very expensive, but by that time a certain fascination had started to build. They are much more in use, although there are not a large number of us who edit *only* on the KEM.

Some editors prefer the Moviola because it lets them handle the film intimately, unlike the KEM. Video is virtually removing that experience.

Very definitely. Film editing is a tactile process and the Moviola has meant a lot to all of us. When you edit on the Moviola, you're running at twenty-four frames a second, and I think unconsciously it begins to develop a rhythm of twenty-four and variables divided into twenty-four—eight, six, twelve, whatever. I had this theory for a while that my cuts had a six-frame lead before the dialogue would start, or a four-frame lead, or eight-frame. Five or seven? No, somehow it didn't work. Wait a minute, that's crazy! So on the KEM I played around with odd numbers. Certain patterns emerge and have a similarity, and there is the desire to break those patterns.

As you started work in features, you also continued in television with some unique shows, didn't you?

There was a musical variety series called *Something Else* sponsored by the American Dairy Association, true to the forerunner of MTV today. We would get a group of maybe four artists, lip-sync the songs and shoot in natural locations all over the United States. There was always a choreographed dance number for each show and John Byner was the host. I started directing those right after *Easy Rider*, we'd do maybe four shows back to back, traveling all over. I called on so much of my editing experience to pull me through. I had ideas how to shoot the dance numbers, how to cover them, how they would go together. I also directed a National General series of shows on outstanding music groups. I did Blood Sweat and Tears on tour behind the Iron Curtain, twenty-one concerts in twenty-seven days. Five cameras—the equipment came out of Samuelson in England. A full planeload of camera equipment, lights, musical equipment, everything except generators which we used from wherever we were. We would do shows in large arenas, hockey arenas, twenty-five thousand people. When I came back, I did more of *Something Else*, but realized I didn't want to continue directing musical shows. I wasn't experienced in directing and not really that experienced in editing. I wanted to get back into the editing room and learn what it was about. With all that behind me, I edited *Drive He Said* for Jack Nicholson; that went into *The Last Picture Show* and *Steelyard Blues*. Each film helped me get the next picture, which is truly what happens to us in this business, particularly getting started. Almost every editor I know, even today, as successful as we can be, always wonders where that next picture is going to come from and how soon it's going to come. It's a facet of the business. I also became an editor during the time the major studio system was changing. We were losing studios. There used to be editorial departments. Now you don't work for a studio; you come in, do a movie, and when you're finished, you leave and go to another place. You might edit the movie in an apartment suite—I did *Jo Jo Dancer* in a medical building. I went through that era, which was really great because I had started while the major studios were still functioning strongly and had the opportunity to develop as they started their demise. That was instrumental in my grasping the idea of working not only independently, but feeling free to work independently and going after projects. At times it turned into a real scrap to get films under all kinds of circumstances and I think that added to the experience of editing film. When you are without certain resources that you have always taken for granted, you devise new ways of editing.

Does that independence affect style of film editing?
    The film dictates the style to me. Somehow out of the energy you develop a significant style for that film. Working independently as we are now, without central people to run the department, each film is a totally new entity. You deal with the film so that it's going to be unique and entertaining, and make a lot of money so you can keep on working. It's a never-ending pattern. You are still presented with the same set of cinema problems to make it entertaining and do it in the shortest amount of time, to make sure that the spine of the story is solid and strong in everything you view so that it can be easily followed. You have to find those sources that give the picture its unique strength. Editing is really a funnel, we get all of the input. It's almost overwhelming because you realize that this production entity has so much energy which comes through the camera and the microphone and ends up in your hands. When it works, you're so pleased that it is telling the story. There are techniques to reveal that story, such as taking out redundancies. Finding a way to remove that redundancy factor, make the point cleaner, further the story more crisply.

Did you risk redundancy in Easy Rider *by including the repeated flashing sequences?*

That came about in looking for a way to simply make a transition from one scene to the other. We literally had to experiment to find how long those cuts needed to be in order to convey the idea. They were six frames, quarter-of-a-second cuts. They didn't always work. At first, we said, "Ah! We got something great here," so we started pumping it every place. Speaking of redundancy, it got to be absolutely indulgent. I don't remember how many times it's used, but it's not that much. But people remember the technique. We learned that it worked depending upon the imagery, that it had to be clean, easily recognized. If it wasn't, it was simply a confusing blur of film. But if the imagery was clear and contained a certain emotional investment as well, then the audience accepted it and was not confused by this bleep-bleep-bleep-bleep.

One example is when you flashed from the road to the campfire.

That's right, flashed to the first major campfire sequence.

How did you develop the "acid trip" sequence at the end of the film?

That was the last scene I cut for the whole movie. Before *Easy Rider* was shot, Dennis and Peter Fonda went to the Mardi Gras and shot that acid scene on 16mm with Karen Black and Toni Basil and some actors they picked up there as well. It was a highly charged, highly emotional experience for everybody. It was about twenty-five thousand feet of 16mm film, between sixty and seventy thousand feet in 35mm. Tremendously wild footage. For the longest time, I had no ideas. While editing the entire movie, I think there was a part of me always working on that acid scene. There was also a tremendous cost factor, so the first thing I did was slowly start looking through the 16 and having only certain portions blown up. Adrian Mosher did the blowups here in Los Angeles. Wonderful blowups. *Easy Rider* was shot in 1.85 aperture—16mm is full-frame aperture—so Adrian would reframe for 1.85 and that helped enormously. I did the first cut in about three days' time and it came to be under eight minutes in length. It went down to three and a quarter over less than a week. By that time, I simply had locked into it with a firm idea of how this film could express an acid trip. I used a documentary approach, meaning taking film around a generality and weaving it into a story. I had to realize the storyline myself. It was like writing with film. Everyone left me to my own devices and once I showed it, we made suggestions to shorten it.

How much of it was scripted?

It was scripted the way that in a Western they say, "The good guys are leading, the horses are here, and now the battle starts."

Then you create it in the room.

Then you go for it. It was right in the very early days of the drug culture, the very early days of a turnover in thinking. I wasn't really a counterculture person: I was happily married with children, but I was still partaking within my own structure, so it gave me a sense of freedom to try. If that sequence had been attempted five years before, it would have been entirely different, much more structured and far more limited.

There was a structure to it, regardless.

Oh, definitely a structure to it, and it had to be written on the film. It was my first experience of getting an emotional rhythm rush out of the work, and that's where my past music experience and education came in so well. It wasn't structured like music is per se, but I recognized the emotional rhythm, when it would fail and how to keep and develop it so that the imageries became more clearly defined. They were chosen for the emotional moment that would take the story just one notch further.

I believe you did not use any dissolves.

It was all straight cut. I had never done acid, but I thought that it was very impressionistic and that individual moments would be clearly defined. They didn't gradually go from one to another as you might in a dissolve. They would be just a series of emotional impressions. That's the reason for the straight cut, to create the sensibility of capturing an image for a moment and going on to the next image.

So images might be distorted, but not transitions between images?

Yeah. It would be like writing in very short sentences, in bursts. In fact, when you look at poetry spread across the page in a unique way, it's done for word imagery, focusing momentarily and moving the eye to another plane. That would be applicable in the acid trip, which is also part of the fun of the trip and part of the fun of film editing. We can do so many things if we understand what the audience's eye is looking at at a particular moment. Shifting the rapidity of the eye is another way of engendering energy to the audience. You have the energy of the image, the energy of how that image moves, the energy of where a particular image is on the screen. And we're talking the big screen, so the eye literally has to scan to do it. Normally, your eye searches for the strongest image. If you are editing a dialogue scene, the audience's eye will go to the eyes of the characters first. It seems to be a landing ground. Knowing that, you can cheat certain things. If you look at the film on a cut-to-cut basis, you'd say, "These two pieces will never go together." But they *will* go together because you know that the audience is looking elsewhere. The art of cheating is the art of film editing, truly. In *Hooper*, we had a wonderful bar fight where one character is dressed as a Roman gladiator, with breastplates, a sword at one side, and a toga. He draws back his fists in a wide shot and the cut happens as he swings. Then we cut to another angle because that's where the hit is the best as far as the person who gets hit and what happens to him afterwards. But on the cut, the character doesn't have his breastplates! In the frame before the cut, he's in full regalia; in the frame right after, he's not. I've never heard anyone mention that they saw that, and it's flat in front of your face. The eye is on the moving fist and you never see it. That's a direct cheat. Some people might even say, "We can't use the film." Sure you can, you just don't let the audience look at a particular thing. In *Steelyard Blues*, Donald Sutherland wants to get Jane Fonda's attention on a bus by throwing a handball. Donald never did the same thing twice, and in this case, he threw the ball with one hand or the other. In order to complete the cuts, to get action-reaction, I had to go from the take where he threw it with his right hand to the take where he threw it with his left. You make the cut at the apex of the swing, and because of the break in angle, where the right hand is sticking up on one cut, it's in the left hand on the incoming cut. The audience never sees that because of the rhythm. On *The Dick Van Dyke Show*, it was difficult to cheat with three cameras shooting simultaneously. When you have an A and a B camera recording exactly the same information, it's more difficult to cheat because one camera is simply mirroring the other except there's a change in angle. When you have single cameras, you aren't faced with that situation. So again, in the acid trip, I was aware of moving the audience's eye and letting the eye stay even though the image changed. That creates within itself another kind of rhythm, a rhythm past the rhythm of imagery. The rhythm of the audience's eye movement. It's like boxing, it's done in a series of combinations which are taught. Jazz musicians learn riffs, and no matter in what area they are playing, they will use that riff as a technique. In editing, you have certain riffs. There were some "eyeball riffs" in that acid trip! Plus you're getting all the audio input, and that was chosen very, very carefully. Sometimes it would be in sync, sometimes it would have nothing to do with what was going on per se but with the emotional content. Of course, we never wanted music. We wanted the trip to be that sense of a real experience, not one supported on the underpinnings of music. But at times there was a repetitiveness about the audio choice. Sometimes the audio would change because the imagery started to change. Sometimes the changed imagery would make me go back and say, "There's something missing in the audio here," and I'd work on it for a while to get it right.

When did you know the sequence was complete?
    I think musical experience teaches you when that climax hits, it hits.

It happens a lot in film editing, having a sense when that climax hits, that's the time to stop. It felt full and it was time to move on.

What was the climactic scene in the acid trip?

It was tied in with religion, with Captain America sitting on the statue talking about the death of his mother—which was very real, Peter *was* talking about the death of his mother. The imagery kept getting loftier, not only in height but in recognition. In essence, it started to become overlapping onto itself. The only way I can explain it would be that you've gone high enough, the clouds are there, you've seen it all. It left specific imagery behind. There was the imagery of the sun seen through the zoom lens, as if the film was burning, you could literally sense it. I saw that as the climactic moment. But maybe it's that time when you're on an acid trip and you fall asleep, you've run out of energy.

Were you also working with subliminal images?

Yes, there was a lot of subliminal imagery, in terms of short cuts. I don't remember doing two- or three-frame cuts, they were longer but still had that subliminal sense. You would sense it more than focus. That would be the riff I was talking about. Get five of those, then settle on something for a longer period of time. Before the acid trip, when Captain America and Billy are in the whorehouse looking at different paintings, suddenly there's a short burst of the exploding motorcycle in the scene, like he sees his own death. That's very subliminal, but it's there, long enough to catch the imagery, but not so long to focus. At the end, with the motorcycle accident, was a shot of an exploding red blob. Sometimes when you're doing an action sequence, a very short cut of a very strong image conveys a sense of impact. The impact became part of the overall imagery that you couldn't define, but you felt its emotional wallop. The sensibility that something terrible is happening.

Did Easy Rider *influence your cutting of the drug trip in* Jo Jo?

Probably. I think you make use of all experiences. Hopefully having grown, there'll be different aspects. I'm sure I used some of my experience with *Easy Rider*, but I wanted to do something different, too. It's the result of a different time, a different drug. Audiences have learned to see more than we saw twenty years ago. They have been weaned on television that throws imagery and audio at them. Audiences have been bombarded not only through their eyes but through their ears. Having seen more, it's more challenging to keep something new and fresh.

Did working in television affect your film editing?

I'm sure it did. I recognized very soon that in television, because of the tremendous time restraints placed on it on a consistent basis, certain shows develop patterns—story patterns, performance patterns, direction, shooting, and editing patterns, which all become part of that series. I'm oversimplifying, but once you learned that pattern, staying within that pattern kept a part of the show real to itself. So I recognized patterns and what a trap they can be when you're doing a feature. As a result, maybe what I learned more from television was not to fall into certain patterns and consistencies within a picture, even within a scene. There are many different methods of changing consistency, to keep the audience on their left foot, in a sense. Going back to a musical expression, I will literally edit on more of the offbeat than on the beat. Many times, the dialogue, coupled with the editing itself and the way those lines are linked, are elements that immediately create rhythm. Then there is the imagery itself, the person moving, whatever is going on within the frame. Many times, I'll know a scene will need further work because I've broken my own rhythm. I literally find myself beating time in that scene, and when it begins to hold in an interesting way, which has nothing to do with the scene per se, the downbeats don't fall on every cut. Once there is a certain consistency, I feel I've found the rhythm of the scene and I can make the bones a little barer. All this works at a subtext level within the scene. A well-written, well-performed piece will have subtext, and revealing those subtexts pictorially, say, by playing on a person's reaction rather than on the speaker, brings out the subtext of what is going on in the scene. You have so many ways of imparting information to an audience. You can overlap sound to picture so that the sound edit and picture edit don't happen in the same place. If the technique is forced, it doesn't work. It's a game I play sometimes.

How does that work in a dialogue scene?

I'll start overlapping the particular dialogue to the picture, coming out of story reasons, and the dialogue is moving closer and closer to the picture cut so that at a given moment, when the emotional crux of that scene happens, I can in essence land on what we call a straight cut, meaning both picture and dialogue happen at the same time. It is as if the dialogue rhythm has been slowly creeping up to that moment.

How do you know that technique will work best?

I've always felt that film talks to you, and if you listen to it, it will show you its strengths. It's up to you to recognize that and find a way to use that. Devising that way is really a test of your technique and experience and skill. When I look at dailies, for example, I will flag certain moments on certain takes because they bespeak to me very strongly either in performance, the meaning of that scene, whatever. As I start to edit that scene, I know that unconsciously I've already begun a series of ways so that when I arrive at that moment, I'm on that piece of film. Dailies can be misleading, comedy particularly. But it's that flag that goes up with me. In *Cinderella Liberty*, the real fun was in the birth of a baby. That was an actual birth. Because I have children and know people who have children, it is a common emotionality. Therefore, it had the opportunity for a wonderful emotional release. And the single-most moment—I flagged this right off the bat—was when the doctor took the real baby's footprint for identification and the baby let out a yell. It was the real first cry—not of life, because he had already gasped a little, but the first one that said, "I'm an individual and I don't like that!" I would have bet money that the audience would laugh with that genuine, common, shared experience. Not only is it a wonderful moment, but it's placed in such a way that it even becomes grand. One of the best moments in a film—I didn't do it, but I wish I had!—was in *Steel Magnolias*, edited by Paul Hirsch, when Sally Field is in the midst of her fury over the death of her daughter, and Olympia Dukakis pushes Shirley MacLaine toward her and says, "Hit her!" The time of that is absolutely, excruciatingly right. It's a shining example of what good direction produces, without question, and how it makes those performances so real that they're unforgiving. But it's also the *placement*. It would be comparable to writers having a sensibility of what is the essence of a particular chapter and knowing that eventually they will arrive at the essence. They will not manufacture it and just place it there, but it will come as a result of what goes on before.

In a way, Easy Rider's *"placement" in film history was timely too. Did that film break the editing tradition of the time?*

I think it differed tremendously. Because I didn't know the rules, I wasn't worried about them. Editing then had generally far fewer cuts and had certain ways of cutting into a scene—like at the end of the line, *then* you go into your over-the-shoulder. "I said I will not do that." Cut. "Yes, you will." Cut. "I will not!" Cut. "I said you will." Cut. *Easy Rider* gave me a sense that I could try other ways, cutting in during a line—schlepping in, as I called it, diving in. *Easy Rider* demanded more cuts coming at you. I devised all of the riding montages to convey an overall emotion. Like the first time you're on the cycles: a sense of freedom, the beauty of the machines, the largeness of the country they were riding through.

You again risked being repetitive with so many outdoor montages.

Oh yes. That's where the music came in so wonderfully, because just thematically you could change what it was about and therefore recolor that imagery for yourself. One of my favorites is after the acid trip and they're back on the road, not particularly happy, and the music has a very hard drive to it. Once we chose the music, I went back and cut very distinctly against or with that music so that the musical impacts would give us cut impacts to get that jarring sense. The journey was somehow beginning to come to an end. It's not a very long sequence, but it ends with a dialogue where Captain America says, "We blew it!" which is really the crux of the whole movie. How do you get to that scene? Languidly? No. You get there with hard ferociousness, with the underlying sense that something is terribly wrong, and therefore the ride creates tension. I think my musical background allowed me to quickly see and develop a technique to be applied to making that aspect work.

How is rhythm important to comedy?

Oh, comedy is, amongst other things, pure rhythm, and if you're off rhythm, you literally kill the jokes. One of my favorite scenes is in *The End*, the first time that Burt Reynolds meets Dom DeLuise. It's about a seven-and-a-half minute scene, and I think it took me three days to cut. Dom was the comic and Burt the straight man, and you had to cut that way. You let the straight man give the setup line or the beat or reaction to the joke and, at the same time, let the rhythm flow on to the next line. That scene is pure rhythm. When you start to get a scene where one line creates a laugh, and another line creates a laugh, and a third line creates a laugh, you can deal with it in several different ways. If you cut too soon to your second line, you step on your laugh and the audience literally doesn't have a chance to get it out. If you do it a third time, you've cut down on the extent of your laughs. By the same token, if you wait too long, the audience laugh will die and it doesn't take them into the second line and therefore into the third line. So the trick is to sense how long the audience will have their laugh up to its optimum and, just before it starts to go, the other line comes in. They'll start chuckling again, and just before that goes, you take them into the third. When I was music editor on *The Dick Van Dyke Show*, Rose Marie taught me a lot. One time there was an actor who had a smaller part with Rose Marie, and he was not experienced in comedy. At the rehearsal I sat in on, she would throw out the punch line and he would move just as soon as she said the line. I could see her starting to steam because he was stepping on her laugh. You never step on a comic's laugh unless you want to be killed! Finally, she grabbed him by the arm and said, "Don't you move! Wait. *Now* you move." It illustrated to me very clearly how the science and art of laughter are not only created, but are allowed to blossom. Film doesn't have that live audience to play against, you know. You are the live audience, meaning the editor, the director, whoever. We learn a lot from our previews. It's wonderful when you're in a theater because you can hear the roll of audience laughter coming back. I always stand at the back of the theater, that's the best place. You hear the audience responding to the rhythm by their laughter. They get that intake of air and start laughing again, because they know something is going to be funny and you give it to them.

Twins must have provided a similar experience as Danny DeVito and Arnold Schwarzenegger played such opposite characters.

I coedited that with Shelly Kahn and when we're working together, I'll do the music scenes because of my background. There was a lovely scene between Danny and Arnold, where Danny's going to teach him how to waltz and he sings. Once that waltz started, its rhythm never stopped as a waltz even though Danny wasn't singing. That was all editing. Danny is very rhythmical, but those rhythms would change from take to take a little. So the fun was sliding to get that to build to a faster and faster waltz rhythm, just as wonderful waltzes do. As people begin to dance to a waltz, suddenly, subtly, the tempo increases just a bit.

Does it actually increase, or is it just a perception?

No, it actually increases. It's subtle, but it's there. In that scene, the idea was to help the excitement get even larger as it went along. In the next scene, they dance with the girls. The dance was choreographed, but the way it was shot, the couples were split in order to pinpoint certain parts of the action, so you have to recreate the choreography. But as long as they were dancing in tempo, you could change things around if you kept the rhythms going. Again, it's the art of the cheat. You can cheat turns as long as you understand the rhythm and the choreography. Another dance I had fun with was in *The Tempest*. There is a scene where Raul Julia is with his goats. He's talking to his pet goat—she's kind of skittish, but a darling goat, if goats can be darling—and he says, "I'll play a song for you." The other goats gather around, it's a lovely pastoral setting. He sings a Greek love song and, through cuts, she indicates boredom. He realizes and says, "Ah!" so he picks up his clarinet and starts to play "New York, New York." Upon that, we sneak the orchestra in underneath and he and the goats do a wonderful dance to "New York, New York." We always thought of the goats as a chorus line and he the lead dancer. I did all the second unit, shot all the goats, and I was able to get cuts where the goats respond to the music, just a series of single cuts of the goats looking up and down and chewing to the rhythm. To get the goats looking up and down, we held a fishing pole over them and a piece of food at the end of a string! For the climax, the goats are leaping through the air—we actually stood off to one side, threw them up in the air and shot up, and they'd go right through the frame! Everything in rhythm. The joy of the moment.

There was a beautiful moment in Romancing the Stone *when Kathleen Turner and Michael Douglas dance. You start with fiesta music and move into romantic music. The tone just changed before your eyes.*

Yes, there was a series of cuts to the point when it stopped being a fun dance and started to develop a romantic intent. It was in the cutting.

They do a series of turns, it's wide, and then at a particular moment, it cuts almost straight in. Those are hard cuts. A lot of people shy away from a straight-in cut; they'd rather break the angle, then come around. The cut always happens at the precise point where the bodies were moving and at the same plane each time. So it sets its own rhythm. Speaking of cuts, on *Harry and the Hendersons*, I was literally making more picture edits there than I've ever made on any movie.

Really?

It was the nature of the piece. The director, Bill Dear, started in commercials, and commercial thinking is short spurts of imagery. So a lot of the movie was shot in those spurts with a lot of action pieces. There were days when I could only cut sixty feet of film, forty seconds of film. You know, you try to set some time schedule for yourself to keep up with the camera as best you can while they're shooting, and if I get a thousand feet or a reel a week, I'm doing fine. So if I'm doing *sixty* feet a day, I'm not up to it! But I couldn't go faster. There were scenes when Harry first enters the kitchen and starts his rampage through the house. Some of those cuts were twenty-four frames, sixteen frames. It was cut after cut after cut.

Was it necessary?

It was, and it all flows, it doesn't feel like a cutty film at all. I started thinking of it as MTV, in terms of the frequency of edit, to keep this high energy level going. Harry's into everything, he hits his head, knocks something, drops something into the fishbowl, picks it up and drops it. And to convey that, it demanded the cuts. Bill shot the film, it was there to do it with, and that's what it demanded. It came to nineteen-hundred-some-odd cuts for the movie, which is an enormous number of edits. Our negative cutter was grumpy! That's not counting any of the sound cuts, because many times there were two or three sound cuts for each cut of film. In specific scenes—like when Harry is going through the house, John Lithgow comes in and they confront each other, then little Ernie comes in and is so pleased—there was a choreography to be dealt with, the movement of the people around the creature. Once that movement got on the film, it took too long, so immediately you're working for compression and compression in this case means more edits. You couldn't take a portion out, join two pieces and cover that much distance. It was always kicking the tempo, but never letting it appear as if it's being done. Keeping the frequency to keep the laughs going. It's a given that if you can keep the audience laughing rather than restarting them, you're going to give them a lot more enjoyment. When an audience becomes offended, they drop out and you have to find a way of bringing them back in or remove that which is offensive. When an audience is offended, there's nothing you can do.

I would imagine a film like The End *risked offending people with its touchy treatment of death.*

I saw that probability and then it was just a matter to what degree. There were a lot of Polish people, I'm sure, who were terribly upset with the Polish jokes. But I think that the film was done with such a *joie de vivre* that it's hard to take offense. It wasn't mean-spirited. That can account for a lot. It's interesting that in the 1970s certain words started to come more into usage and were in every film. Into the 1980s, people started to get offended again. It's a pendulum. I've worked on a picture that was shot, tested several times, and failed—I was called in to "doctor" the movie. Language wasn't the reason that the movie failed, but it had to play to a PG–13 and the language in that movie would not allow it. I cleaned it out and it doesn't affect the intent of the movie. If it's gratuitous, it can offend a lot of the audience. It's easy to take a stance: if the audience doesn't understand it, that's just too bad. But in reality, if you listen to your audience, they're going to tell you what offends them and whether something is funny or not. I'm a great one for wanting to test, particularly when you're doing comedy.

I would imagine the same is true about confusing an audience.

When an audience is confused, they pull out of a movie while they try and figure out what's going on, and then you have to pull them back in and it's much more difficult. *Jo Jo Dancer* contained flashbacks within flashbacks; it was first cut to mirror the script which was convoluted in its original form. In the screening, the audience just left us. So did Richard Pryor! We took cards, did a focus group, did the survey, and Richard came up with an idea of rejuxtaposing scenes. After I got into about thirty minutes, I said it was more confusing than before. But I had an idea to make it as much a narrative form as I possibly could. *Jo Jo* opens on Richard talking on the phone, trying to hook up with his junkie. That scene did not happen in the script until the end of the first act. I had to restructure the film so that the audience knew immediately that this is a picture about this man's struggle with dope. They were confused the way the film had been originally shot because the main character they thought they wanted to laugh at wasn't delivering anything for them to laugh at. When we tested again, it improved in all the scores. Ultimately the film didn't do well anyway, but I learned from that audience preview. On the other side of that coin, you are not trying to let the audience tell you everything in totality, but fit it into your vision, the director's vision of the movie.

Can you elaborate further on what "doctoring" a film involves?

If I am called in to doctor, my terms are simply to leave me alone, I really don't want to hear what the problems were. I start with Scene 1 and look at all of the film on Scene 1, analyze what I think the problems are, then reedit accordingly. I found myself enjoying it a lot. I realized that some of it is that I am not going through the difficulty of putting it together. Doctoring can be practically a no-lose situation, really. I think the biggest pitfall can be—and I'm speaking generally—that you allow your own ego to get out of hand. If you want to help the film and have a concrete analysis of it and a way to approach it, then it can be very enjoyable. I've heard sometimes that people become so involved in their egos that it becomes "their film." Speaking of egos, I learned a wonderful thing from Bob Wise when I was editing *The Hindenburg*. Of course, Bob had been a film editor, having edited *Citizen Kane, Magnificent Ambersons*, and a few of those great movies. When I sat down to run the first cut with Bob, I was nervous because here was Bob Wise, you know? As we started running, he reached over, patted me on the shoulder, and said, "It's looking fine." It was a very gracious thing for him to do to put me at ease. There was one scene with George C. Scott that Bob suggested doing another way—George was talking with one of the other main characters in the body of the airship, a rather simple dialogue scene. I had all these intellectual ideas as to why it should *not* be, *cannot* be, the way Bob suggested. He listened, let me talk myself all the way out, then said, "Well, why don't we just try it the other way? If it doesn't work, fine." We tried it and it worked so much better! What I learned is that it is possible, particularly with egos strung as high as they are in our business, to get into long discussions about how to do a scene. *Long* discussions. When, in essence, if you go right to the film, it will tell you faster than anything.

Is it easier to make changes in film now than it used to be?

Before we had the butt splicer, film was always cemented together and when a change was made, the film had to literally be cut and a black frame put in its place. You don't have to do that anymore. I admire the old-time editors: they had to do some incredibly intricate edits and couldn't give themselves the latitude for trying things except intellectually. Then they would commit by making the cut. You know, a huge amount of money has been spent on a picture, there is a lot of pressure, so there is no time for a lot of intellectual "isms" about how a scene works or doesn't. Keep working on the film, put it together, bust that splice apart, put it back. We have so much more latitude than we used to, which is why people who are not experienced tend to overcut simple scenes. Simplicity is an important part of filmmaking.

Well, it depends on your material, though, because with Harry *you had to cut like crazy. But it was so fluid you don't even see the cuts, like all the little joints in a bone that connect a moving finger.*

That's right.

Can you explain why sometimes a film is two hours and one minute long? Why couldn't they lop off that one minute to make it even?

Well, in the years that I was studying music, Toscanini would conduct "The Pines of Rome"—all those performances were timed. Thirty years later he would do "The Pines of Rome" and would hit it within a second. Thirty years later! All those inner rhythms would always work. That's why the film is two hours and *one minute.* When everything has been done to it, that's why: because it *is* two hours and one minute.

So if you took one minute out, maybe it wouldn't fall apart but—

Somehow you would disturb the rhythms. Some people will go through and take a frame off every cut. Somebody once told me, "Sure, I can get two minutes out of this film," and he told me what he did. Take frames off the cuts. I couldn't believe this was the arbitrary way of doing it. I immediately asked him, "Why did you decide to cut where you cut? Why didn't you make it one frame later or one frame earlier? What kind of thinking are you doing?" He said, "Aw, who cares." Well, I care. I care a lot and one frame is crucial. One frame is literally crucial at times.

Perhaps "style" then is not so much which techniques one uses but the degree of caring about the film.

I think you're onto something. You don't want to impose onto the film a certain technique, a device, because it plays as a device. That's not style. Some editors say, "What you give me is it, verbatim." But those aren't the editors whose work I really admire. In order to be successful and to achieve the enjoyment that's possible, you have to take risks. It's part of the process, taking risks. It can get pretty lonely sometimes. When the film is finished shooting and everybody is gone, it's like the loneliness of the long-distance runner. You are with it longer than anybody else, except perhaps the director and producer. Sometimes you're there longer than both of them.

With all the risks and tension of the business, what keeps you going?

The drive home! Coming home, the fire's going, a glass of wine, you begin to let go.

You're relieved to end the day?

Oh, when I get in the automobile in the morning, I'm happy. I'm literally happy going to work in a wonderful fantasyland filled perhaps with enormous problems. It's the joy of creativity in what has always been one of the most astounding mediums to me, the motion picture. You don't really know whether you can solve the problems. But you know that if you draw wisely on your experience, you can.

13

Seeing the Invisible

Evan Lottman

Evan Lottman quickly puts one at ease with his soft-spoken and exacting descriptions of the movies he has worked on. He believes that the bottom line of film editing is communication with the audience (who, he knows, doesn't even begin to understand what an editor does), and that this is accomplished through meticulous attention to point of view and other rules of the game.

Evan Lottman's interest in photography and cinematography led him to work for Carl Lerner in the mid–1950s on the neorealist documentary *On the Bowery*, followed by a job at a commercial house, which he claims was the only steady job he's ever had. He eventually managed to swing into what for him was the freer, more appealing world of feature films based in New York, and proudly speaks of his uncredited montage contribution to *The Hustler* as one of his early ventures into this arena. As do many editors, Lottman formed a regular collaboration with his first major director, former fashion photographer Jerry Schatzberg, and cut his first film *Puzzle of a Downfall Child*, followed by the acclaimed *Panic in Needle Park*, *Scarecrow*, *The Seduction of Joe Tynan*, and *Honeysuckle Rose*. Many of Lottman's current films are directed by Alan Pakula.

Without hesitation, Lottman will admit that the majority of films produced today are not good, and his own enthusiasm for editing motivates him to carve the very best vehicle of communication out of the mass of footage at his disposal. He keeps up with the latest technical developments in film and sound editing to discover the most attractive or economical ways to execute the finished product. His discussion of the subliminal impact of editing broadens the discussion in earlier interviews of the power of editing to manipulate the audience in "unseen" ways. Lottman, like many other editors, believes that the editor's work should remain invisible to the viewers in order to affect them successfully on deeper levels.

You started in documentaries. What made you switch to features?

I felt that there was a sameness about documentaries. Their structure had become codified and regulated, and everything seemed to be done in the Edward R. Murrow style. Nothing had ever really progressed beyond that technique. I started working in documentaries in what you might call the Golden Age of television news and public affairs shows. The age of Jack Kennedy as President and the best FCC guy they ever had, Newton Minow. He coined the phrase "vast wasteland" for television. The networks were stung by his remarks and documentary programming burgeoned. Old black-and-white stock footage was no problem because most television was black and white. But when Kennedy died and new administrations came in, the networks lost their momentum and their taste for public affairs programming. Football started to replace everything. They insisted on the "balanced view," every viewpoint balanced with its opposite. It became very equivocal and wasn't standing up for anything anymore. Predictable and boring. I was restless and needed a career change.

As an editor, could you have done something to change that trend?

I did the best I could, and I worked with good people and did some movies I'm proud of. NBC *White Paper*, *CBS Reports*, and *Twentieth Century* were terrific. I worked at one point with a Canadian woman named Beryl Fox on *Saigon* for *CBS Reports*. It was a great battle to make that film the way she wanted it. I began to feel that feature films were where it was really happening and you could be expressive and creative in feature films in a way that I had never before thought possible. I made the move, which was not easy. Two separate worlds, separate casts of characters, contacts, producers, directors. If you grow up in one, it's very hard to swing over. I just kept my ears open a lot.

How did your work on The Hustler *fit into your career change?*

I had just become an editor, with one or two credits as an editor in documentaries. Dede Allen was editing *The Hustler* and there were a few montages to be done. The montages were movies unto themselves, mini-productions within the main movie. Robert Rossen had shot thousands of feet of wild pool games, with Jackie Gleason (who played his own game) and Paul Newman in long shots, but Willie Mosconi (the great pool champion of the day) in the close-up of the trick shots. It was wild, unscripted footage. The script said, "Montage," period. That's all it said. I'm not credited on the movie, but it was a wonderful experience.

What was going through your mind as you were creating these montages?

I thought I knew what montage was, exemplified in the work of Slavko Vorkapich, the granddaddy of the Hollywood montage. Meaning,

I thought, superimposed shots of spinning locomotive wheels, newspaper headlines whirling around and coming at you, pages tearing off the calendar. They used to say, "We'll do a Vorkapich here" or "We'll Vorkapich out of this." I thought this technique was kind of old-fashioned and corny. When Rossen and Dede hit me with this, I thought they certainly didn't want me to do *that* kind of stuff. But it turned out they did! I kept asking Rossen and he'd say, "You know, kid. A montage. Do a montage!" I said, "Maybe if I just do a lot of fast cuts?" And he said, "No, I mean a *montage*, a *montage!*" So I finally admitted to myself, "Well, I guess what the guy wants is a *montage!*" Rossen explained that we had to compress this pool game which takes thirty-six hours into about two minutes. The composer Kenyon Hopkins said, "We'll do the whole thing in rhythm and I'll give you a click track." That's an audiovisual method of indicating a steady beat, a rhythm, and you can translate it into film time by frames-per-second computation. I took a piece of film leader and marked every couple of frames to get that beat and rolled it through a synchronizer, timing the cuts to the beat. But the click track was too restricting and I told Kenyon I'd rather not do it that way. Then I figured out something that I thought was terrific. I used superimposed images, which is what Rossen had always wanted, but I used them to react dramatically to each other in a real-time situation. For example, if the pool ball was hit by the cue, then the supered image would be the spectator reactions to that ball in the other level of the visual. Everything was blended visually with everything else and every image reacted to every other image so that there were no disconnected visual entities. I thought I hit upon something original and fresh, and apparently so did Rossen because he loved it and they used it in the film. Dede, who is wonderfully adept at technical things, showed me how to adjust the Moviola to enable it to view three thicknesses of film at one time. We had a special Moviola prepared, and Dede was right in there designing it. The only way you could see my cut on a screen was actually to create the optical. That took a lot of time to execute, going back to the optical house and having to readjust the film for any changes. They were constantly testing the densities of each visual level and it became very, very technical. But at the same time it was very creative.

How long did it take you to edit the montages?

I was not on the movie very long. For eight, twelve weeks. I did five montages. Two wound up in the movie. The one of the thirty-six-hour game, the one at the end, and there were other montages that never got used in the movie. One was Paul Newman's trip through various pool halls.

Was your experience with unscripted footage helpful for Panic in Needle Park?

I had to edit a lot of wild (i.e., unscripted) scenes in the cutting of that movie. It was filmed in a documentary manner. In fact, Jerry Schatzberg insisted on true documentary sound and we shot the picture on Broadway in New York, in what used to be called Needle Park. The sound was not wonderful, and to this day, looking at a tape of the movie, it's hard to hear some of the dialogue. But Jerry was insistent on real sync sound and nonlooped dialogue. The actors were New York actors, and it was done in a very realistic manner. A lot of handheld, documentary-style photography. The heroin shooting-up scenes were shot in the sleazy hotels that used to be located around the neighborhood. I remember that one room looked terrible when I walked into it, dingy, chipped paint and dirty walls, but it looked bright and wonderful on film tests. Something about color film glamorizes. I think we've come to learn that even war gets glamorized by color. They had to make the room look worse than it was—painting it different colors, smearing dirt on the walls.

Are you usually on location during the shoot?

Much of the time. Especially in the beginning, before enough film has accumulated to start cutting. I'm almost always hired on the movie during that period, although I may or may not be present on the set.

Is it usual for an editor to be present?

It depends usually on the budget more than anything else. But it makes sense because, in the first place, you can view the rushes every day with the director. Secondly, you're available for any consultation that might be required. Finally, most important for production managers, you're actually cutting the picture during the time they're shooting it, so that you've got a first cut about a week or ten days after the shooting is over. They feel they're far ahead of the game, and they are. Not having the editor on board for principal photography means, among other things, waiting a long time for the first cut. Certainly major Hollywood movies that can afford it always have editors during the shoot.

Do directors or cinematographers envision a film one way while the editor sees it differently once it begins to be assembled?

I don't think a finished film is ever anything that anybody envisions initially. This may be a cliché, but film has a life of its own. It always comes out somewhat different from anyone's expectations. Actors change the meaning and rhythm of the words, cinematographers change the look, directors reshape it. It's just not the way it was on the written page. The look or pace just doesn't come out as it was written.

Have you ever requested a scene be redone?

Many times. It doesn't always get done, but I never stop trying. There are occasions when I may suggest ways of doing things better or more cheaply. I was momentarily a big hero on the Muppet movie because they were going to do an expensive reshoot of a scene in the Empire State Building and I figured out a way to do it more simply and cheaply.

Did the Muppet movie pose special editing difficulties, or were the problems more in production?

Production was very complicated. All sets had to be built at least four feet off the floor because the puppeteers work underneath and hold the puppets above their heads. They're rigged with television monitors and earphones because they have to see themselves perform. This means that, in the normal course of shooting a scene, they start with one side of the set, and it would be sometimes a week before I would get the reverse angles from the other side. They really had to plan everything on storyboards. I would get a good idea of what the scene was going to look like by seeing the boards. I was in fact consulted and worked on the movie for several weeks before they started shooting, particularly on some of the optical work that was planned. Remember when Fozzie Bear is singing on the train and the heads of the other Muppets appear in a circle around him? We worked that out carefully beforehand. Of course, there was a major optical planned for the wedding at the end of the movie that never got made, too expensive. What we wound up with was considerably cheaper, but no less complicated. Kermit and Piggy go up into the moon and the credits roll up below them behind the New York skyline.

What was the original plan?

All the Muppets were going to get into an old '62 Buick convertible, they were to drive into the wedding chapel, and afterward they would rise and pass through a stained-glass window and continue moving up into the stars, circle the Empire State Building, and turn into the moon. Then one day, Frank Oz got the news, "Sorry, it's a little over the top for a three-minute scene to cost half of the rest of the movie!" So they worked out the alternate optical scene.

Did you develop an editing style that you repeated in these features?

Not really. I think the film dictates the style of the editing, not the other way around. The director, the writer, even the actors set the style of the film. Now, yes, the editor can do things too, he can move it around a little. If it's an action scene, it has a pace to it that is necessary and demanding, and every editor will treat that scene in his or her own creative way, but still conform to the overriding style of the drama. I don't think editors really impose their own style onto a film. Which is not to say they don't make tremendous contributions, but it isn't usually a matter of style—if that is an understandable word. I think of Orson Welles with *Citizen Kane* or *Lady From Shanghai*, or John Huston, who was wide-ranging in his subject matter. Is there a single style in any of those movies? I don't know whether there is a consistent style, other than a striving for excellence. But each movie, each situation demands its own form and pace, its own manner of expression.

Then how does an editor develop from a mechanical approach, following a script, to becoming uniquely creative?

Everybody starts out following a script when he or she does the first cut; it should be that way. Unless there's discussion about another way of doing it in the process of shooting the picture, I follow the script as closely as I can when I'm doing my first rough cut. I make a great effort to serve the script, even when I'm dealing with things I know aren't working or are going to be changed later. It's my obligation to do that, and I think the director deserves to see the film the way he directed it. What happens after that first cut may be a free-for-all. Nothing is sacred, everything is subject to interpretation, changing, elimination. Your imagination may run wild. Especially if the structure or the performances have particular problems, or you think you've got trouble at the end. Pictures often seem to have trouble with their endings.

In Scarecrow, *the editing flowed with the characters and the story. Was that intuitive, or was it scripted? For example, the lengthy shot between Al Pacino and Gene Hackman at the counter.*

I love that scene. First of all, I think it's a minor masterpiece of exposition in writing. One of the toughest things in a screenplay is for a scriptwriter to give the audience a series of facts disguised in believable dialogue and action. This scene is a wonderful elucidation of character and plot, all in one conversation. The scene was partly extemporaneous; no two takes were exactly alike. I am a pragmatist as an editor (maybe in other areas as well), and I saw that that one very long and uninterrupted take was working well. It was a three-quarter shot on Hackman over Pacino's shoulder. Hackman had most of the lines, the performance was perfect, the timing was right, the actors were working properly together, there was no reason in the whole world to cut. Of course there was coverage—it wasn't designed to play in only one angle. So it was a matter of choice—not necessity—to let the scene play as it does. There was only one cutaway in the finished sequence. If we didn't feel that it would be very confusing when Hackman turns around and says to someone, "Mind your own business" or whatever he says, I wouldn't have used the shot of the guy putting the money in the jukebox. But we felt you had to see that guy. Then we went right back to the same take and stayed there.

In that film, I was struck by a difference in styles—that word again—between the sequences you did and those done by your assistant, Craig McKay. That is, your lengthy shots versus the more rapid cutting of McKay's sequences of Hackman's stripteasing and Pacino in the fountain.

Yes, but it's another example of the material imposing the style. Take the opening of the movie, the hitchhikers. That scene went on endlessly, and we knew that it shouldn't last more than two minutes. But there was so much material, Pacino was doing that funny stuff and Hackman was sitting there, glancing occasionally at Pacino and figuring out things in a notebook. We knew it had to be drastically shortened, so what happens, of course, is that the film appears to be very stylistically jump cut. But the underlying reason was really that the sequence was too long. The first cut I made was fifteen or twenty minutes long. We simply couldn't afford to take that time in the opening of the movie.

How did you divide editing responsibilities on The Exorcist?

We divided the movie into distinct parts. I was given the middle to the end of the movie, initially. We each worked separately, editing our own sections independently. Norman Gay did the scenes in the hospital, among other things. Jordan Leondopolous edited the first part. Billy Friedkin didn't want to destroy his objectivity by screening the movie too many times, so he would have the three of us screen the picture. Then we would have a rap session in Billy's office, perhaps once a week. Jordan, Norman, and I all hated the end of the picture. Originally, it went something like this: Lee J. Cobb was the kindly old Jewish detective and a movie fan, and in the last scene, he says to the priest, "Father, let's go to the movies," and they go off together down the block. Oh, it was awful! Trivializing and sentimentalizing the whole film, we thought. We convinced Billy that it was a terrible ending, and he challenged us to come up with other ideas, which we did. Together we three editors worked out the ending as it is now: we eliminated the detective and used as the final shot the priest standing at the fatal stairway and looking up at the boarded window. The ending was shaped and created in the cutting room. We restructured the entire end of the movie from the time Linda Blair goes away with her mother in the car, which initially we had removed because Billy disliked it. We restored that part, recut it, and found the shot of the priest looking up at the window. I think it was taken from an earlier part of the scene. The structure of the ending was a major contribution by three editors working in tandem. I remember the chaos of the scene in the cutting room, ideas and bits of film flying all over.

Although the content was frightening enough, did you make particular editing decisions to enhance the atmosphere and tension?

The raw material certainly helped. I learned more from a director on that movie than I think I've ever learned before. In one scene, Ellen Burstyn comes into the room and furniture starts flying around. The material was there to be edited, the continuity was there, and yes, the dresser was supposed to move forward and all that. But Billy said, "I'd like it faster, make it shorter, you don't need eighteen frames, do it in twelve." He was right. I learned a lot about being bold and outrageous and taking chances. Then I had a terrific idea that worked, and I became a big hero for five minutes! The changing of the eyes at the end.

The priest's eyes?

We were planning a complicated optical, but I felt it could be done in a very simple and straightforward manner. I thought I could match his head, even by repositioning it optically perhaps, then jump cut from Jason Miller's demon eyes to his natural eyes, since he was able to maintain his expression in the two takes. I tried it and it worked. The other thing that Billy thought was terrific was the priest falling out of the window. It was very effectively done in about six or seven cuts, maybe more. It was covered by a lot of angles, and there was a stunt man and also a dummy. There was even a camera that was put in a carton and thrown out the window while its film rolled.

The atmosphere was also enhanced by the way the sound carried over from one scene to another. Was that your doing?

I really had nothing to do with the sound. We locked the final cut in New York and the film went to California. There was a sound company in Chicago that did much of the work, experimenting with weird noises from slaughterhouses and oh, just awful stuff, running it backwards and forwards. I was not really party to any of that at all. But a few times during the picture editing, they sent sound from Chicago and we listened to it and laid it experimentally over the picture.

Why do you like to use The Exorcist *most when you lecture?*

It's such a crowd pleaser and there's a lot to talk about. Everybody always asks me about the dummy with the head going around. Linda Blair started her head turning, and it matched to a perfectly made dummy in the same position that completed the head turn.

Whatever the scene, you work from a sense of pacing with the action.

Sure. But a lot of things can occur to you. You might say, "Well, why don't we orchestrate the scene differently? Let's have a piece of drawer and then cut to the other side of the room, then cut to that and back to the drawer, and so forth." This is how a scene can be shaped and fashioned in the editing room. On the other hand, there has to be on a piece of film a picture of a drawer flying out, and a picture of your cutaway, and a picture of the other side of the room. Somebody must have created that stuff in the first place and photographed it. But how you put it together in such a scene is certainly discretionary and is really what the editing process is all about.

You have to consider how to make an audience react to the scene.

That's the challenge. How do you make them jump out of their seats? I can look at the scene the way it was cut the first time and the director will say, "I am not jumping out of my seat. Make me jump out of my seat." Then I'll go back to the cutting room, work on it, and try to make it better.

How do you keep from getting inundated by the material?

I always felt that one of the biggest challenges in being an editor is to control your material and not to be intimidated by the weight of the footage you can be confronted with in a big film. But organizing it in some way, cutting it down to size, eliminating the dross as quickly as you can, and zeroing in on the good stuff is the best way to attack the scene. Not necessarily to walk away from it and do something else.

What are other work habits that you've settled on over the years?

It's not unique to me, although I'm pretty fast, but I think that after you've been doing it for a while, the technique of editing becomes secondary and commonplace. There's really little I can't do technically, so I can devote more time and energy on creative things. Also, of course, speed depends on organization and having a terrific crew, and a first assistant editor who thinks the way you do and prepares the material beforehand. Being an organized person is very much part of being an editor, and having a respect for organization.

Of your musical films, The Muppets Take Manhattan *and* Honeysuckle Rose, *were there editing difficulties inherent in the genre?*

Well, those two musicals themselves were two different styles, totally. *Honeysuckle* had concerts covered by up to seven cameras at one time. I edited the last six or seven reels. *Muppets* was much more formally planned, with playback, storyboards, pre-scripted, prerecorded. There is a certain difficulty to cutting to playback, it doesn't always work the way you want it to. You are constrained by the rhythm and the recording of the music, and there must be a lot of accuracy in order to match action in dancing, and so on. It involves compensating for slight errors in rhythm or dance steps, and maintaining a flow with the music. But *Honeysuckle* was multicamera-ed, nonplayback. We had a multitude of material and handling it was a massive job.

There, you also wove the story into the songs played away from the concert stage.

In the last part of the film, there was an opportunity to be very creative, with Willie Nelson and Slim Pickens rushing back to a concert in progress, intercutting between them and the songs on the stage, keeping the storyline moving. I think the picture's main problem, as far as box office was concerned, was that it didn't know whether it was a concert movie or a love story. I'm sorry they cut some of the musical numbers that I think should have been kept in their entirety.

Was Orphans *difficult for you, being a stage adaptation?*

I would say that Alan Pakula faced the major difficulty. He had to direct a movie that was a small play, with only three characters, and he had to make it visually forceful and exciting. There were a lot of things done to accomplish that. For one thing, he had the set built in a way that created an island in the middle of the room with a staircase going upstairs, creating a lot of opportunities for imaginative blocking of the action. Also the cameraman, Don McAlpine, used a Steadicam and handheld cameras to create more visual excitement. The editing really had to do with the pace and selection of the performances, and creating and maintaining the proper point of view of the characters. For instance, creating a feeling of distance between Albert Finney and the two boys, especially Philip, by using only long shots. Then when the intimacy grew, to change to closer angles of the characters. Maintaining the proper point of view was something that was definitely part of the editing challenge. *Sophie's Choice* was also a great challenge in that regard.

How so?

A narrator is telling you the story. Obviously the story is told from his point of view and there can be no scene that takes place that he isn't privy to. That's a major constraint put upon the film's framework, and sometimes it becomes very difficult to maintain. Let me give you an example. There's a scene in which Nathan leaves the house and Sophie is very distraught, and the narrator Stingo comes in and sits with her. It's late at night, they sit on this window seat, she tells him the story of the ghetto and the concentration camp, and she falls asleep in his arms. In the morning she wakes up and he raises the window shade; she looks out and strongly reacts to something she sees. Now at that point, we could have cut to Nathan who was sitting on the curb outside. But that would have been a violation of point of view because Stingo hasn't looked out the window yet and hasn't seen Nathan. He doesn't know what she's reacting to. So deliberately holding back the shot of Nathan sitting on the steps until Stingo looks out and sees for himself is an example of what I mean. If P.O.V. weren't a problem, we might have cut directly to Nathan from Sophie's reaction. There are many other scenes like that in the movie, and we were very careful to not violate point of view.

Is that similar to The Seduction of Joe Tynan, *when Meryl Streep and Alan Alda are in his office? The phone rings, it's Alda's wife, he answers, but you remain on Streep for her reactions.*

Sure. That was an editing choice! Streep's performance during the call was much more interesting than Alda's, so much more revealing of the character. When you've got a wonderful performance going, stay with it as long as you can. If there's one axiom about film editing, it's that you must show what the audience wants to see at any given time. Why do you cut suddenly to something, why do you *not* cut to it? You try to anticipate what an audience would expect to see, and would want to see. So here was Meryl listening to the phone call and she was really reacting, fidgeting, playing with something on the table, and so on. All we had of Alda was his back to her (P.O.V., again!) and his occasional glances over his shoulder at her. We *know* what *he's* doing, but we're curious about *her* reactions. So you stick with her. In this case, it was not the conventional thing to do. It's going with the performance. Having respect for actors when they're good. Or when they're bad!

You've been able to save films when they're bad?

No!

That's a myth?

It's a myth. You can help a good performance. I suppose an editor could destroy a film by making it really look bad, and if everybody concerned with the picture were equally untalented, it could be done. But you can't *create* a good performance. If an actor is bad, you do the best you can, accentuating the positive, eliminating the negative, so to speak.

What if the editing is criticized as troubling the movie?

It's usually a bum rap! The editor plays an invisible part in a movie. The only people who know what goes on in a cutting room are the editor and the director, anybody else who happens to be there, the flies on the wall. You can't evaluate the work of an editor unless you are there, in the cutting room, because an editor can do wonderful things with a lot of bad footage, or he can perhaps destroy a lot of good footage, or a director may deserve much of the credit for the editing decisions, good or bad. There are all kinds of permutations, and you just can't put your finger on why it's a wonderfully edited movie or who exactly deserves the real credit. I'm in the Academy and vote for the Best Editing Oscar every year, but my decisions are based more on intuition than knowledge, and I suspect that's true of the other voting members, too.

Audiences often overlook editing. Even I, in reviewing your films, would drift with the movie and forget to look for cuts and transitions.

Then it's a well-edited film. Editing should never call attention to itself. The experience of seeing a movie should be an experience that is divorced from its technique. Anything that suddenly pulls you out of the totality of the experience, a beautiful shot, a gorgeous piece of photography, even a tour de force performance, can hurt the overall effect. The dramatic experience should be the smooth, seamless integration of everybody's work on the film.

Editing then has an almost subliminal effect on the viewer.
Absolutely.

How about the effect of montages and so on?
Unfortunately, it is a kind of editing that is taking hold in some areas. I think TV has had a lot to do with it. TV has had a momentous impact on film editing. Imagistic kinds of stuff, random, meaningless, disparate images. It's not my style. I believe that communication is really what it's all about, you have to communicate a story. You have a dramatic tale to tell and you try not to let the editing show. Of course, that doesn't mean that you have to spell everything out, and it doesn't mean you have to hit people over the head and tell them fifteen times. Editing can be subtle and evocative and surprising, but it must always be communicative, and that's the bottom line. I suppose that's true of anything, poetry and painting, playwriting, sculpture. If that's a definition of my style, then okay, I'll go along with that. My style is to communicate.

You must also follow the story's rhythm to communicate it well.
Sure. The circumstances of the drama define the rhythm. And the rhythm is part of the communication. I'm very exacting about screen direction and eye lines, because I think this is all part of the communication, the seamlessness. A bad cut will disrupt your concentration in a way that you may not even realize. Most audiences are not that technically sophisticated, but they can sense, even subconsciously, that something is wrong when a mismatched cut goes by. Another thing you learn in feature films is that audiences are generally way ahead of you. They just know what you're doing immediately. Perhaps that's a good side of TV's impact.

This may be another myth, but how do you feel editors are regar—
Unappreciated!

No hesitation there!
Underappreciated. Most people don't know what editors do. People in the movie business don't know what editors do. Editors are perceived as special people who work in dark rooms away from the madding crowd. If we're on location, we're usually located in a hotel or a lab, and while the others on the production are off on the location working on their

tans, we're in our dark cutting room all day, appearing only at night with the rushes. We are kind of gray eminences on the production, not really seen as part of the regular production crew. In some ways, there may be a certain amount of jealousy. Editors are usually closer to the director; when they view the rushes, the editor sits next to the director, and there's a lot of muttering and whispering between them. And why do we work so much overtime and have so many people on the editing crew? The work seems *so* arcane and specialized, and nobody even understands what they're looking at when they see an edited scene or why it turned out that way. That it wasn't inevitable!

Have you worked in video at all?
No, not really. Now we're getting into electronic editing and I'm investigating it. It's a tool, but the way it is now, it's neither timesaving or moneysaving, but it *is* another way of presenting and keeping a lot of different versions of a scene. Very expensive. Presently, the memory capability of these computers is not sufficient to hold all the footage for a feature film. The system works well with commercials and TV sitcoms. But on a feature, there's the moment when you want to see the cut on a large movie screen. At that point the computerized cuts have to be manually made on the work print, and once that is done it seems counterproductive to move back to the electronic editing machine. So it has a limited use right now in feature film, but I won't say that this isn't going to change in the future.

Do you see new trends in feature film editing?
The technical part of editing, yes. Sound editing has grown into a major new adjunct of postproduction. When I started in features, we had one sound editor, maybe two, plus an assistant. Now it's routine to have five or six sound editors, all highly specialized: Foley editors, looping editors, ADR, music editors. Sound itself has become technically more sophisticated: Dolby sound, stereo sound, the quality of high fidelity.

As for the movies themselves, has there been a change over, say, the last thirty years in the approach to material through an editor's eyes?
I would say there was a period in the 1950s in Britain when they were doing some remarkably interesting cutting. Tony Richardson's movies, outrageous jump cutting, which is something I think seems not to have changed too much since then. If you look at a lot of old movies on television, you can see the changes that took place in the 1950s which permanently influenced editing and editing style. The elimination of optical fades and dissolves (although now we're going back to them) was probably a television influence.

Even with changes, what remains the focus of the editor's work?

Let's say we're the sculptors who shape the film into a coherent, unified, dramatic piece. I find editing interesting and challenging, and being a free-lancer helps a lot. Keeps me meeting new casts of characters, in front of the camera and behind the camera, and no two situations are alike. The movies themselves are something that I love, I always have. Most of what comes down the pike is not wonderful stuff, you're not always editing *Citizen Kane*. I've had to impress this on students a lot. These kids think they're going to go out and work only on wonderful movies. It's not true in Hollywood or Paris or Rome or anywhere. Maybe one out of thirty-five movies is a good movie, and one out of fifty is a great movie. Of course, it's thrilling to be associated with a terrific picture, but if you're going to make a career in this business, you have to realize that's really not the way it's going to be. So what is left for you is to try to carve out something in any project that will make it challenging and interesting enough for you to keep going to work every day. Something to make it better, change it, make it more worthy.

Have you ever wanted to try another area of film, like directing?

From time to time I've thought about it. I feel I could be a very good director, but I don't like all the peripheral stuff that has little to do with directing. Meetings and lunches and deal making. That's not me. I guess I'm not an "A personality," but a "B personality"! A lot of editors tend to be quiet and introspective people, not usually the kind that it takes to be a director. Obviously many editors have become directors, but I never pursued it seriously enough. I always liked editing, I still like editing. I love editing. Why change? I've stayed in it because there's a kind of inertia when you're doing something that you like and you're making a decent living out of it. As a free-lancer, you're never in any situation for too long, no matter how bad—and it can be pretty bad—and there's always something to look forward to around the bend, another movie, another location, another set of realities. It's kept my creative juices going. What more is there?

Remaining Versatile

Peter C. Frank

FILM EDITOR

1972   *Towers of Frustration*, directed by Scott Neilson

1973   *The Race for the Yellow Jersey*, directed by Tom Spain

1977   **The Fire Next Door: CBS Reports*, Bill Moyers
         The Aliens: CBS Reports, Bill Moyers

1978   *Lifeline*, NBC

1979   *Harvest* (Bill Moyers' Journal)

1980   *A Texas Notebook* (Bill Moyers' Journal)

1982   *The Verdict*, directed by Sidney Lumet

1983   *Daniel*, directed by Sidney Lumet

1984   *Under the Biltmore Clock* (American Playhouse), directed by Neal Miller

1985   *Compromising Positions*, directed by Frank Perry
         Home Town (TV Series)

1986   *A Walk on the Moon*, directed by Raphael Silver

1987   *Dirty Dancing*, directed by Emile Ardolino
         Hello Again, directed by Frank Perry (Coeditor: Trudy Ship)

1988   *The Equalizer* (TV Series)
         The Appointments of Dennis Jennings, directed by Dean Parisot

1989   *Miss Firecracker*, directed by Thomas Schlamme

1990   *A Shock to the System*, directed by Jan Egleston (Coeditor: Bill Anderson)

SOUND EDITOR

1976   *Andy Warhol's Bad*, directed by Andy Warhol

1978   *Holocaust* (TV Series)

1979   *Just Tell Me What You Want*, directed by Sidney Lumet
         Melvin and Howard, directed by Jonathan Demme

1980   *Honeysuckle Rose*, directed by Jerry Schatzberg

1981   *Reds*, directed by Warren Beatty
         Prince of the City (Supervising Sound Editor), directed by Sidney Lumet

VIDEOTAPE EDITOR

1984   *Thirteen Days Through the Looking Glass*, HBO

* See Appendix for complete list of editing awards and nominations.

Peter Frank comes from a family who worked in the film business for generations. His step-grandparents worked at Deluxe Labs. His mother, Margaret Frank (whose cousin was Willard van Dyke), was an editor during World War II and a teacher at the Brooklyn Film Institute. She also cut the first episodes of *Candid Camera*, for which her husband was unit manager. Before World War II Frank's stepfather, Lloyd Frank, was a union organizer and business agent of the lab workers' union, Local 702. The family left New York for personal and political reasons (they were members of the American Communist Party during the 1950s) and became farmers in Connecticut.

Frank returned to New York for a brief stay in college before dropping out, and made the acquaintance of documentary editor Lora Hays. She directed him to a job on the CBS program *Twentieth Century*, carrying negatives to the Pathé Lab on 106th Street. Eventually he was promoted to apprentice editor and free-lanced afterwards as an assistant. While pursuing studies in the violoncello at the Mannes College of Music, Frank worked peripherally in film. From his connection with *The Happy Hooker*, on which he worked as Marc Laub's assistant sound editor, Frank landed odd jobs until moving full-time into the film business. He was also Foley editor on *Andy Warhol's Bad* and grins at remembering how he created sound effects for snipping off fingers, breaking legs, and throwing babies out of windows. After working sound on *The Missouri Breaks*, Frank cut *The Fire Next Door*, the award-winning documentary with Bill Moyers, produced by Tom Spain; he won a special Emmy and John Glenn read the show's transcript into the Congressional Record. Frank had frequented cutting rooms as a kid, but admits he didn't really understand the process until he edited *The Fire Next Door*. "That experience established me professionally," he says. "From then on, people said, 'Oh yeah, he's the guy who cut *The Fire Next Door*.'"

The two lines of Frank's work in documentaries and feature sound progressed separately until he was made supervising sound editor on *Prince of the City* by colleague Jack Fitzstephens, who incidentally had been an editing student of Frank's mother. Sidney Lumet then requested Frank to be picture editor on *The Verdict*, and ever since, he has cut features for Sidney Lumet and Frank Perry, among others.

Frank's expertise spans commercials, video editing, sound, and picture editing; he advocates versatility in many areas of film for potential editors, not only to increase job opportunities but also to understand the inter-relationship of all facets of production. His remarks on sound introduce concepts on the complex union of audio and visual to affect tension, subliminal reaction, and emotion. Above all, Frank attributes his keen sensibilities largely to his study of music, the closest thing he had to self-expression. He says he could not have cut *The Fire Next Door* without his musical training. Through music, Frank found the confidence that is now securely expressed in his editing.

The interview was interrupted for an urgent screening of a trailer for *A Shock to the System*, edited on the latest technology, the Montage Picture Processor. In the shadow of the Moviola at the side of the room, Frank demonstrated the ease of cutting with computerized video.

You've worked extensively in sound editing, including as supervising sound editor for Prince of the City. *Would you distinguish between the responsibilities of sound editors and picture editors?*

I'm not a sound editor. I did it for a while, and it matched in to a large part with my musical training. In terms of responsibilities, they're totally different. The sound editor has a reel of film and he has to do the work on the reel to make it play in the dubbing mix—what's called on the West Coast a dubbing session, in the East it's a mixing session. He has to pre-pare it so the mixer has access to the various levels of the sound and can work with it, and he has to have enough imagination to understand what that will entail. Once he's done that, he's done. There are occasions, like Jack Fitzstephens's work on *The Pawnbroker*, where he can supply an exciting dramatic sound idea that will focus the film. Every sound editor hopes to be able to do that, and every sound editor attempts to do it, but it happens relatively rarely. The picture editor is responsible for the film being a success, period. No matter what it takes. Sure, he can hide be-hind the director and the writer and the producer, but the mandate is simple. He's just supposed to make it work, and if it was shot wrong, he's still supposed to make it work. If it was misconceived, he's still supposed to make it work. And if it was miswritten, yep, he's supposed to fix that too. There is really no limit to the responsibility, in the ultimate sense, of the film editor. However, to have a sound background and be a dramatic editor is vital, I think. Film is at least half sound, and certainly the marriage between film and sound, even in its simplest sense, is the essence of what an editor does. So to be technically secure in sound is vital, and the best way to do that is to have been a sound editor. I don't know that everyone has to do it for a long time. It certainly gave me security. I came to Sidney Lumet on my first job as an accomplished sound editor, sure that I could handle anything that came up in that line. And relatively new to the idea of dramatic editing, I was essentially taught by Sidney how to approach dramatic picture editing and continued learning from there. Sound is very important, just as picture is. You need to be fully fluent in both aspects. Then the real challenge comes in how to marry them. Whether to do different things or the same thing, and how to do them, is the essence of editing.

Were you responsible for the heartbeat motif in Prince of the City?

Yes. Jack Fitzstephens and I made that contribution in that film. Sidney Lumet had some sense that heartbeat was an issue, so in talking with Paul Chihara, the composer of that film, and in talking with me and Jack, he said he thought some sound that would resemble a heartbeat or could be confused with it might be worthwhile. The banging of a shutter, a bump in the night, he wasn't sure. We made some raw sounds, manipulated them, worked our way up to a heartbeat, got a heartbeat, worked it out. We played it for Paul who then was able to write it as a musical theme. It was like one of those articles you read in film magazines—it all worked out! Paul is a very fine composer, and he came up with something that was very convincing musically. Then the effect was fairly easy. Actually it was an old director's chair that was banged around the studio! That sort of stuff is funny—the prosaic origins of sound effects—but the sound was right and that was the point.

People find such significance in these little things, and they're really quite accidental, aren't they?

Well, in Sidney's movies, not much is accidental. He set out with the intent of creating those moments. With *The Verdict*, he knew exactly how what he wanted went together. *The Verdict* was cut in twenty-one days. There were virtually no unanswered questions in the assembly of that film, and what you see is the film he cut virtually the first time. It was familiar material from *Twelve Angry Men*, the whole sense of it. He liked the script, his attitude was, "We'll knock this one out, make some money, and then have money to do one I feel more personally about." So he did that successfully. The next film was *Daniel* which he had wanted to do for a long time and felt intensely about, and had a script by E. L. Doctorow and Doctorow as producer. That was a hard job and a long process. All of us worked for probably six months of editing. The film got very little notice, but I think it was a very interesting film and a much better job than that. It was devastating to Sidney, and to all of us, that the film wasn't at least discussed and accepted on its merits, but only on the merits of the Rosenbergs, which wasn't the issue. The issue all along had been the violence done to the kids, the true injustice of railroading someone, not their guilt or innocence—which was dealt with but was not the central issue of the movie. There were some very fine performances in it, and some real attempts to get beyond linear filmmaking and into something that reached for more. But I guess audiences have to decide.

You were film editor on Compromising Positions, *but did you contribute to the sound for the opening murder in the dentist's office?*

That sequence was, in large part, created in the editing room. The raw material had been given me. Having cut it once, we then looked at it and said, "Yes, this is working, but we need more material," and Frank Perry went back and did get more shots, among them the ring on the hand and a little more explicit material of the water in the sink and so forth. There had been shots to use for that and we sketched it out that way, but then we supplied it with better shots. That was an arrangement done in the cutting room, it wasn't part of the written version of the film. It certainly was indicated by the footage that was shot and by the acting. It wasn't manufactured to impose itself on the material, it came from an aspect of the material that was presented. I try to do that with material. I don't really believe that you can impose an idea on material. You can try, sometimes you get away with it. But it usually doesn't work on the deeper levels, and what you really need to do is find a hidden aspect that can be brought out openly, an undercurrent that can be made overt in the editing. Then you can do rather radical things, as long as there's that hook that says, "*Yes,* that's why you did that! Oh, now I get it. Sure, I was feeling that, but I didn't even know it. Now you've cut that way, I really know what you meant!" Sometimes that's hidden to everyone. It's hidden to the editor, writer, actors, but it's there. There's a theme or a tension or something. Of course, when the material isn't working, you especially look for something you can work with.

Can you relate a specific incident in the film?

I'd be hard put to tell you a specific one. The sense of the water running—Frank had always remarked that the sound of those suction things that dentists use was really pretty awful but could be interesting there. When he shot it, the sound was on and he had a real dentist chair going. We were fooling with it and it became a real strong element. We actually cut to it. It hadn't been scripted that way, but because the sound was there and it was an undercurrent and it fit, we worked with it. Even in this current film, *A Shock to the System*, there's a moment when Michael Caine leaves his house for work and says in a funny voice, "Slay the dragon, darling! Bring home the bacon, darling!" He's being sarcastic, he's just had a fight with his wife. It was okay in its original context, but now in a much tighter film, placed where it is, it becomes alive. It becomes an aspect of the character you hadn't read quite that way before. Everyone is looking for a connection, a random connection that will make sense in a context. That's what editing is.

The way you're describing it, so much seems based on intuition.

I think on the best level it is. There are all sorts of mechanical things to do. You start on the master, cut to the close-up, follow the lines. But that only takes you so far, and then you have to go a lot further. A film that is a mixture of comedy and murder and fright and all sorts of things tests you that way because you need even more connections. You almost need the random connections of a madman. It's a jagged personality, a crazy personality, so the film, maybe the rhythm of the film, is a little that way. It jumps and takes wild leaps into fantasy. Maybe we'll make literal leaps into fantasy. We're playing with ideas, even radical ideas. We're not talking about the careful working out of a scene so that you never notice the camera has shifted subject, which is the meat-and-potatoes and also the frosting of editing. But even radical ideas need to go by seamlessly. When they impose themselves, it better be for a damned good reason.

Was that true in Dirty Dancing? *You jump cut to show the passage of time, such as when Jennifer Grey's sneakers turn into heels, or when she practices on the bridge and you jump cut to show her improvement.*

There we were looking for fun. It was a long take of her improvising on the bridge, and the nature of the song "Wipe Out" was such that to cut to the music, you almost didn't mind. It could leap around a bit, and she was leaping around a bit, and it fit. I think when you put music over it, it's like music videos, it covers a lot, it carries, it creates continuity that isn't there even though you're jump cutting the pictures. They feel continuous, unified. We did it in "Hungry Eyes" also, where she performs the same gesture over and over, and finally she giggles and breaks up, which was a very effective part of that. That style was, in fact, conceived by the director Emile Ardolino; he intended that originally. The dancing on the bridge was done in the editing room, but I think he actually shot that repetition and intended for it to be used that way. People who looked at the dailies said, "What the hell is he doing? Can't he get it right the first time?" When it was cut the way he meant it, it worked nicely. He was constrained by terrible schedule, little money, and a lot of pressure.

But he did get a tremendous amount of choreography and was extremely good at that.

Was there any desire to shoot the dancing full-body, à la Astaire?

Emile did that. He comes much later than Fred Astaire, and our sense of how fast things should move and how close they should be is very different now. When Emile directed films with Baryshnikov, he made sure he stayed back so he could see what the guy was doing. This wasn't Baryshnikov. In spite of a really good job by both Patrick Swayze and Jennifer Grey, there were moments when we were better off close for dramatic moments in the story, not dance moments. They worked six-day weeks, they only had six weeks to shoot the whole thing. The realities are no one can be that good, and there were times when it was better to be close. There were also times when Emile directed it close because we felt that we needed to be with the girl and not with the dance, and he was absolutely right. The dance was romantic and sensual. The choreographer really worked it so it would be where Emile needed to be.

You also cut nonmusical films to focus on where you need to be from an audience's perspective. Do you put yourself in their position?

Always, always. But that's very tricky because I can never be an audience. From the very first, I know more than an audience knows. So the profession, in one sense—and I'm talking now about all editing—is in gaining enough experience with audiences and with film to have some seat-of-the-pants knowledge about where the audience will be at any given moment. The rest is just plain pleasing yourself; that's the most important part. But, you know, it is something an audience has to see and understand, and if they don't get it, you haven't done it right. All of the screenings we do with people present—I mean friends as well as anonymous audiences—are very important. You feel when they understand, when they sympathize, when they laugh at your presentation or are involved with the characters. It's vital to get experience with it and to use that experience every time you work.

For the sake of audience, you have to approach the material fresh.

The material is never fresh, to me it can't be. What can be fresh is the way it takes you from place to place. What can be fresh is the ever-changing meaning of each shot in a new context. If you can keep your mind open to it, every time you make a change in a film, everything changes. I'm being extreme about it and very hyper-artistic, but it's true. You restructure a film or take out scenes, and the next time you see the film, every scene means something a little different, sometimes something very different. As you work with that, you can stay interested in what happens. However, there is a point where exhaustion sets in and you just sit and can't have an idea. You get through that. Directors feel that way too, and writers. Everybody says, "Well, let's fix all the easy things we know are wrong and try it again." You work through it, but it's hard work.

[Screening of the trailer for A Shock to the System.*]*

Since I've had this opportunity to see you in action, could you talk about what went through your mind as you were watching this?
What you just saw isn't strictly representative of what I do. I was asked to do this outside of the role normally taken as a film editor. A trailer or presentation reel is something that we sometimes have to do because of the business interests involved. Money fuels everything, so we have to help out when we can. What you saw was a very hastily put together presentation, a sampling of the movie, intended to show people who are interested in buying rights to the movie what they are getting: that Michael Caine is in the movie, that there's an explosion and some pretty girls, that there's funny moments, sad moments, scary moments. What the movie has to deal with—that was roughly the idea in assembling it. To that end, this process I'm using, which is called the Montage Picture Processor, is very useful. It's the functional equivalent of a word processor for a movie. I can have within it the present cut of the movie and yank pieces from anywhere almost instantaneously. It is not perfected, it has many drawbacks and problems. But at its best, it's wonderfully freeing, especially for something like this. That being the case, when they wanted this reel, I did it very quickly. I see endless things that would be improved, and by listening to my coeditor Bill Anderson, who was also observing it, I get clues to even more things that should be fixed that might be invisible to me without someone's response. Also by seeing a different version done in L.A., I saw some more good ideas. Overall, as a unit, the L.A. version didn't work, it wasn't good enough editing to make it work. The ideas could have worked if they had been done with more finesse, perhaps. I think they tried to tell the story more linearly. I tried to combine different moods and levels of energy so it would be more like a quilt of things that would have more interest. But my version doesn't represent the ultimate of what I could do, given a clear situation; neither does theirs. It's in that gray area of what's best to do with a mixed-up situation. It is more in the realm of commercial editing, of visual design, of rhythm, of producing and writing, than it is in the actual feature film editor's realm of creating a dramatic moment that feels real and yet is symbolic. Creating a moment that conveys some subtlety of human experience. All of those are not involved here. This is actually taking moments that Bill and I have done for this film, ripping them apart, putting

them together in an interesting crazy quilt to sell it. It's not typical and not entirely comfortable.

Just a chore, then?

At best it can function as a way to free your mind of associations and look at the material a different way. Unfortunately, it was done under pressure, so it was frustrating. I couldn't take three or four days and refine it. I also didn't want to rip apart the film completely. I wanted to keep my pieces in discrete blocks, for financial reasons, whereas within the blocks I could have made changes that I avoided. Ultimately, we'll see what Frank Perry says about which one he wants.

Does working with videotape require a different mindset than film?

There are more than two ways to look at film editing. Everyone looks at it differently. But the bottom line is what you see when you run it back for yourself. You made an edit, cut a scene, create a scene—whatever you want to call it—and then look at it. What you do then becomes the controlling issue, because no one cuts it absolutely right the first time, except in those rare instances where you're on the beam. Even then, it's subject to change or adjustment. Even then, the issue remains: what do you see when you look at it? Do you see that it's right or do you go ahead, change it, and just ruin it? Do you see things that are choked off or overly attenuated? Can you heighten them and connect them and make them seem real? That experience is true on every level of editing. However, what you're allowed to do, and what you're after ultimately, are very different. In commercials, you're after a short, intense, uncomplicated response. I recently finished some spots for New England Telephone directed by Chris Menges. A series of spots that told one story; one was the beginning of the story, one was another stage of the story, and it became a serial as they unfolded. That was interesting, but both he and I were frustrated by the reality that the complexity of experience that you hope to get out of or into a film was limited in this form. Some people are very satisfied by that. It's an intense discipline with such short amounts of time to tell a story well and fully. When it comes to videotape editing, the problem is on the technical side. Within film, we have complete random access to any frame, fairly easily and simply, mechanically by hand. When you work with videotape, you don't have that anymore. The editing is the same. Images go together the same way; the rules of what will or won't work, or the lack of rules, are the same. But your access to it is very different; it's totally dependent on the technology. *Thirteen Days*, an HBO special, was an attempt to dramatize a war game scenario, written by a professor, as a speculation on how the United States might end up in a nuclear war with Russia. It was done through a TV newsroom, with stories coming in from all around the world, mostly the Gulf of Oman and Arab Emirates, and a confrontation over access to and from the Gulf, a nuclear exchange, and finally a full-fledged nuclear confrontation. "Looking Glass" was the President's plane that takes him out of harm's way as the world blows up. This was an appropriate form for videotape, with the stories coming in on videotape. So I cut the stories, then they photographed a newsroom and did that part of the story, then we assembled the whole thing. The original stories I cut were done on the most crude three-quarter inch decks, with the simplest controller. It was not frame accurate and was very frustrating. I had to do it many times to even get it close when I had picked a place I wanted to cut. When we cut the dramatic scenes, that was frustrating because, in terms of dialogue, I couldn't get anywhere near the kind of timing I wanted because the machinery wouldn't let me. Finally, the producers realized this and hired another editor who was versed on the CMX system, a more sophisticated computer-operated videotape system. We were then able to do what I wanted, assemble the whole show, and get on with making it work. Now, in fact, on *A Shock to the System*, we're cutting videotape. Eventually the film is conformed to what Bill and I do. But in this Montage Processor, I have virtually random access to any piece of footage. It approaches the freedom that a writer has with a word processor. There's a tremendous amount of backup support needed, which is both expensive and time-consuming, and only one-sixth of the film is available to me at one time because that's all it holds, so there are severe limitations. But within those limitations, it really is very free and it's been exciting to learn. It's the first time I've used it.

Could you give a little demonstration?

Briefly, the images you see are the head and tail frames of a piece of film, and you can manipulate these images. So in this trailer, you saw the train go whipping past—here are the first and last frames of the train. Then you see a scene in which two guys are talking, and that's the first and last. Then another scene, another scene—these represent whole cut sequences out of the original film. [Presses buttons to edit while speaking.] But I don't like the train here—it's gone. I want to put it in here—it's there! See, uh, no, I don't think so, that wasn't an authorized change, so it's back in there. It's that simple. Now to see it, I just go like this [turns a dial] and I'll see all of the clips up to that point in reel.time, 6 minutes, 22 seconds, and 9 frames. In 107 seconds, it will play all of that. It also will do dissolves and fades, it has two different tracks. Not with the accuracy I would like, but within one frame of film. It can't go *in* the frame, but it can do anything up to one frame. Sometimes the computer that operates it is sensitive and breaks down, creates a lot of heat. It's terribly expensive; it is not cost effective for anything but a very large-budget film.

This is not a large-budget film, but the producer believed in the system and felt because we were under enormous time constraints that it would be worth it. I think he was proven right. We got done very fast; the first cut was done the day after the end of production. That's the idea behind this machine.

As much as it has simplified your work, do you miss the feel of film?

I missed it terribly when I first started cutting on this. Everybody was afraid to come in here, I was so grouchy. Every time anybody asked, "How's the machine?" I'd shake my head in disgust! I don't feel that way anymore. The better I got with the Montage, the less I missed the Moviola. It's converted me. I'm well aware of its frailties. I would never insist on having it on any given job, but I wish this was the way we did it from now on.

It may make other editing equipment archaic.

Hand cutting of film is too sophisticated and too simple to ever truly be archaic. It's like saying carving wood is archaic. It's too immediate. There are lots of other ways to work with wood, power tools are wonderful. I'm a woodworker, I love all that stuff. It's just another way to do it on a different level, and a probably more immediate level. So is handwriting. You can't say that the word processor has superseded handwriting, and there may be intimate moments in writing when, for many people, the only thing to do is to get a piece of paper and a pencil and do it that way, then later put it in their processor if they need to. It should never be dismissed as an option, nor should hand cutting be. But in the larger sense, this is the future in some form. I'm not advertising for Montage, I'm just saying that this kind of a system probably will reach that point. But we're dealing with extremely sophisticated technology which is very sensitive and, really, all I need is a razor blade, tape, a block splicer and synchronizer, and a Moviola. [Lovingly points to Moviola at the side of the room.] We call it "The Fern." It's big and green and sits in the corner. It looks like an instrument of torture! Yet it's been around for sixty-odd years and does its job quite simply. It's a complex subject, but that's the essentials.

Equipment notwithstanding, can editors make or break a film?

There is no film until it's edited, however badly or well. There are moments in films when editors are vital. The problem is that you can't say *the* editor made or broke the film, except in a specific case, because almost everyone can improve a film. They may not be able to sit in a room and edit, but they can look at a film and say, "Oh no, wait a minute, all that is too much! I just need this and this." If they have to live with it on a subjective basis, they probably would be as lost as anybody. But you can't show a film without being told that the editing works or doesn't work, so even the worst editing is subject to fine criticism and fine tuning. I do think that in documentaries, certainly in *vérité*, the editor writes the stories to a large extent, but still not totally. If you haven't got it on film, you can't cut it. The editor does create a line, the tension, the interest, directs what the story has to say to an enormous extent. But also, in a feature film, and one that reaches beyond the most obvious storytelling, it's the editor's perception of the reality of the footage that makes the first cut, that has a pervasive influence on the film. Sometimes that is reversed and changed or wiped out. Most of the time, though, that first intent and interest and approach pervades the finished film. Some people have a knack for the technical side of editing or making a good cut, of making it flow; some don't. Some people have an internal rhythm. I mean, what's a good composition? What's a bad one? What's a good shot? A good editor senses the venue of the shot and knows a good shot in terms of what's needed in the film. Also, different directors have different senses of what they want in a shot, and *you* have to sense that. You have to say, "This guy wants action" or "This guy wants subtlety" or "This guy wants visual contrast." Different agendas for different people, as many as there are people who direct. Sensitivity to that is essential. Editors need to be literate, interested in lots of things and widely educated—at least by self, if not formally. On the other hand, I do know a few people with extremely narrow views and extremely limited experience who are just absolutely wonderful editors by some natural talent. Nothing more to be said. They just do it and do it well. They seem to always be in the right place in the right shot at the right time, without a lot of discussion or philosophy or breast-beating, or even necessarily a lot of ego. They just seem to do it right, and it feels right when you look at it. There are very few of them, but I've come across some. I'm not one of them, I don't think!

Would you want to be one of them?

I'd love it if I were. I guess I would go home and feel really confident of everything I ever did. I don't. I go home and I question and I wonder. People like it and I think, "Oh, well, I guess I did it right." Then I think a little more. "Well, maybe I didn't!"

Back to your films, The Verdict *had a number of lengthy master shots which you chose not to interrupt with close-ups. Did you feel you might lose your audience with such distance? Was that scripted?*

Sidney Lumet intended right from the start that these should be played as one-shot scenes, and they were. That's a style that Sidney adopted that I think at times serves him well and at other times I question, but it was his intent and there was no option. Certainly these long shots work better in a movie theater. They are not possible on television. If you see it on a video screen, you lose nuances. If you see it as Sidney intended it, on a big screen—and Sidney himself sits in the first row, he doesn't even want to see the edge of the screen, he wants to feel immersed in the story—but even if you don't go that far and sit in the fifteenth row, you will get all of that, and you will get it easier and more fully than you would at a Broadway play where you're sitting in the center of the house. You have to take that into account. As an example of interpreting a script, when we did *Daniel*, Doctorow was with us in the cutting room a lot. He aided and abetted us in our attempts to change the way things had been scripted. Faced with the immediacy of the scenes that we had in the house, not what had been written necessarily, he recognized (as we all did) that things had to change and be used differently. That which seemed good in the written word was not necessarily the same quality in the finished image. In his original script, for instance, the interruptions were paintings of torture. In the film, the idea of paintings was too literal, it wouldn't work. To see tortures and hear a voice describing them, drawing and quartering or whatever, was too disjointed, didn't connect. However, to see close-up images of preparation for the electric chair, to which this whole film was rushing, was shocking and of a piece with the rest of the movie. Doctorow agreed, as did Sidney. They struggled and both of them are awfully good at what they do, so it took them a while to arrive at it. But they did, and those images came from the movie. They weren't intended that way, but they were eventually successfully used that way.

Is it easier to pace a dramatic film like that than a comedy?

I think there are a lot of differences in pacing. Comedy is hard. What the hell is funny? And certainly, what the hell is funny the hundred-and-fiftieth time you've seen it? After a while, a joke becomes the most tired, awful thing. You want to take it out and that doesn't allow for the fact that the audience might think it's wonderful. I thought *Compromising Positions* was a mixture of social comment, comedy, snappy lines, interesting moments from Susan Sarandon, and a murder mystery which was so complicated that to this day I'm not exactly sure who did what to whom! It didn't matter, of course. In editing the film, we concluded that it wasn't that we had to make sure everybody knew who the murderer was, but that we had to understand the stages in Sarandon's character's growth. The comedy had to come out of that.

When you say the comedy came from the character or the situation, was that already scripted or did you develop that as you cut?

I think Susan Isaacs has a very good sense of comedy and she had put it into language quite well. The problem is that when you shoot a film, what looks like enough comedy in the script suddenly is inundated in tons of prosaic actions that are needed to get people from here to there and in and out of the door. What does the editor do to get rid of all of that? My function, with Frank Perry's active encouragement, was to drop as much of the ordinary as we could and allow those lines to be highlighted. There had also been a love story in it between the cop (Raul Julia) and Sarandon and it turned out not to be interesting enough, so we dropped it.

That did seem like a vestige of a larger situation.

Yes, and it was. It wasn't believable. The film seemed to be more committed to the marriage than the book was, which left us in a difficult place at the end. If she gets really involved with this guy, then where does that go? And we didn't really have the material to show what they might be thinking about that. In the end, the love affair wasn't that convincing so we gave it up. I think that made the film move better. Clarified it. It was a distraction.

It fit the character's personality to stay with her husband, anyway.

Exactly. We were aware that to do that to a film does leave vestiges and a sensitive viewer would sense something missing, but it seemed more her personality not to leave her husband and that was what we were guided by. You have to be clear about the point of view. It's usually subtle. It's usually in the editing. In *Miss Firecracker*, our feeling or our point of view of that character was in the editing, what we chose to show and what we didn't. Also the photography. And of course, ultimately, in selecting who played who and how they played it. Holly Hunter's version of this character was very much her concept.

How did you develop the comedy in the Academy Award–winning short film The Appointments of Dennis Jennings?

That was an HBO special with Steven Wright, a comedian, who wrote it and Dean Parisot who directed it. They understood what they were doing on some intuitive level. I felt it was very hard because it was a much slower kind of comedy, not snappy one-liners. It was an odd comedy that needed a full play-out, a snappy one-liner with a long double take, almost. Very different rhythm. My instinct, my experience, was not to let it run; in the cutting, I let it play as long as I felt it would go. Dean pointed out many instances that it could go longer and be funnier! I did so with immense trepidation and he was right. We shortened some of it later because the pace of the film picked up, but it was an object lesson in "You never know it all" and "You can always learn something."

It sounds like there are no rules for comedy editing—or any other?

I think there are rules, but boy, it would take a smarter person than

I am to really get them! All I know is you've got to look at it, and if it doesn't look right, you've got to find out why. The more experience you have, the quicker you know what's wrong. But you *never always* know. You're always thrown back on how to get it from an unexpected angle, how to jog your brain loose from its accustomed ways of looking and see a new way to find a solution. It's the creative process. You have to do that.

What makes award-winning editing?

In all honesty, so many people contribute to the editing of a film, you never know who did the actual work. Even editors don't know who did the editing. Who was the sensitive person? Did the director sit back, like Dean with me, and say, "I think that could play longer"? Do I get credit for making the edit longer? It doesn't work like that. Every movie I've ever been on had people who made contributions to the editing who were not the editor. No question about it. Yet editing should be recognized as an important creative process, even though it's hard to define in any given circumstance who did what. There are times, in some productions, when the editor is the only person who stands between a film and chaos, because he's the one who has to say, "Wait! I can put it here or there, but you can't have it in both places at once! One of you has an idea that isn't going to work and we've got to decide. I'll do it, we'll look at it, if you don't like it, we'll change it." Everything floats through the editor. He becomes the center of the final efforts to write the film, to score it, to give it a voice. His experience crosses over to other directors and he can bring in outside knowledge. He gets bored with things more quickly and says, "It's a nice shot but let's only use a little of it."

Even so, many editors feel underacknowledged or anonymous.

Certainly film editing is an accompanying position, like a pianist accompanies a soloist. It's artistic, it's sensitive. I don't in any sense mean to demean or belittle the accomplishment or role, but it's one at the service of other people's ideas and intentions—essentially, the writer's and director's intentions. Some people can be comfortable in that role and some people can't. Just because you can be comfortable doesn't limit you to it. But if you're always fighting to be the boss, you'll have at the very least an extremely stormy career. If you can feel your own abilities, even though they're at the service of others, that's an essential for at least a satisfying experience. There's a corollary with editing which is that everyone's point of view is valid, and everyone speaks for some portion of the audience, no matter how outrageously they've misunderstood what you meant. I would be suspicious of anyone who thought that editing was a career for them until they've been in it for quite a while. There's a lot of different jobs, crafts, skills in film. Someone might be intensely interested in film and want to be an editor, thinking that's where it's at. I think they should try to write, direct, edit, shoot, act—do it all and follow their instincts. There'll be people out there who should be editors. There'll be people who are editors but shouldn't be. People have to find what they want to do. It's no good being an editor when you wish you were something else.

15

"Good Stuff" Never Changes

John D. Dunning

* See Appendix for complete list of editing awards and nominations.

"Jack" Dunning chuckles many times as he remembers moments as coeditor and, briefly, second unit director with the "sweaty Italians" and the "stupid little thing that cuts the guy's spokes off" and the "leper stuff." Of course, he speaks of one of Hollywood's most honored films of all time, *Ben-Hur*. Looking back on his forty-year career at MGM, Dunning revives the playfulness of those moments. Although he watches current movies, he almost laments how seldom they entertain him as the oldies used to.

So, too, the business end of moviemaking today troubles Dunning as he recollects the security of the old studio system. He lived within walking distance of the Queen of the Studios, MGM. Upon graduating from high school in the depressed 1930s, he gravitated to MGM, which he calls "the only sizable local employer" at the time. He was employed on the night shift as an editorial, laboratory, sound recording apprentice for the dream salary of twenty-five dollars a week. He attended UCLA during the day and received his B.S. degree. MGM movies fascinated Dunning both for their quality and their promise of steady employment, and he joined MGM ranks during the best possible time, the so-called Golden Age. His three-year service in the army, which he thought would ruin his movie career, in fact enhanced it: he served under Col. Frank Capra making army information and orientation films, including Capra's famous *Why We Fight* series, and acquainting himself with the vast stock footage library at the Astoria Studios in Long Island, New York. He was able to integrate that experience in his first Academy Award–nominated film, *Battleground.* He continued working at MGM as a film editor until 1960 with "big-name directors" and "big pictures."

When MGM embraced television in 1960, Dunning was promoted to Supervising Editor for MGM-TV Production for the next decade and worked on such shows as *Dr. Kildare, The Man From U.N.C.L.E., Flip-*

per, The Courtship of Eddie's Father, and *Medical Center,* to name a few. In 1970, he became Head of Postproduction (Film Editing, Sound Recording, Music Recording, Film Library) and retired in 1978 as Vice-President of Postproduction.

For Dunning, editing theories and concepts miss the point. "It's a question of judgment every single time."

What was MGM like in the Golden Age?

In those days, it was a great place to work because you knew everybody and you were part of a team. You were considered a permanent party. If you did an adequate job, they took care of you. Unlike today, where you're hustling for every job. You did a lot of pictures, a lot of overlapping. Sometimes you'd have two or three pictures in the cutting room, and you worked a lot of hours, six days, seven days a week. It was automatic, you just did it. My start in film was coincidental. I lived near the studio in the 1930s and when I got out of high school, that was the only place you could get a job. So I used to stand around the gate and finally met somebody who gave me an interview with somebody important and I got in as an apprentice film editor. I made around thirty-five, forty cents an hour. They had night jobs then because they worked around the clock. MGM made fifty-two pictures a year and it was a big business. I went to UCLA while I had the night job, graduated from there, then got an assistant's job and worked at that several years. Assistant film editors made a dollar an hour, a dollar for every hour you worked regardless of the number of hours. No one made a lot of money. Five thousand a week was a gigantic salary for an actor like Clark Gable. Money wasn't like it is today, terribly paramount. You have to make a deal when you make a picture now. But then they just threw pictures at us and we did them! And loved it! You felt you were part of it, they took good care of you. When I got out of the army, I went back to MGM because of the Bill of Rights and started editing almost within a year. In those days, your foundation was the big studios. You joined one and stayed there, that was your home. You were part of the whole group. I stayed there for, well, till 1978!

You could see the change in the studio system.

Oh, the change was terrific. Our studio, like all of them, was taken over by the corporate raiders and pretty soon went to pieces and doesn't exist today. Louis B. Mayer was very emotional about the studio, he liked it and liked everybody, and he tried to keep it together but it started to fall apart. When the theater divorcement came in, production fell off because we did not have a guaranteed release situation for the movies.

Were you on a rotation system, working on whatever film came next?

We had a big cadre of producers and directors under contract and you kind of got with some of them. Usually they tried to get you on a show and you would string with them, then you'd change. Certain editors did B pictures and certain editors did A pictures. Once in a while somebody would make a mistake and they'd get a better picture than they usually had, but that was coincidental. Nobody knows when it's going to be a good picture. Everyone tries to make a good picture, but it doesn't happen every time. I usually jumped all over. The most I ever did in a row was after Dore Schary got there, I did a lot for him. I did his first picture, *Battleground,* and it was a huge success so he liked me. It was a great family affair and a wonderful place to work, now that I think back.

Before you worked on Battleground *as editor, you spent some years with Frank Capra. What was that like?*

During the war I was 1A so I went in the army and I thought that was a terrible crisis, but all the background I had in the business came to fruition. I got an MOS as a film editor and was shipped to Capra who was starting what I guess you'd call a field unit to make movies. Did mostly orientation, information for the troops. I worked for Capra for three-and-a-half years, and of course it was a great experience. He happened to be a great guy and we had a great rapport with the whole outfit. They were all Hollywood and New York and Chicago guys with a lot of experience. We made films like the *Why We Fight* series, they called them "orientation films." We made a couple we never released like *Battle of Russia* and *Battle of China*—we didn't know what the hell to do with those!

As an editor, what were you asked to do on those films?

Well, they were all stock film things, you know. We had several writers and we found film for them. We shot some for that series. We did the African campaigns. John Huston did *The Battle of San Pietro.* Capra made a little unit that everybody worked in, a family affair.

Essentially you created those films in the cutting room, then.

Yes. They were all created in the cutting room. They wrote a narration but you covered it and added sequences. They did a lot of animation for them. We used Hollywood and New York, and I went to England with Capra and did a couple of shows with the British film unit, kind of a combined effort. We brought the film back and ran it for General George Marshall in the Pentagon. I was a little buck private standing in the corner! That was very exciting.

How did that experience help you in cutting Battleground?

That's really why I did *Battleground.* They wanted to create a feeling of the actual war, so I went back to New York and the Astoria Studio on

Long Island, where they had a big library of army film. I knew most of it, so I went back and got duplicates. The script had locales in it, so they needed fog film and snow film, and I got enough to cover all the sections where we would match into something. The art director would build the sets to match the army film. I was pretty well involved with that show, setting the whole thing up before they started to shoot. I used several hundred shots of actual combat film to work into it and, you know, today I look at it and I can't tell which shots are which. William Wellman, the director, was a pretty realistic guy and he matched it great. *Battleground* was a story of a patrol of guys and the film that I got was of little patrols. It was a big help to have seen it all and know where to go and get it. Being black and white, you could use the combat film to fit it right in. Then we did a lot of adding of snow and fog. It was difficult to match, so we did a lot of optical work until it all went together. It was a good film editing job, one in which you were involved.

Would you attribute the success of that film mainly to the editing?

Not really, but it enhanced it to a degree. Wellman was particularly good at characterization of men, he was good at zeroing in on a character and being consistent with it, so that's what made that movie. It was a story of individuals. A lot of comedy, unlike today's war stories. It wasn't as grim a war. That was an emotional war that everybody wanted to be in and they carried the American humor along with it.

Were there editing techniques that you used to enhance the tone or convey the story? Effects with music or dissolves to grab the audience?

I don't think so. You were striving for a real look more than anything. As far as the stock footage was concerned, you were trying to make it not look like stock footage. Work it in so that it looked like part of the picture was shot. I don't believe there was any special technique. Well, the only technique of film editing anyway is trying to be innocuous with it. I think today they make a personality out of film editing. That isn't what we used to do. We tried to make it as natural as we could. Not too many effects.

MGM used to say they had "all the stars in heaven." Were you asked to favor stars by cutting them into the film in a certain way?

Only because of the part. I think most film editors really don't favor anybody in the movie except the one who's outstanding in the scene. Most scenes are directed to a certain person and the scene bounces off that person, that's the one you feature. Possibly in some of the Norma Shearer films, you were a bit more inclined to give her a close-up! Generally, no, I think you favored because of the script, because of what part they were playing and how well the part was played. I don't remember anybody telling you to favor anybody. There was a different system of producer and director in those days. Film was a producer's game. The directors were hired artisans, except with certain big, big names. But most of the time it was the producer's show and he did pretty much what he wanted to do. The producer made the movie and the directors complained. So you took your direction from the producer more than from the director.

Even the editor?

Yeah, that's really the fellow you're working for. The director goes pretty much to finality today, and that's good. But producers were paramount then, they called the shots, they put the package together. We had a junior writer group, a writer group, big names—they used to bring in Hemingway. The producer worked with them, then a director was hired. Sometimes the director was in on it, but generally it was the producer who got the thing started. Good, bad, or indifferent, that's the way it was.

On innumerable opening credits on films of the 1930s and 1940s, the editor's name was lumped in with others on one card, often at the end of the list. Did that reflect how editors were considered?

No, it didn't. The editors had a pretty good position in those days. Nobody got a very prominent screen credit, even the writers were down in the corner. It wasn't a big thing then. You felt lucky to get on the title, you didn't care much how. You didn't get a separate card. You got mixed up with the cameraman, art director, makeup in various orders. Some film editors were pretty important people in those days. Today everybody gets a separate card pretty much. Never in those days. That didn't start until the 1950s. We were always considered part of the team.

Did they involve you in the picture before you even started?

Well, they involved us in that they talked about it. They chose us somewhere "up there," we didn't know quite where. But they put a lot of emphasis on who did the pictures, and certain people did a lot of pictures, like Arthur Freed did musicals and he had a little group who did most of them. I did one of his, *Show Boat*, but generally I didn't do his pictures. They had favorites and they used them, and of course became buddies. We had a woman editor, Margaret Booth. Margaret was Irving Thalberg's editor to start with, he made all the great pictures and Margaret became very close to Thalberg. Thalberg was big on correcting movies, he could order retakes. He was smart enough to know what would work and he fixed a lot of movies that were mediocre. The studio kind of inherited his ability to redo pictures. We shot a lot of retakes and tried to make them better. It's not easy to fix a movie. How much can you shoot? Are you going to shoot 10 percent over? How much better is that going to make it, unless somebody made a big mistake to start with? When Thalberg died, they used Margaret a great deal in the selection of editors and she supervised many productions. She had one of the biggest spots in the film editors' area in Hollywood. She had a lot to say about the pictures, worked with the producers, worked with the head of the studio. They relied on her. She was good. We had Blanche Sewell who did *The Wizard of Oz* and a lot of musicals. She was very good, a quiet lady. We had Adrienne Fazan and Margaret. Only three lady editors on the lot. There were some at Fox. I think there are more women today, but there were some prominent women then. All the women in that day were fairly outstanding in the business as editors. They went way back to the silent days, Margaret's generation. We had no women assistant editors, none.

I understand that at MGM there was a separate montage department.

There was a separate department, starting with Slavko Vorkapich. Peter Balbusch used to work with him and a couple of editors who did all of that. Montage sort of fell out of favor in the 1950s, I don't know what happened. I see they're back with little montages, but they're more subtle today. Back then, you really could notice them.

Why were they treated as a separate entity?

Mainly because of the economics of shooting. It takes certain kinds of shots to make a good montage, certain movements, and they didn't tie up big shooting companies with that. These fellows went out as a small second unit and shot, it was cheaper. It's a technique that required certain kinds of film. We're not talking about a lot of footage, maybe thirty feet. We used Vorkapich and Balbusch pretty heavily, then they got into "Coming Attractions," which worked well for them. It was a technique that feature directors didn't want to fool with and didn't know as well.

So the script would indicate "Time passes" and then it was up to them to show that.

They'd dream up something. They tried to build them up, of course. They'd make some, we'd throw them out, they'd make others that were great, and sometimes they'd make them elaborate and we'd cut them down to size.

Was there a special department for newsreels?

Most of the newsreels were done in New York in an interesting way. They cut the negative. I met some of the editors when I was in the army and they just pulled it together, spliced the negative, and made prints. If you go back and look at them, you can see that they were pretty cursory. They had a narrative and they had to get them out. That's what took the place of CBS Evening News, that's all there was. The studio per se did not make Metronome News, it was made in New York. We saw the finished product once a week. That was the case with most newsreels.

Why was New York such a hot spot for the news?

Isn't New York more involved with the world than Los Angeles? Hollywood's involved with itself. You have to get *Time* magazine to find out what happened in Romania! We also had a trailer department. We had three or four producers of trailers and a whole department of advertising. They had their own editors, very specialized. Everybody had different theories on that. Disney told you the whole story in trailer form, which I always liked. We ducked that, we didn't tell you anything.

What editing work habits did you eventually develop once you started?

I liked to have all the film on the bench, pull it out and look at it on the Moviola, four, five, ten times until I memorized it. After I came into the supervising capacity, I got into the flatbed or KEM a little bit, but only for reviewing. I've never edited on a KEM. I'm sure that if you grew up on a KEM, you would be just as proficient and the Moviola would be in your way, but the reverse is true also. I don't like interference of mechanical things when I'm cutting a film. I like to be with the film, I don't want to make the splices or thread machines. Your mind is racing when you're editing, you're racing ahead to get something together. I didn't want to be bothered with splicing. If I could get the right pieces clipped together, that's all I wanted to do. Today with electronics, all the information is stored and you can push buttons and retrieve it. I liked to keep it in my head. I knew each take and every part of it from the whole movie, good, bad, and indifferent. It was part of your training, you knew what was in the film. If you wanted a different feeling to a scene, you knew where you could get it.

On some films, you must have had a lot to remember.

Yes, but there was only so much good stuff, and you would eliminate what wasn't. How you qualify good, I don't know. It's judgment, I guess. It looks like it plays the scene better. Here's an interesting story with Bill Wellman and the first picture I did with him. Those involved with shooting the film would run dailies everyday, that's the highlight of the day. So I went down to Wellman the first day of shooting and I said, "When do you want to run dailies?" And he said, "What do you mean, run dailies?" I said, "When do you want to look at the film?" He said, "I don't want to look at the film. I shot it!" I said, "But you shoot a lot of film. Don't you want to pick and choose the material?" He said, "Just use the good stuff!"

He left it all up to you?

It was pretty obvious what he wanted, by the time he got all through.

If you looked at it closely, pickups and things that he did, you knew what he was after. William Wyler was the same way. Wyler hated his film. We asked him to view it with us and he'd say, "Oh God, did I shoot that? Oh my God, isn't that awful! Oh, I don't know, you do something with it!" He hated to look at his films. And then some directors wanted to nail it down to the frame what they wanted.

Did you enjoy looking at dailies?

Not really. I liked to look at them by myself. I didn't like to look at them in a room of people. Too much talk. They're looking at things like camerawork and photography. I'm not looking at that at all. I may look at that tomorrow. But I have to put the scene together, that's what I'm looking at. You don't get much out of a run with a group.

Did you have to cut differently when you worked in different genres? For instance, was there a certain style for cutting the musical Show Boat?

Not in that particular musical there wasn't. That was a dramatic musical. If you're talking about a musical like some "Extravaganza of 1929," that's different; they've got chorus girls and not too much else. But *Show Boat* was always with the story. For instance, you played a solo by Warfield for its best possible appreciation of the singing and the picture, the mood. Lift it out of the story itself and play it for his great voice and the presentation of that song. Some of the songs involved Ava Gardner, you played on what her part was in the movie. Howard Keel and Kathryn Grayson songs were pretty much straight songs, you played them for the song, then went back to the book. Usually there was a pattern to it. You'd end up with a big close-up. I'll never forget, we had a controversy between Freed and George Sidney, the director, about how a particular Warfield number should end. Freed wanted to move in on the big head and George wanted it another way. He did it both ways, but he wanted the pullback. Freed's was more effective. He had a fit, he just couldn't stand it when it went the other way. George's way was more scenic but it lost its emotion. Generally, when someone is singing a solo with a great voice, you end up moving in on it. There may be variations, but you try to end up big. If you have a solo person, that's as big a head as you can get. It's more emotional. Sometimes you have to guess at what that is or what you feel. Really, you're not editing for yourself. You're editing for what the audience is going to see and how it's going to affect them. That's what you have to think about.

Were there patterns of editing defined in some handbook?

There really aren't any patterns or any answers. There's nothing cut and dried about editing. It's different every show, every sequence. Although it may have a similarity, it has a lot of variations, and I don't know that anybody can tell you exactly how it should be done. I've tried sequences many ways, and some informative sequences you can lay out pretty simply. But when you come to an emotional sequence, I don't think you have a lot of answers. You've got to play with it.

I'm thinking of the buildup of emotion in the chariot race in Ben-Hur. *How did you pace such a long sequence?*

We fooled with that for a long time. Ralph Winters did most of that, but I kibitzed. We just got together and discussed it, and finally we ended up killing off a guy right away. We had a little argument about that. We thought that if we killed him right away, we'd show you that it was dangerous. It worked! You had to treat it like an Indianapolis 500. That's what it is, it's an exciting race for the public. That's all it is, it just happens to be in chariots! And the stupid little thing that cuts the other guy's spokes off—we made inserts forever of that thing. That was the fun of it. I always looked at a sequence as to what a person who was seeing it for the first time needed to see to get the full impact of it. You have to go to whatever he's expecting to see, or what he needs to see to enjoy the sequence. Just a bit ahead of him. You're painting a picture, you're trying to involve the audience with that particular sequence, and you have to paint the picture as lucid as you can.

So the chariot race sequence was built in the cutting room?

Oh yeah. Wyler wasn't involved with the race except maybe to kibitz too. But he didn't shoot any of that film. He shot the pageantry ahead of it and behind it, but for the actual round-and-round, we had several second unit action directors. We all knew that was the highlight of the movie, that was going to sell it. Sam Zimbalist, the producer, was on top of that race and everyday they'd go out and shoot. Ralph would put it together, then they'd decide to reshoot it. They did that for weeks and weeks and weeks. Ralph was so tied up on the race with a roomful of film that he called me frantically from Rome and asked me to come and help because he couldn't get off the race. Three months he was on that damned thing! They shot film, they'd do a trick, it wasn't quite right, and they'd do another one and another one. They had four directors. There were stuntmen and a lot with Charlton Heston and Stephen Boyd—not the dangerous stuff. But it was important, they had to do it. That movie was important to MGM. We were broke and we were dumping a lot of money into it. Seventeen million—ridiculous today. And if that picture didn't go, we were in tough shape. It was a sink-or-swim movie. I did a lot of work in the galley scene. That wasn't even written when I went over. Christopher Fry rewrote a lot of the script. We had reels and reels of the miniatures of the boats in the galley sequence, shot two years before in Culver City. So I cut that together and Fry looked at it and talked about it. He wrote the book, the dialogue, and Dick Thorpe directed. Then Dick had another commitment and he had to go back, so they asked me to shoot a lot of the interior of the galley ships with the slaves and the crash. I spent two weeks on that. I got a little taste of directing there with a galley full of sweaty Italians. And I couldn't speak Italian! It was a lot of fun.

Were you thinking as an editor as you were directing?

Yes. All the parts I would need. It's an illusion, you know. I'll never forget how we tried to make it gory, so we got hold of a one-legged Italian, with his leg off at the knee. We had a bone put on there and blood and everything. We brought him up the ramp to get into the galley, half on crutches and half hopping and this bloody knee sticking out! The rest of the extras in the galley took a look at that and they thought it was real, that we had cut his leg off!

I don't remember him in the movie.

Oh yeah, he's in there. It's not that long because we didn't want to be in bad taste!

You really had two climaxes in that sequence: when Jack Hawkins was driving the slaves with the different rowing speeds and then the actual sea battle. When faced with all that footage, how did you begin?

Wyler took one look at the miles of footage and said, "Oh my God." He shot anything with Heston and Jack, but a lot of that he didn't shoot. He said, "Oh my God, what are you going to do?" I said, "I don't know. We gotta get it down to size." It went on for days! You had to shoot whole takes of everything and then use what you want. You had to put it together with the miles of film, put it the way you think it read in the script and then start from there. You have to do that with any sequence—put it together the way it's intended even though you know it's too long or something's wrong with it. And *then* start working on it. You can't shortcut anything and come up with what you're after. But you have to do an individual job on each sequence, about what you think it should be in the scheme of things. A movie changes from script to film. Two different things. It doesn't always play like the script. It has another personality once it's on film. The first cut of *Ben-Hur* ended up about four-and-a-half hours, and it was all good. We didn't lose anything, we condensed it without losing it. That's the trick. Everything was important. Later when they decided to show it on TV, Wyler called me up and said, "You had ideas for some great cuts at the time, but we didn't want to make them. What were they?" I said, "Hell, I don't remember. What do you want to cut it for, it's working!" He said, "It's gonna play on TV." And I said, "Well, let it play on TV! I think it would be a mistake to cut it." We didn't cut it. We tried.

What could you have cut?

Some of the leper stuff. But it all had a meaning in the movie, you know? It's called *A Tale of the Christ*, that's what it's really about. That's how Lew Wallace wrote it. Everything with Christ in it was tough because you couldn't have anybody speaking. The Sermon on the Mount, but you can't talk! But you kind of thought you heard something, hopefully.

Did you decide on when to use music? During the race you used the pounding of the horses and the chariots and only music before and after, but throughout the galley sequence you were rich with music.

I wasn't really in on that. Miklos Roszas did that. In those days, composers would run the movie and write up their impression of it, then you would comment on that. Miklos Roszas was an expert on dynamic Roman music. He did *Quo Vadis* and a lot of it is very similar.

Speaking of Romans, you also worked on Julius Caesar.

That's kind of an interesting story. It was Shakespeare, but it was colloquial too. I thought Joseph Mankiewicz did a good job on that. He made Shakespeare that everybody could enjoy. It's not easy. You usually have to be a student to enjoy Shakespeare. It was the first time I could understand Marlon Brando! He was just a kid. He was running around the stage with a water pistol, squirting people in the ear! He was very interested in photography, used to come into the cutting room and talk about the film. It was interesting with that soliloquy, where he sways the crowd with his speech on the steps. I wanted to do it not as a soliloquy, but as a speech with reactions of the crowd. And John Houseman didn't think that was so good. I cut it two ways and I felt it was ten times better as a "contemporary" sequence where the guy yells and the crowd yells, you know, not as a soliloquy. We looked at that for a long time and Houseman finally said, "Yeah, you're right."

Is that because of the nature of film, where you need to see close-ups, as opposed to a stage play where distance is easier to sit through?

I don't know. To me, it wasn't as impressive when you didn't bring everybody into it. He was trying to excite the crowd, so that's what you should do with the sequence, excite the crowd. If you want to break the famous speech and do things in the middle of it, you should do that. The guys who look at this are not Shakespeare buffs, they're a motion picture audience. We kicked that around a long time. As I say, I cut two separate sequences and it was most exciting when you made it exciting.

Is a talking film like that harder to cut than an action film?

Dialogue is action to a degree. Well, I'm not a fan of Shakespeare. Some of the sequences were boring, you had to get through them. I suppose students of Shakespeare would look at the film and say, "God, what the hell did you do to it?" But you've got to do it with a movie like that. You can cut dialogue when they talk, but usually there's more to it than being on the guy who's speaking. I think dinner table sequences are difficult, just like courtrooms. So many little things that you can slip in. Everybody's looks and reactions while somebody else does something, that makes them difficult. The director is very important. He can give you angles that include things where you don't have to bounce around so much, to keep it from being a ping-pong match. I don't like those kinds of sequences. You never know when you have them right, you're never finished. You change them all the time, at least I do. Some editors can do it quicker, but I have to play with it.

That must have been true with Raintree County, *where you were always playing among three principals.*

Raintree County was the first 70mm. Big screen, big camera. So everybody says, "What do you do? Do you make big scenes?" You do it like 35mm, but it took us a little experimentation. Eddie Dmytryk directed, he had it set in his head how it should be when shot and he wanted to play that shot all the way, but he had other material in there. We had an argument. He said, "Play it simple, just play this shot and this shot." I said, "What do I do with the other good stuff?" He said, "Well, I don't think you need it." I said, "Well, let's try." So we ended up doing a lot of cutting that we didn't expect to do with that big film. We did 70 just like any other picture. Although you could get a wonderful panorama with it, you still had to do the story.

Dmytryk was an editor in his own right.

He was an editor, but strangely enough, he didn't like to cut. He didn't like to change shots. He liked to play the scene through. He was kind of afraid to break it up too much. Seventy millimeter posed problems for the editor in that you couldn't cut 70—no Moviola to view it. You had to print it down to 35 so that you could properly see it. We didn't know how to make a printdown of 70 to 35—different proportions. Seventy is about three to one, and 35 is three-by-four. So you're going to lose some here and gain some there and squeeze some other place in the printdown. You know there are four sprockets to a frame? *Ben-Hur* was shot in 70mm, and on that we only had a two-sprocket picture on the 35mm. The printdown was still experimental. Two sprockets were all we had as an image of that. We had to block off the other part with black. When you looked at a two-sprocket image, you didn't even know what you had until you cut the negative. We'd print up the 70 now and then, and project it to see what we were getting against what we were seeing in the 35. We really did it blind. When they made *Around the World in Eighty Days,* that happened to be more panorama vista shots and group shots. The editors on that pretty much cut 70 by hand. Seventy is big, you can almost look at it right in your hand, and if you don't have a lot of intricate dialogue cutting, you can get by.

When you moved into TV, how different was that from cutting for film?
We tried not to make it different. We used more close-ups because of the size of the screen. If we could play in close-ups, we played in close-ups. It was better. You get back in a full shot and there's nothing to it. We went round and round about that, because unfortunately we viewed it all in a projection room. I used to try to get them to look at it on a tube, the way you're going to see it. Everybody's working hard when you're starting something new and you want to make it right. I was relieved when they finally gave me postproduction supervision.

Did you miss cutting?
Yes, but I'd had enough of it. How much can you do? Oh, I'd still go in and do a little something, but just for fun. It was better for me because I didn't have to get involved with each product so specifically. All I had to do was be sure it ended up as effective as possible. Cutting really is all-encompassing. It takes your whole being. You get involved with that show and you just can't do a little, you have to do the whole thing. That's why so many editors never move out of the craft. The fellows who did the best were the ones who broke from editing when television came in and made the jump to directing. That was a good move because when TV started to get better they had the background to do well.

Have you found that editing has changed over the years?
Well, it changes per picture, but I don't think the basic idea of editing has changed at all. The idea of painting a picture for the audience. The approach is the same. Techniques look the same to me. But I see things I would change. I don't like a lot of movies today. I don't know what they call it, sensationalism or whatever. That isn't the way I was brought up. I was brought up that movies were to be entertaining. We tried to involve the audience with the emotions and action that the actors were experiencing. In a great many movies today, the audience seems to be a spectator rather than a participant. Perhaps it's me.

Do you think film schools help students learn editing the way you learned it in the studio system?
I guess you have to go to school now. We never went to school. I haven't really looked at all the things they have in their academic programs, but I think they're pretty elaborate. They do a lot of hands-on that we never had a chance to do. I don't think it hurts to be schooled, but I don't think school makes an editor out of you. It familiarizes you with it.

The electronic age is now beyond me. It's fascinating what they can do, but I don't think it changes what you put on the screen. You're still being pretty simple. Simply tell that story so it's dramatic, emotional, funny, whatever you're trying to be.

From your experience, would you say that editors have the final word on how the film comes out?

Not really. But I think if the editor does his cut well, the chances are 75 percent of it is his cut. Even though somebody else cuts on it another three months, they're playing with little parts of it. But your basic first cut is generally acceptable in 75 percent of the cases, maybe more. I used to laugh at Sam Zimbalist, who was an ex-editor. Sam made it a point to change everything, shorten it or lengthen it. I'll never forget Frank Sullivan, who was an excellent editor, did a picture with Sam, *Thirty Seconds over Tokyo*, I think. I wasn't assigned to it but I was in the room helping. Sam was running back and forth on the machine, back and forth over one little cut. I looked at him, what the hell is he doing? And finally he stopped and said, "We never changed that cut, did we, Sully?" And Sully said no. Sam said, "Take a couple of frames off, will you?" He *had* to make that change! I worked with a couple of editors who were lazy. One, Ben Lewis, would let me cut and as soon as he discovered I could cut, I cut all his pictures! He was very good, he'd correct them, fix them. But by the time I got through working with him, I did about six different pictures starting with *For Me and My Gal*. And Busby Berkeley knew it. He and Benny were old pals. Benny fixed it all up, but nevertheless I did the first go-round. Berkeley used to look at some of it and he'd say, "Nice work, Jack! Where is Benny?" But I think most editors' cuts hold up pretty well, even though everybody works on the films and does all kinds of things. The whole movie is usually pretty correct if an accomplished editor has done it.

Can you summarize what editing has been over the decades?

Film editing is getting the chaff out and thinking all the time you're making it for somebody else. You're trying to present a story as well as you can—paint a picture, so to speak—in the best possible way. It's a question of judgment every single time. Every single frame you put through, you have to say what it is doing.

You've said "paint a picture" a few times. Do you paint now that you no longer edit?

Do I? Well—

I knew it was important. Is painting like editing?

You're really doing the same thing, trying to get all the thoughts in. You're just doing what Bill Wellman said, "Use the good stuff."

16

Subliminal Truths

Ted Winterburn

1973–83   *American Sportsman,* ABC Sports Series (also Supervising Editor)

1978   *Flight of Double Eagle II,* ABC Sports

1980   *Winter Olympic Games,* ABC Sports

1984   *Race Across America,* ABC Sports
If I Can Do This, National Handicapped Sports and Recreation Association, National Ski Finals
Summer Olympic Games (Associate Director), ABC Sports

1985   *Race Across America,* ABC Sports

1986   *Giant Panda, Spirit of Adventure* series, ABC TV, produced by John Wilcox
Mississippi: Portrait of America (Sound Effects Editor), produced by Turner Broadcasting

1987   *New York City: Portrait of America,* produced by Turner Broadcasting (Coeditor: Merle Worth)
The Divided Union, BBC for Arts and Entertainment Network (reedited five one-hour documentaries)

1988   *Antarctica Odyssey, Spirit of Adventure* series, ABC TV, produced by John Wilcox
Iditarod Sled Dog Race, ABC Sports, produced by Ned Simon

1989–90   *Great Britain: Portrait of the World,* produced by Turner Broadcasting

1990   *Codependency, 20/20* ABC, produced by Ene Riisna
People Magazine: Lawler the Brawler, produced by Merle Worth, CBS (Coeditor: Joan Morris)

* See Appendix for complete list of editing awards and nominations.

To hear Ted Winterburn speak of editing is to be there, in the midst of his passion for cutting, whether it is a sports event or a portrait program. His animated expressions reflect the "emotional line" that guides his editing. For more than twenty years as editor and supervising editor of television's *American Sportsman*, Winterburn sought the heart of programs about celebrity duck shoots and deer hunts that were not always congenial to him. In all his work, from *Race Across America* and *The Olympics* to *Great Britain: Portrait of the World*, he endures the watching of dailies (which he hates as passionately as he loves editing), and looks to people rather than events to make a successful program.

Winterburn wanted to be a fashion photographer before he discovered film school at Columbia University in New York. Film "was magic to me," he says, recalling how he used to bring lunch to his brother who worked as a theater usher, then sit transfixed at the huge images. After a film history and editing course, he knew his ambition. "When I made my first splice, when I put two pictures together, something happened. All I remember was I found something that I could do all night long!" When he learned that people actually got paid for it, his choice was irrevocable.

At college, Winterburn met a most important influence, fellow student Merle Worth, who herself became an editor, director, and producer. They coedited *New York City: Portrait of America*, a job that Worth warned "may ruin our friendship." It became an enduring collaboration. "When Merle told me about the emotional line, I knew exactly what she was talking about. I just had done it differently. I felt my way through the *Sportsman* shows in a different way."

Winterburn worked as an assistant music and effects editor for a small music editing house in New York which bid jobs with the Army Signal Corps, and did film research on the Roosevelt and Truman documentary series. He studied alongside many documentary editors to learn as much about editing as they would teach him. His voice catches slightly as he reflects on turning down a feature-film apprenticeship to Dede Allen and Jerry Greenberg. But he dreamed of editing documentaries and switched to that route with a sense of determination if not security. Now he has found a comfortable niche in the sports arena and has won numerous Emmy awards and nominations for his work.

Winterburn's position (sometimes as a "disgruntled sports editor") has made him terribly aware of the sensitive questions involved in portraying reality. In feature films, audiences are automatically capable of suspending their disbelief to accept a fictional reality. Documentary editors who build scenes must be continually aware of the responsibility they have to audiences who demand greater reality—the "truth"—from this genre. The issue is all the more apparent to him as he had worked on *Antarctica Odyssey* with Mike Hoover, who later became embroiled in a controversy over his coverage of the Afghanistan War. Winterburn speaks carefully— and realistically—about the editor's view of truth in stories of adventure, broadcast journalism, and documentaries.

When you were starting out, it took a lot of courage to turn down Dede Allen's offer to work with her, didn't it?

Really. I worked at 1600 Broadway in New York City where there were a lot of editing rooms, and my goal was to work for as many editors as I could in one year, three or four weeks at a time. I was helping one get ready for a mix, helping another sync up dailies. Dede Allen walked in and said, "You've been very highly recommended." She looked twenty feet tall! I said, "Oh my God, it's Dede Allen!" Jerry Greenberg was working for her at the time as an assistant, and she wanted to train me as an apprentice. To me, it was a step backwards since my goal was to edit documentaries and I really felt this was going to stop me. Dede said, "I'm leaving town to go on location in Texas. Jerry will train you with the footage so that when I come back, we'll be ready to go." I said, "I have to think about this." She said, "What? I'm offering you a very good opportunity." I said, "I realize that, but . . . " and I didn't take the job!

And the film she was about to begin was—

Bonnie and Clyde! I look back and say, "Ted . . . Ted . . . what the . . . ?"

Still, somehow you knew the feature world was not for you.

I later worked on *Slaughterhouse 5* for five weeks as a sound effects assistant. Working there, I just knew I didn't miss anything. I hated looking at the scripts. I always loved what Dede did, but I thought, how could

I listen to this stuff all day long? And the pressure of the star trip, I call it, distorted everything. It distorted everyone's working relationship. I really liked doing my own work. To me, documentaries were people dumping footage in your room, telling you they don't know how they're going to solve this stuff, and you look at it and say, "I'll see you in a month." People would begin to trust you to do that. Which I guess brought me to sports. *American Sportsman* was a weekly afternoon television series with Curt Gowdy, and movie stars hunting and fishing. Shooting ducks, shooting elephants, shooting everything that walked, and drowning fish. It was a challenge to edit. I had been an assistant on the series when it opened. I worked on the very first season and the show ran for twenty-two years. What I really wanted to edit was important major documentaries. Never got a chance because I was always involved in *Sportsman*, which people weren't taking seriously in our business. If you worked on *Sportsman*, it was sort of like working on *Candid Camera*, and if you stayed through lunch, you were staff! It was sort of a joke. But over the years, it became a bona fide series in the sense that people knew it was around and began seeking work on the show. The editing became better and better because more people wanted to do it.

Why was it so challenging?
It was where I learned to edit. They called me back one season and said they would promote me to an editor if I came back. I was working for a CBS documentary at the time and I thought I was where I wanted to be, where I thought the real important work was. Instead, I was doing this stupid history of rock and roll with Leonard Bernstein. It was grim! The material was awful. Talking about the serious music of the Beatles and illustrating it by following a rock group on tour—but the group they selected as the focus of this documentary for serious rock and roll music was Herman and his Hermits! And Leonard Bernstein at the piano saying, "When the Beatles wrote 'Penny Lane,' the baroque trumpet was so—" What *is* this movie about? It was the time they were having freak-outs in Los Angeles and Zappa was this cult crazy man. *Sportsman* sounded sane after that, so I took it. It was hard work, I was terrified. I had to learn how to cut action footage.

Was there a formula you had to use?
The fishing show and the duck show were the hardest. They would go out in the field and shoot ducks flying over, and you'd have a lot of kills— they called them kills. Then you'd have these little conversations, set pieces, in the duck blind, usually funny or trying to be funny. With Phil Harris and Bing Crosby, there'd always be a song and a lot of patter back and forth, in between which you had to kill ducks with the action footage! You had to find ways of doing that. There were different elements that

allowed you to do it. There was always the duck caller in the blind with the horn, quack-quack-quack, you could cut away to him, break off anything that was going on. There was the dog that retrieved, you could put lines over that that got you back to the next set scene and bring in the next joke. The most important thing with duck kills, you had to have close-ups of ducks flying over, one or two, because they'd always go, "Here come two!" So you had to cut to two, and you'd go through your reel, all these ducks, singles, doubles, kills. You learned the formula for doing these shows to the degree that if you didn't have enough ducks or kills, you'd blow them up so they would look different, or you'd reverse them so they flew the other way! Fish jumps were treated the same way. We had one fish we swore was getting residuals, he was jumping through every show! We had a disclaimer that said that certain production techniques were used in these shows to enhance clarity or dramatic continuity, so we considered this as one of those techniques. We weren't into the current criticisms of Mike Hoover and the Afghanistan War of "You set that thing up." It was obviously set up, you had to in order to get a show. Even Robert Flaherty set things up!

These weren't serious sports events anyway.

Yeah, but they were doing some serious killing. Cleveland Amory was writing for *TV Guide* at the time and bombarded us with hate reviews. Finally they stopped the killing and went into adventure shows. Hang gliding, kayaking—we did a ton of kayaking shows, mountain climbing.

Did you also have formulas for cutting those sports shows?

Oh yeah. *Sportsman* had trouble finding directors who could deliver good "*vérité*" yet "controlled" footage, and if they didn't have a good cameraman, you didn't have a good show. It really was a series trying to develop a style, which it eventually did. There was nothing like it on television. We selected and edited the music, and I imagine we were doing what you would be doing in features in terms of making the scene play. The actor's dialogue was the important element that carried the show and supported the footage. We wanted you to feel that you were right in the middle of a hunt or a stalk or a big fishing trip. It was a conscious attempt not to repeat the travelogue technique of footage supported by a narrator with a polished script. You had to learn how to make a scene play and get some dramatic build, so maybe that's where I relied on working out of my feelings. It was hearing what they were saying, knowing what it looked like when they were doing it. But it was what I *heard* that really directed me towards where this thing was going. Then it was filling in the pieces and pushing it along with the sound. If they didn't say it, then *you thought it* by saying, "Well, now the narrator can say *this* to get me to this." And the writer would come in afterwards. You were orchestrating the show and there was nothing, nothing that you couldn't do. So even though others may not have taken the show seriously, we did a lot of technical work on them and a lot of emotional work on them. We were true to the material, I thought. A lot of times we just stepped back and said, "No show." Not a lot, but there were times when they didn't get a good kill or they didn't shoot enough ducks or the celebrities were terrible. There were some shows that just didn't work.

Did you find that some sequences you labored over and were sure would work still had to be omitted in the final program?

Yes. One good example was in 1972, during the Summer Olympic Games in Munich, Germany. I was with a team of editors who were suddenly turning out hard news pieces (editing negative on Steenbecks) to feed the world the tragedy of the death of the Israeli athletes. Lost in the shuffle was a piece I had done on diving. It was a slow-motion ballet of bodies falling from a high diving board that had caught a lot of people's imagination, but never made "air." I was crushed because I had been so strongly influenced by the diving sequence from Leni Riefenstahl's *Olympia*. Also Leni Riefenstahl was living in Munich then and *Olympia* was playing at a theater in downtown Munich, all very heady stuff for me. I first saw the diving sequence from *Olympia* in a film history course at Columbia taught by Cecile Starr. I remember her saying that once you could do that, you could do anything. It was just a passing remark, I'm sure, where Cecile was expressing her admiration for the editing, but I took it quite solemnly and the power of that piece of magic was indelibly stamped on my retinas. Almost ten years later when I was assigned the diving sequence for the Munich Olympics, I felt as though I were competing in the Olympics myself. I felt an obvious comparison with the work of Leni Riefenstahl in a way that approached reverence. I was inspired when I cut that piece, and not to have it make air was such a sad feeling. For many around me, it was just another day in the trenches of sports journalism, and just another piece that didn't make air, but to me it was a link to the greatness of the past, of all the elements that make our work so fascinating. Through that experience I somehow brushed against those giants of film history.

Although it's debatable that editors can make or break a film, would you say that you "made" some of those sports events, or even entire Sportsman *shows, through the editing alone?*

I ended up supervising on that series and it's very true. Some editors could kill a show, and my job would be to come in and figure out how to unkill it. You could see that they weren't getting it somehow, or their focus was different, the timing was terrible, the cutting was terrible. Some weren't used to doing work where they had to figure out the storyline. How many kills, when the kill should occur, when the joke should occur, to give it life. Sort of like the story of the sculptor—to find the life in the stone. Where is the life? Like when you go through the dailies. I hate screening dailies! Some editors love dailies, they come alive when they see them. I hate them. I go into a depression.

While watching them? Or before or after?

Before, during, and after! It's like apprehension before they come, how much did they shoot. It's all negative. I don't know what the hell it is, except I know it's healthy for me. It's a part of my process, to get rid of all that negative crap. I guess that's how I do it. The fear of "I don't know what to do with this stuff. I don't know what the key to this puzzle is." You think you're making an ass of yourself, or you get lost, or your demands are so high and you think the material isn't up to the demands. It's very creative and I have to trust that I'm developing something good and keep telling myself that I'm good. I feel that way all the time, it never goes away. I heard an editor actually admit those feelings of terror, and we've been best friends ever since. I allow that to go on. I don't sit there and say, "Look at these great shots!" But I try and remember where I came alive, when I perked up at something. Those are the keystones for me. Usually there's one sequence I'm anxious to cut, and it never has to be the beginning, the middle, or the end. It's just a sequence I want to get started on because it has a certain life to it, and then the rest goes easy. It's getting started for me that's hard. I panic when there isn't a sequence I have a feeling to cut. That's because I haven't figured out where the life is. The life has not become obvious to me, if there is any life in it. Usually there is. Hearing the concepts from the producer or the director helps you understand where the life is supposed to be. I believe that my job is to transcend, to go beyond what they thought and what I thought, and get to the third place which is something mystical about that footage. I really believe that there is something—in documentaries anyway, especially about people—that we all have a life of our own, an energy of our own that you can tap into. For the portrait of Great Britain, I did a sequence on this character from Scotland, Ivor Cutler, who's a cult figure and humorist. He writes stories, poetry, songs, and he performs on stage. The guy is marvelous, he's so over-the-line that you don't laugh, you wonder, "What is he doing? Is he serious?" The director shot sequences of him writing stories with a flashlight pen in a dark aquarium sitting in front of a fish tank. Walking barefoot over grass. Nothing had specific links as to why he was doing them. They were wonderfully shot, but what was forthcoming to me was not gripping or lively, it didn't tell me who the guy was. What I had to do was take it another step further. Merle Worth happened to have all his records and most of his books. I took them home and, as I said to Nonny Majchrzyk, my assistant, I imbued myself with Ivor Cutler. I gave it the dailies treatment, I let all this stuff go and I listened to it. Not judgmental. I started liking some of this stuff. "Oh, that's a funny song. That's a very sad poem." There was a wonderful story about "Fish Fright." This guy comes into a drugstore and he says his girlfriend has Fish Fright and does the druggist have anything for that. And the guy says, "Oh, she looks like a fish!" And he says, "Well, yes, she has Fish Fright!" I thought, wouldn't that seem wonderful for the fish tank scene as if he's writing that story! None of this came from the director, it was something I had to do because I wasn't satisfied. I felt there's more to this man than I'm getting, there's more life to this than they shot.

So you picked out the life from listening to his records and reading his books. How did you then interpret that life into the film?

I went for my feelings. I had to disregard the director's outline, which worried me because I didn't want to do that, I didn't want to deviate, but I had to. For me, this was only going to work a certain way, it had to be a little zany. When I try to analyze how I made this sequence tell you who this guy was through his material, against the material that was shot, it was what I *heard* that led me to understand what I saw. "Fish Fright" made me understand the aquarium sequence. I listened to "Fish Fright," I put it aside, I looked at the aquarium, and I said, "Now what are the best shots of the aquarium?" I cut the sequence according to the shots I liked in an order that would lead me, through understanding that someone was sitting here writing a story about fish. Then I laid over the "Fish Fright" story, which I had to edit down. The images that I liked told me how much of the story I had to tell, and it told me how to edit the story, so it wasn't like the story told me how to cut the picture. The story told me *why* to cut the picture, really, and then the *picture* told me *how* to cut the *picture*. One shot too many, it would be boring or repetitive. It was like an amazing marriage.

Sounds like you made little leaps between different elements. What you heard led you into the picture, then led you back into the sound. Do you think it works for an audience that way too?

I think what I'm doing is making myself the audience. I really have a lot of empathy for an audience. I don't want the audience to be bored. I don't want them to not be entertained, I don't want them not to understand. I want them to feel something. Merle calls it an emotional line. Once you find the emotional line, which is, "Where can I take you on this journey?", if you can feel that, it sure is going to be easy. So a lot of that to me is what it sounds like. I know the pictures I have to work with.

But what do I want to hear? How do I want it to sound? Which means bringing in a lot of other sounds.

Would you use sounds that have nothing to do with the subject?

Well, not that have *nothing* to do with it, but that have everything to do with it emotionally. Drones, I think, are very useful for tension which you wouldn't be hearing in a room. There's a sequence of a guy who has a radio museum, a wireless museum. He was obsessed with electricity, that was the idea of the museum, and I had a wonderful time creating an opening that made you feel as though electricity and radios had their own life. So it was just a lot of sound. Electric hum—now that would be a natural sound, that's not too bright. A radio being tuned from station to station—that wasn't too brilliant, that's just another layer. But the thing that I pulled out of nowhere, something I heard just by auditioning sound for another show, was a little girl singing "Seesaw Margery Daw" in an echo chamber. It was so spooky, but it sounded wonderful. He happened to have a picture of a little girl with headphones on, like an old RCA ad, and I knew I wanted to use that picture. When I saw that picture, I *heard* that voice! So that's the connection for me, making this magic out of what you hear. I had had a hard time with the director because he would not allow me to put any sound in when we worked physically together. He would say, "No, we'll do that later, it's very important you get the images correct and you get the intellectual line." And I'm dying for the emotional line. It's like it goes nowhere because who's going to listen to it without feeling? But if you're intrigued from the very beginning by what you hear, by what you see, you'll watch almost anything to find out what's going to happen next.

Are you inclined to choose image above sound, or sound above image?

No. They're always together, but they're really inseparable. They're really so codependent. But they come in different ways. A way of working for me is to go through the transcript and take out all the lines I like—that would be almost like sound cutting. I go through the producer's outline and pull all that, but I also pull the stuff I like and I type them on index cards. Then you have this little "stack of sound." Sound elements, sound material. It's not even sound effects, just voice. I haven't done that with sound effects, it would be interesting to try. Then I start to cut the picture, a sequence, but I'm really thinking about what I read, what appealed to me and what am I hearing over this. You know you want to say something emotionally, you want to get this emotion across that this person is talking about. It doesn't always work out. A lot of things you think are there don't stand up against the picture or go off in their own direction. But it's fascinating to cut the picture after you've done this work on sound but not cut it. I used to cut the sound, what the person said, and let that lead the picture, and I would illustrate what they said. It was a horrible way to work. It was so restrictive because it didn't allow you to imagine a sequence in terms of images that you might not have put together another way. There's much more freedom cutting images without that guidetrack holding me down. But having that guidetrack in your head and right at hand so you can refer to it—like in the middle of cutting, I'll go, "What am I trying to say here?" and I'll go back to the cards. "I'm trying to say this," and "Oh, that was dumb, why did I think that was so wonderful?" And I'll flip through the cards and "Oh, here's the same thought, it's said another way. Oh yeah." Or I'll try it against some of the picture and it tells me whether it works or not.

Are you adding random lines that you like to random pictures?

They're not random. They're concepts. I had a sequence in Ireland, a children's school for Catholics and Protestants, and wonderful lines from the teachers. They were off-camera, wonderful lines, and part of a story I wanted to tell emotionally about how they tried to reach these kids. Now I also had a lot of pictures of the kids in school, and I didn't quite know what was going to lead what. I knew that if you didn't like looking at the kids, you wouldn't follow this emotionally. So I cut what I liked of the kids, nice shots of them doing all kinds of things. One happened to be a shot that I liked of a teacher putting straws in milk bottles, and the light was hitting the straws so that they actually looked like tapers, candles. There was another shot of a kid sipping from a straw in that same kind of light, so I just put that together. I really wasn't aware of anything other than it was a nice flow of images and it followed through to kids cutting out things in paper and being helped by the teacher. Then I started putting in what the teachers were saying, and something one teacher said came close to the milk bottle shot, so I moved it even closer. And what she said was something like, "We're in the business of lighting candles in the darkness."

That's uncanny. None of that was shot with the candle image in mind.

It might have been subliminal. In that case, I don't think so. I think I was just close enough and I said, "Ahh, this would be great here." It's a very free way to work. It's not undisciplined and it's not chance, really. It's very controlled, but very free. I never worked like that until I worked for Merle on the *New York City* film. It scared the hell out of me. She made me work that way.

That was portraiture. Quite different from the Sportsman *films.*

No, they were all action-oriented and entertainment. There were some similar ingredients in terms of the emotional line. When Merle told me about the emotional line, I knew exactly what she was talking about. I just had done it differently. I felt my way through the *Sportsman* shows, in a different way. Which is why it was so scary when I started cutting. They literally would drop footage in your room. The producer would be off on another show and they'd say, "We have to see this in two weeks." I think it was longer, four weeks to cut fifteen minutes, and sometimes it wasn't done in four weeks, that's how hard it was to figure out. It had to look real. With portraiture, there's no action continuity, you can go anywhere you want. But in sports networks, *you are there*, and if they were sneaking up on a deer, you had to be with them while they did it. You couldn't feel that you were cutting to a crowd cutaway. You could cut away to the deer if you had that footage, but you had to make this thing progress and make it feel like you were quietly stalking the deer. I learned a lot from it. I can't believe they were paying me to do that.

Because you enjoyed it?

To teach me. I was struggling with it so much in the beginning, I didn't enjoy it, and the pressure was terrific. I really wanted to be doing serious documentaries, or portraiture with Merle. I was a disgruntled sports film editor. I did some nice things there. I won five Emmys for that work, I worked on the Olympics. Then they started doing *Race Across America*, the ten-day bicycle race. I did all five, five years in a row. Now I was doing serious documentaries even though they were sports events. They were really portraitures.

Each contained dramatic lines as you followed the major cyclists in depth. How did you keep the threads interwoven while still separated?

All the directors did that job. I thought they were exceptional and they only had two crews. One crew followed the leader of the pack and one crew followed the stragglers or the women. The drama of the story really was with the director. He was on the shoot so he knew what the event was, why he shot certain things, what he missed so that he could tell that story even though he missed it. Decide whether to use stock footage, up-close and personals, where to put those. That's pretty much all the director's call. The thing I was very good at was the flavor. Again I would get the emotional feeling, the sounds, the choice of music, and the rhythm of the cut. They would give me the outline—"We wanna go here, here, and here"—and then it was up to me to make that work.

You were following the race, so that was pretty straightforward.

And you knew who the winner was. You knew if you had a good finish line shot or not.

But all that was shot as the race was progressing, not restaged.

No, no, that was catch-as-catch-can.

In these large-scope events, how does everyone get covered?

They really can't, but it looks like they are. Amy Sacks sent me on location to direct the stragglers in St. Louis one year. I never want to do that again. I was sitting at the bridge in St. Louis and all I had to do was catch them as they came across, but you didn't know where they were. They were out in the country somewhere. They had spotters; you would call up the checkpoints to see if they'd seen them yet. Because they didn't see them didn't mean they hadn't passed. It was a nightmare. My spotter called me in the hotel room that this one girl we were supposed to shoot had just gone by *her* and she just *happened* to see her. Our report was that she wasn't due in St. Louis for another two hours! I had sent the cameraman to lunch. I went to the men's room and threw up! It was awful, awful. Of course, I never got the shot of her crossing the St. Louis bridge. When the cameraman came back from lunch, I said, "Uh, Peter, get in the car, we have to go!" At least we knew the race route and we drove until we found her, shot an interview with her somewhere near St. Louis. Another one I had to stay and get, the very last woman in the race, and Amy said, "Stay there until she comes through." I kept going out on the race route, up and down, back to St. Louis—I saw that bridge so many times. I thought, "That woman, she's *got* to come through." I wanted to kill her. In fact, I wanted to leave St. Louis and say I couldn't do it. The very next morning, it must have been six o'clock in the morning, I saw her. It was like a mirage! I found the soundman and the assistant cameraman (the cameraman already left). It was the wildest interview. She ended up being the darling of the race and said the most wonderful thing on camera: "Hey, how'd you guys find me!"

Did you use that line in the film?

Absolutely. It's the end of the film. It didn't make me want to go out and direct films.

Did you cut as you received the footage or wait for it all? And what was the ratio?

Probably twenty to one. By the time we got the film processed, I think the race was almost over. We waited until we got all of it, and then the producer came off the race and screened everything.

How did you discover your focus?

Mainly by who won the race, and you worked backwards. Usually there's a story in the last two, three days of the race. What you don't want to do is give away the story too soon. You don't want to end the race too soon since it's obvious that at this point on Day Five, the race is really between these two guys, or there's no race at all.

In one of the years, you intercut Super 8 film in black and white.

That was the idea of the producer, Joe Feld—he wanted to do something different that year, and he gave a couple of crews 8mm cameras and said, "Shoot whatever is funny. Don't document the race, just side attractions. Give a feel of what it's like to be on the road." He gave them color film and it was a little too bad in color. You thought it was our footage but bad, so we de-colored it, made it black and white so you always knew you were watching something different than our coverage. The joke at the time was that if they ever showed it on TBS, Ted Turner would colorize it and it would get mixed up with our footage! We took our chances.

You often created moods through your background music selection. You used popular theme songs too, like Jaws, Psycho, Close Encounters, Flintstones, *and* Twilight Zone, *all in one year's race!*

One year Amy Sacks used *Halloween*, the theme for the whole show. A lot of the racing was at night and it was kind of a spooky duel between these two guys. In sports at ABC, you can get away with using a lot of different music. ABC has a onetime usage right for any kind of music.

Do you cut to music?

Not any more. In *Sportsman*, I always did that. I laid the music down and, like a video, cut to the music. In sports they do it all the time, lay the music down, then illustrate it. I thought that was the way to go until I met Merle. She wouldn't let me do that. Two things happen. One is that you find out you have an internal rhythm, so whatever visual is going on, once you lay down some music to it, you'd be amazed that what you cut is falling into the music. The other is that the music is not that important, not that prominent, and it shouldn't lead the picture. The picture should be rich and lively on its own, and the music follows it. Supports it, I guess is better. Supports the feeling or the mood. The only exception is when I'm cutting someone who's singing. I have to lay the song down. I do let that dictate what's going on.

Is it a prerequisite for sports shows to have a lot of music?

No. We just felt it was important for the feeling of the show. It either told you what part of the country you were in, or it told you what we wanted you to feel that you might not have felt without it. There was this guy who entered the race with one leg, an amputee. At one point they were scraping him off the ground after a rest stop and putting him back on the bike, his brother helping him. It was a tender, poignant moment. And Amy Sacks said, "This is where I think we can hear 'Amazin' Grace'!" That was the feeling. The producers would come in with a lot of records they liked, that they wanted to hear. They didn't know where they wanted to hear it, but they wanted to hear it. When that sequence came up, we tried it there. It was made for that.

Do you find different sports require different cutting? Like the handi-capped skiing program compared with the bicycle races?

Sure. Skiing to me was more sequential, you had to show them coming down the run—which really made me crazy in that ski film because they didn't have it. It was obvious from the beginning that this was not a race film, this was a talking head film. A lot of feelings and every now and then you'd see an event, with no results. Even though you had to create a feeling that an event was going on with all these people competing. On the portrait of Great Britain, I got accused of cutting a cricket sequence like a commercial. The vision for the cricket sequence was, here is some-thing that we in America just don't understand, we don't know what these guys do and why they play, and why this passion for a game that has no ends, no innings, no runs, and could play for days. I cut this real action-oriented, and it didn't work. The director didn't like it because it looked like a commercial. Merle didn't like it because it didn't have any feeling of disorientation—you knew what was going on even if you didn't know what was going on. The footage to me didn't suggest disorientation. I re-member saying to Nonny, my assistant, that I didn't look forward to recut-ting it. She said she would like to and I was so relieved. She took my whole cut apart without any grace whatsoever, just tore it apart!

Were you too close to the material that you couldn't see it anymore?

That could be part of it. I think it's a rhythm, or I like to see the footage in a certain way. I thought that the nonsense I created in the action was frantic. Actually, as it turned out, it was just the opposite. You needed *no* action or little action. Instead of quick shots, a guy hitting a bat, some guy's knees, some guy catching a ball, some guy throwing a ball, Nonny took one shot of this guy running back and forth after he got the ball, just running back and forth, screen left, screen right. That was the key. Doing very little of anything, but it looked like the sport. It was great for me to let go and see somebody else do it. Nonny has been a wonderful, sup-portive assistant with remarkable instincts. She saved my life! I learned from that too.

What do you do editorially to keep sports events from becoming redun-dant or repetitive, especially a race that goes on for ten days?

When I did the bicycle race for the fifth time, I'd make a cut in Kansas, and I *know* I've made this cut before. They shot it in the same way on the same damned street and the guy is making the same damned turn at that building! I don't think anybody else noticed that. It's the feelings that are different. It goes back to the sound, what were you hearing there? It'd be interesting (if you could stand it) to show the races one after another. The events refresh themselves because they're different people. We keep watching the Olympics and who's going to win the rings or the vault or whatever. You don't ever get tired of that, they're different people, different stories. You could do it more faithful to the race. It would be interesting to do a show more faithful to the race in the sense that it's really tough and boring, and there is a sense of disorientation. I think those people would never want to be filmed that way—it's difficult to know when to be around them anyway. I would like to do something a little more realistic and not as stylistic in an event. I don't know how people would stand it.

These films tend to be glossy and slick, with vibrant colors. Is that for audience appeal? Are they trying to gloss over reality?
I think it's larger than life. That's part of what we do in television. It all has the same entertainment mentality. It's what they're yelling about with the Afghanistan War, it's too real and too good, it's too controlled, so they think it's contrived.

When I was watching the Antarctica documentary, I thought it was a "Hollywood movie" and I kept reminding myself it was not.
That's right.

There was only one official photographer, Mike Hoover—of the Afghanistan War controversy—with three other people trekking across the ice. Yet at the end, when they're risking their lives in a storm to reach the mother boat, how did we suddenly see each person in two separate boats, with no camera in sight?
That was wonderful. They really did that.

How?
They handed the camera over.

While they were trying to save their lives in that rough water?
Well, were they really saving their lives in that rough water? Did they really endanger themselves when they shot that sequence? Is it important to know if it's a set-up sequence or a case of good filmmaking? They did a similar thing in the tent. Mike Hoover did all his lines and Mike Graber photographed him, then Hoover held the camera on Graber and Graber did all his lines back. The acting was wonderful, they did the lines very well, and it was fun to cut. I marveled. You don't get stuff like this from these treks! As an editor, I want more dailies like Mike Hoover's. Hoover is really a wonderful filmmaker, he understands the craft. But there's that fine line between the responsibility of reality and filmmaking. To him, what he does is not a breach of reality. There's a shot in *Antarctica* where you see all *four* of them in the frame pulling the hang glider up the cliff.

I was wondering about that. Who else was there shooting them?

A guide went with them that far, and they were going to take him through the whole trip so that they could have four of them in the frame. I don't know why Hoover felt that was important, I would think just the opposite. But this guide got tired or something and went back. Then they were worried there would only be three from now on—which to me was a godsend. Who wants to worry about who shot all this?

In the gyrocopter sequence, I could see the foot of the pilot, Beverley Johnson (Hoover's wife), in part of the frame but there were also some beautiful aerial shots without her foot. Who else was flying around?

The only aerials were from the gyrocopter, even if Beverley's foot was not in them. Then other shots from the boats, and shots of her landing and taking off. Hoover got very upset about the way I cut the ending of the gyrocopter flight. You could see her going way over this clifflike thing for the landing. Then I cut to a close-up where she landed. He got real upset with that. "No, you can't do that. You have to stay on the long shot because people will wonder who was shooting the landing. We're on the boats." I argued and it stayed. She flew around for six minutes, an extended flying sequence, and it really was hairy. I thought it was an emotional cheat not to be with her when she landed. That was her moment and people wanted to know she was safe. If she landed in the long shot when she disappeared behind this bluff, you might not know she landed. For all you know, she went out into the ocean. In light of the Afghan War, I laughed that we even had that conversation! That he was worried about someone thinking who might be shooting her close-up.

While it didn't bother him that the four "only" people on the trek were in the same shots together.

Exactly. Again, that goes back to my emotional feelings. I felt the payoff was you had to be with her when she's landing.

Wasn't there loyalty to presenting a realistic scenario?

I think they worked very hard to make it look real. To *make* it *look* real.

Would that still be considered documentary?

To me it is. It's not really a breach of truth or faith, because they were there, they shot that. I don't care if he walked around in circles. The guy got off the boat, shot the stuff, set it up, they climbed the mountain, he got in the damned boats. They understood that it would not be a story if they just schlepped around, tested the snow in Antarctica, came home and said, "Well, it was wonderful." If there wasn't tension at the end, we didn't have a good story. The bike races, that's realistic. You may enhance it and the people themselves who are in the event may play to the camera.

They had one guy, he'd be on the road, really tired, and they wanted to catch him tired. As soon as they'd bring up the camera, he'd act up! You have altered reality in any documentary as soon as you turn a camera on. What is real? It's all propaganda, in the finest sense of the word.

You can't do that in broadcast journalism.

I don't know, they're doing it now! It concerns me about where does that go. You don't know, you just don't.

Having a "portrait," then, must be more of a relief because you're free to take artistic license.

I don't know about these portraits. To me they're still propaganda. They still give you a very limited view of a subject. There is a question of censorship in the form of what you decide to show and what you decide not to show. That could scare you too because you don't know what's the intention of the portrait. When I look back on *New York City* as an information piece, not as a film experience (it's a wonderful film experience), I think they liked *New York City* because it wasn't controversial. It didn't show how the city didn't work; in that sense it was not negative. It was very romantic, very spiritual. Almost like a journey. I think they were relieved that it didn't deal with race issues or the Mafia or the traffic or the mayor. There were two things I really always wanted to do: one was to work on a New York City film and one was to work with Merle Worth. And I got them both at the same time. The collaboration was wonderful *once* I understood how she worked. That was scary, I had to let go of a lot of stuff. But it was easy because the way she worked was so wonderful. It was the best film experience I ever had and I learned so much from her. It freed me up in many ways. She is fascinated by a lot of visual that is atmosphere and emotion that you wouldn't normally put in or try to figure out how to use. In the New York subway sequence, there's a brief clickety-clack section, with a shot of a hand in a subway window, kind of still, sort of floating. It's intriguing. I began to have another sensibility of being able to say it doesn't have to make sense, it has to fascinate or feel right where it is.

Would that be a difficult symbol for the viewer to interpret?

No, it's not symbol. The sequence has to shift direction and stop. You go bom-bom-bom and stop, bom-bom-bom and stop. We used the hand to stop it. It's not that kind of vision, it's just a wisp. In college, one of the biggest things my editing teacher, Manny Kirchheimer, taught me was that the images you put together had to be clear—which we were not to confuse with simple. He said you can be very complex and still be clear. In two or three shots, you had to let people know what was going on. Even today, I have trouble with anybody who uses symbolism, because symbolism is so many things to so many different people, it really isn't clear.

Isn't there a danger with inserting too many symbolic shots that the editing begins to be noticed?

My greatest gratification is when audiences don't know it's edited. I like the cuts I don't see. I don't want you to see the cut, I want you to feel the cut, feel the impact.

What's a cut that you would see?

Merle commented almost every time this cut came up: a woman sits writing at a desk, sort of medium shot, then you hear a bongo beat on the shot, an intro like something else is happening. I cut to a close-up, you see her hand come up in the frame with a pen, she kind of twirls it, and the bongo is beating. Then cut to a close-up of hands on bongo and you're off to another sequence. Every time this cut came up, Merle said, "I love that cut!" I didn't know where else to put the shot. I thought, "Oh well, I have to start this bongo sequence, maybe I'll insert this."

You didn't like the shot?

It's not that I didn't like it, but I didn't get a kick out of that. I don't get a kick out of people saying, "That's a great cut." I like the cut you don't see. I had a sequence of just ocean, ocean, ocean, shot after shot after shot, spooky, quiet. I had to break it. In Scotland they threw torches down a well and all you saw were red things that flew by the screen, whoosh, and went down into the darkness. I cut to that, what the hell! I didn't know where to use that shot anyway. I wanted to break something and that was a wonderful way to do it. When the producer Judy Reemtsma saw it, she jumped off her chair. "Oh my God! What a cut! Stop the machine!" I didn't know what to say. "Yeah, it was good." Those are not the ones I admire. To me, they're just big cuts.

Could it be that the images connected are really far apart?

No, it has to do with sensationalism. Ego. The Big Statement. "He did it! Look at that cut." The work I like is the work I feel I don't do. The work that is inner, that emerges or evolves. The cuts I don't see reflect that feeling more than these cuts. I don't like to go to movies and watch for the good cuts. I like to feel the film, feel the story. Then I have a feeling it was well edited. Sort of an inner—

Continuity?

Yeah. Inner worth. It could be very exciting, a lot of emotions. Maybe "seamless" is better. Not showy.

Did you somehow always feel you could find that inner worth by being an editor?

I envisioned myself as an editor when I made my first splice. It wasn't an illusion, it was an awakening. I didn't know how to edit, but I knew that I was an editor. My friends were moving along to directing or producing or becoming filmmakers, and I wasn't. All I wanted to do was edit. I thought, "There's something wrong with me!" Even my kids would tell me, "Dad, it's about time you became a director!" But when I sit down and start cutting, I can't stop. I want to see how this is going to turn out. I jokingly said to my assistant that, for me, it's like *The Red Shoes*. I spend a lot of time hating the dailies, organizing the material and not getting started. It's all preparation time that is valuable. I know I'm postponing sometimes, but the reason I postpone is because it's like *The Red Shoes*. When I make that first cut, it's all over. I know I'm going to be in this emotional turmoil because I work emotionally. I take a journey when I take on someone else's vision. I have found an outlet for my skills and my emotions, and I'm reaching some audience on some level. I don't know why that's important, but it's gratifying. The biggest audience I reach is me.

17

The Inner Voice

Sidney Levin

Listening to Sidney Levin, one almost feels that editing is philosophy. He echoes the words of many editors who seek the humanity within each film, but often are faced with obstacles erected by the "powers that be." Finding equanimity was easier once he established a smooth, cherished relationship with Martin Ritt.* "He was what I thought everyone in Hollywood was going to be like when I first started." Levin describes the lessons he has learned working with Ritt on such emotionally intense films as *Sounder* and *Norma Rae.*

Levin began doing still photography when he was eleven years old; by the time he was thirteen, he was photographing at a legitimate Hollywood theater where famous stars would perform onstage. He moved into animation and documentaries, and credits the latter "scriptless" genre for developing his inventiveness. His first formal editing experiences were on low-budget features from the American International Company. "The fact that there was a rape scene in every single film didn't matter to me, it was just the fact that I was able to experiment with images." Accepting the sordid genre as only a means to a greater end, Levin developed a rapport with the silent image. He was put to the test in *The River*, in which the trailer was constructed purely with music and images.

Levin is fascinated by layers, a personal trait extended into his choice of C. P. Snow as favorite author and J. S. Bach as favorite composer. He also believes that simplicity contributes to the rich textures and emotional depth of a great work of art. He illustrates this concept with a reference to his favorite director. "Marty will say *one* word that will complicate a scene and suddenly actors have to reach so deep within themselves that something sparks." Levin remarks with delicate conviction that editing holds the same sublime challenge for its practitioners.

* Martin Ritt died in 1991.

Your collaboration with Martin Ritt was almost made in heaven.

I was amazed and delighted that after working in Hollywood for eight or nine years I finally met someone I was truly comfortable with. He was from the theater, his sensibilities were so familiar to me, and he was what I thought everyone in Hollywood was going to be like when I first started. I was surprised to find that most of the people who were working in Hollywood didn't really love film. They didn't really care about it in the way that I cared about it, and certainly not in the way that I thought they would. So I had gone through a great disappointment until I met Marty on *Sounder*. On that film I was able to prove to myself as well as to someone who was established that I had the qualities and abilities to do first-rate work. Marty has a way of working with people that is particularly meaningful. I learned from him by example rather than by specific dictums. He taught me, and taught the actors, that the place of greatest richness is within yourself. He inspires everyone around him to search for the unique things they have to offer at that moment. As a result, the quality of work around him is higher than is usually found on most productions, where the director's ego, and his need to be powerful, takes over the production and doesn't allow for individual creativity generally. Which, by the way, I think is often true.

Can you give examples of how you were inspired on Sounder?

That film was a gem. *Sounder* is one of the nicest films I've ever seen as well as worked on. Essentially, it required little modeling after the initial editing was done. I had a real sense of rightness about how it should be put together and felt as inspired in the editing as everyone else did in the shooting. One poignant moment for me was during the filming of the father's homecoming. It was the scene of the mother running down the road towards her husband who she hadn't seen in many years. John Alonzo was shooting Cicely Tyson with a long lens. None of us could see her face clearly, only John could because he was watching through the viewfinder. When Marty yelled "Cut" and John moved his head away from the eyepiece, I could see that John was crying. While I was working on that end scene, I had a vision of how it should be constructed. I think I put it together the first time exactly the way it is today. And every time I worked on that scene—and I must have looked at it twelve, twenty, thirty times—I cried. For me, it was a striking example of what "acting truth" can do to you. I saw Marty's uniqueness in action on that scene, too. The scene wasn't quite jelling until he had said something to the children. He told them to yell, "Momma, Momma, what's wrong?" when they heard commotion on the front porch. Not just "Momma, Momma," but "Momma, Momma, what's wrong?" A child yelling "What's wrong?" to its mother is powerful. Children are supposed to be protected. When you hear a child say, "What's wrong?" the audience lets its guard down.

They're being seduced. You're going down to the base metal of fear. It triggers a response so visceral that it made this scene make you feel like you're on a roller coaster that can't be stopped. At that moment, I learned something very valuable: one little push of a barge can move a huge ship.

I also noticed you did not use music in the homecoming scene.

No. If something works, you don't have to falsify it. To me, Marty is very Japanese in the way he approaches film. He has a sense of purity that I think all great artists have. Honesty does not need to be adorned, it would get obscured. It makes no sense to push it beyond its form.

Do you find editing can help build the personality of a character?

Editing is a very manipulative device, obviously. When you don't have a strong performance, you have to search and find whatever devices are available to create what isn't there. My documentary background comes in very handy when I have to steal moments, a look or glance, and construct something that didn't exist in the shooting. That can be dangerous too, you can really get into your own ego. I think it's an artistic sin to make yourself, rather than the work, seen. The chief element to me is what is touching and moving. When I look at film in the "daily" form, I'm watching not as an editor but as an audience that has suspended disbelief. I jealously guard what I felt in those moments of first viewing so that during the next six or seven months, I can recall those initial feelings, and I can't lie to myself. There's a lot of self-delusion in filmmaking. It goes on everywhere, and in filmmaking, where the stakes are very high, it becomes even more prevalent. I have been with producers, directors, and writers who have seen what they've wanted to see rather than what existed on the film. My role, then, is to fulfill the film's promise with what exists, not with delusion. Hollywood is very incestuous, and if you're not careful, you will believe what everyone else believes rather than the truth.

Is that a legacy of the studio system from the 1930s and 1940s?

I guess in some measure it is, but it seems to me that wherever there's power and money, there's self-delusion. Hollywood reminds me of a feudal court. I think of myself as an artisan, or a puppeteer or jester in the king's court, someone they like and allow to come and eat with them, but I know I don't belong there. I have to leave the castle each night and go back to my place. That's what Hollywood is like. For anyone involved here who cares about the artistry of what they do, it's a real battle, an eternal battle.

How do you define "artist"?

I believe an artist is someone who stylizes life in such a way as to make the truth comprehensible for those who are watching the work of art.

That's how I see my role. I'm an artist and I believe that many of the people I work with are artists. Ultimately and fundamentally, I'm here to help clarify and explain the phenomena of the life around us. The difference between Marty Ritt and a lot of people I've worked with is that when you say to Marty, "I don't think this is working" and explain why, he'll listen carefully and move on it. With many others, you can have a lot of defensive arguing. It can be just like a husband and wife who don't get along.

How do you see through these difficult egos?

You can see through them by recognizing that movie power structures are basically the same. That the most ego-centered are as frightened of you as they wish you to be of them. Their posturing, that is often so cruel and heartless, is done because they're frightened and insecure. You won't take it personally. If you understand these things, you can swim through the turbulent sea without drowning, and even enjoy the swim. That's better than fearfully gasping for breath all the time.

And not feel bitter.

No! If you feel bitter, you may as well be dead. You need to become calm and helpful to the director, you can't do that if you're bitter. I have worked with directors and producers who have been quite cruel, and surrounded by sycophants. Even with them, I've tried to maintain my humor. I remember during my first interview on a major film, the famous director asked me, "Why do you want to do this film?" I said, "I think I have something to learn from you." And then I added, "I think you have something to learn from me." He didn't smile, he kind of nodded, and he hired me.

I'm sure he didn't appreciate that insight.

He didn't like it but he hired me. At one point in the making of the film, he said to me, "I don't like you, but I like your work." He's a rebel, Hollywood people distrust him because he doesn't conform, but he's brilliant. But then I'd ask myself: what is the value of someone's brilliance if in the end it serves the purpose of being alienating? I believe that each moment can increase our understanding of human beings in a way that is compassionate, and yet still remain mindful of the foibles of being human.

How do you insert your own compassion in editing?

Well, for example, in *Nashville*, I tried to find a moment of each character's humanity. That film had a big impact on filmmakers. It was innovative and out of Hollywood's mainstream. Before I was able to edit any of the film, I had to edit the soundtracks and construct the scenes in a way that was consistent with the script. *Nashville* was essentially an improvised film and each actor had his own soundtrack. There could be five or six or seven actors in a scene, and each was "miked" individually, with one of the eight-track channels devoted only to him. He could say whatever he wanted and not interfere with anyone else's soundtrack. Different takes could be wildly dissimilar and still be used. If all the actors spoke on the same soundtrack, you wouldn't be able to use different takes because you'd be forced into using one take. I was faced with having to put together one smooth, comprehensible flow from as many as eight different improvisations. There might be five hours of film for a scene that lasts ten minutes. After constructing the track, I constructed the picture to match the track. That's another time when documentary filmmaking experience proved to be very helpful. I'm very pleased with the editing of *Nashville*. In it, I tried to insert persistent little stones—I've got to explain something. I worked as an assistant for a year to an artist who did Italian mosaic murals, and the Italian stones, *tessere* they're called, are very small and very beautiful. I learned a great lesson from this artist that I never forgot. One time he pointed to the sky portion of the mural; it was composed of blue and grey stones. In the center of that field, he put one red stone and the entire mural changed color. In *Nashville*, I tried to put in my little *tessera* in each scene, one smile, one look, one moment of compassion.

Would you say editing is a paradox because it is both a mechanical occupation and an art?

Editing requires a certain kind of technical facility. All art does, but technique is just icing on the cake. What is important is the *humanity* of the work. We're not machines. The uniqueness that each individual can bring to the task is of the greatest value. It's a sensitivity that is created from whatever common sufferings we've gone through that produce our unique set of sensitivities that is important. The task is to remain alive and not bury those sensitivities and hide them behind fear. I'm trying to unmask our common fears so that everyone can see their commonality, and be more comfortable with exposing their own. If I keep sounding like I'm proselytizing, in a way I am. It's my desire that my work reflects the common good.

Do scripts sometimes restrict you from doing that?

Funny you mention that. I recently read a script that someone wants me to do. As the script unfolded, I felt it was somewhat distasteful, dark and angry. Then as I read a little further, I suddenly saw that it wasn't what I thought it was, it was funny. At first, I didn't see the twist on it. When I decided I really liked it, I asked myself if it's something I want to live with for six or seven months. I can't live with someone who's unpleasant or who I don't believe in. But I'm skillful at dropping everything when I go home—except at three in the morning when I think about life, death, and my work! I enjoy the game of it all, because filmmaking *is* a game. Mark Rydell was over at my house the other day and I told him, "You don't work, you've never worked, you've played your whole life." He laughed and said, "That's right." And if you work in film, you realize you're playing a game.

When I saw Stanley and Iris, *I think I saw one of those stones you described which brought out the humanity of Robert DeNiro's character: when he stands at the bus and says to Jane Fonda, "Teach me to read."*

That's Marty Ritt. That's a pivotal scene in the film. I saw Marty ruminating and trying to figure out what it was that he had to do to make it work well. What he decided was to complicate the scene with rain. An interesting thing to do. That allowed the actors to be broken down a bit— less comfortable, more raw, you can be more real. He's an extraordinary actor, DeNiro. I was sensitive to his acting. What I did was to not interrupt him, to be thoughtful, not harm it. The scene is exactly the way it was in the first cut of the film. It spoke itself. That's a tribute to the directing and to the acting.

You recognized that as an editor.

Yeah. I have nothing to prove. *Sounder* was the first time I worked with a major director and I was so concerned to find out Marty's reaction. After the film had completed shooting, I had a month to myself to work on it, then I ran it for Marty and he simply said "Good job" and walked away. I was disturbed that I didn't hear more. I wanted him to say, "Golly, this was great!" I remember saying to John Alonzo, "I really don't know whether he liked the work or not." I was too young to realize that some people say what they mean. John went up to Marty, I found out later, and said, "You didn't tell the kid that you liked his work." Marty's reaction was "That's his problem." That was a lesson from Marty that I haven't forgotten. It taught me to be more observant, more careful, quieter. Just quieter inside. Marty has often said that everyone who has talent will eventually make it. You do eventually, you just have to believe in yourself during those dark moments of your life. Marty radiates a quality of trust that can't help but warm you. I've learned from him to get the best of the people around you and help them understand their strengths. I do that with my assistants. I believe that my job in Hollywood has not as much to do with editing as it has been to teach and pass on this understanding of self-trust. I'm not doing it because I'm altruistic. I'm doing it because it's the most fun about being alive. It's necessary and, besides, I have no choice.

If you watch your films years later, do you forget you edited them?

Oh yeah, I have no idea what's happening next. None. When I edit a scene, I have ways of working that are very quick. I don't physically handle the film myself when I begin editing. I work on two KEM editing machines, I have four rolls of film up at a time, and I mark and number each cut on the film with a grease pencil, then write descriptions and those numbers on paper. Then my assistant tears them apart and reconstructs them into what I planned on paper. That way, when the film comes into my hand in its edited form, I no longer feel like the editor. Now I become my best friend who's helping and who's not going to tell anybody of any mistakes I've made. I can look at it and help myself through the next step. I'll spend a couple of hours working on the scene, polishing it, removing excess cuts that I put in—I'll always do that to see if it works, and then I'll set the scene aside until I forget it. My short-term memory is three days, generally. In that time I'll forget the problems on a particular scene—I can do that trick to myself—and I can watch it like an audience. Writing and editing are so similar in many respects, though not the same in its initial creativity. They're both phenomena that require forcing yourself to sit down in a chair—which is almost impossible to do sometimes.

It also involves disappearing into some realm of the unconscious.

Exactly. To the "other place." And that other place is where all artists go, otherwise they're producing nonsense. It will always be imitative if it is not from that deep place. Even the same story, same events, if it's from the deep place, becomes original and creative. That's what I strive for.

The human element is not always discovered in the obvious or traditional way. For instance, a close-up is not always more emotional.

Not at all. You have no idea what it's going to be. For example, I had another big lesson on *Sounder*. One of the last scenes in the film, where the father and the boy are sitting on a river bank. It's a very touching scene, shot in a two-shot and two singles. The two-shot was very good but the singles were even more powerful. When Marty and I looked at the dailies, we felt that the two-shot was so good that it shouldn't be tampered with, we should just let it play and not try to cut in the close-ups. But at one point, I said I would like to try to cut into close-ups and Marty said, "Of course, try it." So I inserted the two close-ups that I felt were really better and destroyed the scene because I interrupted the natural flow. A scene has its own life that mustn't be tampered with. So if I didn't know it before, I learned it then: that you're not supposed to edit unless you're *supposed* to edit. Sometimes the human element can even be a shot of something inanimate.

As in The Autobiography of Miss Jane Pittman *where you include a shot of the two rocks which represented a pivotal point in her early life.*

Right. You can construct a scene between two people, end it on the shot of an inanimate object, and still be brought to tears. I had a great deal of freedom on *Jane Pittman* because it was a TV picture; that meant that the director was gone after it was shot. It was a film that was well directed and it maintained the energy and power of the story.

Do you find cutting for a TV audience different than a film audience?

No. I'm doing the same kind of work, looking for ways to be clear, to clarify.

Of course, you can't please everyone in the audience.

You can't, and some directors and producers try to please everyone because they are unsure of their abilities as filmmakers. They lose sight of their original vision. I was on a film where after the preview, the director, having read every comment, tailored the film to please just one person, even if that person had no real understanding of what the film was about. It was astonishing to watch. It was madness.

Speaking of madness, you once mentioned that Nuts *was a technically difficult film to edit. Could you elaborate?*

It was the physical problem of editing a film that had so much coverage on it. There were five or six major actors in each scene. That meant that every ten-minute scene had an hour's worth of film on each actor so I had five or six hours of film on each scene. To go through that much film and not miss one important moment required a disciplined approach. We had a video hooked up to the camera, there was a videotape of each scene, and from that, one frame was blown up; that I would put on a large board so that each time I was editing a scene, I'd have three or four artboards full of stills with scene numbers on them in front of me. I would look at each piece of film very carefully and make notes on everything that touched me. I'd number each line so I'd know that Line 7 was particularly good in this take of that actor. By the time I was done, I had voluminous notes on what was good or not good in the film. Then my assistants pulled out all the important moments for me and put them on new daily rolls so I'd be dealing only with selected material. That brought down five hours of film to maybe an hour and a half. That was manageable. I could then feel confident that nothing valuable was lost. I've seen some editors take the closest soundtrack at hand and construct a scene from that. I couldn't do that. I know what it's like to shoot, it's the hardest damn work imaginable. I feel an obligation to all that effort.

That reminds me of Norma Rae *where it seems John Alonzo must have worked very hard to create a documentary look for a feature film.*

He had a lot to do with that. *Norma Rae* was an unusual film. John prelit the entire factory with daylight fluorescent bulbs and was able to shoot without elaborate lighting setups. Not only that, he handheld most of that film. He's strong as an ox and was able to do it. He has the sensitivity of an artist so that he knew when to move an inch this way and that, to move slightly in or out. It's a tour de force of sensational camerawork as far as I'm concerned, and it allowed the actors, everybody to work at high speed. The energy in that film pops out of the scenes. I can't disregard all that energy so I look at every single piece of film very carefully. If I'm tired, I'll walk away and play for a while, then come back.

Do you find it more difficult to edit a film where there is little or no dialogue, as in The River *where you had so much purely visual material?*

I love it. I did a trailer for *The River* which I thought was wonderful. Some audiences seemed to enjoy it, but the studio was very nervous about it. It didn't have one word of dialogue. Just music and images. I felt it conveyed the essence of what the film was supposed to be. I can't think of any more enjoyable task than cutting film to music. I'm working with images and emotions. Once you put in dialogue, you have forever labeled that particular work. You have grounded it in a certain way that images are not grounded. Images have the same fundamental spiritual contact with an individual that music has. An image goes past the verbal part of the mind, and can reach the emotions much more quickly than words can. So it's a very powerful tool. I love words, I'm not in any way saying that words can't do that too. I'm just saying it's a different task. Words can, certainly, but it requires an intellectual process to get to that next step.

Words almost tend to alienate people. If you don't understand a language, you are lost. For example, silent films were more—

Universal, that's right. I recently ran Chaplin's *The Gold Rush* for my five-year-old daughter. It was a sound version put out fifteen or twenty years after it was shot and Chaplin had written narration for the new version. It destroyed the scenes. Here was an example of words destroying the scenes. The great moments were choked because Chaplin was *talking* about them. Rather than letting you see them, he wanted you to *think* about them. "Now the Little Man is puzzled over . . . " It took the elevated and made it mundane. When I was a teenager, I worked with Chaplin in the theater. I watched him work with actors. He was wonderful.

What do you look for when you have to link image upon image?

You're looking for the best way to tell the story. In *The River*, it's the heartbreaking destruction of what these people have built. There's an image of water running under a bridge. At that moment I felt such pain at them losing the bridge they spent so much time building. Just that one shot of the bridge during the flooding sequence was so touching to me. The flooding sequence is one of the best directed scenes I shall ever work on.

Do you look at the way one image flows into the next?

Always. Editing is not just controlling a flow of moments as it is an accumulation of emotion. It's not so much the process of finding individual moments as it is of creating the flow of all those moments together. The images themselves would become boring unless they were truly part of the whole. So you're always looking for the *backbone* of that whole being. When you're initially editing, you're not thinking in terms of the overall, you're thinking in terms of the individual moment to moment in building a scene. When you've done that and then you look at the whole, you often realize you have reinforced the same point too often in the film. Now you can take them all out with the exception of just one, your strongest. The wise constructor of films knows to distill and refine. Again, it's a Japanese attitude about artistry. Down to the essence. Any appendage to the essence will dilute the impact.

So if you used ten river shots in a row, you knew that those were the best and the sequence was as distilled as you could make it?

Oh absolutely. There isn't a moment in a film I've edited that hasn't been carefully worked out and investigated. It's like Henri Cartier Bresson and his "decisive moment." For me, it's the "decisive cut." Each thing I do is inevitable for me. I'm not trying to compare myself with Bresson or Leonard Bernstein, who said that one of the most amazing things about Beethoven was that every note was inevitable. But in a much smaller way, the work I do has that same inevitability. It *has* to be cut. I've had two other editors recutting some of my work on *The River* because of time pressures. They told me about what they called the "Sid Levin Inevitability." When they investigated what they thought might be a good idea in redoing something, they found that I had already investigated it. They started with the attitude, "Why was this disregarded?" and when they went through all my film, they found that it couldn't have been done any other way as well. That was a reinforcement. If you are as honest as you can be with yourself, you'll end up doing what you're supposed to do.

What is the correlation between music and images?

The heart. It's in the heart. On all projects where music was important, I started by listening to the music until suddenly something goes bang in my heart and I know it's the right piece. Suddenly I'm inspired and then I cannot work fast enough to fulfill what I have to do. Sometimes if I'm writing, I like having the right piece of music behind me because it pushes me into that place for the words to start coming out. It's sheer joy when it flows! The most fun I've had in editing is when the music is right, the engine is running, and all I have to do is hop on the train and pick things off the trees as we go as fast as we can.

How influential is the beat of music in your cutting?

If you cut to the beat, you're being predictable, which is okay. And it will help you if you want to pull the rug out from under the audience later by an unexpected change of rhythm; that's fun to do. On an emotional scene, I will often cut rhythmically until something's about to happen, then I'll throw everything off so that you get tripped. It's the art of seduction. You're always seducing. You're seducing the audiences, your lovers, your readers. You're seducing everybody into giving away their protection. By setting up a structure, you're allowing them to be protected. Suddenly you pull the structure out, they're unprotected but they feel safe, and that's the art of seduction. Then you go ahead and do what you have to do. I don't know if I can say any more than that because how can you articulate something that's instinctive? You just know. And the process of becoming an artist is to trust when you know. The problem with many directors and producers is that they don't know what they know! They see it, but they don't believe it. They're afraid to believe what they've seen. You have to learn to trust that inner voice that never lies. But if you're full of fear, you can't hear that voice. And then you'll try to codify what it is that makes something right. You realize, of course, that can't be done.

Is seduction best achieved through editing?

It's accomplished by *everything* because in film there ain't no rules! Ain't no part of it more powerful than another. It *all* goes hand in hand. The D.P. has his role during the shooting as a constant collaborator of the director. On the set, my role at that time is to whisper in the ear of the director once in a while and to be a helpful pair of eyes during dailies. Marty says the most important part of directing is in the casting, and he may be right. When you cast the right person for the right role, he says 90 percent of the work has been done. That's something to think about. In the end, though, you need a cohesive, coherent agent to make it work right and that is the director. I think there's no particular aspect of filmmaking more powerful than the other. In *Sounder*, the chemistry of the words "Momma, Momma, what's wrong?" with sensitive camerawork, wonderful acting, followed by sensitive editing—and you're dealing with a scene that's a gem. It becomes a classic.

And the director knew all the elements would work together.

He knew. But we all knew something special was happening too because we were watching it happen. As an editor, your problem is not to destroy a good scene in the editing. The hardest thing to edit is a well-directed film because your work is naked. If you see dailies that are great, you *know* that you have screwed up if the edited version isn't better than the dailies. If you want to have trouble, be handed really good film.

Does it scare you to touch it?

It doesn't scare you. You just know that you're on the line, you will stand out.

But then the director can help you along.

Yes, but you don't want the director to go, "Oy gevalt, who's this idiot?" And God knows I've seen that happen. My ego demands that when the director looks at the film, they just go, "Wow." I want them to walk away feeling they have seen the best work possible. I don't know where that comes from because I'm very lazy.

You don't sound lazy.

Well, I am and I'm not. I'm lazy and laid-back about life, yet I care immensely. I think they go hand in hand. It's a balance. Everything I've said to you has had to do with that same refrain, which is "Listen to the inner voice." All the editing I do, *all* that I do, is being attuned to that inner voice.

Regardless of what anyone else says?

Especially regardless. That's the struggle! To divorce yourself from the popular conception. I've been to dailies screenings on location—those are the most dangerous screenings for an editor to go to. The crew's all laughing at the slightest thing and saying "That works great!" to make the director feel good, to make themselves look good. I remember the dilemmas I'd have after the screenings. I'd go back to the cutting room and say to myself, "Something's wrong. I don't see what they saw." In time I realized it wasn't there. Now I go to those screenings like I would to a teenage party where I know everyone's on the make and they don't know quite how to deal with it, and they're all scared. You don't go to a teenage party to learn philosophy! Accept it for what it is and understand the structure. You can learn a lot from that, but don't get caught up in the game. If you do, you may as well go home because you ain't going nowhere. You've got to be sure of yourself and know that that inner voice never lies and you can hear it. And that everybody, *every*body is in the same boat you're in.

Some people don't know how to row, though.

That's right, they don't. I figure it's our job to help show them.

At least throw them a lifesaver.

Yeah, they're going to get thrown over, so that would be nice.

Do you teach at school?

I go to USC once a year and speak to the graduating film class. Recently, I was told by the instructor that when he read the student papers about the speakers they had, it was mentioned that I was the only person who didn't talk about money. I read some of the term papers and I was surprised to see that they all mentioned how much I loved my work. I don't remember ever saying that, but I guess it comes across. I'll probably end up teaching and I'm accumulating videotape of dailies. I also have cut versions, recut versions, final versions of scenes. It's interesting to watch the process that takes place. Nowadays dailies are saved on videotape and I can collect the material more readily.

Would you ask your students to recut a scene that you did?

I might run a scene and ask them how they felt about it. Then run the scene again in a recut version, and then another recut, and help them understand the process. The actual cutting would be marvelous to do, but I don't know whether I have the patience to teach the physical technique in a school setting. I don't care about that as much as the emotional part of editing. Technique you can learn. What I have to offer has more to do with the contact that I want those people to make within themselves to be unique rather than to be like everybody else. They will not be good unless they are unique. That's my mission in teaching, though I also would like to pass on some very disciplined skills in the cutting room. If you don't have a good system of working, you work in chaos and fear.

Have you seen sloppy editing rooms?

I have, I have, and the work that the editor had to go through was tenfold of what it had to be. Editing is like working on a word processor. You want a real good one and you want to know all the moves and macros, and not think about it again. I've seen people work on word processors who aren't benefiting from the technology. As a result, they'll spend an hour doing something that should have taken them ten minutes—that was fifty minutes of creativity lost. They have to get a coffee after that, they're too tired! After you figure out what the hell's wrong and what to do about it, you're too tired, but if you have the skill, then it flows.

What do you want your classes to understand about editing?

I've spent all my time trying to keep my editing hidden. Even in the quick scene in *Stanley and Iris* where DeNiro says, "Teach me to read," the editing is subtle and hidden, I hope. You're not aware that it's being cut. You know? I can't answer that question easily. All I can say is I want them to understand that this editor tries as hard as he can to bring them along for the ride I know is there. The magic happens and I don't really know how. I'm trying to connect with their deep part. Connect all the deepest parts of ourselves. To help each other through this process.

And to make the images move.

To make them moved by the images. To tell them that just one small element can make such a difference. If you were to try to understand what makes editing powerful, and what makes an editor unique, you have to think in terms of those little *tessere* being placed in a large field. Take ten good editors, put them to the task of editing ten good scenes, and they'll come up fundamentally with the same construction. But what will be different will be a little stone here or there that changes the entire color.

18

Drawing the
Emotional Line

Merle Worth

1989–90 *Great Britain: Portrait of the World* (Series Producer/Director), Turner Broadcasting

1990 *People Magazine: Lawler the Brawler* (Producer/Director), CBS

1991 *The Gerasene Demoniac* (Producer/Director), American Bible Society
The Big Apple Circus (Producer/Director), HBO

* See Appendix for complete listing of editing awards and nominations.

Merle Worth has had the extraordinary advantage of crossing a number of specialized fields in film with ease. She has been editor, director, scriptwriter, and musical composer. She recently produced *Great Britain: Portrait of the World* for Turner Broadcasting, following her multifaceted, award-winning contributions in *Portrait of America*. Worth speaks authoritatively of the rigid, unadorned demands of broadcast journalism, having worked for many years with *CBS Reports*, NBC *First Camera*, and Bill Moyers. But she prefers working in "portraiture," a term she uses to describe a genre that she feels has not yet been adequately named. Of the various fields in filmmaking for which she has won numerous accolades, her first love remains editing.

Worth warms up most when she contemplates the power of editing to excite and illuminate the senses of the viewer. She traces her powerful, sometimes frightening drive to assault the senses to her early days at Columbia University Film School, where she built a loving and enduring network of support among colleagues—Ted Winterburn, Nonny Majchrzyk, and in particular, Howard Worth, who encouraged her to pursue her dreams and express her unconscious visions. Her first venture, a short theatrical film called *The Kite*, unleashed both an exhilarating and a disturbing quest to express the heart or the "emotional line" of her subject. This quest consumes her in every project she undertakes.

From *The Kite*, to the East-meets-West experience of *Raga*, to the uniquely personal and visually arresting *New York City: Portrait of America*, Worth's style fuses her intuitive, sensory, almost spiritual perceptions with her subjects and material. As much as she wishes to assault the viewer with sights, and especially sounds, she finds her work a tool to link the humanity of the viewer with the portrait she is painting. Her desire to probe the most hidden recesses of emotional expression has reached out to create a global village in documentary filmmaking. She is developing a training unit in Ghana that will essentially marry Western technology with African sensibilities and help to break barriers between cultures.

For Worth, editing and living are intertwined and inseparable: order, discipline, analysis, intuition, and emotional expression are vital for both to be successful and fulfilling. She believes that by fully understanding their craft, sensitive editors will discover unlimited potential to communicate on levels that transcend the physical. She is in awe of the risks involved in opening oneself to these hidden potentials. She knows, however, that tapping into these rich sources is the only way to seek and find art.

Why did you feel drawn into film?

I backed into film from another discipline. I was taking a doctorate at Columbia University in French history. But I was probably more committed to the *drama* of history than the actual content, so I switched graduate schools and took a course in the history of documentary film. All my apertures were suddenly opened. I had tremendous difficulty as a child communicating. Reaching out to touch people in ways that were nonverbal suddenly seemed to me a magic wand. Once, I heard Dick Cavett ask Sir Laurence Olivier in an interview why he acted. What he said made me burst into tears. As a child growing up in a small town in England, he used to run into the local theater and focus his eyes on the dark purple velvet stage curtains. The lights would go down and the curtains would part, and he said, "My passion had nothing to do with theater, it had everything to do with humanity." He wanted to be an instrument of healing, which is how he perceived acting. Well, I always have and continue to perceive making films in that way. You can touch the miraculous; with great courage you can do that. The miraculous, meaning the light and dark sides of life. You can comfort by the communality of experience. You're not alone.

Do you find that more possible in documentary than in fiction film?

I haven't worked on fiction films, I've worked on theatrical documentaries and theatrical shorts. In nonfiction films, you're dealing with real people and you have the timidity as well as the temerity to ask some very intimate questions that touch nerves and sometimes unleash an extraordinary flow of emotion. I've always questioned how a total stranger such as myself could dare to come into a home and ask things you might not even ask of dear friends. But people are so responsive and I'm responsive. I think it's because film production is very much like a ship at sea. You tell strangers on board intimate things because the journey is finite. There's an atmosphere in film production that burns intensely. All the senses are heightened, of the person participating and the interviewer. Nothing else dissipates that moment.

But through film, you are also making your subject immortal.
Yes, even though frailties as well as strengths surface in that context. It's very beautiful. I'm in awe of the process.

How did you make your first film?
My first job combined history and film in stock footage research. At that time, there were many stock footage series such as *The FDR Series, The Truman Years, Walter Cronkite's Twentieth Century.* I would research the whole show before the editor came on. I think I was probably cutting in my head while I was viewing the footage for the editor. I used the income from that job to make independent theatrical films such as my first short film, *The Kite,* which was produced and believed in by Howard Worth. Being so innocent, not only did I have no concept of what we were supposed to do, but I had no fear. Now I'd be paralyzed! Jess Paley, a professional cameraman, and I went up on rooftops and created a fantasy. I shot it in 35mm, the whole film cost four thousand dollars. I never edited before, so I rigged a setup on my dining room table, cut the film on the viewer with rewinds, and used network cutting rooms at night when everybody went home. Miraculously, *The Kite* was released theatrically with Joseph Losey's *The Servant.* It thrilled me and also terrified me because it was a controversial film; it actually created riots in the theaters. I don't understand it to this day. The audience would applaud and seconds later they'd boo. Drawn by the controversy, *The New York Times* came several times to review the film.

What was so controversial about it?
The Kite was an eleven-minute apparition conceived by a young woman who had absolutely no understanding of the creative forces being released in her. Looking back on it, I would say it's one of the unsafest things I ever did and one of the most fearless. It was a film with a narrative line that had no people in it, no dialogue. The entire film was an impressionistic, somewhat terrifying dream of inanimate objects coming to life. It was a total sensory assault. I show it to people when I teach classes today and they're very disturbed by it. There are similar moments in *New York City* and *Mississippi,* but they're much more mature technically than in *The Kite.* That film is savage in its energy.

You wrote, directed, and edited it yourself?
Yes. My first editing job!

How did you feel the editing contributed to the savagery of the film?

The editing was everything. It was the juxtaposition of really assaultive abstract sound with lyrical imagery that I think made the film so remarkably disturbing. What you were seeing was so soothing and beautiful, and what you were hearing was so abrasive. It's very Japanese in its highly delicate, fragile style, yet with a great seething pumping beneath it. I used electronic pulses which, at the time, were very new and unsettling. My friend Ted Winterburn was editing a sports show at ABC. "Could you use sound effects of catapults being released?" he asked. I said, "Bring it over!" When I slowed it down, it became a whipping sound. Very early on, as an editor, I experimented with a variety of speeds in sound, layers of speeds. If I have a wind track running at normal speed, I'd be interested in slowing down that wind loop and running that on top of the normal one, phasing them in and out. The instinct to use different speeds was developed at that time to an extraordinary degree. When I went to India to edit the Beatles–Ravi Shankar theatrical documentary *Raga*, all of a sudden I was thrown into the world of drones and tones that suspend. I learned a great deal from Ravi about that concept and applied a number of the principles to editing. In the same ways that Eastern music alters your state of consciousness, those were the ways I tried to develop in film editing, to drift you off center, off the concrete reality into a more intuitive one. You need to do very concrete things to create an ephemeral context. In *Mississippi*, during the Willie Morris sequence in the cemetery, there are a number of drones humming inaudibly that create a dream state. I even used them during some of the on-camera interview material to create another level of consciousness.

Does music inspire you when you're editing?

I sometimes pick the music before I cut to focus on the spirit, the soul of the film. Just listening to certain pieces of music gives me impulses for cutting the sequence, and sometimes I don't even use the music after that. I'm totally disinterested in cutting for information, in the specific sense of the word. I'm absolutely *not* in the business of telling you what to think. I am very experiential in my approach. I really don't want you to know what you think until you have had the experience, until you know what you feel. Then you can draw whatever conclusions you want. For some people it's an exhausting style, for some it's exhilarating. I rarely get an in-between response.

Why is sound so important to you?

As an editor, sound is the critical issue for me. It's always been my lead rather than picture. I need to have the sound equivalent of a feeling or a sound representation of a character before I could even begin to edit. Maybe because I was trained as a musician first. The soundtrack has always interested me, at least as much as the picture. But again I'm more interested in interpretive sound than actual sound. I mentally score sound effects while I'm out in the field shooting. Here's a perfect example. In *Mississippi*, we were in the Delta at the peak of the cotton harvest. It was high noon and we were standing in a vast, steamy field. The actual location sound I was hearing never captured that vaporous feeling of miles and miles of blinding white cotton, a commodity that shaped the destiny of this nation. Standing in the middle of that stretch of whiteness, you couldn't help feeling enveloped by the history of slavery, and by the sheer human effort it took to survive those conditions. I was trying to anticipate for the editor—who was going to be me—how to find the sound that gave that sense of oppression and heat and otherworldliness. I wouldn't have worried about the sound, anticipated it, had I not also been an editor. Right then and there, Roger Phenix, the sound man, and I were experimenting with how to translate heat waves into sound. The first thing we did was to record cicadas at a variety of speeds. The normal sound of a cicada on the recording did not give you the floating, disassociating feeling that you had standing there. Playing with speeds, slowing it down many times and playing with two tracks overlaid was one way to do it. What we ultimately did was create an electronic drone that most closely approximated the *effect* of those cicadas and made a loop of it. That seemed even more effective because drones have such a quality of suspension.

Having the enviable position of being both director and editor, how did you find each helped the other?

Directing and editing are inseparable. I'm preediting when I'm directing, and I'm directing when I'm editing. They fuse together. I try to second-guess the editor, who might be myself, when I'm out in the field directing. I find I'm far more sensitive to things than most directors who are not editors. For example, in *Mississippi*, when I was directing Son Thomas, the blues player, I noticed that he had a tendency to drift in and out of his own thoughts, that inner and outer reality. As a director, I knew that it would become an editing problem to translate that reality onto film. In order for it to work in the cutting room, it had to be solved in the field. There was no way that an editor could make that concept work, if the director wasn't aware that the editor had to do it. I worked out a technique in the field for the editor whereby I had Son Thomas speaking to me and then lapsing into long silences which were precipitated by my talking to him, knowing that in the cutting room I would take a lot of his thoughts and run them voiceover himself in between the sync takes that he did on camera. Son Thomas would stare directly at you into the camera, voiceovering his thoughts, and then *without a cut*, he suddenly would begin speaking directly to you in sync. It was a way of changing one's inner reality and the outer reality of the ideas. You almost felt as if there were two Son Thomases talking: the Son Thomas who was longing and reflective, and the Son Thomas who chose to speak directly in words that were bitter and measured. In fact, it was the same interview. There was no way you could successfully edit Son Thomas without respecting the rhythm that he finds within himself to express himself. The director would not have engaged him in conversation to hold those pauses long enough for an editor to build a voiceover introspection, had the director not been aware of the cutting technique. In editing narration, the editor plays a vital directorial role as well. Since the narration is usually not recorded to the picture, the editor must make the words and image correspond by building in or removing pauses in the reading of the narration. In other words, you are repacing the delivery. The actor, even the director, would not think of including those pauses since they would have no concept of how the narration has to be laid into the track at the most timely points for dramatic impact. When you have voiceovers, as is the case with most documentaries, often these narrators are not professional actors, and it is up to the editor to determine the most effective emotional pacing in the cutting room. Actually, the editor is directing all the time.

That's also like being a scriptwriter, seeing a potential in a character that can evolve throughout the script.

I guess so. That's what total filmmaking is.

Did you have scripts for these programs?

No. You write a treatment roughing out your focus, locations, and characters, then go out and shoot. The concepts and locations you want to explore are pre-cut in your head. It is pre-scripted in the sense that you know where you're going, who you're interviewing, the setups. The script is written to a cut picture rather than the other way around. In the *Mississippi* program, there was a twenty to one ratio with the footage, so as an editor, I was working with about forty thousand feet of film to two thousand. I am very interested in interpreting what is going on through sound and image, in the *spirit* of the people uttering those words. The words are necessary, but they're merely a vehicle for something larger. And then, there are always the accidental miracles. I was going to interview Dean Faulkner, William's niece, outside on the traditional front porch steps. We were setting lights in Faulkner's bedroom for indoor shots when she walked in. I said, "Why don't we just shoot you at the door for cutaways?" and she said, "Fine." We started to roll. She couldn't stay still, she couldn't contain the memories, it all came rushing out. About halfway through, she put her hands up and said, "Stop. This is too painful." I had barely asked two questions. There is a moment when you're torn between being a human and being a filmmaker. I was paralyzed. I decided to do nothing and let Dean make the decision. We stared at each other in silence for some time and she asked to leave the room. I don't know what this hypnotic allure is about movies, but minutes later, she came back in and resumed her flow of reverie. We, of course, had never stopped rolling.

Were you always on location during the shooting of these portraits?

A lot of them, yes. It seems obvious to say that it's an advantage. But sometimes it's not, because you become attached to the memories of achieving that sequence. If it was particularly arduous, you have to fight hard with yourself in the cutting room to throw it out if it doesn't work. But it does give you an atmospheric edge that you don't have any other way. When I was editing for other people, especially the networks, there were no real directors, there were producers. I think most of the producers in the networks assumed that the film would be formed in the cutting room, much to the burden of the editor, and much to the excitement of the editor, depending on how you viewed it. For me, it was thrilling because you could go anywhere with that material. You weren't confined. But as a rule, you were deluged by footage and the burden was on the editor to make sense of it.

Might that be a reason why some editors feel underacknowledged?

I can't speak for the feature film world, but I feel it certainly in television, especially because budgets are being slashed, unbelievably now. It's a funnel effect. People consume a lot of time and budget in research, development, and production. By the time you get down to the editing, you're running out of money, running out of weeks, running out of nerves and patience. So the editors get squeezed at the end. Everybody *thinks* they understand what editors are doing. But nobody understands the magic of that process with a great editor. It's pure magic, as a brilliant magician would approach his craft with the proper tools and an understanding of the concrete aspects of it. And the more you know the rules of your craft, the more you can leave them behind. What gives one editor the edge over another is, in my view, that you're drawing deeply on your intuitive self—depending, of course, on how refined an instrument your intuitive self is. In my opinion, that's what creates the difference between good work and brilliant work. You sit down with all this material, you know what the assignment is, and you know what the producer's requirements are in terms of what the show has to say. Now you could cut it together from the basis of logic, you could cut it together from a thematic approach. Or you could make that grand leap of imagination, combine both, and transcend into some other place where these objectives are transformed. When I ask myself, "Why does that moment work?", I'm thrilled when I *can't* answer that. The confluence of what I am feeling and what that material is feeling is like two lovers in a room. There's a little dance of courtship in the beginning. What goes on between you and that material is so sensual, so seductive, so intimate, that it whispers in your ear, you whisper in its ear. If the affair works, it transcends the material and the talent of the editor and the producer's objectives. You create a spark of life.

That sounds so private. How does it work for an audience?

The common denominators are there for all of us. Intimacy is intimacy. When you experience it directly, you're stirred. Transmitted to the screen, it has a unique power of its own. I don't believe that you should be engaging in such esoterica that you leave your audience behind, but I don't believe that what touches me is going to be radically different from what touches the viewer. Second-guessing an audience is a hopeless pursuit. I know, because I've worked for networks and cable stations where the concern is to second-guess your cut based on ratings and what people will like or not like, rather than on the intrinsic value of the piece. I've given up on that because there are no two people who will agree on what the audience will or won't like, and then you play that hideous game of the lowest common denominator. But I don't think of myself as being so removed from the audience that I am impervious to what is touching, absurd, or surreal.

You believe that certain emotions hold true for every audience?

The humanity part, first and foremost. And as a director and as an editor, finding the way to clue the viewer into how unbelievably layered our existence is. How profoundly layered it is. Everyone walks around with contrapuntal responses. The editor has the most exquisite art form to explore that. It's a real challenge and a real responsibility.

Your editing style does seem "layered," in fact. Or dense, with overlaps of sound and images. The New York portrait was very much like that, which was also appropriate to the city's sensory nature.

I specialize in sensory assault! There's a woman composer who released a recording of accordion music played in a well in Cologne. Just as the reverberations created a whole new set of tonalities overlaid on what she was already playing. That's ultimately what we were hoping to create in that film. Living in New York, we can't separate out the tracks because traffic and birds and kids and sirens all fuse into some other presence. If you ran that film silent, it's a striking film visually. But the layers of sound, not merely the images, move you into the darkness and light of this town. We experimented with overlaying two music tracks on top of each other, and on top of that, starting a rhythm beat and then sound effects. We were working with a very compressed editing style, overlaying several simultaneous tracks to see what would happen.

Did you feel a compulsion to keep adding sounds to each other?

Yes, and we did, and then we lost definition. Believe it or not, we knew when to stop!

Many times you also include images that don't seem to belong in the sequence. In Mississippi, *for example, as Willie Morris reads to the children in a library, you suddenly cut to a bicyclist, a bouncing ball, and fade out with a rocking bench.*

Morris was reading to the kids about the town he grew up in, Yazoo City, and I felt so cheated not to see that town. His reading had such a feeling of "memory chips" breaking off and floating to the surface. That is exactly the phrase that occurred to me as I was listening to him on camera. I staged the ball and the swing because they're so quintessentially Southern childhood, a kind of dream living. It was all done in his town, Yazoo City, but it was staged. Willie Morris reading was a real event. There's a real crossover. *Vérité* people would shoot me at dawn! That's why these programs are portraiture, not journalism. This form of filmmaking has become so controversial because it's real, but interpreted.

How would you define your genre?

I've never thought about it. Well, my own life is processed always, first, through my senses. Then I deduce from my whole being what I need to know. So the experiential aspect of my film style is just an extension of the way I need to live my life. I'm amused by *cinéma vérité*. You either like *vérité* or you don't, but it's not reality; it's some little piece of your notion of what's going on. I mean, what reality are we talking about here? Whose reality? In editing or directing, I'm never interested in reproducing the event. I'm interested in *interpreting* it. For me, the enthrallment comes from that altered state of perceiving. I've spent enough time in West Africa and in India to understand that what we call information in this society is so pallid. With the help of some extraordinary people in Ghana, I began to understand different sources of information; for example, "awe" as a source of information. My *idée fixe* is to find sources of "information" about a place or a person that are far more intangible, and to me, more valuable than the ABCs of what they're saying. Editing for me is a tool to explore the intricate ways a human being, given this finite interlude we call a life, can touch the world, can connect to the world. It's just a tool. I'm not in love with editing, I'm not even in love with filmmaking. It's just the most appropriate tool I have to tap into the incandescence of what I feel.

Especially in the New York film, you tapped into the incandescence of the city. I am thinking of the time lapse shots of dusk to dark.

Yes. You know that moment in New York when it's dusk and suddenly it's dark, and you *never* know how that moment slipped from dusk to dark even though you keep watching the sky. I just interpreted that feeling of awe and mystery, and the only way to do that was with a time lapse shot. Merely finding the miraculous in the ordinary, or what we've come to think of as ordinary, because we expose ourselves to it the same way every time.

That feeling is also conveyed in the story of Doug Lee, the genius behind the night illumination of New York skyscrapers. You turned a technological tale into a magical one.

In shooting footage for that sequence, I asked the cameraman to shoot searchlights, the beams themselves, and the guy cranking the spotlight machine. I was in love with that image and I thought for sure we were going to do an electricity sequence when we got back to the cutting room. But all of a sudden, the magic was gone when you saw the machinery. That would have served us well if we were making a film about the technology of lighting buildings, but I was making a film about a mirage that this old fellow had for the city. He had an apparition, and you shouldn't show the machinery of that. But I decided to intercut the beams in the middle of his interview. Who would have known we would be using that shot in that way?·

In that sequence, you also had a startling insert of his eyes at an angle. How did you use cutaways in the middle of his story?

Cameramen often love to give you cutaways of people's hands or feet in order to give you the capacity to cut within an interview, if you don't have the interviewer covered in cutaways. I loathe those shots! I never use them and I beg the cameraman never to waste footage on that because I know in the cutting room I'm never going to use them. I passed them up when I was an editor, and I pass them up now as a director. As an editor, I know that those are Band-Aids—they are covering a cut! I'd rather see a jump cut than an artificial Band-Aid. I'm not interested in staying with the surface reality of what's being said. So I use shots to impressionistically advance your interpretation of who that person is. Doug Lee is a visionary. That was the perfect extreme close-up for a visionary: his pale blue eyes lost in some reverie of what skylines bathed in light at night would look like. I choose shots that are true to the representation of the character, not just to cover cuts.

Sometimes the impressionistic image unexpectedly contrasts with the personality, such as Jerry Clower, the tall-tale teller, juxtaposed to the falling tree in Mississippi.

Jerry was such an enormous presence, and I faced the challenge of how to end his sequence. He was a lumberjack who became a renowned comedian. In one scene, he stands onstage with his arms outstretched and suddenly we cut to a series of shots of trees falling. We cut back to his empty dressing room and fade out with a voiceover of his laughter. His whole personality had a tone of absurdity, he's such an exaggeration, such a Southern fabrication, that I was looking for an extreme image to resolve him. So I chopped him down! But Jerry would find that funny, so then I put his laugh in over the empty room. He absolutely adored that piece.

By the way you cut images together, you may be creating more of a personality than the personalities realize they have. The portraits seem to be rich in personality profiles.

The controversial profile, but I think the one that's winning all the awards, is the sequence in *New York* that begins with a telephone voice and moves to moments seen through apartment windows. Private moments. There was no character development—the character was the city. The only window scene that was staged was that of the woman walking back and forth on the phone, but all the other window life was voyeuristic, shot with a long lens. We were just careful not to reveal anyone's face. So much of New York life is in windows, don't you think? I'm always very curious as to what the hell's going on in there. So I wanted to give an impression of moments lived behind the walls. Plus I grew up in New York. As a little girl, I used to tap dance in the hallways holding on to the doorknob, so I wanted a little girl dancer to be there, I wanted to pay tribute to that. The local cemetery near where I grew up is in the film. It's just a lot of my own childhood, fragments of memory in that sequence. I often think of film editing as a midwife to memory. It can give birth to new ways of feeling, seeing, remembering. It reproduces that moment in which our hearts first opened to experience. We can manipulate sound and image across time and space, to bypass the cognitive for the intuitive realm, to free the audience to swim in that state of dreamy remembrance. I think the editing process can make or break these kinds of sequences. You can get a lot of images and sounds into a cutting room, but you have to find the dark and light sides and juxtapose each with the other. However, you have to be real careful about the character with whom you choose to do that. It has to be appropriate to the character.

Do you feel a responsibility to the character you are portraying?

First and foremost. What a moral responsibility you have as an editor.

When I look at a set of dailies, it's a real trust for me. I think fiction films would be easier on the soul. I wouldn't have so much moral wrestling as I do in documentaries. These people have given you something precious. You've come in and asked unusual, sometimes inappropriate questions. They've shared their emotions. When you get into the cutting room, you have to be respectful of that. After all, it's people's lives. I think editors have such power in terms of making someone look like a fool or like a sage. I've done news shows as well, broadcast journalism. Totally different sensibility. In broadcast journalism, there is an ethics manual, a series of no-no's in addition to what you learn in the field. For example, you cannot add music to editorialize. The Westmoreland case was quintessential. You have to be careful about the way you abstract material and connect it to another abstraction. The concern always is about material not appearing out of context. In broadcast journalism, it is very clear-cut. You are cutting for information, balancing the issues. It is totally unadorned, stripped down. Otherwise, you are accused of interpreting, manipulating the character, enhancing an issue through atmosphere that simply was not intended. It's a whole other sensibility and that's basically why I left.

So you prefer interpretation through portraiture.

People who want to be very purist about documentaries get real nervous about interpretation. That's a can of worms as old as filmmaking. But there is no such thing as noninterpreting. Everybody who knows the ABCs of editing or of camera angles knows that there is no way to avoid making an editorial, whether you shoot low angle, high angle, what you choose to leave out or put in. There is no such thing as a cold objectivity. Everyday in life you cut your "dailies" and choose to define their meaning and line. It's no different from what you do in editing.

How do you reach a respectful interpretation of your subject?

Find the emotional line of a piece first. As a director, the greatest struggle I have with most editors I work with is forcing them to grasp the emotional line. Once you find the emotional line, a third of the dailies will be irrelevant, no matter how beautiful they may be. It's the way I choose to work all the time. As we know, you could cut the same dailies a million different ways, from lukewarm to passionate, depending on the line you construct to begin with.

What can you tell an editor who doesn't understand your focus?

To use the mind and spirit simultaneously to serve the moment. To look into the film with a rhapsodic intellect. What is a character about? How does he develop emotionally so that you're thoroughly captivated and drawn into his journey? Most people can get the emotional line of a *scene* or a *person*, but often they will miss the emotional line of the whole film. Depending on the nature of the film, of course, I have often watched dailies silent, especially interviews. When you watch interviews silent, there is a range of subtle emotion on the character's face that you don't catch when you hear the track. It gives you other insights. Psychological clues, temperamental clues.

As director, though, you would have heard the character during the interview. Wouldn't that bias your outlook?

When you're directing, your adrenalin is at an all-time high. You're praying that all systems are go, that the questions you ask are productive, that the answers you get are coherent and developing a concept. You don't have the opportunity, as in a feature film, to do Take 23. You don't have the opportunity to focus on the emotional expression of the face because oftentimes you can only shoot it once. When you get back to the cutting room and run your interview silent, for the first time you might realize a deep streak of melancholia in this person. But their voice was so animated and their ideas so vibrant that you never caught it. Once you catch it watching the dailies silent, you're able to build another dimension in music and sound that serves the total character.

When you're viewing silent, have you ever been taken with the image and then find that the sound that goes with that image doesn't match?

Oh yes. But I think it's always a question of not having picked the wrong emotion, just having picked the wrong sound to accompany that emotion. Once you understand what overall mood this person or place represents, it's a matter of orchestration. For the Faulkner sequence in *Mississippi,* I wanted an oboe concerto, which didn't work because the orchestration was too heavy for the languid, nostalgic atmosphere of that place. It buried the delicacy of that feeling. So I found a piano solo in a minor key, almost identical to that oboe concerto in feeling, but with a different texture and orchestration. Everything about a character or a place dictates the rhythm, the metronome, of that material. An editor has to let go of preconceptions, serve who that person is and what his or her atmosphere requires. Most people choose to get their line of development conceptually: "What does it mean?" I need to ask, "What does it feel like?" Only then can I grasp the meaning. It's not better or worse, it's just radically different. Working from the inside out.

How did you manage to let go of your Western preconceptions for Raga?

It was a very humbling experience. I had to substantially divest myself of notions of rhythm, space, and time as a Westerner and subjugate myself to what the culture was telling me. My God, I called into question everything I'd known about Western sensibilities for the first half of that film, which took place in India. I reverted back to Western sensibilities for the American part of the film. What a difference! Each raga that is performed runs about two or two-and-a-half hours, and I had to cut them down to maybe ten, eleven minutes each so that we could weave other material throughout. Nothing I edited worked for me. Musically I knew where to cut, but it had no magic. It absolutely tormented me. Then the most extraordinary concept hit me: that I was imposing Western sensibility by always cutting on the beat. Indian music has a sustaining drone to it all the time. So in the slower parts, if you cut on the beat, you break its floating dimension. After the first rough-cut screening was over, Ravi Shankar said, "It's musically perfect, but it doesn't work." He taught me something about Indian music and editing which, of course, filtered into my own life forever. He said I did what a lot of Western people do, which is to neglect the middle section of the raga because it appears to be so melodically uneventful. But in the middle section, all the themes of the first section are being resolved and the seeds for the third section are being planted. It seems as if nothing is going on, but it's the subtlest change, a complex shifting of the rhythmic and melodic patterns, and you cannot be impatient with it, you have to make it work. That was true in my own life. I'm terribly impatient with what seems like plateaus, and his comments changed my life.

How can you encourage students of editing to think this way about the material?

It's not conscious. If they think it's going to come in some conscious selection of material, it doesn't. There is another reality that creeps into you when you're looking at the material over and over again. It's not cognitive in the conventional way that we understand that word. You are looking from inside the bloodstream of what's going on. Initially, you are working exclusively in the realm of intuition. No matter how well structured and intellectual and verbal you are about why you did what you did, that second of creative ignition is intuitive.

Do you think that the images that reinvent memory and emotion in your films actually create editing that jars the audience?

Two shots together shouldn't have such an arresting effect that it's inconceivable that they go together. It's arresting because you never thought of the common denominators between those images. Some editing is seamless because it's like velvet, you're taken on a trip that has no bumps. There seems a direct determination to get from A to Z along a smooth path. Then there is seamless editing where you shift perspectives, but it's jarring in that the sensation it causes is arresting. It's not that the two don't belong together. It's that A plus B sends you out into inner space!

So editing really is a collaboration between the film material and the senses.

To give that sense of fusion and wholeness to a person's existence is the most edifying thing you can attempt to do for a viewer. You can do that in sound, in image, and in pacing. As an editor, you can control the pace of whether someone looks longingly at something for three seconds or fifteen, and force the viewers to lose their defenses, to discover something about themselves in looking at that face for the extra six seconds. How long do you decide to hold something? We deal with frames. One frame, two frames make the difference, if a cut works or if it's sluggish or abrupt. There's a normal period; if you hold it a little longer, it's attractive; if you hold it longer than that, it runs the risk of being boring. Past the point of boredom you can sometimes reach anguish or awe. It's that zone that interests me most. The uncomfortable moment when you feel you need to look away is the moment I feel that real drama is beginning. It's finding the moment of drama in the viewer, in the viewer's discovery of self.

Is it possible to concretize what an editor does?

We build sound and image in ways that reinforce how unbelievably layered our existence is. We all move through life with contrapuntal responses to things, and we as filmmakers have the most exquisite tools to recreate that. What we do is make *compressions of human experience.* At our best, that's what we do! When I'm eyeball to eyeball with other humans on the screen, I face my own fears and strengths over and over again and I send my responses back. That's the real meaning of the global village to me, finding that moment of drama, that split-second intersection of me, subject, and viewer, in which we all rediscover yet another piece of ourselves. Editing is my form of rebellion in a society geared to demystifying the universe. This society, unfortunately, does not respond to much that is shimmering beneath the surface. I wouldn't hesitate to spend the rest of my life putting some of the mystification back in. Once in India, I saw a great Kathakali dance master who had such control over his being that he was able to make one half of his face smile, while on the other half, one eye would weep. That's how I feel about the process of making films. You have to keep those two halves simultaneously in balance all the time. Half of you is worldly and scrutinizing, the other half is innocent and vulnerable. Without that fusion, without that measured incredulity, what you wind up with is merely footage. In the end, however, there's no concrete explanation for the magic any more than there is for human chemistry and why you fall in love. We could logically explore this together forever, but there is still something so mysterious about the editing process that I would hate for the moment to come when I no longer feel that way.

19

The Supreme Collaboration

Barry Malkin

1981   *Four Friends,* directed by
        Arthur Penn (Coeditor:
        Marc Laub)

1982   *Hammett,* directed by
        Wim Wenders (Coeditors:
        Robert Q. Lovett, Marc Laub,
        Janice Hampton)

1983   *Rumble Fish,* directed by
        Francis Ford Coppola

1984   ** The Cotton Club,* directed by
        Francis Ford Coppola (Co-
        editor: Robert Q. Lovett)

1986   *Peggy Sue Got Married,*
        directed by Francis
        Ford Coppola

1987   *Gardens of Stone,* directed
        by Francis Ford Coppola

1988   *Big,* directed by
        Penny Marshall

1989   *New York Stories,* directed
        by Francis Ford Coppola (one
        story, *Life Without Zoe*)
        (Editor of Martin Scorsese
        story: Thelma Schoonmaker)
        (Editor of Woody Allen story:
        Susan E. Morse)
        Meet the Applegates (Con-
        sultant), directed by
        Michael Lehmann (Editor:
        Norman Hollyn)

1989–90 *The Freshman,* directed by
        Andrew Bergman

1990   *The Godfather, Part III*
        (Supervising Editor), directed
        by Francis Ford Coppola
        (Coeditors: Walter Murch,
        Lisa Fruchtman)

* See Appendix for complete list of editing
awards and nominations.

Although his wife has presented him with videotapes of many films he has edited, Barry Malkin cannot make himself look at them. Watching films on a TV screen just isn't the same, he says, and besides, he would think of all the things he would want to change. His current film matters above all, and what he has learned along the way has become as second-nature as breathing.

When given a lead question, though, Malkin can spill out details of a busy life that was diverted from a major in psychology when he met a childhood friend who introduced him to an editorial house. His early career hopscotched through army instructional films, industrial films, documentaries, and commercials. Luckily, Dede Allen urged him to direct his talents to feature films, and he became her apprentice for a short time on *America, America*. Through this experience, Malkin met his mentor, Aram Avakian, who challenged him to explore more subconscious, convention-breaking approaches to cutting, and hired him for work on *Lilith*. It wasn't until *The Rain People* that Malkin met another long-lost childhood friend, Francis Ford Coppola, and began an editor-director collaboration that has lasted over twenty years.

Malkin's casual but sensitive comments on editing reflect the influence of his studies in psychology, often touched with wry humor. He speaks with great understanding of the position of the editor in the business wheels of the movie industry, and presents an unjaundiced description of what can happen to a film in the hands of nonfilmmakers—or even overzealous filmmakers. Because of his longevity in the business and with Coppola, Malkin presents an ideal case study of how an editor can achieve the ultimate working relationship with a director.

Your career editing feature films closely parallels the directing career of Francis Ford Coppola, since you have edited nearly all of his films. How did you form such a steady collaboration?

I was offered what I would call my first "A" feature, *The Rain People* (though technically speaking it was low budget, but there was a major studio involved) and this film marked my initial work relationship with a childhood acquaintance named Francis Coppola. We lived in the same neighborhood as teenagers. I probably hadn't seen him since I was seventeen years old. One day, while visiting Aram Avakian, who was editing *You're a Big Boy Now* for Francis, I happened to idly look at a script and noticed that it was written by Francis Ford Coppola. And I said, "I used to have a friend when I was a kid named Francie Coppola (pronounced KA-*POE*-LA). I wonder if it's the same guy?" Some months later, when Aram inquired, Francis said, "I knew a guy named Blackie Malkin," a nickname of mine from those days. Aram arranged for us to meet, and some time later, Francis called me about working on *The Rain People*. We solidified a friendship that really had never previously existed. Francis was much more a bookish guy than I was as a kid; I was totally involved in athletic pursuits. He was also a gadgeteer, the first kid in the neighborhood with a tape recorder, an 8mm camera, and other interesting playthings. Many years later when I was working on *Godfather II*, his sister, Talia Shire, found home movies of a birthday party at Francis's, and there I was among all of the fifteen-, sixteen-year-olds doing the lindyhop, wearing my nifty pink shirt with upturned collar and sporting a pompadour! Anyway, *The Rain People* was my opportunity to edit a class feature film. Since that early collaboration, Francis and I have been involved together in many productions. For me, he is the easiest director to work with. For starters, we don't have discussions about which take to use: our tastes are very similar and there's a mutual trust. There's a lot of timesaving, as crazy as the editorial process might get, because we're often on the same beam. Communication is done in shorthand.

What was the editing setup on The Rain People?

The film was a real journey and I was required to deal with the production during the entire shoot. We began in Garden City, New York, and wound up four months later in Nebraska, shooting in many cities along the way, often winging it on the move. Francis had by this time directed two or three films. He had gotten special sanction from the International Alliance, and we were composed of members from New York, Chicago, and Los Angeles union jurisdictions—unusual at that time. We were just twenty-five people, including the two stars, and we moved in a caravan of seven vehicles, one of which was a mobile home called a Dodge Travco in which my "cutting room" was situated. I taped a label to the home's exterior titling it "The Magical Mystery Tour." We also had our own band, comprised of crew and cast members featuring Jimmy Caan on piano. Rewinds were mounted on the side of the sink, a Steenbeck was wedged into the original kitchenette space, and we also doubled as the dressing room. I didn't get to do too much editing while we were traveling during the first half of the shoot, but we spent quite a bit of time in Nebraska, at which point we moved into an empty store, flew in additional editing equipment from the Warner Brothers stockpile, and started editing full scale.

Your earlier work with Aram Avakian influenced your style in editing films for Penn and Coppola, didn't it?

I learned a lot from Aram. Learned about breaking rules and trying to do things less conventionally, not for the sake of breaking conventions, but to attempt originality or a fresh point of view. Aram was one of the few feature film editors in New York at that time and he offered me a job as his assistant on *Lilith*. I had gotten to know him during my work on *America, America*. He was a friend of Dede Allen's and used to drop by our cutting room. He became my mentor; he felt like a big uncle. Aram had a montage style that involved multiple images. He was in some way influenced by the work of still photographers; in fact, he had been one. I remember once asking him what I could do to learn more about film editing. I don't know if I ever asked that of anybody, I never really read books about editing. Most of what I knew came intuitively or just from looking at movies. But Aram said to me, "Look at collages and do collages." I started cutting up newspapers and magazines at home and hanging things on the wall, playing with images and moving things around, doing assemblage, so to speak. We used to talk about different jazz musicians and their approaches to music, how tempo and harmony influenced our putting film together, whether this was a subconscious kind of thing. I also realized that film editing had its parallel in musical arranging, and I started paying more attention to "arranging."

Did you cut to jazz music?

Oh yeah, almost everybody has done that. I had been exposed to that in my work in the commercial world. There's a method in which music specifically influences your cutting, certain rhythms dictate your cutting, but I don't mean that. I'm talking about less conscious rhythmic approaches like Miles Davis's use of space in his music. Sometimes we'd say, "Let's put this sequence together and see if we can do it with as few cuts as possible. Let's play cuts as long as we can." Or "Let's cut it like Charlie Parker." Very often the adventurous sequence would wind up in a form diametrically opposed to where we set out. We didn't really talk about "the craft." "Us guys" talked about the "movies." I don't even think the word film entered our vocabulary!

When you experimented, how did you sense what worked and what didn't?

I don't know. You just played a shot until you thought it ran out of steam or somebody made a "mistake," whether that be actor or production technician. Aram made me think less formally about film, although in so doing I developed my own style—whatever that may be. He thought I was a brash young kid who had a lot of nerve. He claimed that the first time he met me, I walked into his room when I needed to borrow a synchronizer and literally pushed him away from his table. I think I *asked* whether I could borrow it for a few minutes, but he perpetuated this myth! He opened up a side of me that was hidden. The work was always joyous. The cutting room was a place filled with laughter.

Once you made the transition, what differences and similarities did you find between the commercial and feature worlds?

I could not tolerate the advertising agency types, which was really what drove me into features. What I found so unusual, when I moved to my first feature as apprentice, was that the editor had tremendous input and a great deal of respect from the director—a mutuality of respect. At the agencies, people were afraid of losing their jobs. There was the whole account group, and one would look at dailies—nine million takes of a close-up of a bottle with a hand coming into frame to open the cap! People would spill their guts deciding which was the best take. This was wearing on my soul. But I learned things in the commercial world that were helpful. I learned speed, because of ever-present deadlines. Commercials are minifilms, same problems, same processes. A dramatic film takes a long time, but as in commercials or documentaries, you're chipping away at a mass of information footage—trying to refine, refine. Ironically, the film business today seems to be populated with "Vice Presidents" of this or that—not far removed in type from my former adversaries at the ad agencies.

What was your experience with One-Trick Pony?

I came in to lend a hand. I wasn't the editor who began the film, nor the editor who finished it. Sometimes I would recut what the other editors, Eddie Beyer and David Ray, did. We traded sequences back and forth, dramatic sequences, performance sequences, transitional montages. I worked on a little bit of everything, as I remember, tried to help them reshape the film, put it into a continuity different from the way it was scripted—often one of the essential parts of editing a movie. After you get past the technical part of cutting all the little pieces together, then comes the important task of moving chapters around.

Was Four Friends *difficult to edit in presenting the viewpoint of the central character instead of splitting it up among his friends?*

I don't recall that being a particular difficulty. The focus was generally on Danilo, and I think we keyed off him. But it was a story of four friends and parents and girlfriends too, and the film was not shot in a subjective manner. Whatever subjectivity there was came from the editing. There was standard coverage, but in certain situations, as in the flag-burning sequence, the subjectivity is apparent or more focused. Though it was essentially Danilo's story, perspectives did shift.

Yes, sometimes the perspective comes through Georgia's eyes. For instance, the wedding scene where the father comes down the stairs before he shoots his daughter and Danilo. You see this through his eyes, then you switch into Georgia's horrified reaction.

I remember I had difficulty in trying to establish the girl's horror, and for want of actual expression on film, I did something that I hadn't done before or after. Not that the technique was absolutely new, but strangely enough, some people credited me with starting "something." I slowed the action down. I multiply printed the girl's reaction, the horror on her face. Somebody at a screening asked Arthur Penn, "What's that?" He said, "I don't know. I call it a 'Malkin.'" I printed each frame two or three times or I varied the frame multiplicities. For want of slow motion, I used that technique. Her reactions didn't last long enough, at least didn't strike me as lasting long enough to have the emotion that I wanted. I remember doing that with Georgia's close-ups.

You also used "slow motion" when Danilo is watching the flag-burning and the flag runs across the windshield of the car as he sits inside.

I multiply printed, that's right, and superimposed some of it. That may have been done to counter what I had earlier done. But rather than trying to create an effect, it became a practical way of doing something. The flag whipped across too quickly to give it impact. By optically slowing the action, it had a new impact. The same way that a person hit by gunfire or some other dynamic action has in slow motion.

I gather that effect was not written into the script.

No, that wasn't stated in the script. I put the sequence together and it wasn't happening. It wasn't working because I wasn't getting any emotion out of what the actors were doing, or what I felt one should feel for those characters, because of the duration of expression, so I had to manipulate it. One does this in editing in various ways. Sometimes when something is lengthened, it's not apparent to the viewer. There are ways to optically extend: freeze the frame, print in multiples, print it forward and backward—part of the everyday vocabulary. You use whatever technique is best for that given moment. Or sometimes simply by double or triple cutting. That is: repeating the action.

Your main concern is always the emotional impact on the audience.
Yeah, yeah. You use the technique that works best to spotlight the emotion or event.

Speaking of perspective, Rumble Fish *was shot in black and white except for some startling inserts of the fish in color. Was that done because the Mickey Rourke character could only see black and white?*
I'm not sure that was the impetus for the decision, but it was certainly partly that. That film has gained some sort of underground status. The black and white, splashes of color, painted shadows of the German Expressionist cinema, and the soundtrack have garnered a following. The music itself was a first effort by Stewart Copeland, a former member of the rock group, the Police. Francis Coppola gave him some vague idea of what he thought he was going to do with the film and Stewart recorded some music based on these notions. I used this as temp music all along as I was cutting, where I thought it worked. What was unique about that movie was that we tried to integrate the timbres, the emotional feelings you get from certain sound effects, into the music, so we kept a close communication between our sound editor, Ed Beyer, and Stewart. Ed would provide Stewart with the prominent sounds we planned to use in sequences and Stewart would use them as a point of departure, written in a key that would complement the harmonics of that sound effect. The amalgamation of music and sound.

Was the rumble scene from that movie difficult to edit? I counted something like eighty-one shots in two minutes.
Oh no, you can find a lot more films with many, many more cuts per minute. Just look at MTV. Some people respond to flash. It's generally easier to cut stuff like that, action scenes, where you have the option to go to any one of many places from one cut to another, where your options are great, than it is to edit a dialogue scene with a lot of characters sitting around a table. That stuff is a million times more difficult to cut than your average flashy shoot-'em-up razzle-dazzle sequence. That kind of cutting is what traditionally gets honored with awards, though. I know anytime I've ever won anything, or if people talk about it, even my peers, it's the

razzle-dazzle, it's the flash, it's the quick stuff. The average dialogue sequence is more difficult to edit than the rumble scene. That's why I so admire Dede Allen's work.

It's quite a contrast to a film like Gardens of Stone.

That was an elegy of sorts, a film about death. In my first cut, I constructed certain sequences to exactly document the way the honor guard did their ceremonies. When I began that film, it was impressed upon me that in the end we would allow the army or the people who performed the ceremonies to look at the cut and make sure we had done it properly. But in the end, they relaxed their demands and we were allowed to skip over certain parts of the ceremonies because it took too long. But the first time I put the sequences together, I followed the ceremonial rites to a tee. They originally had many, many more cuts than they eventually did. But it's a different kind of film in total. It's brooding, purposely so.

A far cry from the army instructional film of your early career.

I still remember the name of it: *Use of Teletypewriter SP22PT for Switching Teletypewriter Circuits,* the first thing I ever cut. A technical adviser was supplied by the army and stayed in the cutting room with me. There really wasn't a script, just a lot of shots, what are called inserts, of various pieces of machinery. The adviser made sure I assembled the film in a technically correct way. When the film was in one piece, the first cut was very close to the intended length—I guess the army knows how to shoot these things economically. I then had to take the silent workprint, which ran about a half hour, to the Army Pictorial Center (now the Astoria Studios), and screen it with some civilian executives of the Defense Department. I sat in the back of the screening room holding the intended narration and read it aloud as the executives viewed the film. It was very difficult for anybody but an experienced narrator to read almost continuously for a half hour, watch the screen, and make sure the voiceover was coming in at the right spots. I was absolutely winded!

It's no wonder features gave you a sense of freedom. Did you feel you could define your own voice in feature films? Or is it possible to identify an editorial voice?

I don't have great philosophies to expound about this, but it's really hard to know what the film editor does by looking at the finished product. You can say something is nicely put together and it's sometimes apparent that something special has been done. But it's really hard to appreciate what the film editor's input has or has not been, unless you're there observing how it's done. It's unlike beautiful photography which is apparent to the eye; beautiful costumes or production design are quite visible. But film editing is much more amorphous, it's not palpable. One can say Shot

1 lasts seven feet, eleven frames; Shot 2 is a particular length, of a particular angle. Cutting from the master to the close-up, one can explain it in
physical terms. But not what the options were, whether the choices were
right or wrong, how it improved a moment in an individual sequence or
in a cut-to-cut analysis, what a new perspective is after eliminations are
made, points of view, ad infinitum. Things have become very different
today. The alleged pace of the audience is much faster now. It's conditioned by television. We're always being told by the powers that be,
the studio execs, that "It's too slow." The audience has to be titillated and,
for my money, you're often forcing the material when you shouldn't.
People count numbers at previews, it's a game of statistics. It's very hard
for someone to see his conception through. Pace is very often forced. Jazz
it up!

Did you find that to be true with The Cotton Club?

Yeah. *The Cotton Club* was a film that got compressed to its detriment,
in my opinion. My opinion may not bring in more movie dollars, but as
an execution of the script, we did some violence. We started crosscutting
and moving things around. Right from the very beginning, there's a dance
piece involving the Cotton Club girls, and it's intercut with titles. Originally, the titles were a self-contained title sequence, live action shooting
of specially-lit architectural letters. We compressed two ideas—titles and
that dance sequence—by intercutting. I preferred it when it was two
separate sequences. Sometimes it's the fault of the filmmakers going in.
People start with scripts that are overly long that really should be abbreviated for commercial demands. If you're going to work in this arena,
you've got to know that the average picture can't last more than two hours
because it must be shown a certain number of times a day. But *The Cotton Club* was special. I think it would have been more successful in a
longer version. Sometimes we think of ourselves as artists or crafts-
men, but there are these commercial demands and restraints, and they
very much impinge upon the work of the film editor in the commercial
cinema—the whole testing process of a film. After you've reached a point
you think is right, the response of the test audience is paramount—rules
the roost. It used to be that the filmmaker had to go begging to the studio
for extra money to shoot a new scene. Now it's kind of imposed, now it's
the studio telling the filmmakers, "We really need a happy ending."
Sometimes you agree and often you disagree. I recently worked on a film
where the head of the studio begged us to shoot "a happy ending." I was
personally against doing that. Some of my superiors almost relented, but
finally we ended the film as had always been planned, as it was scripted—
without the happy ending. And the film was a tremendous success. One
would have to say the studio was very wrong in feeling that the original

ending was going to hurt, despite the preview reaction. But there are all sorts of accountants and lawyers running this business—it becomes the bottom line, the tail wags the dog.

There's conflict all the time in media-related business, then.

At a late point in postproduction, people who I never see are somewhere behind doors making decisions about what lies out there at the box office. Is this film going to be a winner or should we minimize our losses at this point? Or do we think that if we improve the numbers this much at the next preview that it's worth spending millions more to shoot more stuff, redo the music, or create a flashy opening sequence? Most of these things are done in vain. It usually compromises the script.

Would Apocalypse Now *be of the same situation you're describing?*

No, because that was all the filmmaker's doing, the director's option. That was a film that went to great lengths and great costs and great time for various reasons, a lot of them having nothing to do with filmmaking per se. But whatever was done, was done rightly or wrongly because the filmmaker decided to do it that way, to reshoot a scene, recast an actor, shoot second unit stuff after the fact. To help the film as he sees it, not somebody else saying we'll make a lot more money if we do it *this* way. I had begun *Apocalypse Now* and worked on it for about four months in Manila. About the time of the first hiatus, we got knocked out by a typhoon and I left the film at that point for personal reasons. I brought Evan Lottman in as a replacement and came back to New York to put both of *The Godfather* films together for television, adding a lot of new material that had never been in either of them. Did it out of guilt because I had to leave *Apocalypse*. Then I got involved again with *Apocalypse* during its second hiatus, when everybody just needed a break at Christmastime. But *Apocalypse* was not the situation I was describing earlier, something that's really gotten hot and heavy in the business over the last three or four years: heavy previewing, all sorts of marketing experts, people surveying. They took films to Pasadena in the early days of moviemaking, but now it's *de rigueur* and you're flying all over the place on a few weekends from this city to that city. All these supposed pockets of Americana: Phoenix, Minneapolis, Denver, San Jose. Everybody looks at their numbers. All I know is that films that have gotten very high marks, have tested well, don't always make money. It's all very much geared to a young audience. Generations of people brought up on television rather than on movies or even books. It leans toward the lowest common denominator and that's frustrating.

Big *was a tremendous commercial success.*

Probably the biggest commercial success of any film I ever worked on.

Despite the numbers game, or the ultimate success of a film such as Big, *it seems that you as editor still strive to follow what you feel is the best for the film itself.*

I'm dealing with the reality of the film. Up until the time it's filmed, it's a concept—a writer's concept, then a director's concept, then a production design idea. It's rehearsed. Then the reality of it exists in the rushes—the raw film. It reaches a certain performance level or it doesn't, it's photographed well or poorly, or there are problems with the light because the sun was lost or because the second day of shooting wasn't like the first; an actor had acne that day and we've got to minimize this or that. So I'm viewing the myriad problems of that particular scene and looking for what I think are the highpoints. How can I do the best with what I have? I try and remember what attracted me at first viewing in a particular take, in a particular moment. Still, an editor's input varies. Who is to say that a given sequence that one sees in Film X was something that the editor had a great deal to do with? It may have been written that way, it may have been the director's desire that it be that way, or it may have been a very original piece of work by that film editor. An idea may have been unscripted or edited in a manner so different from the original intent. There's a lot of stuff in feature films that is created in the cutting room. People who don't work in that area have the conception that everything is scripted and planned. There is a tremendous amount of planning, there's always a script and rewriting is commonplace, films are sometimes storyboarded before they're shot. But a lot of that is thrown by the wayside once you get into the cutting room. The buck stops there. So I don't know what Editor X's contribution is to a film. I can say, "I really like the way it's put together" or "I don't like the way it's put together." But I don't know what his options were, how he overcame the lapses that exist in every script. His signature isn't in the corner of every moment. Film is a collaborative effort in that the finished product has passed through a lot of hands.

Given that it's so hard to pinpoint specific contributions by an editor, what would you say is the overall effect of editing? There is, regardless of Editor A, B, or C, a concrete movement of images that results from somebody's efforts.

Along with a lot of other things that you are doing, you are essentially telling a story. There are various points of view from which you can tell a story. One doesn't know when you see the film how you would feel about a given sequence told from another point of view, whether it would be more effective or less. It's like reading a book. I don't know while I read a book what hasn't been included, what's been shifted around, what little word was changed to improve. Nor should these questions enter my thinking. An editor attempts to make it better. A film, when it is edited, is redirected. It is first directed and then there's a chance for redirection, involving the director and the editor and whoever else may have input into the situation. One hopes that in the editing of the film, in the redirection of it—given the reality of what exists *on* the film, both good and bad—that you're coming up with the best. You have a closet full of clothes and you hope that you put together the right pieces of apparel each day— with originality, flair, pizzazz to coordinate your outfit. An editor makes thousands of decisions while cutting a full-length film. And you often keep changing your mind as the film evolves, as the editing evolves. You start out chipping at a big block of stone, hours and hours of film that are refined to eventually reflect the essential script. But nothing *is* written in stone. You remove something for whatever reason. "It's a good scene but it's really slowing us down." "It's a lousy scene, do we need it?" So you take something out. The scenes that originally appeared before and after this "no-longer-existing-scene" now follow each other back-to-back. Well, now that they follow each other, a brand new continuity exists dictating the modification of the ending of one and the start of the other—there is a need for a better transition. You constantly reorder your priorities. You may have started the sequence long shot, medium shot, close-up, and change to close-up, medium shot, and ending loose, in its simplest, most basic form.

You must be flexible.

Yeah. Sometimes to achieve those things, you wind up having to break rules that you make for yourself, rules of structure and form, and you have to teach yourself to accept another way, a way that didn't originally fit neatly into your personal philosophy.

It struck me that in Peggy Sue Got Married, *you indeed broke a rule of perspective. Because Peggy Sue is unconscious, the audience is seeing every character and episode through her dream perspective. But in one scene, she talks to the Nicolas Cage character and leaves, but we remain with him until he is rejected by a musical agent. How did Peggy Sue know what happened if she wasn't there?*

Right. It's funny, that particular shot was done as an afterthought. We were trying to make his character more sympathetic. So we may have swayed from whatever subjectivity we had established and done that to gain a couple of points for the character. Sure, one tries to stick with point of view, but you sometimes box yourself in. When you set up rules for yourself, especially when you're less experienced and you have certain formulations in your mind, you tend to leave a lot of good stuff out. There's a lot of film you precensor because it doesn't fit into your little personal window. You close yourself off a priori to a lot of goodies. That's it, pick the good stuff and then you get rid of the bad—that's the bottom line of what we do. We could talk about a lot of fancy theories of montage, but it's all very boring. Essentially that's what you want to do.

Pick the best for the best effect.

Let's see what is good and let's get as much of that into the movie, and let's get rid of the stuff that doesn't work. We're faced with a lot of problems in doing that, the mechanics—it's not like erasing a word from paper! But then you rely on your technical abilities to get from point A to point B to point C. The film is constantly in a state of flux. Once you realize that no matter how hard you work, there's a very good chance that you're going to change it for one reason or another, then you become much more relaxed. When you first start editing, you marry yourself to everything that you do and you hate to think about the physical difficulty of undoing. Just the physical part of the job is often arduous. What a drag if you have to make a change! But you have to think of it more as a first draft, as in writing. I think most editors tend to overcut when they're younger. You try and show the world what you can do, how you can use it all. Make a lot of cuts. Before I really knew what I was doing, I used to think, "Well, he shot it, I guess he meant for me to use it!" Then you realize a lot of directors really are unsure or uncertain as they're shooting a film that they are "covering" a scene, and one has to be selective, one has to refine. Why use two shots when you can make do with one? Sometimes you have a beautiful shot, but it's gilding the lily, it's beauty for beauty's sake. Along the way, you start breaking rules, become less orthodox. Sometimes there are the usual matching problems which a young editor pays undue attention to and wants everybody looking exactly the same way from shot to shot. Why let that rule your editing?

Wouldn't audiences be aware something is mismatched?

As you become more experienced, you realize that most people aren't going to see it, they're not inspecting it cut by cut as you are. Unlike the editor who's stopping it on his Moviola or flatbed, they aren't going to see that a character is looking down instead of up, or using his left hand in one take and then his right hand. Let's go for performance, let's not rule that out just because it's not as cosmetically attractive a cut as we would hope it to be. When I was a kid there was a guy named Sidney Skolsky who wrote about the movies in one of the New York newspapers; he carried an item called "Boner of the Week" and he'd mention some glaring error in a movie, about how some actor's hair or costume or whatever didn't match from one scene to another. I'm sure that most of the audience was unaware as they watched the films. It's not that we don't try to minimize these problems—and they exist in each and every movie, in every scene—but that kind of stuff is small potatoes in the greater realm of things.

You find the story or performance dictates what you edit.

Hopefully so. This tells us what we want it to tell, it moves us, it achieves the intent. How do we spotlight it?

Is it easier to choose the best shots in a film like The Godfather *where everyone is covered with tons of backup shots?*

Usually there's never time to do all that you would like to do, but yeah, on a picture like that, you have ample coverage. But when we don't have the coverage, when there hasn't been time to shoot it, you can't hem yourself in. You break rules, you jump the axis, throw matching out the window and do the best you can. You have to say, "Screw it, all right, so it's not the greatest cut, but at least I used what I thought was best and made it play."

Did you work on Godfather I?

No. Just *Godfather II* and the TV version.

Godfather II *seemed to be so much more psychologically oriented to understand the background of the major characters. Was that your own approach to the film?*

The film in its eventual form was different from how it was scripted, that is, in the way different eras were intercut. The TV version was chronological: the early 1900s scenes from *Godfather II* to start, and then *Godfather I* in the middle, and ending with the more contemporary stuff from *Godfather II*. *Godfather II* was scripted chronologically. But along the way we decided to crosscut the old and the new, so we had to find transitions, make transitions, figure out how to do it every time we veered from the scripted continuity. Maybe that's why you found it more psychologically oriented.

There were some beautifully fluid transitions. Each time you moved from the "old" Robert DeNiro section, you superimposed Al Pacino picking up with a similar action in the present.

Sometimes it worked. It involved repositioning shots and designing a nice optical effect. Maybe flipping a shot to create a nice graphic. I think the film is better for it that way. In the TV version, we could often take "commercial breaks" to get around transition problems.

As for Life Without Zoe, *which was one of the trilogy of* New York Stories, *did the three editors meet to discuss their techniques or goals for each story's effect on the whole film?*

There couldn't have been three more dissimilar films, which I think was one of the attractive things about the project. When all three were finished, we assembled them as one movie and screened it, and I suggested switching the continuity and the other editors and directors agreed. When we first screened the project, the continuity was: Coppola, Allen, Scorsese; it was changed to: Scorsese, Coppola, Allen. I thought it best to start with the most dramatic, segue to the fairy tale, and leave 'em laughing at the finish. But they were three individual productions really, separated by fades at ends and beginnings of each. Our segment left me unhappy. We abbreviated it and removed some material from the film to make it more palatable to the audience. It was a film that was not conceived to be quick. I felt we rendered the story less faithfully and hurt it. And I know Francis feels that way too. I think he yielded to commercial demands, and I was sorry that a number of things wound up on the floor. But I'm unsure that it would have made people like the segment any more.

Do you find there are different principles for editing comedy and drama films?

My first real experience with comedy was *Big*, and I am working on another now called *The Freshman*. Oh, I had cut some comedy stuff for TV years and years ago. People are always talking about pace and timing in comedy. While that's all true, I think it's somewhat overblown. I think the same rules govern all kinds of filmmaking. I don't think one takes a specific beat for comedy. It's got to vary from film to film. It's a cut-by-cut business. Every action, every line, every look is different. From cut to cut, whether it's dramatic, whether it's action, whether it's a heavily dialogued film, or whether it's a film with a lot of jokes.

Cut-by-cut. That's exactly what your work comes down to, doesn't it?

Each cut is a new and fresh decision. Sometimes situations seem to repeat themselves in a technical matter of speaking, but there's always a new wrinkle, always something different to consider. The words are never exactly the same from take to take, the performance is never exactly the same, what you're seeing beyond the person performing, the background, is ever changing. All those elements and many more impact on where you make the cut. We're building a house but none of the bricks are the same. When to get off the shot or how long you hold the shot, cut it tight, give it two beats, or whatever. My extra beat is different from your extra beat. You change it the next time, you change it the third. A dictum of mine is to try and retain (during a long process of editing a film) my early reaction to moments, takes, scenes. We as editors see the film so many times, more than anybody else will ever see it, and one gets used to or immune to those moments that originally made you laugh, made you cry, etcetera. You can get used to it to the point of boredom, but you have to try and say, "Gee, I liked it for this reason. I thought it was good before, it must still be good." How many times can I laugh at that joke? You tend to often become too critical, hypercritical.

Have you had to put something away for a while?

Sure. Sometimes it's not coming, you've got to let your subconscious take over and go back to it later. Used to be I would wrestle with something till I thought I had it licked, then I'd come in the next day, look at it, and say, "Oh God, that's awful, I should have gone home and gotten a good night's sleep instead of staying up all night." You learn, if it's not coming, don't push it. You get blocks. Sometimes there are too many trees, you can't see.

Have you ever had any desire to go into other areas of film?

I have. I've rejected them along the way for one reason or another. I think I will eventually wind up doing something else. Film editing is pretty rigorous work. I think it's essentially a young man's or young woman's craft. When I reach the point where I feel I don't have the strength to give to it as I used to, then I'll throw in the towel. I have passed up a lot of opportunities to direct. I don't think it's in my personality. I have had various opportunities to move in different directions, but I'm not at all unhappy with what I'm doing. I'm not a frustrated editor—there are a lot. I find my work fulfilling, and I think I make a contribution.

And from your collaboration with Coppola, it sounds like your work always comes full circle. You always return to your old friends.

Yeah, that's happened a lot. Those from the old neighborhood and the ones with whom I've grown up in the business. I have maintained friendships. I've never been fired from a job. Oh, I've walked off a couple, but have come back. I've worked with a lot of people I respect. I really haven't been exposed to many of the jerks, and there are a lot of them in the film business. I have a good time doing what I do. I think I've been very lucky.

20

Diplomatic Takes

Rudi Fehr

1940   *My Love Came Back*, directed by Curtis Bernhardt
Honeymoon for Three, directed by Lloyd Bacon
The Great Mr. Nobody, directed by Ben Stoloff
Alice in Movieland (short subject), directed by Jean Negulesco

1941   *A Million Dollar Baby*, directed by Curtis Bernhardt
Navy Blues, directed by Lloyd Bacon
All Through the Night, directed by Vincent Sherman

1942   *Desperate Journey*, directed by Raoul Walsh
Watch on the Rhine, directed by Herman Shumlin
Devotion, directed by Curtis Bernhardt

1943   *In Our Time*, directed by Vincent Sherman
Between Two Worlds, directed by Edward A. Blatt

1944   *The Conspirators*, directed by Jean Negulesco
Nobody Lives Forever, directed by Jean Negulesco

1945   *A Stolen Life*, directed by Curtis Bernhardt

1946   *Humoresque*, directed by Jean Negulesco
Possessed, directed by Curtis Bernhardt

1947   *The Voice of the Turtle*, directed by Irving Rapper
Romance on the High Seas, directed by Michael Curtiz

1948   *Key Largo*, directed by John Huston
The Girl from Jones Beach, directed by Peter Godfrey

1948–49   *The Inspector General*, directed by Henry Koster

1949   *Beyond the Forest*, directed by King Vidor
The Damned Don't Cry, directed by Vincent Sherman

1950   *Rocky Mountain*, directed by William Keighley

1951   *Goodbye My Fancy*, directed by Vincent Sherman

1952   *I Confess*, directed by Alfred Hitchcock

1953   *The House of Wax*, directed by Andre DeToth
Riding Shotgun, directed by Andre DeToth
Dial M For Murder, directed by Alfred Hitchcock

1954   *The Land of the Pharaohs*, directed by Howard Hawks

1982   *One from the Heart,* directed
        by Francis Ford Coppola
        (Coeditors: Anne Goursaud,
        Randy Roberts)

1984–85 **Prizzi's Honor,* directed by
         John Huston (Coeditor: Kaja
         Fehr)

* See Appendix for complete list of editing
awards and nominations.

Rudi Fehr reminisces about his forty-plus years at Warner Brothers in the very room of his home that his boss, Jack L. Warner, loved to visit. Surrounded by thousands of records, meticulously captioned photo albums, and his collection of unusual hats on a rack, Fehr tells many anecdotes of life at Hollywood's second largest studio of the Golden Age.

Fehr came from a well-to-do banking family in Berlin. When he was fourteen, his relatives asked him what he wanted to be when he grew up; a diplomat, he decided. "Little did I know that Hitler was around the corner, and my being Jewish and Hitler's feeling about my race didn't quite go together." He settled on music, conducting a fourteen-piece dance orchestra in Berlin for a number of years. While he was studying music, the president of the second largest film company in Germany, Tobis-Klangfilm, contacted Rudi (whose father was on the board of directors of the UFA) and made him an offer he couldn't refuse: a salaried job in motion pictures. After three months of observing but never touching film, Fehr was approached again by the president: "We're starting a picture next Monday. Every editor in town is busy. Are you ready?" He wasn't, but said yes and began his editing career.

Urged by a friend to leave Germany, Fehr gathered references from bankers and attorneys in New York before heading to Hollywood. He made the rounds of the studios. At MGM, he lunched in the executive dining room between Spencer Tracy and Clark Gable. Five weeks from the day he arrived, Cedric Gibbons at MGM promised montage work in six weeks; Fritz Lang at United Artists offered him assistant editor's work in six weeks on *Fury*; and Henry Blanke at Warners offered a translation job the next day. Fehr chose Warners, moving into the editing department when an assistant slot opened. He stayed forty years. "That wasn't because I'm slow!" he is quick to add. "My good fortune was that Jack Warner took a liking to me."

As Head of Postproduction from 1954 to 1976, Fehr worked closely with this mogul on some of the studio's great pictures. He sighs when he recalls that he had *The Sound of Music* in the palm of his hand, "but Mr. Warner didn't want to do it because there were Nazis in it." He remembers how John Huston lured him to edit *Prizzi's Honor* in 1985. "But the last time I edited was in 1954," Fehr said. "Oh, it'll come back to you," Huston assured him. For that film, Fehr was nominated for an Oscar with his coeditor, daughter Kaja.

Fehr's work now involves directing foreign-language adaptations, teaching editing at UCLA and the California Institute of the Arts, chairing the Academy's Foreign Language Film Awards Committee, and promoting the sister city affiliation between Los Angeles and Berlin.

Your long relationship with Jack L. Warner is one for the history books. What did he think of editors?

To him, editors were important. Editing was his pet department. He had an instinct for editing and he would listen to the editors.

Was this for any editor?

Well, I was a little more—how should I say? I had a great rapport with Mr. Warner, I knew how to talk to him. There was one editor, a good editor named George, he never said a word. One day Mr. Warner asked, "Doesn't George ever open his mouth?" Once when we were in the projection room and Mr. Warner had to leave for a short time, I said to George, "For Christ's sake, say something, make a suggestion, anything. Just say something!" He never opened his mouth. At one point Mr. Warner said, "Can he talk?" It was very embarrassing.

He knew that without the editor, there would be no finished product?

Absolutely. The editor was not only asked to edit, he was asked to make constructive suggestions. Hal Wallis, who produced *Casablanca*, always wanted the editor to read the script and come to his office to tell him what he thought of it. I remember after *Casablanca* and *Passage to Marseilles*, Wallis made a picture called *The Conspirators*, which I edited. When I read the script, I was shocked. It was terrible. He called me over. "Have you read the script?" "Yes, Mr. Wallis." "What do you think?" "To be very honest with you, Mr. Wallis, it reads as though you are using leftovers from *Casablanca* and *Passage to Marseilles*. I don't care for it." He thought for a minute. "Well, I like it!" "Mr. Wallis, that's all that's necessary." He cast Hedy Lamarr and Paul Henreid. They were

frustrated with the parts too. So Hedy Lamarr became "Headache Lamarr," Paul Henreid was "Paul Hemorrhoid," and the picture became
The Constipators! It was a disaster. I wish I had edited *Casablanca*, it's
one of my favorites. If I had been up for the next picture, I would have
gotten it. Owen Marks edited *Casablanca*. He also edited Errol Flynn's
last picture, *Too Much, Too Soon*. The director's name was Art Napoleon.
Owen and Art didn't hit it off too well, so Owen put a sign on his door
that said "Waterloo." Many editors have a great sense of humor.

It sounds as if pictures were assigned to editors like a lottery.

Not really. Before television made its appearance, each of the major
studios produced about sixty movies annually. The picture that started
shooting was assigned to the editor who had just finished a show. When
I started at Warners, there was a standing cutting department of twenty-
two editors and twenty-two assistant editors. They worked six days a week
and were never laid off. Nor was anybody paid overtime. If you worked
long hours, you received a meal ticket which gave you a free lunch the
next day. The editors did not have a union until 1944. Routinely, the film
was edited until all concerned were satisfied. It was then turned over to
the composer and the sound effects editors. It took them approximately
six weeks to do their work. The soundtracks, dialogue, music, and sound
effects were then electronically mixed onto one track and the picture was
ready for a sneak preview. While this work was being done, the editor
started on another assignment. The preview reactions by the audience
told us if the picture played well or if additional changes were necessary.
If there were a large number of changes, a second editor was asked to
help out on the new assignment so that the editor on record would not
fall too far behind.

How did editing differ in Germany?

When I started editing in the early 1930s, the editor did everything.
In addition to the editing, he cut the sound effects, timed the picture
for the composer, created the backgrounds for the titles, edited the trailers, and created montages. I remember a montage I did for a film called
The Tunnel in Munich in 1933. The story dealt with a tunnel being built
between the Continent and England. Shipworkers concerned that this
would threaten their livelihood sabotaged the construction of the tunnel.
I showed flashes of the tunnel flooding, explosions, shooting, men running, etcetera, to get the point across in a fairly short span of time.

*How did you adapt to the idiosyncracies of the big-name directors at
Warner Brothers?*

Directors get deeply involved in the editing process. Some of them have strong likes and dislikes. John Huston, for instance, did not like cutting in motion. Take somebody sitting down: he or she starts to sit down in a long or medium shot; cut to a close shot and the movement is completed. Huston preferred to have them sitting down in one shot and cut to a closer shot after the person is seated. Not knowing about his feelings about cutting in motion, I made such a cut in *Prizzi's Honor*. He took me aside and said, "Rudi, I can't stand cuts like that. Could you have him sit down in one shot and then cut?" No problem, I did. He was wonderful to work with, he would print two or three takes of the same thing and say, "You pick the best." And every time I showed him scenes I had edited, he would say, "Good, Rudi, very good." After we had shown the first cut to Brandon Stoddard, who was in charge of ABC's feature production, I received a call from him. It had to do with the running time of the picture which was two hours and thirty-three minutes. "Rudi, I look to you to cut this picture down to two hours." I said, "Mr. Stoddard, you're talking to the wrong guy. You should talk to John Huston." He replied, "I cannot communicate with Mr. Huston, but you can." I ran the picture with John and the producer, John Foreman, several times. By pointing out that some scenes were not essential to the plot, I managed to lose twenty minutes. Other directors I worked with were just the opposite. Raoul Walsh, for instance, did not look at the rushes nor did he view the first cut. He'd see the picture put together at the sneak preview. After the screening he would tell me how pleased he was with my contribution. Of all the directors I had worked with, Alfred Hitchcock was my favorite. I edited two films for him, *I Confess* and *Dial M For Murder*.

Didn't he camera cut?

Not on the two pictures I edited. There is one picture that comes to mind: *Rope*. He actually made this film in eight takes and each take ran from nine to ten minutes. It took place in an apartment where a murder had occurred. He moved the camera a great deal and at the end of the film in the camera, he would move in on a painting, freeze the camera, remove the exposed film, and put a new roll in. After the unexposed negative was in the camera, he pulled back from the painting and by doing that at each ending and beginning of a reel, the entire film looked as though it was filmed in one take. He would rehearse each take for three days and then shoot one day. It was a tour de force, Hitchcock was the first to admit that. He shot *I Confess* on location in Quebec. He covered it well and gave me all the footage I could possibly use. In those days, editors were not sent to locations. I worked in Burbank and every day, after having looked at the rushes, I would call Hitchcock and give him a report. Then the film would be shipped to Quebec so that all concerned could look at it. It was then returned to me and I could start the editing.

Dial M For Murder was a different story. It was based on a play by Frederick Knott. Most of the scenes were played in one room; therefore, the camera angles were somewhat limited. I had a great rapport with "Hitch" and he was very complimentary in regards to my work. When I was working with him, he used to take me to Perino's, the finest restaurant in Los Angeles, twice a week for lunch. I remember one night when he came to my house for dinner—a night when he started a diet—my wife asked if it was difficult for him to go on a diet. He responded that it was very easy to decide to go on a diet; the difficult part was to decide when to *start* the diet.

How did your creative input blend in with the director's?

It is my considered opinion that the most important contribution is made by the writer. He has to please himself, the director, the producer, and if it is a major studio production, the head of the studio. The editor plays a similar role. He has to please himself first. He must not try to figure what the director would like. His concept of the way the story should be told is usually discussed after the director has seen the first cut. If the director is open-minded, he'll listen to the editor's creative input. A director with a closed mind presents a problem. I usually present my ideas three times and if after the third time my suggestions are not accepted, I forget about them and do as I am told.

Are editors often considered a pair of hands?

Not anymore. In the early stages of filmmaking, there were no editors. Short films were shot without cuts. One day a director wanted to get closer to an actor and made a close-up. Since projectionists knew how to splice film in case of a break, the director asked one of them to splice the close-up into his film. It worked, and that is the beginning of editing. Over the years, editors have received more and more recognition. The industry has learned to respect them and is aware of their contribution and importance. I have been very lucky inasmuch as I have never had a director in my cutting room. I would not feel comfortable having someone stand in back of me and tell me where to cut. If that should happen I would turn around, hand the scissors to the director, and say, "You don't need me." I have always shown the film to the director in a projection room and discussed changes and problems with him there. I feel that I have been hired because I am a competent editor and I should therefore have the opportunity to put the picture into first cut by myself.

Did you follow the script closely?

I read the script and familiarized myself with the story. I told it the best way possible with the film at hand. Sometimes the writer notes when there should be close-ups, long shots, dissolves, etcetera. What the writer visualizes and what the director shoots are not necessarily identical. I study the film very carefully before I start the editing process. At the end of *Humoresque*, Joan Crawford commits suicide by walking into the ocean. The director, Jean Negulesco, gave me wonderful footage for this scene and the music department gave me a track from Richard Wagner's "Love Death Theme" from his opera *Tristan and Isolde*. It worked beautifully, as though the music was written for this scene.

Were there editing formulas, like master to medium to close-up?

Not necessarily. However, Mr. Warner always insisted that an establishing master shot be made for the audience to know where the various characters were located.

That is very clear in Watch on the Rhine, *where the scenes are almost set up as tableaux.*

I'm glad you brought that up. The director was Herman Shumlin. He had directed the play by Lillian Hellman on the stage in New York; this was his first film. I was assigned to work with him. Every night I laid out the next day's sequence with him, when to make a dolly shot or a pan shot or a close-up. The first time I screened a completed sequence for him, he looked at it and walked out of the projection room in a daze. He turned around, walked back in, and said, "I want to see it once more. What you've done is miraculous." He was very grateful.

Did you freely voice your opinions with more experienced directors?

Here is an interesting story about that. When I was in between being an editor and becoming Head of Postproduction, I was not too busy. They were editing *Giant* at the time, and Mr. Warner wanted to keep me busy so he called George Stevens, the director, and asked, "Would you mind if Rudi sits in on the cutting session?" "By all means, I like Rudi." George had booked a projection room twenty-four hours a day. He sat in the first row with his secretary; in back of him were George Stevens, Jr., and Fred Guiol, the writer. In back of them was the editor, Bill Hornbeck; behind him were two other editors, next the assistant editors, and in the last row was Rudy Liberace, who was the apprentice and the nephew of *the* Liberace, and myself. Mr. Stevens ran the film and stopped whenever something was on his mind. I soon caught on to his way of working. He would stop the film, turn to the writer, and quote a line of dialogue which he felt may not be necessary. He said, "Fred, do you think we need that line?" Fred replied, "I wrote it for a reason." Stevens turned to the editor and said, "Take it out." He continued to screen the picture and stopped again. He turned to Hornbeck. "There is a two-shot of Elizabeth Taylor and Rock Hudson. Do you think it would play better in close-ups?"

Hornbeck said, "It will play very well in close-ups." Stevens said, "Leave it alone." There is a scene in the picture where Jimmy Dean's oil well comes in; shortly thereafter he gets into his car, drives to a hotel, puts on the brakes too late, and rear-ends a car which was parked there. Instead of apologizing to the owner of that car, Dean knocks him down. The scene bothered me; I had just learned to like Dean and now he did something that made me angry. I felt that this scene was not needed. Lo and behold, we came to this scene and Mr. Stevens turned to me and asked, "Do you think we need that scene?" "I think you do, Mr. Stevens." His response: "I think you're right!" I had outsmarted myself. The very next day I had a chance to talk to him. "I want to level with you. I did not think that the scene we discussed yesterday was necessary. I rooted for Dean, especially when his oil well came in. He worked hard for that and all of a sudden he knocks this totally innocent guy down and that bothered me." Stevens said, "That's exactly what I wanted. I wanted to throw the audience off balance in regards to Dean's character. I did not want them to like him that much." I understood.

Were films from the 1930s and 1940s generally cut to be slow-paced?

It depended entirely on the subject matter. I was invited to speak for the ACE [American Cinema Editors] one evening after having screened one of the films I had edited, *Key Largo*. Someone asked, "Did pictures of that era always move slowly?" I responded, "No, it depends entirely on the subject matter. Comedies, chase pictures, etcetera, should move like lightning, but love stories and human interest stories should move slowly." *Humoresque* was such a picture, and so was *Key Largo*.

If anything was fast-paced, it was probably your schedule.

Among the pictures I have edited was *The Voice of the Turtle*, based on a play by John Van Druten. I had this picture in first cut three days after they finished shooting. I called the director, Irving Rapper, and told him that I was ready to screen the picture for him. He looked at it and said, "Your cut is perfect, don't touch it." I couldn't believe it. "You must be kidding, there must be something—" Rapper picked up the phone, called Mr. Warner, and invited him to see the picture. Mr. Warner had the same reaction and the picture was turned over to the composer, Max Steiner, and the sound effects editors the next day. A few years later, Mr. Warner assigned me to edit *House of Wax*. The year was 1953, television had made its appearance, people stayed home to watch the latest fad, theaters were empty. When Mr. Warner called, he told me that the picture was to open five weeks from the day they finished shooting. I asked him about the shooting schedule. He told me that they would shoot the middle part first, then the ending showing the big fire in the Wax Museum, and then the earlier part. I told him that it would be impossible to have it ready in five weeks, what with 3-D and stereophonic sound. After he told me that it was imperative to have the picture ready in five weeks, I suggested that he change the schedule and shoot the picture in continuity, starting on page one. Whenever I would have a reel assembled, I would show it to all concerned, make changes if necessary, then turn it over to the composer and the sound effects editors. I guaranteed that the picture would be in the theater in five weeks from the day we finished shooting. Mr. Warner informed the head of production of this change who was unhappy because it would increase the budget. Warners hoped that the 3-D gimmick would lure the audiences back to the theaters. It worked!

Did 3-D pose an editing challenge for you?

Not really. You work with two filmstrips, one for the left eye and one for the right eye. You actually edit one only after having made very precise notes where the 3-D effect stands out. Then, with the help of code numbers, the assistant editor matches the other eye to the edited film. You really edit it like any other picture, except for scenes where the 3-D effect stands out. In *House of Wax*, there's the scene where the ping-pong ball hits you between the eyes, or where the flames lick out when the Wax Museum is on fire. The same holds true for comedy. You have to know what is going to get a laugh. If there is a big laugh, you have to milk the reactions and not have any dialogue until the laughter in the audience dies down. I love sophisticated comedies and musicals. One of my favorite pictures is *My Fair Lady*. I was deeply involved in the post-production of this wonderful film, and I worked closely with Mr. Warner. I had input on the final editing, worked on the special effects, and suggested who should sing for Audrey Hepburn. It seemed that the director, George Cukor, and the musical director, Andre Previn, were slow in deciding whose voice was best to sing for Hepburn. Both were hoping that the other would make that decision. One day Mr. Warner called me and asked, "Have you heard the seven tests we made of the singers to sing for Hepburn?" I replied, "Yes, I have." "Which one do you think is right?" "My choice would be Marni Nixon." He responded, "She's got the job." He was very proud of this picture and when the first print was delivered by Technicolor, he decided to take it to London and screen it for his peers and prominent friends. A few days before he left, he invited me to go to London with him. I was thrilled. A special screening was arranged on a Saturday morning at the Leicester Square Theatre. He asked me to sit next to him. When the film had finished running and the house-lights went on, the audience rose in a body and gave Mr. Warner a standing ovation. He turned to me and asked, "What should I do?" "I suggest you stand up and take a bow." "Do I have to?" "I'm afraid so." He stood up, took a bow, and sat down. The audience kept applauding. "What do I do now?" "I'm afraid you have to stand up once more." Without the slightest hesitation, he said, "No, you stand up." This came as a total surprise. "Why me?" I asked. His response, "Don't argue with me, that's an order!" I stood up, took a bow. It felt wonderful!

Your relationship with Mr. Warner will probably surprise many people, especially since an editor shared such a privileged position.

I was privileged indeed. Because of the nature of my job, I spent one to two hours alone with him in a projection room every working day to look at the rushes, the film shot by various productions on the previous day. With one exception, I never asked him for anything. The one exception was simply my asking him if I could take my family on a two-week vacation. He looked at me and said, "When I'm here, you're here. You take your vacation when I take mine." When he left on his vacation, I went to see his right-hand man, Steve Trilling. "Steve, now that Mr. Warner has gone on his vacation, may I take two weeks off?" Steve replied, "Are you crazy or something? When he's gone, I need you more than ever. You want me to carry the ball for you too?" From 1956 to 1963, I did not get one day off, except for weekends, of course. When *My Fair Lady* was finally finished, Mr. Warner asked me to go to Europe to supervise the foreign-language adaptations in the four dubbing countries: France, Germany, Italy, and Spain (I speak French and German). This is a painstaking job, and Mr. Warner asked me to make sure that the foreign versions look as good as the original English version. One day, when I was in Rome, I received a phone call from him. He wanted to know what progress I was making. I assured him that everything was going well. Then he said, "I hear you are working too hard." I replied, "Not at all, I'm doing fine." "That's not what I've heard. I have instructed our Paris office to arrange for you and your family to spend a week at the Hotel Majestic in Cannes as my guests. All you have to do is to let the Paris office know when you can go." We had a great time in Cannes and I am forever grateful to Mr. Warner for having been so thoughtful. One day, when a meeting broke up in Mr. Warner's office, he asked me to line up a screening of a film that had just finished shooting. He also asked me to invite the director and producer to the screening. Before I left his office, he told me that he would have a bite to eat in his office and that I should go home and meet him in the projection room at 8:30. Later that afternoon, after we had screened the rushes, he turned to me and said, "I don't feel like having dinner by myself. Why don't you and I go out to dinner?" Before I had a chance to think it through, I said, "I have a better idea. Why don't you come to dinner at our house?" Without the slightest hesitation, he said, "You've got a deal." As he walked out, I picked up the phone and called my wife, "Darling, guess who's coming for dinner? . . . Jack Warner!" My wife sent one of our daughters out to get some steaks. After dinner, we played some of the songs from the 1920s which he enjoyed very much. I reminded him that people were waiting for us in the projection room, but he was not ready to leave. I kept calling the fellows at the studio, asking them not to leave. We finally arrived there at ten o'clock, one hour and a half late.

What was your secret with him?

Frankly, I didn't have a secret. I simply studied his likes and dislikes, discussed the films I saw with him, offered suggestions how to improve them, listened to his jokes and anecdotes, and told some myself. Some of the executives had contracts, and one day three contracts came up for renewal. Mine was one of them. Word got around that Mr. Warner wanted us to stay, but to forget about the salary increase which was contractual; things weren't going too well and this was not the time for a raise. First, the story editor was called to the studio manager's office and was told that Mr. Warner would like him to stay with the understanding that there would not be a salary increase. The story editor told the manager that he enjoyed working at Warner Brothers and would like to stay without an increase in pay. Next was the casting director; he said that he would have to discuss the situation with his wife. He was told that he would have to give an answer by 6:00 P.M. that day. He did not call by then and consequently was let go. I was the last one to be called, and I was prepared. I suggested that instead of giving me the increase as spelled out in the contract, to give me 50 percent of it. No sooner had I said these words when Mr. Warner's voice came booming over the intercom. "Have you talked to Rudi yet?" The studio manager replied, "Yes, Mr. Warner, he is right here." "What does he say?" "He suggests that you split the difference and give him a 50 percent raise." Mr. Warner's response: "He's got a deal!"

Your diplomacy seemed to have helped you as much as your musical background. Was that your secret with directors, too?

The editor works very closely with the director, and after the director has looked at the editor's first cut, he suggests changes. I have never said that I could not make such editorial changes because I didn't have the material. I always said "Good idea" even though I knew in my heart that I could not make such a change. After I tried to accommodate the director and realized it could not be done, I informed him of that and explained why. Whenever the editor makes a suggestion, he must be sure of what he is talking about. Never throw cold water over other people's suggestions. I remember an incident after we had previewed *Gypsy* and Mr. Warner felt that the picture needed some more tightening. We were looking at the picture in a projection room and at one point, he said to the editor, "I want you to go out of this scene a little sooner." The editor said, "I can't do that." I wanted to sink through the floor. Mr. Warner asked the projectionist to stop running the film and to turn the house-lights on. He turned to the editor and asked, "What did you say?" He repeated, "I can't do that." To my embarrassment, Mr. Warner turned to me and said, "Rudi, show him how to do it." When I talked to Mr. Warner the next morning, he asked me not to give this editor another assignment. It really pays to be diplomatic. An editor deals with so many people and it happens frequently that he is caught between a feuding producer-director team. I worked with one producer who wanted me to make changes behind the director's back. I refused to do that. I suggested he discuss his ideas with the director and have a meeting of the minds. I would be glad to make changes that all interested parties agreed on.

Did your diplomacy ever complicate things for you?

Before we started production on *My Fair Lady*, Mr. Warner called me and told me in no uncertain terms that he wanted a Warner Brothers editor to edit the film. I assured him that I would do my best. A few days later I met with the director, George Cukor. He was very emphatic and determined to bring his editor in. "I want the editor to work for me and not for Jack Warner." I replied, "I understand that very well but before you do that, I feel obliged to tell you that the best editor for musicals is working right here on this lot." Cukor was interested, he wanted to meet him. I got hold of the editor, Bill Ziegler, who had a long list of outstand-ing credits. Cukor was impressed. He agreed to have Bill edit the film but under one condition: Bill was not to edit anything that George Cukor had not seen. I gladly agreed to that, never dreaming that this agreement could get me into trouble. Mr. Warner was quite nervous during the mak-ing of this film, a lot was at stake. Every morning I had to call him at his home and give him a progress report, how much film had been edited. For the first few weeks of shooting, everything went smoothly, but after he shot the "Ascot Gavotte" on a large set, with a large number of extras and horses, Cukor got tired and went home without looking at the rushes. That went on for about eight days. Consequently, Bill was unable to do his job. Every morning, I told Mr. Warner that two thousand feet had been edited. "Two thousand feet." "Two thousand feet." After the eighth day, Mr. Warner asked, "Isn't Bill putting the film together anymore?" I answered, "When you asked me to use a Warner Brothers editor, Cukor made one condition: not to edit any film that he had not seen. Mr. Cukor hasn't found the time to look at the rushes lately." Mr. Warner was angry. "You mean to tell me that SOB hasn't looked at his own film?" I tried to smooth things over, "He worked on a big set, he got tired." Ten minutes later, his right-hand man, Steve Trilling, called and yelled at me. "Why in heaven's name did you have to tell Mr. Warner that Cukor hasn't screened the rushes? He wants me to fire him now. Are you trying to ruin the studio?" I told him that I would not lie to Mr. Warner nor would I lie to him. I was in a spot where I could only do one thing: tell the truth. Steve's retort: "Are you and I going to cross swords? You come up to my office right now!" When I arrived at his office, he stuck out his hand and apologized. "What can we do to calm Warner down?" I suggested that he and I go to the set and explain the situation to Cukor and persuade him to look at the film as soon as possible. That is exactly what happened. In the long run, Steve realized that there was nothing else I could have done and he respected me for it.

I imagine that's easier to do when you have already garnered such confidence from your colleagues.

I remember one incident where I was up against a very prominent director, George Stevens. Warners had scheduled a preview of his picture *Giant*. Stevens had to spend a few days in New York and when he returned to the studio, he listened to the soundtracks we had mixed during his absence. He turned to me and said, "Cancel the preview in Riverside tomorrow night. There are too many things wrong with this mix and I am not going to preview it this way." I countered, "We cannot cancel it, the preview has been announced as an important event." He then suggested that we preview another picture, which I felt was not in the same class as his picture. The dialogue became somewhat heated and one by one the people involved in this work left the room. Stevens was adamant that we not preview *Giant* in this condition. I said, "Mr. Stevens, if you tell me what your objections are, I will keep the crew here until five in the morning to straighten them all out. I guarantee that all your major objections will be taken care of." That's the way it worked out and he respected me for it. I don't know if you remember a film starring Bette Davis entitled *Beyond the Forest*. In this film, Bette becomes ill. The doctor administers penicillin, a miracle drug, and she takes a turn for the worse. When we showed the picture to Mr. Warner, with the director and the producer present, I brought this point up and we all felt that a scene should be shot that explains why her condition has worsened. That was the scene that showed her getting out of bed, opening the window wide, and cold air blowing into the room. The scene was shot and it worked.

I wonder if audiences would have picked up on that ambiguity.

I am sure they would have. But I'd like to tell you about another incident where the audiences did not pick up. In 1954, Warners produced *Helen of Troy*, a spectacular film directed by Robert Wise. When the film was completed, Warners ordered eight hundred release prints for theaters throughout the country. One day I received a telegram from Norway; it was sent by the gentleman who spots the subtitles for the prints to be released in his country. The telegram read, "Is it intentional that in Reel 3 at 650 feet a four-motored plane flies through the scene?" My first reaction was that the guy must have been drunk when he looked at the film. I had seen the picture about a hundred times and never saw a plane. I pulled the reel out, ran it down, and sure enough, there was a plane on the screen! It was a very short cut, a soldier blew into a fanfare, hundreds of pigeons took off in all directions, and the shot served to signal the beginning of the Trojan War. I immediately changed the cut although four hundred prints had already been manufactured by Technicolor which went out with the plane in the third reel. The studio never received a letter commenting on this flaw. I guess that except for the gentleman in Norway, nobody saw it.

Can you say a bit more about Mr. Warner as you knew him personally?

Whenever we finished running film in the afternoon, he'd ask me to walk him back to his office. We'd talk about the weather, about baseball, which he enjoyed tremendously and to which he invited my wife and me frequently to watch at Dodger Stadium—where, by the way, he had the best seats. Anyway, it was about a five-minute walk to his office and I often wondered why he asked me to accompany him. One day I found out. A gentleman came walking towards us and said, "May I talk to you for a minute, Mr. Warner?" Mr. Warner said, "Not now, I am discussing some very important matters with Rudi. If you want to see me, make an appointment with my secretary." He was afraid that people would ask him for a loan or other favors. He had a snappy answer for them, "We have an agreement with the Bank of America: they don't make movies, we don't loan money."

Can you describe how your relationship began?

It actually started when I was working as an assistant editor. Every day, on his way to the private dining room, Mr. Warner passed the cutting room I was working in. I was a new kid. He called the editor I worked with out of the room and asked him what my name was—that happened at least once a week. When I became editor, he liked my work, that I was ready on time, that I did not look like a bum, and above all, that I contributed some good suggestions. One time, I criticized some dialogue in a picture that I thought was in bad taste. Mr. Warner pooh-poohed that reaction. But it seems he got some mail and telephone calls about the dialogue I had criticized. So one day he came into the projection room and said, "You're the one with the good taste. From now on, whenever you hear or see something in bad taste, let me know!" I also tried to persuade Mr. Warner for eighteen months to have his own record company. I showed him the profits, listed in *Billboard* and *Variety*, that other record companies were making. Even though the Warner executives in New York were opposed to it, Mr. Warner did start a record company in 1958. This company is now one of the two top record producers in the country. I do not take any credit for its success—I only take credit for it being there! And another time, when the *$64,000 Question* was on television, Mr. Warner was impressed with the fact that I had been approved to appear on the show (my subject was jazz). However, he would not give his okay for me to fly to New York until two big pictures were completed. By the time they were finished, the *$64,000 Question* was off the air!

You certainly were devoted to your work—and to Mr. Warner. It must have been a strange feeling to work for others when you retired.

When I was sixty-five, I was mandatorily retired by Warner Brothers. Francis Ford Coppola, who made two pictures for Warner Brothers, heard about it and called me. "I am more interested in your ability than your age," he said. "Why don't you work with me?" It was music to my ears. I joined his company, Zoetrope, when he bought a studio in Hollywood. He knew that I had worked closely with Mr. Warner and he wanted to run the studio he had just acquired the same way Jack Warner ran Warner Brothers. One of the first questions Coppola asked me was, "What did Mr. Warner do when he wanted to fire somebody?" I answered, "He told somebody else to do it!" Mr. Warner loved a good laugh, he enjoyed telling jokes and anecdotes. He did not like people who never had anything to say. I was sad when Mr. Warner passed away. Mrs. Warner passed away just a short time ago, but I used to call her every year on his birthday to let her know that he was not forgotten.

What do you think of the new editing technology these days?

Man is a creature of habit. I still prefer to edit on a Moviola as do many of my peers. Flatbeds like the KEM, for instance, have their advantages—a larger screen, for one. Tape editing machines like the CMX or the Montage have their advantages, too, I'm sure. You must remember that editing is not done by machines; they are merely tools. It is still up to the editor to decide where to cut, which angle to use, how long to hold on to a close-up, etcetera. It is also more economical to work on a Moviola, the rental fee is considerably less than any of the newer innovations. When George Stevens directed *Giant*, he exposed about one-and-a-half million feet of film. It would cost a fortune to transfer that much footage to tape, then edit on tape and transfer the final cut back to film. However, I believe that just as soon as Sony or another company can produce tape that can be projected onto a large screen and look as good as film does today, everything will be shot on tape. I've been called upon twice to

reedit films which did not play well. I screened the films and told the
people who asked me to work on them that I could not create a miracle
and make a good film out of them. But I could make them move faster
and therefore somewhat better. I did that on two occasions and both films
flopped. I won't do that again.

*Did you ever witness major excises from films taken over by the studio,
such as the tragic "face on the cutting room floor"?*
  I remember a film called *No Time for Sergeants*, based on a play by
Ira Levin and directed by Mervyn LeRoy. When it was completed, we
previewed it in Westwood. The first half played like a house on fire, but
the second half looked as though it was written by another writer. It just
died, and by the time the houselights went on, the house was empty.
Shortly after the preview, Mervyn had to leave for the East to start
another picture. A few weeks after the preview, Mr. Warner called and
told me that we were going to run *No Time for Sergeants* that night to
see how we could improve the second half. By the time we were through,
we had eliminated about eighteen minutes, almost two reels. I asked Mr.
Warner, "Are you going to tell Mr. LeRoy about these changes?" "Don't
worry about it" was his response. A few weeks later, Mr. Warner called
again and told me that Mervyn LeRoy was back from location and that
we were going to preview the picture again. I asked, "Does Mervyn know
about the changes?" "Don't worry about it." Before going to the preview,
we had dinner in the private dining room. Mervyn still did not know what
was in store for him. I was invited to ride in a car with Mr. Warner and
Mervyn LeRoy. Suddenly Mr. Warner said, "By the way, Mervyn, while
you were gone, we made a few little trims in the picture." When he
saw what we had done, Mervyn was livid. He paced up and down in the
theater lobby saying, "Rudi does not know comedy; he obviously did
not know what he was doing." It was clear that he was addressing Jack
Warner, accusing him of using bad judgment. So Mr. Warner said, "If
you want to put anything back in the picture, be my guest." Mervyn put
eight minutes back in the picture, but we were still ten minutes ahead.
Another time, Mr. Warner and I were looking at the rushes of another
film Mervyn LeRoy directed, *Gypsy.* Mr. Warner asked me, "Don't you
think Mervyn is covering from too many angles and printing too many
takes?" "We talked about that before, Mr. Warner, yes, he is." He picked
up the phone and asked the operator to get Mervyn on the phone. A short
time later the phone rings. "Mervyn, *we* think you are shooting too much
and printing too many takes." Mervyn was very sharp. He shot back,
"Who's *we*?" Warner: "Rudi and I." I could hear Mervyn's voice bleed
through the phone. "What the hell does Rudi know?" Warner: "A hell of
a lot more than you'll ever know!" How to make friends and influence

people! I am very careful with language. I wish Mr. Warner had said, "*I think you are . . .* " instead of "we."

Well, he must have considered you his right arm.

All I can tell you is that he felt comfortable with me around. I have heard that from many sources. One evening I received a phone call from Mr. Warner's secretary, Bill Schaefer. He said, "There is going to be a story about you and another guy in the trade papers tomorrow. The Boss asks that you not sign with an agent." I tried to persuade Bill to tell me what this was all about, to no avail. The next morning, I dashed out, got hold of the trades, and read: "Jack Warner Gives David Weisbart and Rudi Fehr Producer Status." That was a complete surprise, he had never asked David nor me if we wanted to be producers. I made an appointment to see Mr. Warner, and when I saw him I told him that I never dreamed of becoming a producer. If anything, from editing you go to directing. I'll never forget his answer: "Oh, Rudi, directors come and directors go. As long as I'm here, you'll be here." He kept his promise. As a matter of fact, I was still at the studio ten years after he had sold it. I have no regrets. I thoroughly enjoyed the forty years I spent at Warner Brothers. The wonderful people I've met, the family atmosphere at the studio, and the friends I've made. A couple of years ago, I was on my exercycle watching television. The great violinist Isaac Stern was being interviewed. At the end, the interviewer asked, "Is there a particular episode you would like to tell us?" Stern replied, "I remember one experience I would like to pass on. Warner Brothers made a movie called *Humoresque*. John Garfield played a concert violinist and I was asked to prerecord all the violin solos." Garfield knew nothing about playing the violin. Whenever he was shown playing, it was either in a close-up or over his shoulder. His arms were crossed on his back and the first chairs from the Warner Brothers orchestra were doing the fingering and the bowing. The violinist who did the fingering was kneeling on Garfield's left side, the one who did the bowing on his right. Whenever I used a long shot, I showed Garfield putting the violin under his chin or taking it away from him. In conclusion, Stern said, "I could not figure out how they were going to make Garfield look like a virtuoso, but when I saw the film, I said, 'My hat off to the guy who put this film together.'" All I could do was to yell at the television set, "That's me! That's me!"

21

Creating a Legacy

Richard Marks

* See Appendix for complete list of editing awards and nominations.

At one point in the interview, Richard Marks apologized for being a bit vitriolic on the subject of what film editing classes should teach students. He opts for hands-on, practical education over pure theory, and stresses experimenting and nurturing. "Nurturing is not just being critical, it's being able to offer some encouragement and some tools." With his wife Barbara, a former documentary editor, Marks has developed a course at UCLA which he feels gives aspiring editors what they need to know of the "real world" of the film industry. The course also explains to students, the majority of whom are aspiring directors, what editors do.

Marks finds teaching to be a calming respite from the demands of his daily work. His current project, *Dick Tracy*, had him toiling seven days a week to meet its summer release date. Running between the dubbing stage and the cutting room, checking on assistants, answering calls, discussing the deletion of two frames to smooth out a word from "Pruneface," and wondering about dinner, he mentions the need to maintain a sense of humor.

Marks drifted into editing from a background as an English literature major and, briefly, a labor union organizer. While cutting commercials and trailers in New York, he met Barry Malkin, who urged him on to bigger goals. Then Dede Allen gave Marks the chance to assist her. "That really launched my career. Without Dede, I don't think I'd have much of one." His association with Dede Allen was his motivation to teach as generously as he feels he was taught by her.

Being a die-hard New Yorker, it wasn't easy for Marks to move to the West Coast, but he has not regretted his decision. He poses pet theories about the differences between the coasts, and the evolving profile of editors. Having lived through three relentless years on *Apocalypse Now* as Supervising Editor (for which he shared an Academy Award nomination with Lisa Fruchtman and Jerry Greenberg), Richard feels well equipped to handle the rigors of any feature film.

What was your start in film?

I started work in commercials and trailers in New York. I had been an English lit major in school, but never contemplated working in film. I graduated with a degree in English literature and no desire to teach. For a time I even worked as a labor union organizer. Eventually, being totally bored with my indecisions, I started looking around for an area that interested me, and the film business seemed promising. I drifted into film editing which, by some strange quirk of fate, I had an affinity and some talent for. I often speculate it was an occupation that totally suits my rather compulsive personality. It was a serendipitous thing, and it worked into something I really began to love. My first big break was working as assistant to a free-lance editor in a commercial company who became a very close friend of mine, Barry Malkin. He was always trying to help me get out of commercials and work with him in other areas. Eventually I worked my way into theatrical films which, since I started in film, was what I really wanted to do. Of equal importance was that my then girlfriend, later to be wife, also worked in films as a film editor in documentaries, which opened up a whole new area to me. I think the third most important thing was when I landed a job with the legendary Dede Allen. I was in the right place at the right time. Without Dede, I think my career would have been very different. She is a wonderful teacher and friend.

Did you feel you had to relocate to the West Coast for the features?

Being a die-hard New Yorker, it was very tough for me to move. When I was supervising editor on *Apocalypse Now*, my wife had started writing and moved to L.A. while I was still in San Francisco. Near the end of *Apocalypse*, I realized that of the previous seven years, I had spent close to five outside of New York on location, and I didn't want to live out of a suitcase anymore. If I was to continue to work in feature films, and still have a home and some semblance of sanity, I thought that moving to L.A. was the smartest thing I could do. It also afforded me an opportunity for greater choice in work.

Having straddled both coasts, do you find a difference between them?

I think there used to be. I think it's becoming less and less. When I came into the business, there was an enormous rivalry between East Coast and West Coast film editors. There were differences in the way we worked. There seemed to be a certain rigidity that came out of the old studio system in L.A., although certainly with many exceptions. The backgrounds of people in New York spanned working on all different kinds of films, from documentaries to features to commercials to trailers. To stay alive in New York, you had to be willing to work on almost anything. People in the studio system were used to being treated as a sort of fixture—there's the editor in that little cage in the grungy little building on the back lot and they will be assigned to a particular film. I think New York editors, especially Dede, Carl Lerner, Ralph Rosenblum, and Aram Avakian, pioneered breaking that image. I think the differences between coasts have, as a whole, become negligible.

Is editing style different between coasts?

I think style can't be defined by coasts, but by person. It's a signature, everybody has their own little quirks, their own inner rhythms, their own sensibilities that become their signature in the work they do. It's like looking at two different handwritings.

Do you think your "editor in a cage" idea contributed to the anonymity that some editors feel haunts their profession?

I think so. Editors traditionally have been a "craft" in this business, especially in the studio system in Hollywood, and as a craft they've been treated as below the line. Blue collar rather than white collar. Cinematographers, on the other hand, were treated very differently. I think the image of the editor has changed dramatically over the last couple of decades. It's funny, I worked on a film that Elia Kazan directed called *The Last Tycoon* where an editor is portrayed in the screening of a first cut of the film. One of the characters says to the editor, "Eddie, Eddie, I'm talking to you, Eddie!" And it turns out Eddie has died during the screening of the first cut. There's something very prophetic about that. I ended an Academy seminar I did with that clip of film. I think it represented an attitude within the old studio system of what editors were: a pair of hands who existed in a state of anonymity. You told them what to do, they'd cut out the required number of frames, cut off the slates, and put everything together. They were passed around. Somehow both cinematographers and production designers—as they were called then, art directors—broke that mold more readily. Their profession was recognized for their artistic input way before editors have been.

Could that be because editing is not as tangible as photography?

Perhaps. It also has to do with what part of the process is involved. In the minds of almost everyone, including a lot of people who work in and run the business, the filmmaking process ends when the shooting's over; the editing is sort of an aside. You take off the slates, throw some sound on, and get onto the dubbing stage as fast as possible. There's more money riding on production, and it's obvious money. If the cinematographer is sick one day and you lose one hundred and fifty thousand dollars, it's a lot more significant than if I get sick and we only lose ten thousand dollars a day. This is an economic reality that I think increased the image that cinematographers and art directors have. But the image of the editor has changed drastically. For example, I think in the last five years, if you did a study of film posters, you would probably see a hundred percent increase in the number of editors' names in the credits.

Why did studios object to giving credit?

Like everything else in the business, no one ever wants to set a precedent, but once the precedent is set, people very easily fall into it. The first time I ever got a poster credit was on *Apocalypse Now*. It was almost unheard of to get it. I think Dede got it occasionally, but not consistently. Francis Coppola gave it to me, certainly out of no contractual obligation, but out of generosity. Once there, when you negotiate your deal, they will very rarely tell you you can't have something you've already gotten. Therefore you have created a precedent. Now I think it's becoming much more common, and studios on principle are not objecting to it, which at one point they did.

What have editors done to make themselves more recognized?

I have my own pet theories about this. I think there was a point when the nature of how films were made changed the editor's role. The difference in the editor's role reflected the change in filmmaking, and that probably came about when they started recording on mag stock rather than optical tracks. They started shooting more and coverage became different. More and more directors came to rely on the editing process to create scenes that at one time were created in one sweeping take, where they would rehearse something for three days, shoot it and get it right. All of a sudden they only had a day to shoot four scenes and they would shoot it in pieces. As the shooting became more complicated, the need for relying on the editorial process became more apparent. Editors were no longer a pair of hands cutting off slates, they were people who had to think, have opinions, and have some feeling for the material. The process became more dramatic choice than automatic, mechanical response.

Was it possible for editors to find the feeling in the material even when they were just a pair of hands? Or has the material changed too?

I think the material has changed. If you're dealing with a two-minute scene done in one take, or with a two-minute scene that's done in twenty setups and each setup has fifteen takes, then you're asking an editor to get involved with a whole different set of ground rules. Certainly there are directors who still treat editors like a pair of hands, but they're generally few and far between these days. Sometimes, no matter how big the budget or how complicated the film, a director makes a decision to do a scene in one take—just go for broke and hope it works. Bowing to the economic realities of filmmaking, the only thing a director can do is shoot one cutaway so he can at least change takes if there is a problem. Then again, the filmmaking process is changing. Now almost every film has budgeted a couple of days of additional shooting to be done long after the principal photography is over. Thus the editing process becomes more flexible because there is the possibility of fixing mistakes by shooting the solution to seemingly unsolvable problems.

Having witnessed about ten minutes of sound work on Dick Tracy *before the interview, could you explain why you spent so much time deliberating over two frames?*

There, we had replaced a production line with an ADR line (a looped line), and the ADR line was slightly different than the way I had cut it in production. We start the line off-camera, as a man is hearing it through earphones, and then we cut on-camera at a certain point during the line. The way I cut the original production material, the cut occurred on a specific word. The way the looped line was laid in, the cut on-camera occurred in the *middle* of a word. Cutting in the middle of a word from off-camera to on-camera is very jarring and clumsy. By moving it two frames, we're able to bring it on-camera at the beginning of the word, thus making it more acceptable to your ear.

It's interesting that you were obsessed—if I may use that word?

Oh you may!

—with an issue that will last bare seconds on the screen.

But it's the cumulative effect that kind of thing has. If you make those mistakes every few seconds in a film, you'd walk out of the film twitching! Or you'd feel very uncomfortable and wouldn't know why. You're not dealing with reality, but with people's expectations of reality. There's a funny story from *Apocalypse*, when we were starting to put in all the sound effects of the munitions. There is a standard way we're used to hearing sound when watching old war movies. When someone yells "Incoming!", you hear this whistling artillery coming toward you and exploding, but the truth is that the shell explodes *before* you hear the whistle because the shell goes faster than the speed of sound. So the *reality* of it is that you would hear an explosion and *then* the whistle. When we tried to recreate reality in *Apocalypse*, it was confusing because it had nothing to do with what we expected to hear. In a film that prided itself on realistic sound, we chose to go in the other direction because that's what was expected. By giving them reality, we would have destroyed the moment. Instead of watching the film and accepting the emotions of that moment, the audience would be unconsciously thinking, "Wait, something's wrong here." In a sense, this is a metaphor for everything we do with film.

I wondered if something was wrong for a second with the continuous phone conversations between mother and daughter in Terms of Endearment. *Instead of hearing a faint voice on the other end of the phone, both voices are loud and clear as if they were in the same room.*

That was a very conscious decision. Usually when you're cutting the film, you cut the takes and telephone-filter the voices later. Since this was a film that relied heavily on telephone calls and the intimacy of the scenes, I made the decision, when cutting the film, to ignore the usual way that telephone calls are cut—specifically, ending a cut on a word and then starting a new word when you cut to the other person. I decided that these phone calls were so important to the heart of the story, that I would ignore the convention of how you cut a telephone conversation and deal with it as if it were two people in a room talking to each other. That's what we lived with all through the cutting process, and when it came to mixing the film and we started to filter the off-camera voices, it was terrible. It suddenly pulled you out of the film, out of the intimacy created between you and those characters. So we ignored using telephone filtering because it was destroying the relationships we had so carefully created. As filmmakers, we work toward fulfilling audience expectations, and when we violate conventions, we have to be doing it consciously to achieve a specific effect.

A great example of what editing does is in Broadcast News *when the William Hurt character edits the news to manipulate audience reaction.*

Yes. There were huge choices about whether or not he was actually faking the tear during that news story of rape or recreating a moment when he actually cried. And we manipulated that.

You mean you *did while editing that film?*

Yes, because *we* could have gone either way. We could have made it so that he was this hard-assed guy who just saw a great opportunity and said, "Okay, let me go back and create this tear because the tear would be good." Or we could have made—which we did—someone who had cried and just recreated it for the camera. It was the lesser of the two evils, yet one which intentionally created a narrower moral dilemma for the character that Holly Hunter played.

Is reality in a film partly created by editing techniques that evoke the period of the movie, as the 1930s style for Pennies from Heaven?

No, we didn't really feel an obligation to do that. We've run into the same question with *Dick Tracy* which is a late thirties period piece, although obviously a comic strip. I don't think you can deliver a thirties film to a nineties audience and have them sit still for it. You're dealing with a whole different vocabulary and different audience expectations. One can't easily violate that vocabulary. I don't think you can do what they did in the thirties: use long takes and rehearsed scenes played only in wide shots. There are montages in *Dick Tracy*, and my first thought was to try to duplicate the classic thirties Vorkapich montages with multiple images since very fast cutting was a little used technique. But it just didn't work. With our current MTV sensibilities, it seemed to stop the film. The montages in *Dick Tracy* are very quickly cut, although there are some multiple images that are kept to a minimum.

How about wipes?

We played with wipes in *Dick Tracy* but used very few of them in the final film. What seemed to work well for the film were the iris wipes because of the nature of the image they are used on. I wanted very much to use other kinds of wipes, and I even did a pass on videotape using them as transitions from scene to scene, but what I finally realized is that we, as the nineties audience in the United States, associate most wipes with cartoons. Once you see a wipe, you start to believe that the material you're watching shouldn't be taken too seriously.

Weren't wipes primarily used in comedy anyway?

They weren't. Wipes were standard transitions in films of the thirties that had nothing to do with comedy. It was the way you might now use a dissolve or a fade; rather than a cut, you'd wipe to the next scene. It was a perfectly legitimate tool, but we have come to associate it with a more cartoonish tone. Perhaps wipes are funny by association, but there's a certain seriousness to an iris.

Do you have to adjust material around an iris differently than around a cut?

Basically I cut for it to work, then on the occasions where we would decide that an iris was right, I would adjust the material to reflect using the iris, which would be changing the rhythm slightly.

Would you say that rather than type of transitional device, it's enough that the characters and sets evoke the time?

Well, we don't even have that in *Dick Tracy*. Visually, it's an incredibly stylistic film. It has primary colors like the comic strips, and it's a comic strip world where you go out on the street and you don't see lots of people; perhaps just one person and a car. Everything is the very sparse world of the comic strip, although the characters and emotions are very real.

What editing complications arise out of dealing with the emotions of real characters in your films?

If you love what you do, you get so caught up emotionally that it's difficult to tell the difference between reality and the fantasy you're working with. I often joke that my head thinks in cuts. It becomes a way of looking at things. You do it long enough and work the kind of hours editors generally do, and you start to confuse reality with fantasy. I kid around with people that sometimes if I begin to drift off in a conversation, I'll start to shorten the conversation by cutting it in my head. I'm popping into a close-up, cutting to an over-the-shoulder! In a film, if the emotions are real and true, then they're true to you and you're affected by them. If you're not affected, it shows in your work. Some of the most difficult dailies I ever had to sit through and the most difficult ones I ever had to cut were for the death scene from *Terms of Endearment*. Actually, the death scene was easy. It was the scenes with the children, the husband, and the ability to distill, to focus, and to change the focus of a scene, a character, an emotion. It's wonderful for someone who loves manipulation. Just cutting to the child, Huckleberry Fox, staying on him and watching. Some of his reactions were mind-bogglingly powerful.

Or choosing to stay on the mother's reaction when the daughter dies.

We shot her dying and we shot the mother sitting there. The choice I made on my first cut was to play it off Shirley MacLaine, because the emotion of death seems more powerful for the living than for the dying. The power of the loss was in the person observing the death.

Can you get hardened to dealing with an emotional scene like that?

Eventually you start to feel less. I don't think you can ever keep up the same emotional intensity forever. Certainly it's a value of the preview system where you take it to an audience and you start to hear the handkerchiefs come out and the sniffling, and it confirms that you've effectively done what you set out to do.

Do you always make a connection to an emotion while you're dealing with innumerable pieces of film?

Not always. Sometimes. Cutting is a search to find that connection. Part of the fun for me is having the material pull me in different directions. Cutting is an experiment. Unless you're willing to try new things, you never truly serve the material. *Apocalypse Now* taught me the most valuable of lessons, which is that there's always another way to edit a scene. After three years editing one film, you learn to pull something apart and start from scratch. That's a hard thing to do because you have your own preconceptions and feelings, and you don't want to violate something that's working. But sometimes, by forcing yourself to reapproach the material, you just make a quantum leap. It was a very difficult film and a very difficult experience. It was crazy, it was nuts—and that's what made the film great! *Apocalypse Now* was as much an event as it was a film. The thing that kept me going was the need to be true to the film and finish it. But it was hard to keep going for that period of time, and the film certainly had a lot of problems, many of which we were never able to solve. I'll probably never work on something that monumental again. I don't have another three years to give!

How do you keep the emotions flowing in a multiple-character film?

It's very difficult. In *St. Elmo's Fire*, the director made some very interesting choices. Because of the anamorphic format he chose, which is unusual in a rather contained dialogue film, we were able to keep many characters in the frame at one time. The whole idea was to create an ensemble piece and not have to constantly cut between close-ups. Keeping it in multiple-character shots was what was important in the film, and was what gave it some of its fluidity. It wasn't something I created in the cutting room but certainly I was very conscious of it when I was cutting the film—it was a story about characters and interrelationships as opposed to *a* character. Multiple-character scenes are often very tricky to cut just because you have so many more choices and permutations in the way you cut things. The more characters you add, the greater the number of permutations.

Can you comment on the use of the subtitles at the beginning of Broadcast News *to introduce the three main characters?*

That was in the original script. I think the wonderful thing about those titles at the beginning was that they were laughs and they set a tone for the rest of the comedy. I really believe that a film in its opening ten minutes, even opening five minutes, must lay the ground rules for how the audience is going to accept the film. I think you have to tell the audience what they are going to get. If you show the first five minutes of a murder mystery, make it a hilarious comedy, and *then* all of a sudden lapse into a mystery, you're going to confuse an audience. In *Terms of Endearment*, we tried something: the film opens with a shot of a young Shirley MacLaine standing over the crib and pinching the baby. We tested the film without that scene, and the audience response was interesting. It took them a much longer time to get into the film than when we had that scene up front because that scene gave them the key of how to accept the film. It said, this film is going to be kind of funny, with some bizarre humor, so be comfortable, you're going to be seeing a lot of this. It definitely set the tone of the movie. *Broadcast News* introduced the three major characters with a sense of comedy and it promised you the saga of their lives. It was also saying that we would explain these character traits and you were going to see more of them during the rest of the film. That was the thing that really almost demanded the book-ending seven years later.

So that ending was added afterwards?

No. It was in the original script, but there was a lot of thought given as to whether or not to lose it. Emotionally, the film was over when the Holly Hunter character refuses to go off with the William Hurt character. That decision having been made, the movie could have ended right there. You would have seen her at the taxi cab giving instructions to the driver as she always did and that could have been the end.

It was more poignant, though, to know after all those years she is still alone.

Yes. And that was probably the reason the film didn't do better. I think ultimately the audiences walked out disappointed that we hadn't sewn up all the loose ends and given them a nice happy ending. It may be a function of Hollywood, or it may just be a function of our society, that people desperately need to tie up loose ends and resolve things in this world. The audience gets used to half-hour sit-com resolutions.

Could you describe the purpose of storyboards? There was a storyboard illustrator listed in the credits of Terms of Endearment.

Tom Wright. Jim Brooks was a first-time feature director, and I think the storyboarding process gave him a tool to help him visualize working in a new medium. We talked about the scenes with Tom who then drew the boards. Jim and I then looked at them, made changes, adjusted angles, suggested other coverage and action, and Tom redrew them. Tom was even redrawing on the set. It's a great tool for a first-time director. Storyboards really say, you can figure all this out beforehand and if you get up in the morning and aren't really sure what to do with the scene, you still have your basic storyboarded coverage to fall back on. If anything, it's a jumping-off point. It provides a certain security that you've thought it out and visualized it. You have a safety net that allows the scene and the location and the actors to take you to another place. *Dick Tracy* had a lot of storyboards done by a great storyboard artist who's been working for many years in the industry. It was not a tool that Warren Beatty used very much. I think in some ways the storyboarding was more helpful to the production designer, Richard Sylbert, in addressing the problems in the visualization of the film. A lot of films I've worked on had storyboards because they provide that jumping-off point to find the imagery you're searching for. The first cut of a film is also a jumping-off point. The first cut is like a superstructure, the starting point. You can start to work with it, play against it, see what's wrong and why it's wrong, how you want to build the characters, the subtle changes you want to make in them, and what story problems you're going to address. Working with the director is a very important process in getting feedback, and after the first cut, you're able to get a fresh eye from someone who is seeing the cut with some distance. It's that objectivity that can easily get lost in the editing process.

Can you go back and ask for a shot you didn't think you'd need?

Often. I think it was *St. Elmo's Fire*, I'd come on the set and the crew would yell, "Here comes 'Close-up'! He wants another close-up!" It's notorious when an editor comes on a set—"Oh, oh, what's wrong? He either wants something or something's wrong with yesterday's dailies."

What are your usual last words to your film editing students as they walk out the door?

Oh, just words of encouragement. They're not editing students.

Aspiring directors?

Aspiring directors. I tell them to be nice to editors.

Do they ever say, "I want to be an editor now that I know what it's all about"?

Some of them do. A lot of people who work for me have come from film schools. Some become editors, some cinematographers, some sound mixers. Not everyone becomes a director, or wants to become one. Teaching has become such an interesting experience. Not having gone to film school, I never understood the ground rules, but I guess they are not dissimilar from any other course of study. It can be either a very positive or a very damaging experience. We try to nurture our students by not just being critical, but being able to offer some encouragement and tools to work with. I'm astounded how much I enjoy the work that my wife Barbara and I are doing at UCLA. There was a part of me that just wanted to try teaching as an alternative, less pressured lifestyle. However, it is something I've grown to love.

Do you analyze clips from other movies?

No. We consented to do this course only under certain conditions. We didn't want to teach an editing course about the theory of editing. We wanted to teach a practical course. There is a part of the film school process that I think relies too much on theory and not enough on giving students the realities of what they will have to deal with, or the tools with which to deal with them. The way we structured the course was to make it available to third-year graduate students who are working on their thesis films, who had a couple of films under their belt and who were familiar with the process—we didn't want to teach splicing and rewinding. We screen the films on the flatbed and then do a second pass making recommendations and suggestions. We also open it up to the rest of the class for comments. It becomes a hands-on way to deal with the realities of having to finish their films. This course has been a fascinating experience for my wife and me because it's forced us both to articulate what it is we do and why we do it, rather than saying, "You do this, you do that." It forces you to explain, which is sometimes quite amazing and challenging.

There must be certain techniques that are easy to articulate.

There are, in order to make things technically smooth. I spend a lot of time going over films saying, "Trim a couple of frames over there, it will be smoother if you do it." Certainly for someone first learning to make cuts, that's the sort of thing for which they have no tools to understand the process. I think it takes a certain amount of learning and experience doing it to start to understand where you cut something. Then again, there are people in my class that are just born with an instinct, God bless them. You can explain mechanical things, but you can't explain dramatic taste. They just know emotionally, they feel where to cut, and they're pretty much right when they do it. It's an internal sense of rhythm some people have and some don't. It's a very musical process. I've always been a frustrated musician—gave up piano at eight years old and refused to take another lesson—but I seem to have a rhythmic sense that defies me, and thank God I have it.

Do you advocate cutting to music?

As a matter of fact, I find that distracting. There's an internal rhythm that comes out of the material that you have to find. What I find myself doing is making the Moviola louder and louder when I run a scene back and forth. The louder I make it, the more it forces me to focus in on the picture. Actually, my wife jokingly accuses me of being stone deaf! But every material has its own rhythm and the material often tells you where to cut. Some people can make the cut smooth—cut off or add a few frames—but it doesn't necessarily mean they've cut in the right place, or what *I* consider the right place. We're getting into an area that's so personal that we preface every class we teach with, "These are *our* opinions, they're not necessarily right or wrong. They're opinions. It's a matter of personal taste. But we will sit there and say, 'This is right and this is wrong' because it's easier and clearer to do it that way." I've met some talented people. It's the first time in my life I've carved out some time to do something else besides cutting film. It's a different kind of satisfaction. I feel like I'm passing something on. Dede Allen was probably one of the only film editors I've ever met who had this incredible instinct for teaching. She's taught so many of us and given so unselfishly of herself that I feel an obligation to help other people as she did.

Do you bring in other editors to speak to the class?

Occasionally I've brought in a sound editor and a music editor to discuss their areas. But I didn't want to make it a course about war stories, which a lot of editing courses taught by working professionals are. They tell anecdotes about the strange people they've worked with. That's not teaching.

It must be hard to teach editing. It can be a boring process.

It's only boring if you're not the editor. It's just as boring as going on a set is boring if you're not the director or the actor or the cinematographer. It's damn boring to sit there if you're not directly involved. To see someone roll a piece of film back and forth two hundred times, then make a splice, is not the most fascinating way to pass time. Unless you're doing it yourself, it's very tedious.

If you were to look back on your first film success, do you think you'd see things you would change?

Oh yes. *Bang the Drum Slowly* was the darling of the critics, and the critical success of that film made it much easier for me to get more work. Had that film been a critical disaster . . . But yes, there are things I would change. Every film has things I want to change when I look back at them after a period of time. I very rarely watch the films I cut because I want to change them. What you want to do constantly changes with your perspective. The way I would cut something right now would be different than the way I would have cut it two weeks ago or two years from now. It's constant change and flux. Every time I look at a film I've cut, I remember three more options I didn't try. Highly neurotic! I like to be quoted as saying, "Films are never finished, they're abandoned"—I've probably plagiarized that quote. Ultimately you can work something forever, and at some point you say, "That's it." Mostly you say that because the time is up and you have to release it in the theater. That is functional abandonment. How's that for a last quote?

22

"Locking" Up

Alan Heim

1968	*The Sea Gull*, directed by Sidney Lumet *Blood Kin*, directed by Sidney Lumet	1983	*Star 80*, directed by Bob Fosse
1970	*The Twelve Chairs*, directed by Mel Brooks	1985	*Goodbye New York*, directed by Amos Kollek *Beer*, directed by Patrick Kelly
1971	*Doc*, directed by Frank Perry **Liza With a "Z"* (TV special), directed by Bob Fosse	1986	*Nobody's Child* (TV movie), directed by Lee Grant *True Colors* (Music video), directed by Pat Birch and Cindi Lauper
1973	*Godspell*, directed by David Greene		
1974	*Lenny*, directed by Bob Fosse	1988	*She's Having a Baby*, directed by John Hughes *Funny Farm*, directed by George Roy Hill
1975	*The Silence* (TV special), directed by Joseph Hardy		
1976	**Network*, directed by Sidney Lumet **Holocaust* (TV miniseries)	1989	*Valmont*, directed by Milos Forman (Coeditor: Nena Danovic)
1979	*Hair*, directed by Milos Forman (Coeditors: Lynzee Klingman, Stan Warnow) **All That Jazz*, directed by Bob Fosse	1990	*Quick Change*, directed by Bill Murray and Howard Franklin
1981	*The Fan*, directed by Ed Bianchi *So Fine*, directed by Andy Bergman	1991	*Billy Bathgate*, directed by Robert Benton (Coeditor: Robert Reitano)

* See Appendix for complete list of editing awards and nominations.

As his assistant works industriously on *Quick Change*, Alan Heim speaks of the personalities and films he has known in his lengthy career as sound and film editor. On the windowsill of his New York cutting room in the famous Brill Building sits his collection of vintage editing tools; over his work table hangs a lively original banner advertising Saturday matinees for the kiddies.

A native New Yorker, Heim attended City College in the late 1950s with an interest in still photography. He discovered the film school at City College, a "well-kept secret at the time," headed by Hans Richter and later by George Stoney. After shooting a film, he was urged to "trim it up a little and make it work." He eventually moved into a job at the editing house Ross-Gaffney, then served as sound effects librarian at the Army Pictorial Center. He worked a few years on television shows such as *The Nurses*, *The Defenders*, and *East Side, West Side*, and free-lanced as a sound effects and music editor before he met Sidney Lumet. Following work as sound effects editor on Lumet's *The Pawnbroker*, *The Group*, and *Bye Bye Braverman*, Heim was asked to cut his next film, *The Sea Gull*. While that was shooting in Sweden, colleague Ralph Rosenblum suggested that Heim take over the nearly completed cutting of *The Producers*, directed by Mel Brooks. Essentially, Heim jumped from sound assistant to sound editor to picture editor, without serving as picture assistant.

Perhaps Heim's greatest devotion is to Bob Fosse, for whom he cut one television special and three feature films. At times Heim speaks of him in the present tense, perhaps as an ongoing tribute to this temperamental genius. That Fosse hired him for their initial venture, *Liza With a "Z"*, was all the more amazing as Heim's inexperience with music irritated an already hostile Fosse; thus began a stormy but cherished friendship. Heim's award-winning work on *All That Jazz* is also a case in point of an editor-director collaboration that went far beyond "just a job" and absorbed their personal lives.

Heim speaks of editing musicals, dramas, comedies, and documentaries, of intense relationships with directors, of the vagaries of the public and the industry, and of the attitude and personality of the successful editor. Just as editors "lock the film" when their work is done, in a sense Heim's interview also locks this collection of interviews on editing by linking many principles and concepts into one comprehensive picture.

How did you and Mel Brooks collaborate on editing The Producers?

The first thing I did was kick Mel out of the cutting room for a while. Most of the film was finished, but there was one trouble scene that should have been very funny and Mel said it just never worked right. It was all done in master shots and I said we need some close-ups. It turns out he had shot a bunch of close-ups. I said, "Just let me look at these materials, go away for a few days, and come back at the end of the week and I'll show you something different." And I discovered that not only had he shot a lot of close-ups, but Ralph Rosenblum had at some point made a cut very similar to mine. There were marks on the film, they were a few frames off, a foot here, eight frames there, but the scene was a very different scene. And when I finished it, it was done almost entirely in close-up. We had a sneak preview of the film at the Baronet or the Coronet on Third Avenue in New York City, and the audience laughter at that area was so enormous, I found it just thrilling. I said, "Gee, I really want to do this." I continued with picture editing and here I am!

What made you know what would work with that trouble scene?

It was funny! The whole timing. Mel was a believer—as a lot of people who do comedy are—that the timing is basically the timing of the comics themselves, of the actors. If the actors are not perfect, when you're doing live acting on the stage, you can judge the audience responses and fill in the gaps. If there's a big laugh, you can wait for a laugh. On the screen, you can't wait for a laugh, you just have to keep moving and hope the audience gets it—and usually they do. Mel was afraid of that. So the stuff in the close-ups was hysterically funny. It was funny in the long shot too, but it wore you down. Actually, my original theory was that it wasn't funny because there was an enormous portrait of Hitler behind everybody, and that was sort of putting a pall on the scene. I'm not sure that wasn't partially to blame, but by taking the close-ups, I was able to make the actors really respond to each other and their actions. It's the scene where they sign up the crazy Nazi writer. They go up on the roof with him and his pigeons, then he comes down into his apartment. The close-ups were quite marvelous, things about "Churchill, he was no painter. Hitler was a painter! Painted the entire apartment in one afternoon. Two coats!" And when he said "Two coats," his fingers came up in a "V" and filled the screen and his face was behind them. It was just wonderful. In the long shot, all of this was lost. When Mel saw it, he grudgingly admitted it was good. When the audience saw it, the laughter was so enormous that I began to doubt myself in a way. I felt maybe I should have left more space, but I gave that up pretty quickly. You just don't mess with that kind of laughter. Let them come back and listen a second time. Anyway, I did that and two films for Sidney Lumet, and I went on to do *The Twelve Chairs* for Mel Brooks in Yugoslavia.

Did you have more freedom editing that one?

Well, yes and no. At one point, and I quote, Mel said, "I don't want any fucking editor's jokes!"

What kind of joke is that?

That by changing the juxtaposition of something, changing the rhythms of things, he was regarding that as an enemy action on my part! He actually told a director in my presence near the end of that film to never trust anybody on a film who's getting credit because they only care about their own little department and they really don't care at all about the film as a whole—only the director does. I believe the job of the director is really to synthesize everybody's best work, although I think the only other person who really has an overview of that is the editor who spends the second longest amount of time on a film. Cameramen indeed care about the look of the film but they rarely care about the whole; they just care about the look. I've had cameramen mistime a scene because they feel the close-up looks better pink as opposed to normal skin tones, something I find very jarring and usually the directors do too. But the idea of helping a director through the vision is the best thing you can do.

Did you try to capture the atmosphere of the film through editing techniques?

The Twelve Chairs, stylistically, was very much an old-fashioned movie. In fact, Mel had wanted to use things like diagonal wipes and spins and stuff, but it was after the fact. Had we discussed it beforehand, we might have been able to work out some transitions, but after the fact, there seemed to be no reason. Those wipes in the older movies were quite wonderful. In fact, I used some in an awful film I did called *Beer*. Terrible film. But the motion on the screen called for these wipes, they were planned, and you can't throw in a diagonal wipe or a spin just because you want to. It doesn't make much sense. I don't think they were particularly out of the style of *The Twelve Chairs*. It was set in 1927 and we shot it in Belgrade. There I saw Vertov's *Man With a Camera*, and 1927 Moscow had exactly the same trolley stanchions as 1969 Belgrade. That whole ambience was very similar, although a lot of us didn't know it at the time. I certainly didn't, the costume designer didn't. We could have used things like that. Stylistically, I think the film is pretty consistent. As an editor, I remember showing it once to a class and being greatly embarrassed by it. I thought it was primitive. Certainly from an editorial point of view, it was a pretty primitive film.

What would have made it more mature—say, what you've done since?

It's not so much what I've done since. Mel was always waiting around for the "something" to happen, for the joke to happen, and one of the things I pride myself on is a kind of a flow in my films. I think I'm always striving for a rhythmic smoothness, an imperceptible movement from one place to another, and I think that film just never had it. Mel was always after me to let the speeches play long. In Yugoslavia, he did stop me from editing once or twice; he said, "Don't cut, don't touch my film." I said, "I'm going home, I can't stand it here! If I'm not cutting, I'll be bored witless!" So I started cutting again and he said, "All right, cut for a while." Then when we got back here, he just felt that the long stuff, the stuff I had left long was boring, and the other stuff was missing the germ of the comedy. He would come in every day, we worked on the material, and eventually hacked out something that satisfied him.

Are there principles of editing that apply to both comedy and drama?

I treat both basically the same way. I just feel that the rhythm should be as real as you can get. Now indeed, if an actor or director is playing for a laugh, you have to give a little space for that. But normally I treat them the same way. I just think the truth of any moment has to be played on the screen, and I don't think you can change that.

How do you find that rhythm from so many disparate pieces of film?

I find that often I look at the dailies and pretty much decide then which way I want to go with the scene. But then it becomes a question of the first shot that opens a scene, and then you just listen to the material. You go to the best performances, you go for the sizes you want, for the action you want to emphasize, and it just comes together for me pretty quickly. Even with a lot of material, and some of these scenes have a great deal. In *She's Having a Baby*, John Hughes had half a million, six hundred thousand feet of film. That was more than we shot on *All That Jazz*, or as close to it as any film I ever worked on, and it was a really very simple film. John never came into my cutting room on *She's Having a Baby*. All that film appalled me. When I looked at the material, my eyes rolled back in my head! This wall of film was building up in front of me day after day! I came into the cutting room on Monday in Chicago to discover the lab had called me to say, "We just got Saturday's material in." John had shot twenty-five thousand feet of film. That is four-and-a-half hours of film, printed, plus Monday's material which was going to go into the lab Tuesday morning. I got forty thousand feet of film in one day! The first film I ever edited, *The Sea Gull* for Sidney Lumet, had print total forty-five thousand for the *whole* movie. So to get forty thousand feet of film in one day from the laboratory, you can't sync it, you can barely screen it because you have seven-, eight-minute takes and you just sort of doze until you get awakened by door-slammings. I think it's not possible to focus for that long. Yet you look at it once and you say this is possible, you make a mark and put it aside. Sometimes you end up with six or seven possible areas that are good, and you make decisions based on that. I threw out enormous amounts of film that I looked at once and just wouldn't go back. As a matter of course, I didn't want to look at it again! What I had was perfectly fine.

You really are going by intuition.

A lot of it is intuition. It's not like cinematography where you have to know technical things. We really know very little, we go by intuition. There's a certain dramatic sense that you develop in going to the theater, from reading books. I think life plays a great part in being a good editor. You're always working with the emotion. You have to open yourself to the material. You can't force film. I've always regarded film as almost a plastic medium, almost like sculpture. Like metal, you can bend it in different positions. But there is a point when it stretches too much and you can't go that far. I was working on *Valmont* this year with Milos Forman. He likes to see everything, and so I was just crowding my first cut with stuff that I really didn't love, but I was trying to figure why he was shooting these odd angles. So I tried to show every piece of emotion that the actors were going through in any scene, and it tended to be overcrowded. It's simple enough to simplify things. Usually it's the other way around.

In The Twelve Chairs, *and later in* Funny Farm, *the cuts you made often contributed a visual punchline or punctuation to a gag. Did you see editing as a way of getting jokes across other than verbally?*

I think I try to do that. Let me digress for a moment. One of the thrills of working with Bob Fosse, and I haven't really had this experience with anybody else, is there's a script and it's a strong script, but the pictures, the juxtaposition of the pictures in some way tells the story, the juxtaposition of the scenes. It's very much going back to what they used to do in silent movies. There's a lot of the material that you don't have to listen to so much. The images tell the story, and I like that. I think for anybody making films, that's what you want to do, you want to go for the moment. You do want a punchline. I don't know specifically what you're talking about in the films.

Well, in Funny Farm, *you use the ducks to punctuate some scenes.*

Yes. Well, the ducks were a mixed blessing. The animals and the ducks worked very well in that. We used every frame of duck. The other thing that people don't understand about editing is that a lot of it is serendipitous, a lot of it is accident. The ducks, for instance, went under because there was a guy off to the side wearing boots, knee-deep in the pond, and they had rigged the ducks with monofilament collars (don't tell the ASPCA!). I mean we had a wrangler, a duck wrangler, for God's sake! But this guy would, on cue, schlepp the ducks under water with this monofilament and pulleys under the pond. The ducks wouldn't fly. They built a platform and threw the ducks! If I needed another eight frames, I didn't have them. So a lot of accidents happen, and critics who often write about the "vision" are missing a little nuance in there, it's not that simple. I love to read Pauline Kael, I think she's a tremendously talented critic, but when it involves films I've worked on, she's often writing about things that never run through anybody's mind. Maybe they should have! But we did what we had to.

You mean the deep significance that critics often attribute to films?

Yes, the auteur, the director's grand vision, which is often just—not to knock it, but it's often a lot of accidents, a lot of moments you get forced into. Something's out of focus, or the camera breaks. When we get to Lenny, I'll tell you a few things.

Well, we can move into Lenny *now. The three Fosse films you worked on are similar. For one, they all have an interview format.* Lenny *seems like a documentary. Am I placing too much significance on that?*

That was the intention. It was shot in black and white, partly for that and partly for economic reasons. The film cost, I think, all of two million dollars, which seems like a tiny sum now but was not so tiny then, and they really pushed Bob a great deal. He was never happy with the script. Bob's a perfectionist, he was a perfectionist. Perfection in screen time takes a lot of money and a lot of time. After that, Bob went to a different producer who realized that he just had to make a sort of a fiction budget. He made the budget, we started, and you hoped to be able to get by with it, and if you didn't, you hoped to hustle up a few more dollars somewhere else, which is what happened on *All That Jazz*. You had to give Bob his space; if he didn't have his space, he'd get crazy, he'd feel pressured, he'd develop a real hatred, and the work would suffer all around. On *Lenny*, the documentary intent was always there.

The interview sequences in Lenny *were so realistic, even though they were staged with actors. In one nice touch, Valerie Perrine offered to show a photograph to the interviewer and he answered no. Very natural.*

Bob was the interviewer and we always planned on changing his voice. Then as the film went along, technically there was a problem because of all the backgrounds we would have to replicate, including airplanes going over, because all of that was done on location. But also we realized that that low-key voice, that sometimes you could barely hear, was valuable. It added a lot to that sense of reality. When Bob worked with Bob Aurthur on the script of *All That Jazz*, he tried to use a lot of the techniques in the script that came up with *Lenny* in the cutting room, and we found when we got into the cutting room that it wasn't as flexible, that we were even more locked in to what he had shot than we had been on *Lenny*. It had some of the problems without the easy solutions, or at least we didn't have the obvious solution.

You've mentioned that Lenny *greatly influenced all your work since.*

Lenny was made in the cutting room. The structure of the film was made in the cutting room, and that's what was so exciting about that film for me. Every day was a real discovery. When I read the script, I turned to my wife and said, "You have to read this." She said, "I'll read it tomorrow," because it was by that time quite late at night. I said, "You've got to read it now. I must do this film." So the script itself was tremendously filmic. But then we discovered in the cutting room that, by breaking up the comedy routines and interspersing them more with the documentary and with the interviews, we gave a whole life to the film that it didn't have in its original structure. In our estimation, we also improved Dustin Hoffman's performance immensely because we both felt he never really had the character. He may have sounded like Lenny Bruce, but he never had an edge. Dustin doesn't like to play unpleasant people, and Lenny Bruce was very unpleasant. So there was always that little edge. On one occasion, Bob gave him a whole day, reshot a whole scene because Dustin felt he could do it better. Without even seeing the dailies which hadn't come back yet, Bob reshot the next day. What Dustin had played with a lot of edge the first time, he played again much sweeter. We looked at it once and threw it out, we never touched it. Near the end of the film, we had not shown anything to the producer, and Bob had to show the film to David Picker and we had no ending. Absolutely no ending. The ending we had didn't play, it just was not good. About ten or eleven at night, Bob and my two assistants and myself all went to have a big dinner. About midnight, we went back into the elevator and we started talking about the film again, and I looked at Bob and said, "Listen, why don't we just kill the son of a bitch?" He said, "Why?" And I explained that from the time he gets dragged out of the courtroom until he's lying on the toilet floor, we have an enormous amount of material. We had him saying good-bye to his daughter in a full scene. We had a long scene, I think part of which is still in the movie, where Dustin is going around eating peanut butter from jars and being very paranoid and talking to his wife or his lawyer, I don't remember which. Twenty minutes of material between the time he's dragged out of the courtroom and the time he's dead. It just struck me that that was excessive and not interesting anymore. You lost interest in the character. By this time, he was so self-destructive and so paranoid. And we took out the twenty minutes—like the Frank Capra story, we threw out a reel, we took out twenty minutes of film. We juxtaposed the courtroom with the death, and although we brought in parts of the other scenes later, suddenly the end of the film was alive again. Then when we showed it the next morning, we both knew that we had a lot of work to do to put back those little fragments that we did keep, him waving good-bye to his daughter, but we didn't keep the whole scene, we just kept that part. I don't remember what else, we kept part of the phone call, I think. But that suddenly made the freedom to change with something that came to me out of that movie. Before that, I had done *Godspell* where the director would say to me, "Gee, I had no idea what to do with that material." The picture was wonderful, but I always feel the director knows what he wants done with the material, and if he gives it to me, I try and squeeze it in somewhere. Bob knew what he wanted. Sometimes he shoots two minutes of film for ten seconds, and it's pretty clear what the ten seconds are going to be in a dance number. You know when you're behind the cymbals for that one moment that he wanted to be there. He taught me a way of looking at things and a way of looking at the whole structure of the film that has stood me in good stead ever since. And that's why I love that film more than, I think, any other.

Really?

Yeah. It gave me a lot more freedom, a lot more flexibility. There's a scene that people ask me about. With so much cutting in the movie, there's a scene near the end when Lenny is stoned on the stage, wearing a raincoat, ends up running into the dressing room, gets arrested by the police. But the scene was played in a long shot in a master, and people ask, "Why didn't you cut that scene?" There were several reasons. One is that we felt Dustin was really very good in it and deserved screen time without our own manipulations. It's not that the scene wasn't covered, I could have cut a scene out of it, and I did fiddle with it for a while, but it just didn't seem to be worth it. It wasn't as good as leaving this guy exposed on the screen. The nightclub, as I remember, looked a little bit like a medical amphitheater anyway, and he really seemed like a subject at that point and it seemed right. But the other side of that coin was that there was static electricity, lightning flashes, all through the movie in that area. All this was shot in Miami, Miami Beach, where the humidity was enormous. The nature of black-and-white film—which I discovered only after this—is that sometimes in very humid situations, when you go from an air-conditioned place to a humid place, you'll develop static electricity on the film. So we couldn't give it the treatment that it deserved, and we felt this was also very good for the character and for the film at that point.

There you go, a mix of vision and accident.
    Yes.

In any case, you generally go for performance as your determination.
    In every case, in comedy and serious drama, you go for the best performance, and usually the best performance just waves at you. The director will turn to you and say, "That's the best take," and you know perfectly well from looking at the dailies before they do that that's the best take. Sometimes there's something quirky that goes on, sometimes. In *Quick Change*, the directors hated the performance of a person who's in one scene; when I cut the scene, the nature of it was clear to me to be on this person very little, that most of it is reactive. It was coming from one character, the jokes, the comedy were coming from the situation which involves action going on outside the room that you have to be on at certain points, and it involves a response of another character who is watching the goings-on outside the room. So when they saw the scene the other day, they were rather delighted. The scene was much too long, that would be dealt with later; but they were delighted with the fact that you almost never see the person who said the lines. Now I didn't do that just to get away from a bad performance. The performance isn't as bad as they feel it was, but it wasn't particularly inspired and they developed a real dislike for it. I come to it cold. I'd like it to be different, perhaps, but I know it can be made to work and that's what's really important.

This reminds me of those quiet dialogue scenes in Network, *where during certain performances you chose to cut away from rather than stay on the speaker. Or else you would stay on the speaker for the duration.*
    In particular, you're talking about the scene in the kitchen. There's a film that I knew was a good film, and I expected it to get a good number of award nominations. It ended up with ten Academy Award nominations, and I was really astounded by that because it seemed so easy, and one of the shortest films I've ever worked on—totally, I was on it for seven months. Six days after shooting, I showed Sidney Lumet and Paddy Chayevsky and the producer a finished product. All we really did after

that was shorten two scenes and we took out just about every shot of people walking from place to place that never should have been shot in the first place—they were shot for Paddy. Stanley Kauffmann, reviewing the film, said a great thing about editing in general. He said, "You are always on the person you want to be watching even if you didn't know it at the time." I think it's a tremendously insightful remark and I think that's the editor. The editor should be guiding the audience as to where they should be, and I think that kitchen scene was really perfectly done. You wanted to hear Bill Holden, and the two places I went to Faye Dunaway in there, she was positively superb at just the right moment. That scene was never touched from the first cut to the end of the picture. That particular scene just jumped out and it didn't need anything. It's interesting when you do a Fosse film, there's a lot of fancy stuff that goes into it, and many other films are really pretty tame.

When you're on location, do you get to suggest more coverage that you think you will need for these long scenes?

Very rarely do I do that. I did it just the other night on *Quick Change*. The cameraman always asks me if I have enough coverage. The other night, I said, "Are you going to get me a point of view of the taxi driver?" Everybody looked at me in shock. He said, "Well, what do you need that for?" I said, "Well, there's a very long scene when he comes here. You don't want to stay on him the whole time. What's he looking at?" And they nodded and they said, "Right," and they shot it. But I rarely am in such a position.

How tied are you to the script then?

Oh, we're pretty tied in a dramatic film. This is like a book editor, a story editor. It's the last stages of writing, really. You restructure things within reason, but on most fiction films you're tied up. You eliminate transitions and you eliminate the middle of the scene, but it's clear once you look at it—it's not so clear when you read it. I mean, you look at a scene that runs three or four pages and you think this is a little verbose, but you can rarely talk somebody out of giving it up then— particularly a writer-director. Usually when you go to the cutting room and they look at the cut, they will see that it's wrong and where it's wrong.

Did you create the silent script reading scene in All That Jazz *in the cutting room, or was that scripted?*

Oh, the elimination of the sound. That was in the original script, it just was a question of, again, where the accents go. Bob lived through that, and I did too, because we had finished *Lenny* when he had his heart attack, and a lot of those lies were lies that I was told—that he's resting, he's okay, and it took me a few days to get through to what was going on. *Lenny* opened while he was in the hospital a few blocks away, and I went there to tell him about the crowds which were enormous at the beginning. It was very hard to take, all of it. A film like *Jazz* goes on for a year or more, and you begin to live the things that happen. The guy who was the set dresser had a heart attack during the production. People had babies. My mother died while we were doing the last number of the film. That stopped our rhythm, as you can well imagine; took me away from the cutting room for a few days and put Bob into a tremendous depression because we were rolling toward a completion. Just emotionally, you go through things in a film like that that you don't go through on an average movie. An average movie is work, it's a job, you come in, you cut a certain amount of film, and eventually you go home. The director comes in, you sit and talk, you discuss and argue, whatever you want to do with it, and you go home. But here you carry it with you. It was tough. Unfortunately, Bob was not the most prolific of filmmakers, but I always liked working with him because you never knew what was going to happen. Working with Fosse was a unique experience. He had amazing vision and an untiring search for perfection. It was an emotional and physical strain to work with him, but I'd gladly do it again. I always thought Bob should do a comedy. He was a very funny guy, very witty.

All three of his films are very intense and certainly unique from the other films you've worked on. Jazz *must have been even harder since it was so close to home.*

One of the tough things about working with Bob was that a lot of the material dealt so closely with his own life that he would get very defensive about it. In *Jazz*, at the beginning when he came into the cutting room, I would refer to the character, "Well, here *you* . . . " and he'd say, "It's not me! It's Joe or it's Roy. It's not me." At one point I thought I might have to quit the film because he was being so brutal to me, and I don't like to expose myself to that situation. But I was able to deflect him one day and I made him laugh and he suddenly realized what he had been doing. It had to do with the scene in *Jazz* where I played myself. There was something he had wanted me to do, just a little raising of my eyebrows, and I have big eyebrows, and I did it. He kept the camera running and said, "A little smaller, a little smaller." When I saw the dailies, it was hilarious to me because I got bigger and bigger each time he said smaller! Bob looked at the cut scene and said, "Can we try a take where you do it smaller?" I said, "This is the smallest one I did!" He said, "No, let me see the outtakes." So I showed him the rest of them—he actually did one take but he kept it running—and he walked across the room, kicked the chair and said, "I should really get a better performance than that!" I said, "Bob, I'm not an actor!" And he said, "But you're a human being and I should be able to get a better performance out of a human being." I said, "Bob, that's the nicest thing you've said to me in three weeks!" And he laughed and realized he had been abusive.

How did you distance yourself from the material in Star 80 *that was so violent and disturbing?*

It's movie blood. I once opened a refrigerator on the set of *The Fan* and took out what I thought was a bottle of juice and it was a bottle of blood. It's fake stuff. After I did *Star 80*, the producer I was working with said to me one day, "You know, I know you a few weeks now, you seem like a decent guy. How could you work on such a vile film?" I never felt it was vile. There's stuff I won't do, there's scripts I've read that I find really disgusting. If Bob weren't doing it, I wouldn't have done it. When we looked at the dailies of *Star 80*, we all tried to get Bob to tone down the ending a little. In the final analysis, he told me he wished he had listened to us. But we couldn't. In the cutting room, we no longer could. The fact that Paul attempted three times to rape Dorothy Stratten was one time too many. Structurally, it was not possible to cut it out. We tried very hard. The blood was movie blood. To watch it in the dailies was tough. That was shot at the end of the production because the actors didn't want to do it and have to come back to a lighter scene. Nobody wanted to do that. I think all of us were afraid of it. Fosse was afraid of it. It was inexorable. I like doing action scenes, I've done action scenes in almost all of my movies, there's some kind of action that goes on and it's mechanical and quick. But sometimes there's a moral repercussion that I can't find myself working on. *Star 80* in a way is also a documentary of sorts, and it's a little bit like turning over a rock and filming whatever is under the rock and just watching it. Like an Andy Warhol movie, just watch what's going on. You know what's going to happen, everybody knew it. Apart from the article in the *Village Voice* that the movie was based on, while we were shooting, the television version came on and then the film was released. I think it was Bob's best work, oddly enough, and I don't think it's watchable if it hadn't been so marvelously made. But the audiences hated it, Hollywood hated it. Bob was very disturbed, he went into a real funk after that. He didn't really want to touch film again. Near the end of his life, he was beginning to. We were doing commercials for his shows and he said he really missed the cutting room and was thinking about maybe doing another movie, but that was four, five years.

He was disillusioned with the reactions to his film?

I think so. He was astounded at the degree of hate that came out, both from the Hollywood establishment and from reviewers. We were all shocked. We felt we had made a really strong movie about some very believable characters, and I think that part of the problem was a lot of people were able to relate to the killer Paul in a way that they found very uncomfortable. I think people understood why he killed her in a way that we maybe don't understand in a regular shoot-'em-up, and they were just appalled by it. I think Bob found the story attractive because of its Svengali-like qualities. All three movies have the same kind of man exerting control over women or a woman, and Bob found that fascinating. It was an element of his own life that he put into his films.

Fosse's films weave in and out of documentary and fantasy and past-present-future; they also repeat similar scenes to punctuate time frames, such as with the pill bottles in Jazz *and the murder updates in* Star 80. *Did you have trouble keeping all the different threads untangled?*

In a word, no!

How did you prevent redundancy?

Well, the scenes are all different, they're all subtly different. For instance, the scene with the pills starts off in a pretty straightforward fashion, but by the end of it, there's a low angle shot and the Joe Gideon character is in silhouette, from low behind looking like some crazed bird. Just the whole flow of that, the whole progression would be leading to the destruction of the character. It was very conscious. The one case where we shifted the position had to do with his coughing. After Joe Gideon puts his kid in the car and comes upstairs, you have a very long shot of him in the studio and he begins to cough, then you cut to these giant inserts and suddenly intersperse close-ups of him coughing with the pills. It's the only thing we ever really changed, I think. It got very chilling at that point. At least for me. You go to it at different times, hopefully to keep the audience awake.

The same with Lenny. *You return to him during his last appearance, linking the past with the present.*

Every film has a different problem as far as structure goes. After seeing *Star 80*, E. L. Doctorow (he was a friend of Fosse's) said, "You know, there's flashbacks and there's flashforwards and there's real time. And then there's Fosse time." Which is true. I think in *Star 80*, it's very difficult to follow the time frame. It's just there. That gives you a freedom as an editor to move things around because the time frame doesn't really exist in a linear sense. It's different. That's again part of the juxtaposition of the different thoughts, and the ability to be flexible.

With the volume of film you sometimes get, as you've described, how do you keep your flexibility? Especially for comedy?

It's tough, it's tough. I just have to try and remember my first reaction to the material. One of the problems with comedy is, when you go to dailies, a lot of people laugh and it ain't that funny—or it's a different kind of funny. People say, "Well, we laughed at it at the dailies. Why isn't it good now?" So you try and change it and get the same feel, but the freshness does disappear. There are some editors who flip the film and look at it left to right. I never really tried that. But when I ran fifty-nine minutes of *Quick Change* the other day, I was delighted that with my staff—two of whom hadn't seen the film—the two directors, and the producer, there was some real good laughter there. Afterwards, we had a very sober discussion of what had to go. Based on that screening, I went through and took out a few things. When you make a little change, it's going to change everything. After our screening the other day, I had my assistant make just a few of the trims that we talked about, and the scene suddenly came alive in a very different way. It comes after the first screening, it comes out of the material again, and you go over it and try to make the corrections. Then you just hope. What they do nowadays is play films for audiences a lot and take notes a lot, and you ask people questions. I'm a little mixed about that. We did that for *She's Having a Baby*. We thought we had a very strong ending. The audience hated the movie, and it was clear that they really liked the movie up until that point. Every time, the last memory they had was very unpleasant. One day they had what are called focus groups, they seek ten or twelve people—I didn't realize this, but they actually pay them, I think ten or twenty bucks. The last time I went to one, I was shocked to see them passing out money to these people. But they ask them questions. At one of our last focus group meetings, a woman raised her hand and said, "Look, I'm a nurse and I would never go up and say to somebody whose child was in danger of dying, 'We don't think it's going to survive.'" Suddenly it dawned on us that we had never realized this was setting up the whole ending of the film in a very negative way, with the people resenting that Elizabeth McGovern lived at the end. I think they really did, I think they were expecting her to be dead. They didn't feel an elation that she lived, but they felt we were manipulating them—and we were. The woman who played the nurse was in California, and I recut the scene so that we could put the line on her back and on Kevin Bacon's face. She came in the next day and did the line for us in an office. We finished the movie and screened it and we improved our ratings twenty points or so, from seventy-five to eighty-five or ninety. We got very high ratings on the movie. Then the other question is why the film was hated so when it was finally released because the audiences filled out these cards and gave us very high numbers. I don't know, I never saw the final version.

Maybe it became too sentimental at the end?
    Could be. It did stall emotionally, it didn't seem to play with the rest of the film. John Hughes was doing *Planes, Trains, and Automobiles* and

Paramount Pictures no longer wanted to rush us out because either *Top Gun* or *Beverly Hills Cop II* was ready (they weren't sure they could make them for the summer release and they wanted us to back up, though we didn't know it at the time). Both pictures were able to make their dates, so they sort of sloughed us off. Instead of being the first of the "baby boom" series of films, we became the last.

People were tired out by then.
I think so.

The musical is also a popular genre for you. Does editing a musical pose any particular problems?
I like doing musical scenes a great deal. Again, musical scenes are really the epitome of what I was talking about earlier, they really are all image. People used to complain—and I guess still do in a Fosse film—that you never could see a whole dancer. I don't think anybody ever understood that Bob was not choreographing for the stage, he was choreographing movement in a frame. I regard any musical number I do as moving the eye around in the frame and keeping the audience interested in getting the dancers' very best moments on the screen. This also applies to regular dramatic film editing. When I was a sound editor working on *The Group*, Aram Avakian (a legendary New York editor and director) popped in one day, looked over my shoulder, and saw a close-up in a dialogue scene. He said, "What a marvelous cut that is!" And I said, "Why?" And he said, "Go back over it." So I went back and forth a few times. I saw what he was talking about, which was that the actor moved his hand in a certain way on one side of the close-up and it directed you: as you followed his hand, you then went with the cut to the other side. It seemed like the most normal kind of thing, go from one person to another as he was speaking. But the choice of the moment of when to move carried your eye right into the other; they're basically two still shots. Ever since then, I've been very careful of where the actors are looking. I avoid a little extra blink, I always try to get out of an actor when they're focused on where the audience should be. The same applies to musicals. Musicals also become a kind of a technical puzzle that I enjoy, keeping in sync to the music and getting those moments. Bob had a quirk: he never wanted to see the bottom of a dancer's foot. He said they're dirty. I would slip one in occasionally, because I liked the cuts better from the peak down, and usually you see the foot up at the peak. Bob would always make me push it off a little bit, off the beat—which isn't such a bad thing either. A choreographer once said, "I wondered whether in *All That Jazz* you were cutting on the beat or off the beat, and you're really not. You're *between* the beats somewhere." I guess it was something I learned from Fosse, but it seemed very natural. On the beat is very predictable, and off the

beat can be disorienting. You sort of move around a little. I guess it's kind of a jazz technique.

Did you cut to finished musical arrangements?

In the big musical numbers, oh sure. The opening sequence of *Jazz* was done to a real rehearsal piano, and we put on the George Benson piece afterwards. Though we cut to the Benson piece, the dancers did not dance to it; they danced to various rehearsal pianos. So if you look closely, the piano player in the pit—there is one cut of him, I think—was playing whatever they were hearing; it was an impressionistic kind of thing. It happened to be good in that kind of picture. The dancers do it mostly to playback, and it then just becomes a matter of getting the material in.

In the case of *Godspell*, they shot the opening sequence which plays at the fountain in the park, and I realized suddenly that they kept shooting it with the same bars of music. They were shooting more and more material, and I didn't have enough music to cover the scene. I cut it to the rhythm, I stretched the music mechanically—that is, I cut it, made it longer; the rhythms were similar and I just ignored the playback at certain points. Then they reorchestrated and rewrote the piece. Stephen Schwartz did his music to my cut because the dance was so good.

When *Hair* came up, I was going to take over this one scene which nobody could get a handle on—the draft board scene, "Black Boys/White Boys." What they showed me was a cut that—well, Milos Forman used the term "vulgar," it was vulgar and it wasn't funny. If you're going to be vulgar, you might as well be funny! They had missed the fact that this was a production number. They were trying to stuff it with racial import, and they missed the point entirely that it was an honest-to-God dance number and should be treated like that. So I put it all back in dailies form and did just that, and it worked very well. After I left the film, it got over-embellished. But still, much better, much more entertaining.

We had a small montage in *So Fine*—the Garment Center montage—and I thought we really needed music for it and we could cut to some music for it. I had a piece about a tailor, "I'm Sam the Man Who Made the Pants Too Long." I put it in and we loved it, and the scene was just a lot of fun with this in. Then the studio said, "It's too Jewish. You can't do that." We fought them a little bit, and then to hell with it and changed it to some sort of bland piece of contemporary music. But one tries. I've thrown a few pieces in and it's not that I've cut the scenes to them so much, but that I've embellished the scenes with the music. Usually in the non-dialogue scenes, it's nice to have some kind of rhythm.

Would that define your style of editing? Do you have a style?

I guess I do. Enough people have told me I do so that maybe I believe it.

Do you know what that style is?

No! Yes. Well, I think the one thing that I am very conscious of is trying to make a seamless cut from beginning to end. Trying to make the
transitions. You could either make your transitions very noticeable or
very unnoticeable, and in both cases, I think it can be done with grace
and smoothness. I try to keep the pace of the film to be conversational,
to be believable, to make everything very real, or as real as I can.

As you talk, I recall the audition scene in Jazz *where the dancers change
with every spin. That's very noticeable cutting.*

That was Fosse's concept. He called me the day he shot it and said,
"Tomorrow you're going to get these dailies and I want them cut together, I want to see them the day after on the screen." I put them together and they were never touched again. Once Bob and I were kidding
around about something and I mentioned that scene, and he said nobody
has ever seen anything like that. I said, "Well, there is that commercial
for Coca-Cola where they show all the bottles changing." He was a little
shocked by that. After we did that, suddenly there was a spate of commercials, a lot of fashion commercials where models would be in one position
and change clothing all the time, and I hadn't noticed it before that except
that I had seen the Coca-Cola commercial. It's a big concept, but it was
gorgeous. The opening was a terrific ten-minute piece. I wish I had a copy
of that because the one that's in the film now, which had been cut to
three-and-a-half or four minutes, is not as directed or as smooth, and the
other sequence was really something. It could have been a documentary
about how tough it was to be in show business.

Is that "flash" easier to cut than a sedate dinner table sequence?

I think it is. You know, it's all visual. Because of its placement in the
scene, that had a sense of rhythm to a climax, but in effect, it's all a big
visual climax. In a dinner scene, every nuance has to be gotten, every
look, every dramatic moment has to be searched for. So in a way, it's simpler to do musical things, it's just there.

When you have a long monologue, as in Lenny, *do you treat that like a
musical number and cut to the beat of words instead of notes?*

Sure. Lenny Bruce was like that himself. He would talk about the
rhythm of his speech that way. Every scene is like that. Without being
pretentious, that's what rhythm is all about. It's a pictorial and verbal
rhythm. Apart from the physical content of the scene and wanting to show
the positions of the actors, at a certain point it becomes exactly that, a
rhythmic moving on, hopefully picking up the tempo and getting to the
end. Carrying the audience with it.

So, after all this, what is editing about?

That it's really extremely pragmatic—if it works. That it's important to communicate. The audience has to know what you're doing, and that's very pragmatic. There are no rules, none whatsoever. Directors would say, "Why don't you use the close-up here? It's better, look at it!" You can't really sit down and do a paper cut. Sometimes when you get a script, it's written so that close-ups are described. That usually indicates a writer who doesn't know what he's doing, and it's not something that ever gets done in the movie. The important thing about the movie, about the script, is to take the scene and get the dialogue right, and then the pictures sort of take care of themselves as you start putting them together. It's not that there's one right way to do it, but once you commit to a way, then it's pretty clear that you have to go in that direction or start all over again and try something else. I worked with a television editor from California who used to describe exactly how you cut a Western chase. You'd cut to the close-up, you'd cut to the horse's hooves, you'd cut to the horse. I found that fascinating because there really was a historical right way. But editing is very pragmatic. The other thing is, you can change it, it's only splicing tape.

Where does that spark come from that distinguishes good from bad editors, or good from great editors?

I don't know. A lot of it is the luck of the draw. A lot of it is the film you get to edit. It's very hard, I think, to be a good editor and work on a bad movie. Editing is a real important part of filmmaking and under-appreciated. When you're cutting, they always say that good cutting is basically unnoticeable, so it's very hard to get any kudos for doing un-noticeable work. It's a hard bind we get ourselves in. Once, in a screening of *She's Having a Baby*, some people in the audience said, "You could see every cut." Now I don't know what that meant, except you can see physically the splices in a rough cut, an assembly. There's tape, the focus changes slightly through the splices. But that all gets fixed and smoothed, and people don't realize that. So at the time you see a finished movie, it should be pretty seamless.

Have you ever thought of trying another area of film?

Usually when I'm working on a film with a terrible director, I just feel I could do better. What's that thing in the F. Scott Fitzgerald movie, where the editor has a heart attack in the screening room and dies, and the lights come up and there he is dead, and somebody says, "He didn't make a sound." And somebody else says, "He didn't want to interrupt the screening." That's it in a nutshell! We work in quiet dark rooms, a lot of the times by ourselves, and the time we're not by ourselves or with other people with similar proclivities, we're working with directors who have large egos and very large salaries. In the long run, it's the director's medium. But for the most part, I like this. Fosse used to refer to me as a collaborator, and I think that's a pretty good honor coming from a filmmaker. There's something special about an editor's personality—whether it's for good or ill, I don't know—that makes the collaborative venture an attractive one. I like the process of putting the film together, then sitting down with the director and/or the writer and working out the bugs. I like that editing process. Always felt part of it.

Appendix
Awards and Nominations

The following is a list of nominations and awards for outstanding achievement in editing presented to the editors interviewed in this book by:

- The American Academy of Motion Picture Arts and Sciences (OSCAR),
- The British Academy of Motion Picture Arts and Sciences (BRITISH),
- The Academy of Television Arts and Sciences (EMMY), and
- American Cinema Editors (EDDIE).

Special awards for outstanding achievement in producing, directing, and sound effects, as well as honors in film festivals, are also indicated.

Paul Barnes

EDDIE
    Award: *Wasn't That a Time!*
    Nomination: *Say Amen Somebody*
    Nomination: *Statue of Liberty*
    Nomination: *The Thin Blue Line*

Geof Bartz

EMMY
    Awards: *Lifeline* (for Outstanding Program Achievement and Outstanding Individual Achievement in Editing)
    Nomination: *The Body Human*
    Nomination: *The Facts for Girls*
    Nomination: *The Loving Process: Woman*
    Nomination: *The Wyeths: A Father and His Family*

Donn Cambern

OSCAR
  Nomination: *Romancing the Stone*
EDDIE
  Nomination: *The Bob Hope Christmas Show*
  Nomination: *The Hindenburg*
  Nomination: *Hooper*
  Nomination: *Romancing the Stone*

Anne V. Coates

OSCAR
  Award: *Lawrence of Arabia*
  Nomination: *Becket*
  Nomination: *The Elephant Man*
BRITISH
  Nomination: *Murder on the Orient Express*
EDDIE
  Nomination: *Lawrence of Arabia*
  Nomination: *Becket*

John D. Dunning

OSCAR
  Award: *Ben-Hur*
  Nomination: *Battleground*

Rudi Fehr

OSCAR
  Nomination: *Prizzi's Honor* (with daughter Kaja Fehr)

Peter C. Frank

EMMY
  Award: *The Fire Next Door*

Tom Haneke

EMMY
  Award: *He Makes Me Feel Like Dancin'*
  Award: *Mother Teresa*
  Nomination: *The Second Time Around*

EDDIE
  Nomination: *Mother Teresa*

Alan Heim

OSCAR
  Award: *All That Jazz*
  Nomination: *Network*
BRITISH
  Award: *All That Jazz*
  Nomination: *Network*
EMMY
  Award: *Holocaust*
  Nomination: *Liza With a "Z"*
EDDIE
  Award: *Holocaust*
  Award: *All That Jazz*

Paul Hirsch

OSCAR
  Award: *Star Wars*
BRITISH
  Nomination: *Star Wars*
EDDIE
  Nomination: *Star Wars*

Sheldon Kahn

OSCAR
  Nomination: *One Flew Over the Cuckoo's Nest*
BRITISH
  Award: *One Flew Over the Cuckoo's Nest*
EDDIE
  Nomination: *One Flew Over the Cuckoo's Nest*
  Nomination: *Out of Africa*

Carl Kress

OSCAR
  Award: *The Towering Inferno* (with father Harold F. Kress)
EMMY
  Award: *The Night That Panicked America* (Sound Effects)

Nomination: *Singing Whales: The Undersea World of Jacques Cousteau*

EDDIE

Nomination: *The Towering Inferno* (with father Harold F. Kress)

Harold F. Kress

OSCAR

Award: *How the West Was Won*

Award: *The Towering Inferno* (with son Carl Kress)

Nomination: *Dr. Jekyll and Mr. Hyde*

Nomination: *Mrs. Miniver*

Nomination: *The Yearling*

Nomination: *The Poseidon Adventure*

EDDIE

Award: *How the West Was Won*

Nomination: *The Towering Inferno* (with son Carl Kress)

Carol Littleton

OSCAR

Nomination: *E. T.: The Extraterrestrial*

EDDIE

Nomination: *E. T.: The Extraterrestrial*

Evan Lottman

OSCAR

Nomination: *The Exorcist*

Barry Malkin

OSCAR

Nomination: *The Cotton Club*

BRITISH

Nomination: *The Godfather, Part II*

Richard Marks

OSCAR

Nomination: *Apocalypse Now*

Nomination: *Terms of Endearment*

Nomination: *Broadcast News*

Tom Rolf

OSCAR
   Award: *The Right Stuff*
BRITISH
   Nomination: *Taxi Driver*
EDDIE
   Award: *WarGames*

Ted Winterburn

EMMY
   Award: *American Sportsman*
   Award: *Winter Olympic Games*
   Award: *Race Across America*
   Award: *Summer Olympic Games*
   Award: *Antarctica Odyssey*

Merle Worth

EMMY
   Award: *3–2–1 Contact*
   Nomination: *To Be a Doctor*
   Nomination: *CBS Reports: Murder Teenage Style*
EDDIE
   Nominations: *Mississippi: Portrait of America*
      (as Producer, Director)
   Nominations: *New York City: Portrait of America*
      (as Producer, Director)
   Nominations: *Great Britain: Portrait of the World*
      (as Producer, Director)
CINE GOLDEN EAGLE
   Award: *The Kite* (Berlin Film Festival, Tours Film Festival)

References

An asterisk (*) indicates that the book contains a comprehensive glossary of editing terms.

American Cinemeditor. Publication of the American Cinema Editors, Inc., C. E. Publications, Encino, Calif.

Anderson, Gary. *Video Editing and Post-Production: A Professional Guide.* White Plains, N.Y.: Knowledge Industry Publications, Inc., 1984.

————. *Electronic Post-Production: The Film-to-Video Guide.* White Plains, N.Y.: Knowledge Industry Publications, Inc., 1986.

Ash, Rene L. *The Motion Picture Film Editor.* Metuchen, N.J.: The Scarecrow Press, Inc., 1974.

Primarily a list of editors' credits, including silent films. Useful springboard for becoming familiar with names, but very incomplete.

Avallone, Susan, ed. *Cinematographers, Production Designers, Costume Designers and Film Editors: Guide.* Beverly Hills, Calif.: Lone Eagle Publishing Co., 1990.

Annual directory of names, contact addresses, titles, and awards. Useful resource, but incomplete.

*Baddeley, W. Hugh. *The Technique of Documentary Film Production.* London and Boston: Focal Press, 1975.

*Balmuth, Bernard. *Introduction to Film Editing.* Boston and London: Focal Press, 1989.

Barnouw, Erik. *Documentary: A History of the Non-Fiction Film.* Rev. ed. Oxford and New York: Oxford University Press, 1983.

*Burder, John. *16mm Film Cutting.* London and Boston: Focal Press, 1986.

The 1975 edition includes diagrams with color.

*————. *The Technique of Editing 16mm Films.* 5th ed. London and Boston: Focal Press, 1988.

Crittenden, Roger. *Film Editing.* London: Thames & Hudson, 1981.

Dmytryk, Edward. *On Film Editing: An Introduction to the Art of Film Construction.* Boston and London: Focal Press, 1984.

Dmytryk began as an editor before turning to director. His other companion volumes are *Screen Acting, Screen Directing,* and *Screen Writing.*

Editing. Publication of Editors Forum, North Hollywood, Calif.
Monthly interviews with editors in film, television, videos, and commercials. Editors Forum also serves as a network and resource center for editors.

Eisenstein, Sergei. *The Film Sense.* Translated and edited by Jay Leyda. New York: Harcourt Brace Jovanovich, 1942.

————. *Film Form.* Translated and edited by Jay Leyda. New York: Harcourt Brace Jovanovich, 1949.

*Hollyn, Norman. *The Film Editing Room Handbook: How to Manage the Near Chaos of the Cutting Room.* New York: Arco Publishing, Inc., 1984.

*Kerner, Marvin M. *The Art of the Sound Effects Editor.* Boston and London: Focal Press, 1989.

Lustig, Milton. *Music Editing for Motion Pictures.* New York: Hastings House, 1972.

Miller, Pat P. *Script Supervising and Film Continuity.* Boston and London: Focal Press, 1990.

Pudovkin, V. I. *Film Technique and Film Acting.* London: Vision Press, Ltd., 1970.

Reisz, Karel, and Gavin Millar. *The Technique of Film Editing.* 2d ed. London and Boston: Focal Press, 1989.

*Robertson, Joseph F. *The Magic of Film Editing: An In-depth Look at the Film Editor's Role . . . from Script to Screen!* Blue Ridge Summit, Penn.: TAB Books, Inc., 1983.

Rosenblum, Ralph, and Robert Karen. *When the Shooting Stops . . . the Cutting Begins: A Film Editor's Story.* New York: The Viking Press, 1979.
First-person narrative from the editor of *The Pawnbroker, The Producers, Bananas, Annie Hall,* among others.

Rosenthal, Alan. *Writing, Directing, and Producing Documentary Films.* Carbondale and Edwardsville, Ill.: Southern Illinois University Press, 1990.
Includes a brief section on editing.

*Schneider, Arthur. *Electronic Post-Production and Videotape Editing.* Boston and London: Focal Press, 1989.

Vaughan, Dai. *Portrait of an Invisible Man: The Working Life of Stewart McAllister, Film Editor.* London: BFI Publishing, 1983.
Reevaluation of the life and work of one of England's most important and neglected documentary film editors.

*Walter, Ernest. *The Technique of the Film Cutting Room.* London and New York: Focal Press, 1969.

Index